Casebook to the APA
Clinical Practice Guideline
for the Treatment of
PTSD

Casebook to the APA Clinical Practice Guideline for the Treatment of PTSD

Edited by Lynn F. Bufka, Caroline Vaile Wright, and Raquel W. Halfond

 AMERICAN PSYCHOLOGICAL ASSOCIATION

Published by
American Psychological Association
750 First Street, NE
Washington, DC 20002
https://www.apa.org

Order Department
https://www.apa.org/pubs/books
order@apa.org

In the U.K., Europe, Africa, and the Middle East, copies may be ordered from Eurospan
https://www.eurospanbookstore.com/apa
info@eurospangroup.com

Typeset in Meridien and Ortodoxa by Circle Graphics, Inc., Reisterstown, MD

Printer: Sheridan Books, Chelsea, MI
Cover Designer: Nicci Falcone, Potomac, MD

Library of Congress Cataloging-in-Publication Data

Names: Bufka, Lynn F., editor. | Wright, Caroline Vaile, editor. | Halfond, Raquel W., editor.
Title: Casebook to the APA clinical practice guideline for the treatment of PTSD /
  edited by Lynn F. Bufka, Caroline Vaile Wright, and Raquel W. Halfond.
Description: Washington, DC : American Psychological Association, [2020] |
  Includes bibliographical references and index.
Identifiers: LCCN 2019059295 (print) | LCCN 2019059296 (ebook) |
  ISBN 9781433832192 (paperback) | ISBN 9781433833588 (ebook)
Subjects: LCSH: Post-traumatic stress disorder—Treatment—Case studies.
Classification: LCC RC552.P67 C3735 2020 (print) | LCC RC552.P67 (ebook) |
  DDC 616.85/21—dc23
LC record available at https://lccn.loc.gov/2019059295
LC ebook record available at https://lccn.loc.gov/2019059296

http://dx.doi.org/10.1037/0000196-000

Printed in the United States of America

10 9 8 7 6 5 4 3 2 1

CONTENTS

CONTRIBUTORS

Lynn F. Bufka, PhD, American Psychological Association, Washington, DC

Taylor L. Ceroni, PhD, University of Akron, Akron, OH; now at Southeast Louisiana Veterans Health Care System, New Orleans, LA

Kathleen M. Chard, PhD, Cincinnati VA Medical Center and University of Cincinnati, Cincinnati, OH

Anke Ehlers, PhD, Department of Experimental Psychology, University of Oxford, Oxford, England

Thomas Elbert, PhD, Department of Psychology, Universität Konstanz, Konstanz, Germany

Edna B. Foa, PhD, University of Pennsylvania Perelman School of Medicine, Philadelphia

Matthew J. Friedman, MD, PhD, National Center for PTSD, U.S. Department of Veterans Affairs and Department of Psychiatry, Geisel School of Medicine at Dartmouth, Hanover, NH

Thea Gallagher, PsyD, University of Pennsylvania Perelman School of Medicine, Philadelphia

Berthold P. R. Gersons, MD, PhD, ARQ National Psychotrauma Center, Amsterdam University Medical Centers, Amsterdam, Netherlands

Raquel W. Halfond, PhD, American Psychological Association, Washington, DC

Ellen T. Healy, PhD, VA Boston Healthcare System, National Center for PTSD, and Boston University School of Medicine, Boston, MA

E. C. Hurley, DMin, PhD, Soldier Center, Clarkesville, TN

Dawn M. Johnson, PhD, Department of Psychology, University of Akron, Akron, OH

Louise Maxfield, PhD (retired), Ridgetown, Ontario, Canada

Marie-Louise Meewisse, PhD, Abate, Center of Expertise in Trauma and Anxiety, Enkhuizen, Netherlands

Frank Neuner, PhD, Department of Psychology, Universität Bielefeld, Bielefeld, Germany

Mirjam J. Nijdam, PhD, ARQ National Psychotrauma Center, Amsterdam University Medical Centers, Amsterdam, Netherlands

Julie Petersen, BS, Utah State University, Logan

Maggie Schauer, PhD, Department of Psychology, Universität Konstanz, Konstanz, Germany

Geert E. Smid, MD, PhD, ARQ National Psychotrauma Center, Diemen, Netherlands, and University of Humanistic Studies, Utrecht, Netherlands

Roger M. Solomon, PhD, Licensed Psychologist/Consultant, Arlington, VA

Jeffrey H. Sonis, MD, MPH, Departments of Social Medicine and Family Medicine, University of North Carolina at Chapel Hill

Jennifer Wild, DClinPsy, Department of Experimental Psychology, University of Oxford, Oxford, England

Caroline Vaile Wright, PhD, American Psychological Association, Washington, DC

PREFACE

Raquel W. Halfond, Caroline Vaile Wright, and Lynn F. Bufka

This casebook is meant to illustrate how the treatments recommended by the *Clinical Practice Guideline for the Treatment of PTSD* (American Psychological Association [APA], 2017) are used in practice. As staff members at APA, housed within the Practice Directorate in the Practice Research and Policy Department, we were all involved in the development of this guideline.[1]

The purpose of the APA Clinical Practice Guideline was to make recommendations regarding the efficacy of interventions for treating adults with posttraumatic stress disorder (PTSD; see https://www.apa.org/ptsd-guideline/ptsd.pdf). In addition, a website for the guideline with many resources (including additional case examples) is available (see https://www.apa.org/ptsd-guideline/). The information and case examples included in this book represent each of the recommended treatments for PTSD and are intended to illustrate distinct elements of treatment and how they are implemented in practice. This casebook is educational, and, as is true with the APA Clinical Practice Guideline, it is not intended to be a mandate or required standard for practice. Furthermore, no attempt is made to match particular symptoms to particular treatments. Rather, given that evidence-based practice in psychology is the integration of the best available evidence with clinician expertise

---

[1]Lynn Bufka is the senior director, practice transformation and quality and, together with her counterpart in APA's Science Directorate, oversees development of clinical practice guidelines. Caroline Vaile Wright is the senior director, health care innovation and conducted the additional searches for information on potential harms and burdens for the PTSD guideline. Raquel Halfond is the director of evidence based practice and worked most closely with the guideline development panel. All three editors are licensed clinical psychologists.

and patients' preferences, culture, and individual characteristics (APA, 2006), the casebook describes the treatments, briefly summarizes their evidence bases, and shows readers how some clinicians have used the treatments with particular clients so that readers can make their own clinical choices.

Although the APA Clinical Practice Guideline was approved as policy with a majority vote by APA's Council of Representatives, there was and there continues to be controversy surrounding this guideline. Concerns were raised that the guideline did not include or did not give a strong enough recommendation to some treatments that are commonly used in practice but for which there is a less robust research base than is available for other treatments. This situation stems in part from the decision to follow the standards for guideline development from the former Institute of Medicine (IOM [now the National Academy of Medicine], 2011), which some argue are a poor fit for mental and behavioral health guidelines because they adhere to a medical model. Others raised concerns that insufficient attention was given in the guideline to aspects that are important to care, such as the nature and quality of the therapeutic relationship and patient individual differences. While these areas are indeed important, methods for evaluating the quality of this body of research to inform guideline recommendations do not meet the rigor and transparency of systematic reviews and established standards for evaluating the efficacy of interventions, and the panel determined it could not make recommendations in these areas.

To address these concerns, APA is developing a companion professional practice guideline to address the role of contextual and nonspecific factors in providing evidence-based practice and another to address issues relevant to trauma-specific care. Professional practice guidelines are based in the professional literature but differ from clinical practice guidelines (CPGs) in that professional practice guideline recommendations are developed through expert consensus without a systematic search for and evaluation of the quality of the evidence base. Furthermore, as APA has continued to produce additional CPGs, its process has worked to address concerns raised about the PTSD guideline. CPG development will continue to evolve, and as APA becomes a leader in guideline development, APA will be positioned to identify and incorporate new methodologies to evaluate evidence that could be well suited for mental and behavioral health topics.

Combined, these efforts support the same goal: to help individuals living with PTSD to cope, feel better, and lead productive and fulfilling lives through informed, evidence-based care. Many of us in the mental and behavioral health field have been touched professionally and personally by the horrible ravages of PTSD in our patients, families, friends, loved ones, or even selves, and many of us know firsthand the impact of PTSD and importance of treatment that works. While much remains to be understood about the development, maintenance, and treatment of PTSD, this is a starting point. It is our sincere hope that this book will contribute to efforts to bridge this gap, more closely tie research with pragmatic practice application, and ultimately better the lives of individuals living with PTSD and of their family, friends, and loved ones.

REFERENCES

American Psychological Association. (2017). *Clinical practice guideline for the treatment of PTSD.* http://dx.doi.org/10.1037/e514052017-001

American Psychological Association, Presidential Task Force on Evidence-Based Practice. (2006). Evidence-based practice in psychology. *American Psychologist, 61,* 271–285. http://dx.doi.org/10.1037/0003-066X.61.4.271

Institute of Medicine. (2011). *Clinical practice guidelines we can trust.* Washington, DC: National Academies Press.

Casebook to the APA Clinical Practice Guideline for the Treatment of

PTSD

1

Overview of the Volume

Lynn F. Bufka and Jeffrey H. Sonis

Most people over the course of their lives will experience a potentially traumatic event (Copeland, Keeler, Angold, & Costello, 2007; Kilpatrick et al., 2013; McLaughlin et al., 2013). Those exposed to traumatic events have a range of reactions that include changes in emotions, memories, sleep, arousal, and other psychophysiological responses. Most reactions remit spontaneously within weeks (Nugent et al., 2009; Orcutt, Erickson, & Wolfe, 2004; Rothbaum, Foa, Riggs, Murdock, & Walsh, 1992), but for some individuals, these reactions persist and the person goes on to develop posttraumatic stress disorder (PTSD). Several factors contribute to whether a person develops a disorder or has a particularly complex presentation. Although almost 90% of U.S. adults are exposed to traumatic events (Kilpatrick et al., 2013), the lifetime prevalence of PTSD among adults is between 6% and 9%, with rates approximately 2.5 times higher in women than in men (Goldstein et al., 2016; Kilpatrick et al., 2013; National Comorbidity Survey, 2017). Comorbidities and other related symptoms are common and include substance use and abuse, depression, anxiety, dissociation, nonsuicidal self-injury, and suicide. Despite the high prevalence of exposure to traumatic events and subsequent development of PTSD for some of those individuals, far fewer individuals get appropriate care (Institute of Medicine [IOM], 2014; Mental Health America, 2018). People with PTSD need access to high-quality care and services that have strong support for their efficacy.

http://dx.doi.org/10.1037/0000196-001

Casebook to the APA Clinical Practice Guideline for the Treatment of PTSD, edited by L. F. Bufka, C. V. Wright, and R. W. Halfond

This casebook introduces each of the interventions recommended for adults with PTSD in the American Psychological Association's [APA's] *Clinical Practice Guideline for the Treatment of PTSD* (APA Clinical Practice Guideline; APA, 2017a). The guideline outlines seven psychotherapies and four medications with good evidence for efficacy (see Table 1.1). The interventions are cognitive behavior therapy (CBT) and specific variants of CBT, including cognitive processing therapy (CPT), cognitive therapy (CT), and prolonged exposure (PE); brief eclectic psychotherapy (BEPP); eye-movement desensitization and reprocessing (EMDR); narrative exposure therapy (NET); and medications (specifically fluoxetine, paroxetine, sertraline, and venlafaxine). The four psychotherapies that received strong recommendations are presented in alphabetical order, followed by the three psychotherapies with conditional recommendations, also in alphabetical order. (A conditional recommendation was given when the evidence supported the efficacy of the intervention, but the guideline development panel determined the overall strength of evidence, balance of benefits vs. harms, patient preferences and applicability did not warrant a strong recommendation.) The final intervention chapter is on medications.

Although other interventions are used in the treatment of PTSD (e.g., psychodynamic psychotherapy), the panel did not have sufficient evidence to make a recommendation for or against these. Absence of evidence is not evidence of lack of efficacy; rather, recommendations regarding efficacy could not be made. Future research will contribute to our knowledge about commonly used and newly emerging interventions over time.

TABLE 1.1. Summary of Recommendations of the APA Guideline Development Panel for the Treatment of Posttraumatic Stress Disorder (PTSD)

	Strength of recommendation
Psychotherapy	
For adult patients with PTSD, the panel strongly recommends that clinicians offer one of the following psychotherapies or interventions (listed alphabetically): • cognitive behavior therapy (CBT)[a] • cognitive processing therapy (CPT) • cognitive therapy (CT) • prolonged exposure (PE) therapy	Strong
For adult patients with PTSD, the panel suggests that clinicians offer one of the following psychotherapies or interventions (listed alphabetically): • brief eclectic psychotherapy (BEP) • eye-movement desensitization and reprocessing therapy (EMDR) • narrative exposure therapy (NET)	Conditional
For adult patients with PTSD, there is insufficient evidence to recommend for or against clinicians offering the following psychotherapies or interventions (listed alphabetically): • relaxation (RX) • Seeking Safety (SS)	Insufficient

TABLE 1.1. Summary of Recommendations of the APA Guideline Development Panel for the Treatment of Posttraumatic Stress Disorder (PTSD) (*Continued*)

	Strength of recommendation
Pharmacotherapy	
For adult patients with PTSD, the panel suggests that clinicians offer one of the following (listed alphabetically): • fluoxetine • paroxetine • sertraline • venlafaxine	Conditional
There is insufficient evidence to recommend for or against clinicians offering the following medications (listed alphabetically) for treatment of adults with PTSD. • risperidone • topiramate	Insufficient
Comparative effectiveness	
For adult patients with PTSD, the panel recommends clinicians offer either PE or PE plus cognitive restructuring when both are being considered.	Strong
For adult patients with PTSD, the panel recommends clinicians offer either venlafaxine ER or sertraline when both are being considered.[b]	Strong
For adult patients with PTSD, the panel suggests clinicians offer CBT rather than RX when both CBT and RX are being considered.	Conditional
For adult patients with PTSD, the panel suggests clinicians offer PE therapy rather than RX when both PE therapy and RX are being considered.	Conditional
For adult patients with PTSD, the panel concludes that the evidence is insufficient to recommend for or against clinicians offering SS vs. active controls.	Insufficient

Note. These recommendations and this clinical practice guideline are not intended to set a standard of care but rather to be a general guide to best practices. A clinical practice guideline can facilitate decision making for both provider and patient. Adapted from "Clinical Practice Guideline for the Treatment of PTSD" (pp. 4–5), by American Psychological Association, 2017a. Copyright 2017 by the American Psychological Association.
[a]The RTI UNC review refers to this as CBT-mixed therapy. CBT-mixed is a category that includes interventions using aspects of CBT that do not fit neatly into the other CBT categories. In this chapter, this type of therapy is referred to as CBT. [b]The recommendation for the comparison between venlafaxine ER and sertraline is different from the recommendation for SS versus active controls, although there is moderate evidence suggesting no difference between the two treatments for both comparisons (i.e., venlafaxine ER vs. sertraline and SS vs. active controls). The reason the recommendations are different for venlafaxine ER versus sertraline than for SS versus active controls is that the panel made a conditional recommendation for venlafaxine compared with no intervention and a conditional recommendation for sertraline compared with no intervention but did not make any recommendations for SS compared with no intervention or active controls compared with no intervention because there was insufficient or very low evidence. In other words, the panel believed that because there was evidence that both venlafaxine and sertraline had demonstrated efficacy compared with inactive intervention, it was reasonable to recommend either treatment when both are being considered. However, because neither SS nor active controls had demonstrated efficacy compared to no intervention, the panel concluded that evidence was insufficient to recommend for or against either treatment.

EVIDENCE-BASED PRACTICE IN PSYCHOLOGY

Clinical practice guidelines (CPGs) have been defined as "statements that include recommendations, intended to optimize patient care, that are informed by a systematic review of evidence and an assessment of the benefits and harms of alternative care options" (IOM, 2011a, p. 4). Guidelines are intended to assist clinical decision making, not supplant it. CPGs are tools that synthesize the broad evidence base regarding interventions, thus facilitating delivery of *evidence-based practice*, which is the "integration of best available research with clinical expertise in the context of patient characteristics, culture and preferences" (APA, 2005). This definition of evidence-based practice is variably presented as three overlapping circles or a three-legged stool, underscoring that each domain informs the other and all are important for decision making (Haynes, Sackett, Gray, Cook, & Guyatt, 1996). Whereas guidelines draw primarily from the best available research domain, guidelines themselves are informed by clinical expertise and patient values and preferences. High-quality guidelines not only systematically include reviewed research but also synthesize those findings with additional information about the harms and burdens of care, applicability of interventions, and patient values and preferences (Bufka & Halfond, 2016). And use of guidelines in the context of decision making is typically a complex interaction of the three components as manifested in shared decision making between the clinician and the patient. The evidence-based practice model underscores the need to synthesize available information and knowledge from research and clinical expertise to provide the best care for each individual (Bufka & Swedish, 2016).

Intervention recommendations contained in CPGs are guides for clinicians but do not replace clinical judgment. A clinician uses evidence about efficacy of interventions from CPGs and other sources to reduce the uncertainty inevitable in decision making, but nothing replaces the critical role of clinical expertise in combination with the patient[1] to determine the best course of action. Ideally, guidelines serve to identify and synthesize high-quality research, but the responsibility remains with the clinician to combine that evidence with patient factors and other information to deliver high-quality care. When used appropriately, guidelines can also facilitate information sharing with patients and support shared decision making (SDM; Bufka & Swedish, 2016). Ultimately, a thorough understanding of the evidence-based intervention, along with key personal and contextual factors, allows care to be individualized to meet the unique presenting concerns of each patient.

---

[1]To be consistent with other areas of health care, we use the term *patient* to describe the recipient of psychological services. However, we recognize that in many situations there are important and valid reasons for using such terms as *client, consumer,* or *person* in place of *patient.*

GUIDELINE DEVELOPMENT

The APA Clinical Practice Guideline was developed following the practices outlined by the IOM (2011a) and described by Hollon et al. (2014). Best practices for development of CPGs include transparency, management of conflicts of interest (COI), selection of multidisciplinary and balanced writing panels, use of systematic reviews of the literature as the evidence base, establishment of a system for grading the strength of evidence and the strength of recommendations, articulation of recommendations, use of external review, and development of plans to update guidelines. A brief description of the development process for the APA Clinical Practice Guideline follows; more detail is available in Hollon et al. and the full APA Clinical Practice Guideline (APA, 2017a). See Table 1.2 for a brief description of each practice.

Standards for systematic reviews, which undergird the CPG development process, have been published by the IOM (2011b). Systematic review teams are driven by key questions about populations, interventions, and outcomes to focus the review and identify relevant studies. Those studies are then reviewed for methodological quality (i.e., risk of bias) before inclusion in a systematic review. The entire process has multiple steps intended to foster transparent and fair review, reduce the risk of bias, and adequately address the guiding clinical questions so that users of the review can feel confident in its quality and the conclusions drawn from such a review.

APA appointed a multidisciplinary panel to develop its CPG for the treatment of PTSD in adults. Although the panel was largely composed of psychologists

TABLE 1.2. Best Practices for Developing Clinical Practice Guidelines

Best Practice	Description
Transparency	Guideline development processes and sources of funding described and publicly available
Managing conflicts of interest (COIs)	All involved in guideline development disclose potential financial and intellectual COI and processes to manage such COI are followed
Multidisciplinary and balanced writing panels	Different disciplines, perspectives, and expertise represented on panel, including researchers, clinicians, and community members
Systematic reviews as evidence base	Systematic reviews serve as evidence base and where possible, panel has input into review process
Establishing evidence base and rating strength of recommendations	Both the strength of the evidence and the strength of the recommendation are clearly noted so users can gauge confidence in decision
Articulation of recommendations	Standardized format of recommendations describes what is to be done under which circumstances
External review	Public or peer review is conducted prior to finalizing guidelines
Plans to update	As new evidence emerges, guidelines are evaluated for updating

(both clinicians and researchers), two psychiatrists, a primary care physician, a social worker, and two community members also served on the panel. Careful attention was paid to identifying perceived and actual financial and intellectual conflicts of interest (COIs) and managing such COIs through disclosure, discussion, and recusal. No panel member had COIs that prohibited entire participation in the process. Prior to reviewing the evidence for any intervention, the panel determined that the outcomes critical in deciding whether to recommend an intervention included reduction in PTSD symptoms and serious harms.

The panel used a systematic review that was developed by the RTI-UNC Evidence-based Practice Center, funded by the Agency for Healthcare Research and Quality at the U.S. Department of Health and Human Services. This review (Jonas et al., 2013) was determined to be consistent with the IOM standards: high quality, comprehensive, and transparent. The review was designed to answer specified key questions with clear inclusion and exclusion criteria for studies. For assessment of treatment benefits, the systematic review included only randomized trials, as is standard in systematic reviews of treatments, because they are believed to have lower risk of bias than observational studies, such as cohort studies. Because data on treatment harms are reported less frequently than data on treatment benefits, the systematic review also included large observational studies for its assessment of harms.

In the systematic review, studies were graded for risk of bias using a standard method (Viswanathan et al., 2012). Subgroup analyses were conducted, when possible, to determine whether intervention effectiveness differed by type of trauma; subgroup analyses that had been conducted in the original studies were compiled and summarized. Sensitivity analyses were conducted to determine whether studies that had been excluded because of high risk of bias would have changed substantive summary conclusions if they had been included. The review addressed questions regarding both the efficacy of specific active interventions (compared to inactive interventions) and, when possible, the effectiveness of active interventions compared to other active interventions (i.e., comparative effectiveness; very few comparative effectiveness trials were available for inclusion in the review). The systematic review team searched for studies on both psychotherapeutic and pharmacologic treatment of PTSD, but not all routinely used treatments had sufficient bodies of high-quality evidence to be included in the review and therefore in the final analysis of the panel.

Finally, the review team determined a strength of evidence (SOE) for each body of evidence, that is, the aggregated data for a specific intervention for particular outcomes from relevant studies. The panel made recommendations only for interventions for which there was at least low strength of evidence for either of its two critical outcomes. SOE considers not only risk of bias but also the degree to which the effect is consistent across studies, the degree to which the intervention is linked to that outcome (directness), and the precision of the estimated effect (i.e., the width of the confidence interval around the estimate). For this review, the SOE rating also included consideration of four minor domains: the evidence that higher doses were associated with larger effects, the magnitude of the effect, plausible potential confounders, and the potential impact of unpublished studies. An SOE rating reflects the degree of confidence that the estimated effect of an intervention is the true effect and that it will hold up in future research (APA, 2017a).

When determining recommendations, the panel evaluated the SOE for efficacy and comparative effectiveness of interventions and included three additional considerations: harms and burdens of treatments, patient values and preferences, and applicability of findings to relevant populations. Harms and burdens were evaluated to determine whether treatment benefits outweighed harms and burdens or vice versa. Given that information on harms and burdens was not consistently reported in randomized trials of PTSD interventions, particularly psychological interventions, the panel utilized not only what was reported in the published literature but also the input of community and clinician members of the panel in making these assessments. In general, for each psychotherapy, the panel noted that the length of treatment could be perceived as a potential burden to patients and that some patients could experience a short-term exacerbation of symptoms on the way to long-term resolution, a situation that could be distressing for individuals (APA, 2017a). For medications, harms were more likely to be reported in the literature; the panel considered published information about side effects and other potential harms (e.g., interactions with other medications) and burdens. For each recommended intervention, the panel determined that the benefits of care outweighed potential harms and burdens; however, clinicians will want to discuss these issues with their patients when determining the course of action for any individual because individuals may differ in how they assess and prioritize harms and burdens.

When formulating its recommendations, the panel also considered information about patient values and preferences regarding treatments. A recent systematic review (Simiola, Neilson, Thompson, & Cook, 2015) served as the primary source of information on this topic, although the panel also sought input from the community members and information found in additional searches of the professional literature. Unfortunately, few studies directly compared patient preferences for the specific interventions evaluated by the guideline panel. Thus, although patient preferences and values were an explicit component in the APA guideline development process, they had little impact, in practice, on recommendations. Accordingly, clinicians will want to carefully discuss values and preferences for care with their individual patients.

Finally, the guideline panel considered the applicability of the evidence to various patient populations and treatment settings, using the PICOTS framework (referring to populations, interventions, comparators, outcomes, time, and settings). Panel members concluded that the samples from the studies included in the systematic review included patients with a wide range of trauma types and were broadly similar to most populations with PTSD in terms of racial, ethnic, and gender distribution. Applicability of the evidence to persons with substance use disorders is problematic. Although substance use disorders are common among persons with PTSD (Brady, Killeen, Brewerton, & Lucerini, 2000), most of the trials included in the systematic review excluded persons with substance use disorders (Jonas et al., 2013). Some members of the panel concluded that the findings should therefore be applied with caution to persons with substance use disorders; other panel members believed that the findings were likely generalizable to those populations, based on the fact that treatment-effect heterogeneity by substance use disorders has not been demonstrated.

To clinicians, it is important to know not only whether a treatment works, in general, but also whether it works better or worse for specific subgroups of patients. Accordingly, the panel paid special attention to the findings on treatment-effect heterogeneity (i.e., subgroup effects) in the systematic review. The systematic review team concluded that the evidence was insufficient to identify differential treatment effects by subgroups based on factors such as gender, race, ethnicity, and sexual orientation (Jonas et al., 2013). The panel, therefore, did not make recommendations specific to any subgroup. Clinicians need to be aware that cultural competence is critical for appropriate treatment and may have particular relevance for those who have experienced trauma (Brown, 2008).

IMPLEMENTING RECOMMENDATIONS

When implementing any intervention, whether it is a particular treatment approach, a combination of different psychotherapeutic strategies, or an integration of therapy and medication, clinicians are generally trying to individualize care so that it meets the needs of the specific patient. In addition to determining the target of intervention, such as symptoms of PTSD, clinicians also seek to understand the factors that might require modification of treatment, such as patient characteristics (e.g., gender, culture or heritage, other features of their identities). Clinicians consider any other health conditions experienced by the patient as well as external factors such as social support, access to treatment and other logistics, and personal resources. Certainly, system or setting factors can also affect care, such as any constraints regarding duration of treatment or availability of the provider. Such a careful assessment coupled with an understanding of the processes of different interventions can help clinicians develop a conceptualization for the treatment path to be shared with the patient for decision making.

SHARED DECISION MAKING

The APA Clinical Practice Guideline (APA, 2017a) is intended to serve as a starting point for the SDM process between patients and clinicians. In the context of treatment for PTSD, SDM can be defined as a process in which clinicians and patients collaborate to explore options and make decisions about treatments (including the possibility of no treatment) for PTSD based on the best available research evidence on benefits and risks of treatments, patient preferences and values, patient-specific characteristics, and other health problems (Barry & Edgman-Levitan, 2012; Elwyn et al., 2012; National Learning Consortium, 2013). In SDM, decisions are made through active partnership of the clinician and the patient, each bringing to the encounter unique knowledge and skills necessary for an optimal decision consistent with the patient's goals and needs rather than either paternalistic decision making by clinicians for patients or informing patients of options but leaving patients to make decisions on their own (Hamann, Leucht, & Kissling, 2003). Fostering SDM can equalize the relative power that clinicians and patients bring to the interaction and can facilitate trust, components that may have been affected by the experience of trauma.

Clinicians use SDM as opposed to paternalistic or informed-choice models of treatment decision making for patients with PTSD for four reasons. First, SDM is the most ethically defensible model of decision making because it balances the core ethical principle of respect for patient autonomy (by incorporating patient preferences) with the core principle of beneficence (by incorporating clinician knowledge about benefits and risks of treatment; Beauchamp & Childress, 2012). The bioethical principle of autonomy is consistent with the principle of respect for people's rights and dignity from the *Ethical Principles of Psychologists and Code of Conduct* (APA Ethics Code; APA, 2017b). Second, there is evidence that SDM can lead to better decision-making processes. A recent Cochrane Collaboration systematic review, based on 105 randomized trials and 31,043 research participants with a wide variety of health conditions, showed that patient decision aids, tools that foster SDM, increased patient knowledge, improved accuracy of patient risk perceptions, reduced patient uncertainty about values, and increased congruency between a patient's values and the health decision (Stacey et al., 2017). A pilot study among veterans with PTSD showed that SDM was associated with choice of an evidence-based treatment and receipt of an adequate course of psychotherapy (Mott, Stanley, Street, Grady, & Teng, 2014). Although it is theorized that SDM can also lead to improved health outcomes (perhaps through greater patient engagement), research findings on the effect of SDM on health outcomes, from a variety of fields, are mixed (Duncan, Best, & Hagen, 2010; Kew, Malik, Aniruddhan, & Normansell, 2017; LeBlanc et al., 2015; Stacey et al., 2017). Third, although a systematic review of PTSD treatment preferences showed that patients generally preferred psychotherapy over medication, a substantial minority preferred medication (Simiola et al., 2015). With any individual patient, therefore, it is necessary to identify specific preferences and incorporate those preferences into collaborative decision making. Fourth, SDM is what patients exposed to traumatic events want. In a study of patients who scored high on a screening test for PTSD, almost all of them (97%) wanted to be involved in treatment decision making, and 67% wanted to "make the final decision about my treatment after seriously considering my doctor's opinion" or preferred that "my doctor and I share responsibility for deciding which treatment is best for me" (Harik, Hundt, Bernardy, Norman, & Hamblen, 2016, p. 224).

Although various approaches have been proposed for implementing SDM in routine clinical care (Elwyn et al., 2017; Stacey, Légaré, Pouliot, Kryworuchko, & Dunn, 2010; U.S. Department of Health and Human Services, Agency for Healthcare Research and Quality. 2016), they all share three common elements: (a) building a clinician–patient team; (b) discussion of options, including benefits, harms, availability, and burdens (such as number of visits, costs and homework); and (c) incorporation of patient preferences and values into a decision. Decision aids—tools designed to facilitate the SDM process by providing information about specific treatments and soliciting patient preferences and values—can be introduced at any stage in the SDM process. The recently developed PTSD Treatment Decision Aid, developed by the U.S. Department of Veterans Affairs National Center for PTSD (2017), is an excellent example of a decision aid that fosters SDM.

SDM regarding treatment for PTSD should include nine distinct elements. First, patients should understand that good options are available for treatments for PTSD that fall into two broad categories: psychotherapy and medications. Because the APA and other guidelines have identified effective treatments, clinicians can begin the SDM process with a discussion of recommended treatments. Because some patients have spontaneous remission from PTSD without treatment, one option is to choose no treatment at intake, with close follow-up to assess symptoms and functional status. A recent systematic review reported that, on average, 44% of patients had PTSD remission without treatment after a mean of 40 months of follow-up from baseline (Morina, Wicherts, Lobbrecht, & Priebe, 2014). However, because patients with PTSD of shorter duration are more likely to remit than those with PTSD of greater duration (Morina et al., 2014), choice of no treatment may be more suitable for those with PTSD of recent onset.

Second, the patient's goals, values, and preferences should be solicited from the outset of the discussion, with the understanding that preferences may change as the patient becomes more knowledgeable about treatments over the course of the SDM process. Indeed, at the start of the discussion, patient preferences may be more likely to be related to symptoms (e.g., "I want the nightmares to stop") or potential side effects of treatments (e.g., "I don't want a treatment that makes me groggy during the day") than about classes of treatments (e.g., medications vs. psychotherapy) or about specific medications or psychotherapies.

Third, discussion of potential benefits of the treatments (i.e., the benefit of treatments compared to no treatment or compared with an inactive treatment) may include the strength of the evidence for benefit and the magnitude of the treatment effect. For all treatments considered, the APA Clinical Practice Guideline includes information on the strength of evidence (rated high, moderate, low, or insufficient/very low strength) and magnitude of benefit (rated large/medium benefit; small benefit; no effect; small harm; medium/large harm). It may be useful, depending on patient interest, to incorporate those ratings into the discussion.

Fourth, patients are likely to want to know about recurrence of symptoms after treatment discontinuation. Unfortunately, no systematic reviews of PTSD treatments have reported long-term follow-up data. Patients also may want to know about the effect of treatments for PTSD on outcomes other than PTSD. The additional outcomes for which benefits have been shown for treatments that are recommended by the panel are shown in the Detailed Recommendations for each treatment (APA, 2017a).

Fifth, patients frequently want to know the comparative effectiveness of treatments—which ones "work the best." Unfortunately, there have been relatively few head-to-head randomized trials comparing recommended PTSD treatments with each other. Based on the head-to-head trials that were available, the panel recommended prolonged exposure rather than relaxation therapy, cognitive behavior therapy rather than relaxation therapy, prolonged exposure or prolonged exposure plus cognitive restructuring equally, and sertraline or venlafaxine equally. The panel did not believe it was appropriate to recommend psychotherapy rather than medications on the basis of the larger effect sizes because those differences may be due to methodological differences between psychotherapy and medication trials, as explained in Chapter 10. Head-to-head trials comparing recommended psychotherapies to recommended medications are urgently needed.

Sixth, discussion of common and rare but serious potential side effects of treatments is crucial for the SDM process because choice of a treatment involves weighing benefits and harms. In addition, patients may have strong preferences for potential side effects that they would like to avoid, such as sexual side effects that are common to selective serotonin reuptake inhibitor (SSRI) and serotonin and norepinephrine reuptake inhibitor (SNRI) medications. Medications have different side effects, and those of the four medications recommended by the APA Clinical Practice Guideline are detailed in Chapter 10. Adverse effects have been commonly reported in medication trials, due to FDA regulations, but they are uncommonly reported in psychotherapy trials (Dimidjian & Hollon, 2010). Thus, harms or so-called side effects of psychotherapy are not well described. While evaluating the anticipated benefits of treatments during SDM, one might discuss potential burdens of psychotherapy, such as the regularity of sessions or anticipated homework, along with the possibility that patients may feel some discomfort during psychotherapy when discussing difficult material.

Seventh, patient preferences for a variety of details about treatments may be important determinants of patient choices for treatments (Harik et al., 2016). Logistical details include treatment availability, cost of treatment and whether the patient's insurance will cover the costs, frequency of visits and total number of visits required, and whether homework is required. Some patients may prefer treatments with a particular theoretical mechanism of action, whether it be a medication influence on neurochemistry or a psychotherapy that proposes that change occurs by targeting thinking patterns. Additionally, whether to discuss the trauma experience, and how much discussion, are components of treatment that may influence patient choice.

Eighth, is this the best treatment for this patient, given other health conditions and personal characteristics? This type of personalized health care decision making is the holy grail of SDM. However, as the APA Clinical Practice Guideline states, "At this time, there is little research to indicate which efficacious treatments are most effective for which patients under which conditions" (APA, 2017a, p. 84). For recommended medications, discussion of potential side effects and the effect on the patient's known medical problems may be useful to help choose an appropriate medication. For example, because nausea and vomiting are more common for venlafaxine than for SSRIs, venlafaxine would be less suitable than an SSRI for a patient with peptic ulcer disease, dyspepsia, or gastritis. However, beyond patient preferences, little information exists for choosing different psychotherapy options based on patient health conditions or other factors.

Finally, the clinician should solicit patient preferences for general classes of treatments (e.g., medications vs. psychotherapy) and specific treatments, based on the preceding discussion. The clinician should support the patient to select a treatment (or no treatment) based on the best research evidence and the patient's unique preferences. Consistent with the model of SDM as teamwork, the clinician should raise concerns if the patient chooses a specific treatment that appears to be inconsistent with one of the patient's previously articulated preferences. An example of this type of inconsistency would be a patient who chooses prolonged exposure based on the strength of evidence but has also stated clearly that she does not want a psychotherapy that involves talking about the trauma.

A clinician's use of these principles to work collaboratively with patients is likely to result in treatment choices that are congruent with their preferences and goals. The PTSD Treatment Decision Aid developed by the U.S. Department of Veterans Affairs National Center for PTSD incorporates all these principles of SDM. The effect of the PTSD Treatment Decision Aid on decision making and patient outcomes has not yet been formally evaluated. However, a randomized trial of a previous decision aid for PTSD, also developed at the National Center for PTSD, showed that patients with new diagnoses of PTSD who were randomized to review the decision aid had less conflict about their choice of treatment and greater reductions in PTSD symptoms at 6 months after study entry (Watts et al., 2015).

INTRODUCTION TO THE CASEBOOK

This chapter describes how the APA Clinical Practice Guideline was developed and discusses the process for using a guideline to inform decision making with patients. Chapter 2 lays out the foundations of treatment, including information about the treatment relationship, assessment, comorbidity, and termination.

The author identifies many factors potentially unique to the treatment of PTSD, such as questions of safety and trust, avoidance, and vicarious or secondary traumatization. Chapter 2 also addresses core competencies for providers of PTSD and trauma care.

Chapters 3 through 10 provide useful clinical descriptions with helpful case examples of the recommended treatments: cognitive behavior therapy (CBT), cognitive processing therapy (CPT), cognitive therapy (CT), prolonged exposure (PE), brief eclectic psychotherapy (BEPP), eye-movement desensitization and reprocessing (EMDR), narrative exposure therapy (NET), and medications (specifically fluoxetine, paroxetine, sertraline and venlafaxine). These chapters are intended to provide sophisticated clinicians with information about each intervention so that they can determine which are consistent with their approaches to providing mental health services and might warrant additional training and supervision to develop the skills necessary to provide such care competently. Chapter 11 summarizes the themes of this casebook and identifies gaps in our knowledge and critical opportunities for further research to improve patient care.

Authors were asked not only to describe the treatment but also to illustrate delivery of the treatment with case examples. These case examples are typically composites of individuals seen in treatment, but any references to specific individuals are used with permission. Whether chapter authors used the word *patient* or *client* (or some other term) depended on the focus and orientation of the intervention. Given that experience of trauma is a universal experience, authors were asked to pay particular attention to diversity and to comment on the research base supporting the application of the intervention, as well as any particular strategies for delivering care successfully across different populations and subgroups. However, there was not sufficient space for authors to detail the complexities of culturally adapting treatment.

CONCLUSION

Although the majority of adults in the United States experience potentially traumatic experiences, most do not go on to develop PTSD. Some individuals who develop PTSD may experience a remission of their symptoms without intervention, but many will require specialized mental health care. General psychological interventions broadly result in some improvement, but specific psychological interventions appear to offer efficacy beyond general approaches. A recent meta-analysis found that across studies, patients who received "comparison" interventions (i.e., a psychological or pill placebo) showed some benefit, but those who received a targeted intervention for PTSD experienced a greater benefit, particularly those involving CBT (Carpenter et al., 2018). That said, it is important to remember that some individuals prefer medications to psychotherapy. In either case, unfortunately, relatively few studies directly compare treatments, and systematic reviews typically have little evidence suggesting one specific intervention is more efficacious than another intervention (e.g., Jonas et al., 2013). In the end, research indicates that some specific psychological interventions and medications (i.e., those noted in the APA Clinical Practice Guideline) have specific benefit in treating those with PTSD, and clinicians will likely want to offer these treatments first when initiating care. Because the research does not provide sufficient guidance to select among interventions and every clinical presentation is unique, patients and clinicians will want to consider numerous factors and share in decision making regarding best treatment options.

The challenge is ensuring that patients access those efficacious interventions. A first step is ensuring that more providers are familiar with the range of evidence-based options available. Although this casebook is neither a treatment manual nor a training course, it provides useful guidance about each intervention identified in the APA Clinical Practice Guideline with moderate or strong research support for its benefit. Clinicians are encouraged to obtain additional training and supervision to become proficient in one or more of these interventions and to use this guidance to increase the availability of appropriate care options.

REFERENCES

American Psychological Association. (2005). *Policy statement on evidence-based practice in psychology*. Retrieved from https://www.apa.org/practice/guidelines/evidence-based-statement.aspx

American Psychological Association. (2017a). *Clinical practice guideline for the treatment of PTSD*. http://dx.doi.org/10.1037/e514052017-001

American Psychological Association. (2017b). *Ethical principles of psychologists and code of conduct* (2002, Amended June 1, 2010, and January 1, 2017). Retrieved from http://www.apa.org/ethics/code/index.aspx

Barry, M. J., & Edgman-Levitan, S. (2012). Shared decision making—Pinnacle of patient-centered care. *The New England Journal of Medicine, 366,* 780–781. http://dx.doi.org/10.1056/NEJMp1109283

Beauchamp, T. L., & Childress, J. F. (2012). *Principles of biomedical ethics*. New York, NY: Oxford University Press.

Brady, K. T., Killeen, T. K., Brewerton, T., & Lucerini, S. (2000). Comorbidity of psychiatric disorders and posttraumatic stress disorder. *Journal of Clinical Psychology, 61*(Suppl. 7), 22–32.

Brown, L. S. (2008). *Cultural competence in trauma therapy: Beyond the flashback*. Washington, DC: American Psychological Association. http://dx.doi.org/10.1037/11752-000

Bufka, L. F., & Halfond, R. (2016). Professional standards and guidelines. In J. C. Norcross, G. R. VandenBos, D. K. Freedheim, & L. F. Campbell (Eds.), *APA Handbook of Clinical Psychology: Vol. 5. Education and profession* (pp. 355–373). Washington, DC: American Psychological Association. http://dx.doi.org/10.1037/14774-022

Bufka, L. F., & Swedish, E. F. (2016). Clinical practice guideline development and decision making. In J. J. Magnavita (Ed.), *Clinical decision making in mental health practice* (pp. 105–123). Washington, DC: American Psychological Association. http://dx.doi.org/10.1037/14711-004

Carpenter, J. K., Andrews, L. A., Witcraft, S. M., Powers, M. B., Smits, J. A. J., & Hofmann, S. G. (2018). Cognitive behavioral therapy for anxiety and related disorders: A meta-analysis of randomized placebo-controlled trials. *Depression and Anxiety, 35*, 502–514. http://dx.doi.org/10.1002/da.22728

Copeland, W. E., Keeler, G., Angold, A., & Costello, E. J. (2007). Traumatic events and posttraumatic stress in childhood. *Archives of General Psychiatry, 64*, 577–584. http://dx.doi.org/10.1001/archpsyc.64.5.577

Dimidjian, S., & Hollon, S. D. (2010). How would we know if psychotherapy were harmful? *American Psychologist, 65*, 21–33. http://dx.doi.org/10.1037/a0017299

Duncan, E., Best, C., & Hagen, S. (2010). Shared decision making interventions for people with mental health conditions. *Cochrane Database of Systematic Reviews.* http://dx.doi.org/10.1002/14651858.CD007297.pub2

Elwyn, G., Durand, M. A., Song, J., Aarts, J., Barr, P. J., Berger, Z., . . . Van der Weijden, T. (2017). A three-talk model for shared decision making: Multistage consultation process. *British Medical Journal, 2017*(359), j4891. Advance online publication. http://dx.doi.org/10.1136/bmj.j4891

Elwyn, G., Frosch, D., Thomson, R., Joseph-Williams, N., Lloyd, A., Kinnersley, P., . . . Barry, M. (2012). Shared decision making: A model for clinical practice. *Journal of General Internal Medicine, 27*, 1361–1367. http://dx.doi.org/10.1007/s11606-012-2077-6

Goldstein, R. B., Smith, S. M., Chou, S. P., Saha, T. D., Jung, J., Zhang, H., . . . Grant, B. F. (2016). The epidemiology of *DSM–5* posttraumatic stress disorder in the United States: Results from the National Epidemiologic Survey on Alcohol and Related Conditions-III. *Social Psychiatry and Psychiatric Epidemiology, 51*, 1137–1148. http://dx.doi.org/10.1007/s00127-016-1208-5

Hamann, J., Leucht, S., & Kissling, W. (2003). Shared decision making in psychiatry. *Acta Psychiatrica Scandinavica, 107*, 403–409. http://dx.doi.org/10.1034/j.1600-0447.2003.00130.x

Harik, J. M., Hundt, N. E., Bernardy, N. C., Norman, S. B., & Hamblen, J. L. (2016). Desired involvement in treatment decisions among adults with PTSD symptoms. *Journal of Traumatic Stress, 29*, 221–228. http://dx.doi.org/10.1002/jts.22102

Haynes, R. B., Sackett, D. L., Gray, J. M., Cook, D. J., & Guyatt, G. H. (1996). Transferring evidence from research into practice: 1. The role of clinical care research evidence in clinical decisions [Editorial]. *Evidence-Based Medicine, 1*(7), 196–198.

Hollon, S. D., Areán, P. A., Craske, M. G., Crawford, K. A., Kivlahan, D. R., Magnavita, J. J., . . . Kurtzman, H. (2014). Development of clinical practice guidelines. *Annual Review of Clinical Psychology, 10*, 213–241. http://dx.doi.org/10.1146/annurev-clinpsy-050212-185529

Institute of Medicine. (2011a). *Clinical practice guidelines we can trust.* Washington, DC: National Academies Press.

Institute of Medicine. (2011b). *Finding what works in health care: Standard for systematic reviews.* Washington, DC: National Academies Press.

Institute of Medicine, Committee on the Assessment of Ongoing Efforts in the Treatment of Posttraumatic Stress Disorder, Board on the Health of Select Populations. (2014). *Treatment for posttraumatic stress disorder in military and veteran populations: Final assessment.* Washington, DC: National Academies Press.

Jonas, D. E., Cusack, K., Forneris, C. A., Wilkins, T. M., Sonis, J., Middleton, J. C., . . . Gaynes, B. N. (2013). *Psychological and pharmacological treatments for adults with posttraumatic stress disorder (PTSD).* Rockville, MD: Agency for Healthcare Research and Quality. http://dx.doi.org/10.1037/e553842013-001

Kew, K. M., Malik, P., Aniruddhan, K., & Normansell, R. (2017). Shared decision-making for people with asthma. *Cochrane Database of Systematic Reviews.* http://dx.doi.org/10.1002/14651858.CD012330.pub2

Kilpatrick, D. G., Resnick, H. S., Milanak, M. E., Miller, M. W., Keyes, K. M., & Friedman, M. J. (2013). National estimates of exposure to traumatic events and PTSD prevalence using *DSM–IV* and *DSM–5* criteria. *Journal of Traumatic Stress, 26,* 537–547. http://dx.doi.org/10.1002/jts.21848

LeBlanc, A., Herrin, J., Williams, M. D., Inselman, J. W., Branda, M. E., Shah, N. D., . . . Montori, V. M. (2015). Shared decision making for antidepressants in primary care: A cluster randomized trial. *JAMA Internal Medicine, 175,* 1761–1770. http://dx.doi.org/10.1001/jamainternmed.2015.5214

McLaughlin, K. A., Koenen, K. C., Hill, E. D., Petukhova, M., Sampson, N. A., Zaslavsky, A. M., & Kessler, R. C. (2013). Trauma exposure and posttraumatic stress disorder in a national sample of adolescents. *Journal of the American Academy of Child & Adolescent Psychiatry, 52,* 815–830. http://dx.doi.org/10.1016/j.jaac.2013.05.011

Mental Health America. (2018). *The state of mental health in America.* Retrieved from http://www.mentalhealthamerica.net/issues/state-mental-health-america

Morina, N., Wicherts, J. M., Lobbrecht, J., & Priebe, S. (2014). Remission from posttraumatic stress disorder in adults: A systematic review and meta-analysis of long term outcome studies. *Clinical Psychology Review, 34,* 249–255. http://dx.doi.org/10.1016/j.cpr.2014.03.002

Mott, J. M., Stanley, M. A., Street, R. L., Jr., Grady, R. H., & Teng, E. J. (2014). Increasing engagement in evidence-based PTSD treatment through shared decision-making: A pilot study. *Military Medicine, 179,* 143–149. http://dx.doi.org/10.7205/MILMED-D-13-00363

National Comorbidity Survey. (2017). *Lifetime prevalence of DSM–IV/WMH-CIDI disorders by sex and cohort* [Data file]. Retrieved from https://www.hcp.med.harvard.edu/ncs/ftpdir/table_ncsr_LTprevgenderxage.pdf

National Learning Consortium. (2013). *Shared decision making* [Fact sheet]. Retrieved from https://www.healthit.gov/sites/default/files/nlc_shared_decision_making_fact_sheet.pdf

Nugent, N. R., Saunders, B. E., Williams, L. M., Hanson, R., Smith, D. W., & Fitzgerald, M. M. (2009). Posttraumatic stress symptom trajectories in children living in families reported for family violence. *Journal of Traumatic Stress, 22,* 460–466. http://dx.doi.org/10.1002/jts.20440

Orcutt, H. K., Erickson, D. J., & Wolfe, J. (2004). The course of PTSD symptoms among Gulf War veterans: A growth mixture modeling approach. *Journal of Traumatic Stress, 17*(3), 195–202. http://dx.doi.org/10.1023/B:JOTS.0000029262.42865.c2

Rothbaum, B. O., Foa, E. B., Riggs, D. S., Murdock, T., & Walsh, W. (1992). A prospective examination of post-traumatic stress disorder in rape victims. *Journal of Traumatic Stress, 5,* 455–475. http://dx.doi.org/10.1002/jts.2490050309

Simiola, V., Neilson, E. C., Thompson, R., & Cook, J. M. (2015). Preferences for trauma treatment: A systematic review of the empirical literature. *Psychological Trauma: Theory, Research, Practice, and Policy, 7,* 516–524. http://dx.doi.org/10.1037/tra0000038

Stacey, D., Légaré, F., Lewis, K., Barry, M. J., Bennett, C. L., Eden, K. B., . . . Trevena, L. (2017). Decision aids for people facing health treatment or screening decisions. *Cochrane Database of Systematic Reviews, 4,* CD001431. http://dx.doi.org/10.1002/14651858.CD001431.pub5

Stacey, D., Légaré, F., Pouliot, S., Kryworuchko, J., & Dunn, S. (2010). Shared decision making models to inform an interprofessional perspective on decision making: A theory analysis. *Patient Education and Counseling, 80,* 164–172. http://dx.doi.org/10.1016/j.pec.2009.10.015

U.S. Department of Health and Human Services, Agency for Healthcare Research and Quality. (2016). *The SHARE approach* (AHRQ Publication No. 140034-1-EF). Retrieved from https://www.ahrq.gov/sites/default/files/publications/files/share-approach_factsheet.pdf

U.S. Department of Veterans Affairs, National Center for PTSD. (2017). *PTSD treatment decision aid: The choice is yours.* Retrieved from https://www.ptsd.va.gov/apps/decisionaid/

Viswanathan, M., Ansari, M. T., Berkman, N. D., Chang, S., Hartling, L., McPheeters, M., . . . Treadwell, J. R. (2012). *Assessing the risk of bias of individual studies in systematic reviews of health care interventions methods guide for comparative effectiveness reviews* (AHRQ Publication No. 12-EHC047-EF). Rockville, MD: Agency for Healthcare Research and Quality.

Watts, B. V., Schnurr, P. P., Zayed, M., Young-Xu, Y., Stender, P., & Llewellyn-Thomas, H. (2015). A randomized controlled clinical trial of a patient decision aid for post-traumatic stress disorder. *Psychiatric Services, 66,* 149–154. http://dx.doi.org/10.1176/appi.ps.201400062

2

Foundations of PTSD Treatments

Caroline Vaile Wright

Most of the chapters in this casebook focus on describing the specific components found in various recommended treatments for adults with posttraumatic stress disorder (PTSD), based on the American Psychological Association's (APA's) *Clinical Practice Guideline for the Treatment of PTSD* (APA Clinical Practice Guideline; APA, 2017). This chapter, however, covers foundational issues in the treatment of PTSD that transcend specific recommendations—that is, elements shared across many psychotherapies and not specific to one theoretical orientation, often referred to as *common factors*. The factors included in this chapter are not intended to be an exhaustive list; entire chapters can be—and have been—written about many of these factors. Instead, the intent of the chapter is to give the reader a sense of the breadth and depth of the knowledge, skills, and awareness needed to treat adults with PTSD effectively. Moreover, these factors do not exist in isolation and instead should be conceptualized as interrelated. The chapter concludes with a discussion of the core competencies of providers that are believed to be important when providing effective care in trauma psychology.

COMMON FACTORS ACROSS ALL RECOMMENDED PSYCHOTHERAPIES

This chapter begins with a discussion of therapeutic factors often seen as common across all psychotherapies, including those in the APA Clinical

http://dx.doi.org/10.1037/0000196-002
Casebook to the APA Clinical Practice Guideline for the Treatment of PTSD, edited by
L. F. Bufka, C. V. Wright, and R. W. Halfond

Practice Guideline. These factors include informed consent, alliance or work-ing relationship, diagnostic assessment, comorbidity, goal setting, patient factors, treatment adherence and attendance, outcome measurement, and termination.

Informed Consent

Viewed across treatment approaches as a critical first step when initiating therapy with a client, *informed consent* has been defined as the "legal and ethical obligation to provide information to patients before they initiate assessment or treatment" (Knapp, VandeCreek, & Fingerhut, 2017, p. 83). Others have defined it as the act of obtaining "consent from an informed person," meaning that the patient has the right to refuse treatment and that the role of the therapist is to protect the patient's right to give "informed refusal" (Fisher, 2016). As part of maintaining good practice, informed consent may prevent future misunderstandings and disappointments in therapy by promoting open exchanges, anticipating questions, establishing a shared set of expectations for therapy including around limits of confidentiality, and helping patients understand the process of therapy. All of these are believed to be essential for building and maintaining trust, a critical component because patients who trust their health care professionals are more likely to seek and cooperate in treatment (Knapp et al., 2017).

Informed consent may play a particularly important role when working with adults presenting for PTSD treatment. Specifically, informed consent in PTSD treatment stresses that the trauma resolution work is an attempt to process the trauma directly (Courtois, 2008), may result in feeling worse for a period of time before beginning to feel better (APA, 2017), and could possibly disrupt relationships with spouses or significant others because of periods of resulting emotional detachment, lack of intimacy, and impaired sexual relationships (Knapp et al., 2017). Therefore, it is critical that the informed consent process be active rather than passive and that it continue throughout the entirety of therapy. This process includes going beyond giving patients a standard form to sign or a scripted discussion (Knapp et al., 2017) and may include devising forms that are personalized and accurately represent your policies (Fisher, 2016). Moreover, discussions of the limits of confidentiality and, in the case of PTSD treatment, the potential inclusion of specific exposure-based techniques need to be conducted without sounding uncertain, reluctant, hesitant, defensive, or apologetic out of fear that the patient will not want to proceed with treatment (Fisher, 2016). Instead, championing the notion that informed consent should be a collaborative and shared decision-making process between patient and provider is more likely to result in trust, buy-in, improved patient autonomy, and self-determination, and it ultimately may lead to better patient outcomes and greater satisfaction (APA, 2017; Knapp et al., 2017).

Therapeutic Alliance/Working Relationship

Bordin (1979) is generally credited with articulating the most comprehensive theory of *therapeutic alliance*, which is defined as an agreement between the patient and therapist on the goals and tasks of therapy, within the context of an emotional bond between the two individuals. From both a clinical and theoretical perspective, the importance of the therapeutic alliance to treatment outcome seems intuitive (Zilcha-Mano, 2017). Yet, meta-analyses (Flückiger, Del Re, Wampold, & Horvath, 2018) looking across various treatment modalities have typically found only a moderate relationship between therapeutic alliance and outcome (approximately 8% of the variance), and although the findings are generally robust, some have called into question the relative importance of the alliance particularly within the context of manualized-treatment protocols (for background, see Flückiger, Del Re, Wampold, Symonds, & Horvath, 2012). Research suggests the existence of a nuanced relationship. For example, weak therapeutic alliance has been shown to be related to premature termination from therapy (Swift & Greenberg, 2015); however, this relationship may be moderated by patient education level (Constantino et al., 2017). In general, a good therapeutic alliance certainly would seem to make it possible for treatment to be successful. Overall, such findings highlight the importance of personalization in treatment, in that different patients may be helped by different therapy elements at different stages of therapy (Constantino et al., 2017; Reynolds et al., 2017).

This personalization may be particularly salient when examining the role that culture plays in building a strong alliance between patient and therapist. Hook, Davis, Owen, and DeBlaere (2017) highlighted the critical role that "cultural humility" may play in the establishment of a strong therapeutic alliance. Koo, Tiet, and Rosen (2016) found that veterans with PTSD who were from racial or ethnic minority groups reported lower ratings of bond and overall therapeutic alliance when asked about their relationships with former outpatient providers. Weak alliance between patients from racial and ethnic minority groups and therapists predicted lower treatment satisfaction and perceived therapist incompetence. However, a therapist who is culturally humble is viewed by the patient as "other oriented" and facilitates a culturally safe environment while being emotionally engaged and responsive to the patient's needs. Such attributes have been positively related to deepening the therapeutic bond and alliance between ethnic minority clients and therapists (Hook et al., 2017). Furthermore, Hook et al. (2017) encouraged therapists to explore cultural opportunities in therapy sessions by expressing curiosity and interest in their patients' cultural identities and ensuring that the tasks of therapy are consistent with the patients' cultural worldviews.

Establishing a strong therapeutic alliance has particular significance when treating individuals with PTSD. Many trauma-focused interventions involve the patient approaching, rather than avoiding, painful memories that elicit anxiety and distress, which can put significant demands on both patients and therapists

(Hoffart, Øktedalen, Langkaas, & Wampold, 2013). Moreover, patients with PTSD often report experiencing helplessness, shame, and guilt, which are challenging to reveal to a therapist, especially if an early and strong bond has not been established (Hoffart et al., 2013). Yet, the literature examining therapeutic alliance specific to treatment in adults with PTSD is inconsistent on whether alliance is related to positive outcomes (e.g., APA, 2017), suggesting the need for additional research. Therefore, studies examining the therapeutic alliance specific to prolonged exposure (PE) treatment for adults with PTSD highlight the importance of agreement about treatment tasks and goals in therapy (Hoffart et al., 2013) and suggested that alliance was associated with PE homework adherence and overall treatment completion (Keller, Zoellner, & Feeny, 2010). Furthermore, when examining the literature on pharmacotherapy for PTSD, Keller and colleagues (2010) noted the paucity of research on alliance but found in their study that alliance was not strongly associated with medication adherence or dosage, suggesting that taking medication may not require the same level of goal and task agreement as PE. This finding is consistent with non-PTSD-treatment-specific research examining the role of the therapeutic relationship on pharmacologic interventions (Beutler, Forrester, Gallagher-Thompson, Thompson, & Tomlins, 2012). Finally, despite criticisms about the relative importance of alliance within manualized treatments noted earlier, Flückiger et al. (2012) found no support for the conclusion that the alliance was any less important to treatment outcome in standardized evidence-based treatments, such as those used to treat PTSD in adults.

Diagnostic Assessment

Diagnostic assessment is often one of the first steps in treatment initiation, following informed consent. In addition to being required for billing purposes, diagnostic assessment accurately determines eligibility for services, guides treatment planning, and may play an important role in treatment success (Jensen-Doss & Weisz, 2008). Despite the importance of diagnostic accuracy, the assessment process has traditionally been conducted through informal methods such as open, unstructured interviews in lieu of more valid, reliable methods, including structured or semistructured clinical interviews combined with standardized instruments (Aklin & Turner, 2006; Jensen-Doss & Weisz, 2008). Information gathering through informal methods has the potential to result in invalid diagnoses, which could have numerous negative consequences, including interference with the therapeutic alliance due to a lack of agreement on therapy goals (Jensen-Doss & Weisz, 2008). This may be particularly true when working with ethnic minorities because they are more likely than White adults to be misdiagnosed (Aklin & Turner, 2006). To mitigate this possibility, experts recommend that in addition to conducting a comprehensive assessment (i.e., structured or semistructured interviews combined with standardized instruments), therapists should incorporate collateral information; consider race, ethnicity, and cultural background (including socioeconomic status) in their assessments; and enhance their cultural competence through consultation and continuing education programs (Aklin & Turner, 2006).

Diagnostic assessment and accuracy are uniquely salient when determining whether an adult has PTSD. To begin, Criterion A of the fifth edition of the *Diagnostic and Statistical Manual of Mental Disorders* (*DSM–5*; American Psychiatric Association, 2013) criteria for PTSD has been controversial since it was first conceptualized (Kilpatrick, Resnick, & Acierno, 2009; May & Wisco, 2016; Priebe et al., 2018). Although a thorough discussion of the controversy is beyond the scope of this chapter, Criterion A defines a traumatic event and serves as a determining factor, or gatekeeper, for whether one qualifies for the diagnosis of PTSD (Kilpatrick et al., 2009; May & Wisco, 2016). Criterion A has been modified with each new edition of the *DSM* (Priebe et al., 2018), generally moving toward a less restrictive definition of what constitutes trauma. *DSM–5* (American Psychiatric Association, 2013), the most recent edition, made some significant changes relative to earlier editions, such as including both direct and indirect exposure to trauma in Criterion A and removing the requirement of subjective distress as a result of the trauma (i.e., Criterion A2; May & Wisco, 2016).

How Criterion A is defined can have implications for diagnostic prevalence, as can the way in which the index trauma is defined for individuals who have experienced multiple traumas (Priebe et al., 2018). Some have argued that PTSD has been overdiagnosed, especially among service members and veterans, causing it to lose its explanatory power and clinical utility (Litz, 2014). Others have raised concerns about the challenges of diagnostic accuracy due to overlapping symptomatology between PTSD and other disorders and the subjective nature of symptom descriptions by patients (Bauer et al., 2013). Courtois (2008) argued that the current diagnosis of PTSD does not adequately cover the complexity of individuals experiencing complex trauma (e.g., C-PTSD/DESNOS), such as the reactions reported by victims of repeated, cumulative, and extensive trauma, thereby resulting in possible underdiagnosis or misdiagnosis.

To address these concerns, Litz (2014) and others have recommended using formal structured diagnostic instruments, embedded within the standard psychosocial assessment conducted at the start of treatment (Courtois, 2008). The Clinician-Administered PTSD Scale (Blake et al., 1995), a semistructured interview, is generally considered the gold standard for PTSD diagnosis. Additional instruments with strong psychometric properties include the Impact of Events Scale—Revised (Weiss & Marmar, 1996), Posttraumatic Diagnostic Scale (Foa, 1996), PTSD Checklist for *DSM–5* (Weathers et al., 2013) and Trauma Symptom Inventory (Briere, 1996). Finally, for adults with crime-related PTSD (e.g., domestic violence), it has been recommended that assessment procedures should include gathering information on immediate needs, such as housing and medical concerns, as well as safety and subsequent risk of future victimization (e.g., whereabouts and potential contact with the perpetrator; Amstadter, McCart, & Ruggiero, 2007).

Comorbidity

Comorbidity—specifically the occurrence of two or more *DSM* disorders experienced at one time—is central to treatment planning and sequencing and to the coordination of service delivery (Clarkin & Kendall, 1992; Newman, Moffitt, Caspi, & Silva, 1998). Given the extensiveness of comorbidity within child, adolescent, and adult mental health populations (Newman et al., 1998), the presence of comorbidity in treatment is often considered to be the rule rather than the exception (Clarkin & Kendall, 1992). Although comorbid disorders do not have to be treated concurrently, it is important that the therapist assess multiple areas of difficulty to sequence treatment targets adequately (Clarkin & Kendall, 1992). Moreover, even though comorbidity does not necessarily indicate increased treatment difficulty (Clarkin & Kendall, 1992), comorbid presentations have been found to have a more chronic course and poorer prognosis, due in part to the physical, educational, judicial, and economic problems associated with them (Newman et al., 1998). Specifically, comorbidity has been linked to various lifestyle factors, including job stress or unemployment, physical illness, housing instability, lack of social and familial support, and increased social welfare support, making service coordination critically important for treatment to be successful (Newman et al., 1998).

High rates of comorbidity (anywhere from 20% to 60%) have been documented in adults with PTSD, underscoring some of the challenges in treating this population (Amstadter et al., 2007). Common comorbid disorders and concerns for adults with PTSD include depression, anxiety, panic attacks, alcohol and drug abuse, dissociation, self-destructive or risky behavior, medical and somatic concerns, difficulty with affect regulation, problems with interpersonal relationships, and revictimization (Cloitre, Stovall-McClough, & Levitt, 2004; Courtois, 2008; Gold, 2004; Teng et al., 2008). In addition, veterans returning from Operation Iraqi Freedom and Operation Enduring Freedom have presented in both mental health and general medical settings with comorbid mild traumatic brain injury (mTBI), often the result of increased exposure to dangers such as improvised explosive devices (Davis, Walter, Chard, Parkinson, & Houston, 2013; Holland, Lisman, & Currier, 2013). This group has also been noted to have higher rates of alcohol problems (Erbes, Curry, & Leskela, 2009). These comorbidities have been noted by providers as perceived barriers to engaging in evidence-based treatments such as prolonged exposure and cognitive processing therapy (Cook, Dinnen, Simiola, Thompson, & Schnurr, 2014). All of this lends support to the notion that treatment of PTSD in adults is complex and challenging, requiring specialized knowledge and skills but also some breadth with interventions that target a wide range of difficulties (Gold, 2004). A review of the research suggests that PTSD-specific treatments may be effective at reducing comorbid symptomatology including depression (Amstadter et al., 2007), substance use disorders (Ouimette, Moos, & Finney, 2003), panic disorder (Teng et al., 2008), and mTBI (Davis et al., 2013). Further, although definitive guidance on how to sequence treatment most effectively (i.e., concurrently vs. targeting one disorder before the other) remains lacking, the presence of a comorbid disorder need not discourage the initiation of evidence-based PTSD treatments for adults.

Goal Setting

Another important component of successful therapy involves the collaborative process of therapeutic goal setting, which serves to guide both therapist interventions and patient participation. Consensus regarding goals—meaning that both the patient and therapist understand and accept the treatment rationale and believe the treatment is appropriate and will bring some relief—may help mitigate the strains experienced by both patient and therapist as a result of trauma-focused approaches (Hoffart et al., 2013). Therapeutic goals—the purpose or intentions a patient is attempting to address in therapy—influence behavior and causal attributions (Long, 2001). Specifically, a shared belief that the patient had some control over the problem was positively associated with patient improvement. Further, as noted previously regarding therapeutic alliance, goal agreement may influence treatment satisfaction, premature termination, and ultimate success in therapy (Long, 2001; Swift & Greenberg, 2015). Again, given the demanding nature of many PTSD-related treatments, goal agreement between patient and therapist is vital.

Although the concept of collaborative goal setting is independent of a particular theoretical orientation or treatment approach, therapists often interpret their patients' concerns regarding potential treatment goals via their own theoretical orientations to arrive at a shared understanding (Renninger, 2013). Further, the process is fluid, with goals often changing over the course of therapy, making actual goal agreement—as opposed to perceived goal agreement—challenging to assess (Long, 2001; Renninger, 2013). As such, some have highlighted the importance of establishing a strong therapeutic contract, hypothesized to be an intervention in itself, which ensures explicit goal agreement between patient and therapist (Long, 2001).

Patient Factors

Patient factors, generally defined as nondiagnostic personal qualities that influence response to treatment interventions, can play an important role in case formulation; treatment planning, sequencing, and implementation; and therapeutic success (Beutler et al., 2012; Constantino, Penek, Bernecker, & Overtree, 2014). Patient factors can be viewed as an umbrella term for a variety of attributes, including but not limited to outcome expectations, credibility beliefs, stages of change and motivation, resistance or resistance traits, openness to evidence-based treatments, level of functioning, subjective distress, coping style, attachment style, cognitive flexibility and function, literacy level, demographic variables (e.g., marital status, employment status, gender, race or ethnicity, age, socioeconomic status), beliefs about mental health care, logistical concerns, immediate needs or crises, use of community resources, and cynicism (Bachelor, Laverdière, Gamache, & Bordeleau, 2007; Békés, Beaulieu-Prévost, Guay, Belleville, & Marchand, 2016; Beutler et al., 2012; Breuninger & Teng, 2017; Constantino et al., 2014; Cook et al., 2014; DeViva, 2014; Marques et al., 2016; Miles & Thompson, 2016; Renninger, 2013). Research suggests that when compared with treatment and relationship factors, patient variables produced the largest effect size on positive therapeutic outcome (Beutler et al., 2012).

The patient factor area with some of the most robust extant research involves the role of patient motivation. Patient level of motivation, also conceptualized as readiness for change, is viewed by many as a vital prerequisite for successful treatment. Research suggests that highly motivated patients are more likely to engage in therapeutic tasks, tolerate discomfort, complete homework assignments, remain in therapy longer, and have better therapeutic outcomes (Bachelor et al., 2007; Cook et al., 2014; Philips & Wennberg, 2014). Not surprisingly, lack of motivation is viewed as a prominent barrier to treatment (Grumet & Fitzpatrick, 2016), leading some to argue for the importance of assessing motivation prior to the start of therapy in order to better inform therapeutic interventions (Renninger, 2013). Moreover, DeViva (2014) advocated for the use of interventions designed to increase motivation and readiness for change in patients. Some posited examples include the use of motivational interviewing and pretreatment training and preparation videos (Erbes et al., 2009).

Numerous patient factors have been investigated in adults seeking treatment for PTSD. For patients engaged in exposure therapy and EMDR for PTSD, credibility beliefs (i.e., beliefs that a particular treatment approach is logical) were associated with positive treatment outcomes (Constantino et al., 2014). Some providers working with veterans with PTSD have expressed concerns that compensation-seeking status could interfere with treatment because veterans might fear that improvement would jeopardize their disability eligibility (Cook et al., 2014). The relationships among various demographic variables and treatment responses have also been examined, particularly in veteran populations (Doran & DeViva, 2018). For example, Miles and Thompson (2016) found that veterans who dropped out of therapy prematurely were more likely to be African American and from an era other than Vietnam. Similarly, Hundt and colleagues (2014) found that younger age was associated with low treatment utilization among veterans, and DeViva (2014) noted that being married and being employed were associated with greater treatment completion. Such findings suggest the importance of personalized and targeted engagement methods delivered early and continually throughout therapy.

Treatment Adherence

Treatment adherence is a multidimensional concept and an important contributor to treatment outcome (Dolsen et al., 2017; Kang, Tucker, Wippold, Marsiske, & Wegener, 2016), although the association between adherence and outcome is likely complex and influenced by additional variables (Owen & Hilsenroth, 2014). *Treatment adherence* on the part of the therapist refers to the degree to which treatment is delivered as intended and can be measured with standardized instruments to ensure that prescribed techniques are being performed and proscribed techniques are omitted (Amole et al., 2017; Schoenwald & Garland, 2013). To ensure adequate training and treatment delivery fidelity, some minimum level of adherence is critical, yet it is important to acknowledge that some variability is not only likely but expected in therapists' use of techniques over the course of therapy (Owen & Hilsenroth, 2014). Therapists have the difficult challenge of finding some balance between using specific techniques to address the clinical problem and nonspecific techniques to develop the treatment context and maintain patient engagement and therapeutic alliance within a time-limited session (Amole et al., 2017). Some have posited that this degree of adherence flexibility reflects therapist competence superior to strict adherence (Campbell, Guydish, Le, Wells, & McCarty, 2015), which could have important implications: Overly strict adherence to a treatment protocol has been viewed negatively by some providers (Marques et al., 2016) and may be related to worse treatment outcomes (Owen & Hilsenroth, 2014).

Patient adherence, on the other hand, refers to the degree to which a patient follows through on health-related recommendations (Kang et al., 2016). In the case of psychotherapy, this includes the patient receiving and understanding the treatment as well as enacting it by practicing the treatment recommendations outside of session (Dolsen et al., 2017). Patient factors—including motivation level, receptivity, and resistance to therapy tasks—can contribute to fluctuations in adherence (Owen & Hilsenroth, 2014). Furthermore, perceived provider cultural sensitivity may affect treatment adherence for patients from racial and ethnic minority groups. Ensuring that treatment is both patient centered and culturally sensitive, including prioritizing equitable access to services and effective therapist–patient communication, may increase treatment adherence among individuals from racial and ethnic minority groups (Kang et al., 2016). In addition, recent research on ways to improve patient treatment adherence has focused on the role of improved sleep as a possible pathway to support memory and learning, foster treatment understanding, and improve homework compliance (Dolsen et al., 2017).

Adherence is a particular challenge in the treatment of adults with PTSD. Multiple studies have suggested that providers perceive strict adherence to evidence-based PTSD treatments as having the potential to exacerbate symptoms, thereby making patients worse and leading to premature termination (Cook et al., 2014; Marques et al., 2016). These perceptions persist even though no studies have supported significant iatrogenic effects of PTSD treatment (Marques et al., 2016). Rigid adherence to PTSD treatment protocols have been associated with higher rates of dropout, suggesting that even within PTSD treatment a delicate balance related to adherence flexibility is warranted (Doran & DeViva, 2018). Such flexibility includes taking the time to address any negative process indicators that arise (Doran & DeViva, 2018), as well as calibrating the pace and intensity of techniques, such as exposure, to match the patient's capacity (Courtois, 2008) while remaining cognizant of any resistance or avoidance on the part of the therapist or patient due to unwarranted fears.

Treatment Attendance

Regular and frequent therapy appointment attendance is, not surprisingly, associated with better outcomes and symptom improvement (Gutner, Suvak, Sloan, & Resick, 2016). Patients cancel or reschedule sessions with moderate frequency (approximately once per month) for a variety of logistical, personal, and clinical reasons (DeFife, Conklin, Smith, & Poole, 2010). Common reasons cited for missing appointments include scheduling conflicts with work or family, transportation problems, and physical or emotional problems. Further, clinical process factors are believed to be prominent contributors to missing appointments, namely, low patient motivation for treatment, negative feelings about the treatment model or interventions, and therapeutic alliance ruptures (DeFife et al., 2010; Doran & DeViva, 2018). In addition to leading to inadequate doses of treatment, missed appointments and no-shows are likely to lead to treatment dropout and premature termination.

Premature termination—also referred to in the literature as *dropout, attrition,* and *unilateral termination*—refers to situations in which a patient discontinues therapy before meeting treatment goals, without finishing therapeutic tasks, and typically without experiencing a substantial reduction in symptomatology (Swift & Greenberg, 2014; Swift, Greenberg, Whipple, & Kominiak, 2012). Although universal agreement is lacking in the literature on how best to operationalize and measure the construct, the negative effects of premature termination on treatment outcomes is well documented (Owen, Imel, Adelson, & Rodolfa, 2012; Swift & Greenberg, 2014; Swift et al., 2012). This may be particularly true for patients from racial or ethnic minority groups, who are more likely to receive fewer services and prematurely terminate from therapy than White patients (Lester, Resick, Young-Xu, & Artz, 2010; Owen et al., 2012). Although patients often have several reasons for dropping out of treatment (i.e., perceived improvement, logistical barriers), Murdock, Edwards, and Murdock (2010) noted that "there is little concordance between therapist and client perspectives on reasons for psychotherapy termination" (p. 223). In particular, therapists appear to have a blind spot: They do not notice or acknowledge that a patient is dissatisfied with the therapist or with therapy and do not recognize that this dissatisfaction may be a significant contributor to premature termination (Murdock et al., 2010; Owen et al., 2012). As such, many scholars have highlighted the importance of understanding why patients do not show up for appointments or drop out altogether (Gutner et al., 2016; Lester et al., 2010) and to engage in strategies designed to reduce premature termination. These strategies include pretreatment education regarding therapeutic roles and tasks, obtaining buy-in of the treatment rationale, assessing patient motivation and negative reactions to therapy, fostering the therapeutic alliance and addressing ruptures, attending to cultural differences and expectations, incorporating shared decision making and patient preferences, and routinely monitoring outcomes and progress (DeFife et al., 2010; Doran & DeViva, 2018; Lester et al., 2010; Swift et al., 2012).

The issue of dropout and premature termination has been a topic of great interest within the PTSD treatment literature. Much of the research has focused on determining whether there are differences in dropout rates by treatment approach (e.g., Imel, Laska, Jakupcak, & Simpson, 2013; Swift et al., 2012) and identifying potential predictors for premature termination by individuals seeking treatment for PTSD (e.g., Davis et al., 2013; Doran & DeViva, 2018). Although Imel et al. (2013) found similar dropout rates for patients in various PTSD treatments, others have found lower dropout rates when integrative approaches to treating PTSD (i.e., combining multiple techniques) are included in the analysis (Swift & Greenberg, 2014). Further, studies have generally found differences in dropout rates depending on whether the research was conducted with a randomized controlled sample population or a naturalistic clinical sample, with the latter generally having a higher rate (Doran & DeViva, 2018). Although identifying consistent predictors for dropout has been challenging, numerous studies have demonstrated that dropout typically happens early in treatment (i.e., before Session 3), suggesting that individuals who drop out did not receive the active components of various PTSD treatment protocols and continue to experience significant PTSD symptomatology (Davis et al., 2013; Doran & DeViva, 2018; Kehle-Forbes, Meis, Spoont, & Polusny, 2016). Given this, the engagement strategies mentioned earlier, such as motivational interviewing and cultural humility, may be particularly important for individuals receiving treatment for PTSD, especially individuals from racial and ethnic minority groups or underserved populations.

Outcome Measurement

Similar to other topics in this chapter, there is a robust research literature on the tracking and monitoring of outcomes and progress in therapy. There is, however, apparent confusion among providers because the concept is often labeled with a variety of terms, including but not limited to *routine outcome monitoring, quality improvement, quality reporting, patient-reported outcomes measurement,* and more recently, *measurement-based care.* At its most basic, outcome measurement in psychotherapy refers to the measurement of therapeutic progress by a patient in treatment (Hatfield & Ogles, 2004; Lambert, 2010). Historically, psychotherapists' attempts at measuring change were informal in nature and lacked methodological rigor (Lambert, 2010), and although it is an ethical and professional responsibility (Lambert & Hawkins, 2004), routine outcome assessment remains infrequent, with only 39% of psychologists surveyed indicating they use some form of outcome assessment to measure therapeutic progress (Wright et al., 2017). This finding is consistent with results from 13 years earlier (i.e., 37%; Hatfield & Ogles, 2004), suggesting that little has changed.

These findings are unfortunate, as the use of routine outcome measurement has many notable benefits for both patients and providers, such as improved health care outcomes for individuals and couples (Reese, Norsworthy, & Rowlands, 2009; Reese, Toland, Slone, & Norsworthy, 2010), improved patient satisfaction (Johnson & Shaha, 1996), increased feedback to patients regarding progress (Bobbitt, Cate, Beardsley, Azocar, & McCulloch, 2012; Lambert, 2010), increased feedback to clinicians enabling them to improve care and increase skills (Bickman & Noser, 1999; Johnson & Shaha, 1996), and increased cost-effectiveness (Slade et al., 2006). These benefits are especially important for patients at risk for prematurely dropping out of treatment because of lack of progress or deterioration, and outcome measurement allows for the clinician to make adjustments to the treatment plan as appropriate (Lambert et al., 2003; Swift et al., 2012).

As previously noted, Litz (2014) strongly recommended the use of outcome monitoring when working with individuals in treatment for PTSD, advocating for the use of at least weekly administrations of reliable and validated patient-reported outcome measures such as the PTSD Checklist for *DSM–5* (Weathers et al., 2013). Moreover, his recommendation came independent of the treatment approach a therapist and patient take, as it allows the patient to "become a better consumer of treatment" (p. 201) and is known to promote therapeutic improvement. In the same vein, Amstadter et al. (2007) suggested employing measures with a reasonable range of response options and a shorter time frame for symptom reporting in order to capture sensitivity to change. Furthermore, others have advocated for the importance of measuring and tracking the patient's perspective of the therapeutic alliance in addition to PTSD symptomatology to ensure treatment engagement (Swift & Greenberg, 2015; Swift et al., 2012).

Termination

Regardless of theoretical orientation or treatment approach, all therapy has a beginning and an end (Bhatia & Gelso, 2017). The final termination phase of treatment—distinctive from premature or unilateral termination—is generally associated with feelings of positive growth as well as sad loss and ideally signifies the agreed-upon or planned completion or ending of therapy (Bhatia & Gelso, 2017; Norcross, Zimmerman, Greenberg, & Swift, 2017). Although termination is often considered a significant component of the therapeutic process, the research base is scant (Bhatia & Gelso, 2017; Olivera, Challú, Gómez Penedo, & Roussos, 2017), and practitioners receive little formal training in their graduate programs regarding termination activities. Despite this, Norcross and colleagues (2017) found relatively high concordance among therapists on self-reported termination activities across various theoretical orientations, with great emphasis on identifying patient gains and growth and helping each patient take ownership of said gains while planning for future growth.

Given the relatively small empirical research literature on planned termination in general, it is probably not too surprising that there are no empirical studies specific to termination in the treatment of PTSD in adults. Of note, however, is that many PTSD treatments, including those described in this casebook, are time limited, potentially making the end of treatment less ambiguous for both the patient and the provider (Mueser, Rosenberg, & Rosenberg, 2009). Given research that shows that patients in general report valuing the opportunity to talk and share openly with their therapist their feelings about ending therapy (Olivera et al., 2017), it would seem important that time-limited treatments for PTSD also take this into consideration. Furthermore, given the specialized nature of PTSD treatment, it is sometimes, if not often, the case that a patient may end trauma-specific work with a therapist and subsequently return to a "regular" therapist or other ongoing supports.

FACTORS POTENTIALLY UNIQUE TO PTSD TREATMENT

Above and beyond common factors, certain elements have particular salience when individuals present for treatment for PTSD. These elements include but are not limited to safety and trust, avoidance, type of trauma including complex trauma, and the potential for vicarious or secondary trauma for providers.

Safety and Trust

Safety within the treatment setting is important across a variety of populations and presenting problems; it generally refers to the degree to which a patient feels comfortable taking risks and being vulnerable in therapy, including discussing painful feelings and memories (Escudero, Friedlander, & Heatherington, 2011). In Herman's (1992) seminal work on trauma recovery, she highlighted the essential component of establishing safety, both physical and emotional, as the first stage when working with trauma survivors. Unlike other treatment-seeking populations, adults with PTSD can commonly present in treatment with multiple ongoing safety concerns, including revictimization (e.g., domestic violence), high-risk behaviors (e.g., self-injurious behavior, suicidality, aggressive behaviors toward others), poor self-care (e.g., substance abuse, poor sleep quality), and dissociation (Brand et al., 2012; Heron, Twomey, Jacobs, & Kaslow, 1997; Johnson & Zlotnick, 2009; Myrick & Green, 2014). Furthermore, patients who reported feeling a lack of safety in therapy also reported greater resistance to change (Dowd, 1999) and tended to do more poorly in treatment (Escudero et al., 2011). Therefore, establishing safety and subsequent trust on the part of the patient in treatment is paramount.

Safety and trust with individuals presenting for PTSD treatment can be established in a number of ways. The treatment setting itself can affect how safe a patient feels via positive, encouraging interactions with facility or clinic staff. Larger and more open treatment spaces may feel safer than small, enclosed rooms, which may feel confining to a trauma survivor and serve as a trigger (Hoyt, Rielage, & Williams, 2012; Marich, 2010). Furthermore, the structure of the treatment program, including the development of a strong therapeutic alliance between patient and provider, is a critical avenue for establishing safety (Heron et al., 1997; Marich, 2010). An essential role of the therapist is establishing appropriate boundaries to ensure safety and trust (Myrick & Green, 2014). Boundary setting can include providing structure for how much and when trauma memories are shared by the patient to prevent oversharing, as well as to prevent avoidance (Myrick & Green, 2014). Boundary setting can also include the therapist having an awareness of his or her own presence and behaviors in a session, as touch within the therapeutic setting can feel confusing or overwhelming to trauma survivors (Brand et al., 2012). Finally, many highlight the importance of revisiting safety and stabilization throughout all stages of recovery and not solely at the beginning, ensuring that survivors achieve a sense of power and control over themselves and their environments (Myrick & Green, 2014; Tummala-Narra, Kallivayalil, Singer, & Andreini, 2012).

Avoidance

Avoidance—one of the four primary *DSM–5* diagnostic criteria along with reexperiencing, negative alterations in cognitions and mood, and arousal—has been referred to as the hallmark of PTSD (Doran & DeViva, 2018). This is, in part, because avoidance serves as both a symptom resulting from trauma exposure and a subsequent maladaptive coping response to manage trauma (Reynolds et al., 2017). Maladaptive coping includes engaging in activities such as unnecessary safety behaviors or distraction (Reynolds et al., 2017), including self-destructive behaviors such as substance use (Hoyt et al., 2012), to "restore control over fear" through the avoidance of traumatic memories and reminders (Salcioglu, Urhan, Pirinccioglu, & Aydin, 2017, p. 123). Other examples of avoidance behavior in treatment are coming late or missing sessions and poor compliance with tasks, such as not completing homework. These behaviors are strategies to avoid confronting and retelling the trauma in session, yet doing so is typically a key component of successful treatment for PTSD (Doran & DeViva, 2018). Not surprisingly, avoidant coping can interfere with the development of the therapeutic alliance in PTSD treatment, which has negative implications for treatment retention and outcome (Doran & DeViva, 2018; Keller et al., 2010; Reynolds et al., 2017).

Reducing avoidant coping, therefore, becomes a critical treatment target when working with adults with PTSD. One recommendation involves providing the full complement of a treatment program over a shorter duration. For example, a patient might attend twice-weekly therapy over 6 weeks rather than once weekly over 12 weeks, as this schedule may be successful at decreasing avoidance by providing more support via more frequent therapist interaction (Gutner et al., 2016). Although some clinics and facilities can accommodate this practice pattern, there are numerous practical and financial barriers for both providers and patients. Additionally, teaching and encouraging the development of adaptive coping skills that do not involve avoidance or self-medication can help adults with PTSD build a tolerance for uncomfortable symptoms and emotions (Hoyt et al., 2012). Moreover, earlier recommendations for enhancing the therapeutic alliance and increasing patient motivation for change, such as personalization of treatment and pretreatment training, could also be effective at reducing avoidance.

Type of Trauma

Much attention has been paid to the type of trauma adults with PTSD have experienced and how that may or may not affect treatment, as PTSD rates and symptom presentation differ across types of trauma. Interpersonal traumas, such as physical and sexual assault, are associated with a higher probability of PTSD and more severe symptomatology, and they are the most common cause of PTSD among women (Amstadter et al., 2007; Priebe et al., 2018). For example, adult survivors of childhood interpersonal abuse present in therapy with a myriad of symptoms (e.g., self-harm suicidality, risk taking, emotional dysregulation, revictimization) that add great complexity to their treatment plans (Courtois, 2008). Combat exposure and witnessed violence are the most common causes of PTSD among men (Amstadter et al., 2007). Given the potential difference in presentation, it is recommended that initial assessments should include questions ascertaining exposure to multiple types of traumatic experiences across the life span (Amstadter et al., 2007). However, the current state of the research is insufficient to make any recommendations regarding whether specific treatments are more effective with certain types of trauma (APA, 2017).

Complex Trauma

The experience of repeated, cumulative traumas, referred to as *complex trauma* (or *complex PTSD/C-PTSD*), has been the focus of a great deal of PTSD treatment research (Courtois, 2008). Herman (1992) is often credited with early conceptualizations of complex trauma, which highlighted how the experience of repeated traumas, from which a victim is either unable or perceives oneself as unable to escape, can alter internal structures of identity as well as attachment and external connections with others. Specifically, the associated sequelae can include feelings of shame, self-blame and powerlessness, difficulty trusting others, fear of abandonment, affect dysregulation, lower satisfaction in intimate relationships, and higher likelihood of revictimization (Myrick & Green, 2014; Tummala-Narra et al., 2012). Given this constellation of reactions experienced by victims, some researchers and clinicians have argued that the current *DSM* diagnostic criteria for PTSD does not adequately reflect complex trauma (Courtois, 2008).

Courtois (2008) also recommended a staged model of treatment for C-PTSD that is organized to address specific issues and skills and emphasizes safety, security, and affect regulation. Stage 1 focuses on pretreatment issues, including alliance building, stabilization and skill building, psychoeducation, and establishing safety. Stage 2 incorporates specific therapeutic techniques to address the trauma more directly toward resolution and integration. Stage 3 focuses on moving forward by establishing enhanced daily living through increased self-awareness and the development of trustworthy relationships with others. Although issues of safety and stabilization are especially critical in the first stage of C-PTSD treatment, it is often appropriate to revisit these issues throughout all stages of treatment (Myrick & Green, 2014; Tummala-Narra et al., 2012). Litz (2014) argued for the importance of taking a flexible and idiographic approach to the selection and implementation of therapeutic techniques with complex cases to maximize treatment effectiveness.

Vicarious and Secondary Trauma for Providers

The literature examining the impact or psychological harm of working with trauma victims for providers and other helping professionals is still relatively in its infancy (Adams & Riggs, 2008; Voss Horrell, Holohan, Didion, & Vance, 2011). One of the challenges has been the lack of consensus on the terms used to describe the phenomenon, resulting in often-interchangeable usage (Miller & Sprang, 2017; O'Brien & Haaga, 2015). *Vicarious trauma* and *secondary trauma* refer to the indirect traumatization that can occur to providers who work with traumatized populations; the assimilation of the traumatic material may result in psychological distress and changes to one's view of the self, others, and the world (Butler, Carello, & Maguin, 2017; Johnson, Bertschinger, Snell, & Wilson, 2014; Voss Horrell et al., 2011). Although many have argued that these terms are not synonymous (Killian, 2008; Voss Horrell et al., 2011), others have suggested that there is little evidence for distinguishing between the terms *vicarious trauma* and *secondary trauma* (Johnson et al., 2014). *Compassion fatigue* and *burnout*, though not unique to working with traumatized populations, have also been used in the literature to describe the occupational stress and emotional strain of being a therapist (Caringi et al., 2017; Voss Horrell et al., 2011).

Numerous studies have examined the potential risk factors for health care providers developing vicarious trauma when working closely with traumatized individuals. These factors include a personal history of trauma, lack of formal trauma training or experience, maladaptive defense style or worldview, high level of empathy, combat-zone deployment, repeated and frequent work with trauma survivors, high caseload demands, lack of social and organizational support, and lack of control and autonomy on the part of the provider (Adams

& Riggs, 2008; Garcia, McGeary, McGeary, Finley, & Peterson, 2014; Holmqvist & Andersen, 2003; Johnson et al., 2014; Killian, 2008; O'Brien & Haaga, 2015; Voss Horrell et al., 2011). Vicarious traumatization can then manifest in a variety of psychological effects, including suspiciousness, anxiety, depression, somatic symptoms, intrusive thoughts and feelings, avoidance, emotional numbing, vulnerability, hyperarousal and vigilance, disengagement, collusive resistance, fatigue, uncertainty, and apathy (Adams & Riggs, 2008; Caringi et al., 2017; Holmqvist & Andersen, 2003). Left unresolved, vicarious trauma can lead to clinician burnout and turnover as well as negative treatment outcomes for patients (Adams & Riggs, 2008; Caringi et al., 2017; Garcia et al., 2014).

Fortunately, multiple protective factors at both the individual and the organizational level have been identified. For example, researchers have cited the importance of peer support within an organization, opportunities to process traumatic work, and regular self-monitoring and engagement in self-care strategies on the part of the provider (Caringi et al., 2017; Garcia et al., 2014; Johnson et al., 2014; Killian, 2008). Organizational policies and support, including reduced workloads, variation in patient load or caseload balance, access to professional resources and adequate workspace, having autonomy or input regarding work schedule and caseload, and availability of support staff are all believed to help mitigate vicarious trauma (Holmqvist & Andersen, 2003; Johnson et al., 2014; Killian, 2008; Voss Horrell et al., 2011). Finally, researchers have advocated for improved formal graduate training related to trauma, using a trauma-informed curriculum that spans more than a single lecture or discussion and is instead more immersive and comprehensive, to protect future clinicians against the potential negative impact of working with traumatized populations (Adams & Riggs, 2008; Butler et al., 2017).

CORE COMPETENCIES OF PROVIDERS

Over the last decade or so, the field of professional psychology has shown sustained movement toward competency-based models of training and practice (Rubin et al., 2007). *Competency* generally refers to possessing the knowledge, skills, attitudes, and values to practice one's profession safely and effectively (Rodolfa et al., 2005). Knowledge and skills in and of themselves are necessary but insufficient to demonstrate competency; rather, demonstrating competency requires action and public verification of such action as a means of protecting and benefiting the public. Rodolfa and colleagues (2005) introduced the cube model for describing competency development in professional psychology. The cube model outlines two competency domains—foundational and functional—that are interrelated and developmental in nature. Foundational competencies refer to the "building blocks" or the core knowledge base underlying what psychologists do in practice. These include multiple components typically taught during graduate school, including reflective practice and self-assessment, scientific knowledge and methods, ethical and legal standards, individual and cultural diversity, interdisciplinary systems, and relationships. Functional competencies, on the other hand, include the knowledge, skills, and values critical to professional functioning and performance of the day-to-day activities of a psychologist. These domains include assessment/diagnosis/conceptualization, intervention, consultation, research/evaluation, supervision/teaching, and management/administration. A third aspect of the competency cube describes the stages of professional development (i.e., doctoral education, internship, post-doctoral residency or fellowship, and continuing competency) within which competency is gained, maintained, and enhanced.

One driving force behind the competency-based movement is the shift in the profession of psychology toward specialization in practice. A specialty area in professional psychology is "a specific area of practice characterized by a distinctive pattern of services related to problems and populations that requires an organized and advanced sequence of education, training, and experience that builds on the core scientific and professional foundations of psychology" (Rodolfa et al., 2005, p. 349). The APA, the Council of Specialties in Professional Psychology, and the American Board of Professional Psychology are all responsible for the definition, recognition, maintenance, and credentialing of specialties. All specialties share the same foundational and functional competencies, but are shaped by the particular problems, populations, and settings served in which the specialty area practices. Although trauma practice is not officially recognized as a specialty area, it has been argued that work with this population requires specialized training (APA, Guideline Development Panel for the Treatment of PTSD in Adults, 2015).

Guidelines on Trauma Competencies for Education and Training

In 2015, the APA Council of Representatives approved the *Guidelines on Trauma Competencies for Education and Training* (APA, Guideline Development Panel for the Treatment of PTSD in Adults, 2015). The guidelines are the product of a national consensus conference on trauma, referred to as the New Haven Trauma Competency Group, which convened in 2014. The guidelines define trauma-related competency as "the minimal knowledge, attitudes, and skills a psychologist working with populations exposed to trauma ought to possess. . . . these competencies are designed to apply across trauma-exposed groups, disciplines, and theoretical stances" (p. 15).

The guidelines include nine cross-cutting competencies (i.e., those considered to be foundational to all other competencies) and five specific competencies, each seen as critical and needed for a therapist to achieve proficiency. The cross-cutting competencies highlight the importance of demonstrating an understanding of the impact of trauma on health outcomes, tailoring treatment interventions to the individual, accounting for developmental life span factors, incorporating survivors' strengths and resilience, addressing the complexities of trauma-related exposures such as comorbidities, engaging in self-care as a provider, evaluating and applying available science, and working collaboratively across systems. The five specific competencies outline the knowledge, skills, and attitudes that providers are required to demonstrate as they relate to scientific knowledge, psychological assessment, psychological intervention, professionalism, and relational and system-level awareness. Following the cube model, these guidelines highlight both foundational and functional competencies specific to trauma psychology. And although aspirational in nature, the guidelines illustrate the need for proposed competencies because formal training in trauma psychology in graduate programs is sorely lacking; as a result, evidence-based psychosocial treatments for PTSD are rarely applied by providers (Hundt, Harik, Barrera, Cully, & Stanley, 2016).

CONCLUSION

Despite decades of research, the term *common factors* continues to drive polarity in the field of psychological treatment (Amole et al., 2017). This polarity is due, in part, to the current state of the research. Although it is true that substantial research supports the importance of common factors contributing to psychotherapeutic outcome, it is also true that there are various inconsistencies in the literature regarding their importance and role in therapy (Stamoulos et al., 2016). Furthermore, little research has focused on the extent and frequency with which therapists use both common factors and treatment-specific techniques within their approaches (Amole et al., 2017). The result is a division between the evidence-based practice camp and the common factors camp, which has the potential to interfere in the delivery of effective patient care (Asnaani & Foa, 2014). Although this chapter will not end this debate, it underscores that this tension is unwarranted and counterproductive. The argument need not be phrased as "either, or" but instead as "yes, and," as it has been argued that solely taking a common-factor approach without also applying appropriate specific strategies is insufficient when delivering effective treatments (Renninger, 2013). One delivers treatment in the context of a therapeutic relationship; together good treatment strategies and strong attention to common factors enhance the likelihood of satisfying patient outcomes. A constructive dialogue about what treatments work for which people at which time, and an understanding of the competencies needed on the part of the provider to deliver that treatment effectively, are truly what will advance care for individuals who have experienced trauma.

REFERENCES

Adams, S. A., & Riggs, S. A. (2008). An exploratory study of vicarious trauma among therapist trainees. *Training and Education in Professional Psychology, 2*, 26–34. http://dx.doi.org/10.1037/1931-3918.2.1.26

Aklin, W. M., & Turner, S. M. (2006). Toward understanding ethnic and cultural factors in the interviewing process. *Psychotherapy: Theory, Research, Practice, Training, 43*, 50–64. http://dx.doi.org/10.1037/0033-3204.43.1.50

American Psychiatric Association. (2013). *Diagnostic and statistical manual of mental disorders* (5th ed.). Arlington, VA: Author.

American Psychological Association. (2015). *Guidelines on trauma competencies for education and training*. Retrieved from https://www.apa.org/ed/resources/trauma-competencies-training.pdf

American Psychological Association. (2017). *Clinical practice guideline for the treatment of PTSD*. http://dx.doi.org/10.1037/e514052017-001

Amole, M. C., Cyranowski, J. M., Conklin, L. R., Markowitz, J. C., Martin, S. E., & Swartz, H. A. (2017). Therapist use of specific and nonspecific strategies across two affect-focused psychotherapies for depression: Role of adherence monitoring. *Journal of Psychotherapy Integration, 27*, 381–394. http://dx.doi.org/10.1037/int0000039

Amstadter, A. B., McCart, M. R., & Ruggiero, K. J. (2007). Psychosocial interventions for adults with crime-related PTSD. *Professional Psychology: Research and Practice, 38*, 640–651. http://dx.doi.org/10.1037/0735-7028.38.6.640

Asnaani, A., & Foa, E. B. (2014). Expanding the lens of evidence-based practice in psychotherapy to include a common factors perspective: Comment on Laska, Gurman, and Wampold. *Psychotherapy, 51*, 487–490. http://dx.doi.org/10.1037/a0036891

Bachelor, A., Laverdière, O., Gamache, D., & Bordeleau, V. (2007). Clients' collaboration in therapy: Self-perceptions and relationships with client psychological functioning, interpersonal relations, and motivation. *Psychotherapy: Theory, Research, Practice, Training, 44*, 175–192. http://dx.doi.org/10.1037/0033-3204.44.2.175

Bauer, M. R., Ruef, A. M., Pineles, S. L., Japuntich, S. J., Macklin, M. L., Lasko, N. B., & Orr, S. P. (2013). Psychophysiological assessment of PTSD: A potential research domain criteria construct. *Psychological Assessment, 25*, 1037–1043. http://dx.doi.org/10.1037/a0033432

Békés, V., Beaulieu-Prévost, D., Guay, S., Belleville, G., & Marchand, A. (2016). Women with PTSD benefit more from psychotherapy than men. *Psychological Trauma: Theory, Research, Practice, and Policy, 8*, 720–727. http://dx.doi.org/10.1037/tra0000122

Beutler, L. E., Forrester, B., Gallagher-Thompson, D., Thompson, L., & Tomlins, J. B. (2012). Common, specific, and treatment fit variables in psychotherapy outcome. *Journal of Psychotherapy Integration, 22*, 255–281. http://dx.doi.org/10.1037/a0029695

Bhatia, A., & Gelso, C. J. (2017). The termination phase: Therapists' perspective on the therapeutic relationship and outcome. *Psychotherapy, 54*, 76–87. http://dx.doi.org/10.1037/pst0000100

Bickman, L., & Noser, K. (1999). Meeting the challenges in the delivery of child and adolescent mental health services in the next millennium: The continuous quality improvement approach. *Applied & Preventive Psychology, 8*, 247–255. http://dx.doi.org/10.1016/S0962-1849(05)80039-3

Blake, D. D., Weathers, F. W., Nagy, L. M., Kaloupek, D. G., Gusman, F. D., Charney, D. S., & Keane, T. M. (1995). The development of a clinician-administered PTSD scale. *Journal of Traumatic Stress, 8*, 75–90. http://dx.doi.org/10.1002/jts.2490080106

Bobbitt, B. L., Cate, R. A., Beardsley, S. D., Azocar, F., & McCulloch, J. (2012). Quality improvement and outcomes in the future of professional psychology: Opportunities and challenges. *Professional Psychology: Research and Practice, 43*, 551–559. http://dx.doi.org/10.1037/a0028899

Bordin, E. (1979). The generalizability of the psychoanalytic concept of the working alliance. *Psychotherapy: Theory, Research & Practice, 16*, 252–260. http://dx.doi.org/10.1037/h0085885

Brand, B. L., Myrick, A. C., Loewenstein, R. J., Classen, C. C., Lanius, R., McNary, S. W., . . . Putnam, F. W. (2012). A survey of practices and recommended treatment interventions among expert therapists treating patients with dissociative identity disorder and dissociative disorder not otherwise specified. *Psychological Trauma: Theory, Research, Practice, and Policy, 4*, 490–500. http://dx.doi.org/10.1037/a0026487

Breuninger, M. M., & Teng, E. J. (2017). Safe and secure: Spiritually enhanced cognitive processing therapy for veterans with posttraumatic stress disorder. *Spirituality in Clinical Practice, 4,* 262–273. http://dx.doi.org/10.1037/scp0000142

Briere, J. (1996). Psychometric review of Trauma Symptom Inventory (TSI). In B. H. Stamm (Ed.), *Measurement of stress, trauma, and adaptation* (pp. 381–383). Baltimore, MD: Sidran Press.

Butler, L. D., Carello, J., & Maguin, E. (2017). Trauma, stress, and self-care in clinical training: Predictors of burnout, decline in health status, secondary traumatic stress symptoms, and compassion satisfaction. *Psychological Trauma: Theory, Research, Practice, and Policy, 9,* 416–424. http://dx.doi.org/10.1037/tra0000187

Campbell, B. K., Guydish, J., Le, T., Wells, E. A., & McCarty, D. (2015). The relationship of therapeutic alliance and treatment delivery fidelity with treatment retention in a multisite trial of twelve-step facilitation. *Psychology of Addictive Behaviors, 29,* 106–113. http://dx.doi.org/10.1037/adb0000008

Caringi, J. C., Hardiman, E. R., Weldon, P., Fletcher, S., Devlin, M., & Stanick, C. (2017). Secondary traumatic stress and licensed clinical social workers. *Traumatology, 23,* 186–195. http://dx.doi.org/10.1037/trm0000061

Clarkin, J. F., & Kendall, P. C. (1992). Comorbidity and treatment planning: Summary and future directions. *Journal of Consulting and Clinical Psychology, 60,* 904–908. http://dx.doi.org/10.1037/0022-006X.60.6.904

Cloitre, M., Stovall-McClough, K. C., & Levitt, J. T. (2004). Treating life-impairing problems beyond PTSD: Reply to Cahill, Zoellner, Feeny, and Riggs (2004). *Journal of Consulting and Clinical Psychology, 72,* 549–551. http://dx.doi.org/10.1037/0022-006X.72.3.549

Constantino, M. J., Coyne, A. E., Luukko, E. K., Newkirk, K., Bernecker, S. L., Ravitz, P., & McBride, C. (2017). Therapeutic alliance, subsequent change, and moderators of the alliance-outcome association in interpersonal psychotherapy for depression. *Psychotherapy, 54,* 125–135. http://dx.doi.org/10.1037/pst0000101

Constantino, M. J., Penek, S., Bernecker, S. L., & Overtree, C. E. (2014). A preliminary examination of participant characteristics in relation to patients' treatment beliefs in psychotherapy in a training clinic. *Journal of Psychotherapy Integration, 24,* 238–250. http://dx.doi.org/10.1037/a0031424

Cook, J. M., Dinnen, S., Simiola, V., Thompson, R., & Schnurr, P. P. (2014). VA residential provider perceptions of dissuading factors to the use of two evidence-based PTSD treatments. *Professional Psychology: Research and Practice, 45,* 136–142. http://dx.doi.org/10.1037/a0036183

Courtois, C. A. (2008). Complex trauma, complex reactions: Assessment and treatment. *Psychological Trauma: Theory, Research, Practice, and Policy, S*(1), 86–100. http://dx.doi.org/10.1037/1942-9681.S.1.86

Davis, J. J., Walter, K. H., Chard, K. M., Parkinson, R. B., & Houston, W. S. (2013). Treatment adherence in cognitive processing therapy for combat-related PTSD with history of mild TBI. *Rehabilitation Psychology, 58,* 36–42. http://dx.doi.org/10.1037/a0031525

DeFife, J. A., Conklin, C. Z., Smith, J. M., & Poole, J. (2010). Psychotherapy appointment no-shows: Rates and reasons. *Psychotherapy: Theory, Research, Practice, Training, 47,* 413–417. http://dx.doi.org/10.1037/a0021168

DeViva, J. C. (2014). Treatment utilization among OEF/OIF veterans referred for psychotherapy for PTSD. *Psychological Services, 11,* 179–184. http://dx.doi.org/10.1037/a0035077

Dolsen, M. R., Soehner, A. M., Morin, C. M., Bélanger, L., Walker, M., & Harvey, A. G. (2017). Sleep the night before and after a treatment session: A critical ingredient for treatment adherence? *Journal of Consulting and Clinical Psychology, 85,* 647–652. http://dx.doi.org/10.1037/ccp0000184

Doran, J. M., & DeViva, J. (2018). A naturalistic evaluation of evidence-based treatment for veterans with PTSD. *Traumatology, 24*, 157–167. http://dx.doi.org/10.1037/trm0000140

Dowd, E. T. (1999). Why don't people change? What stops them from changing? An integrative commentary on the special issue on resistance. *Journal of Psychotherapy Integration, 9*, 119–131.

Erbes, C. R., Curry, K. T., & Leskela, J. (2009). Treatment presentation and adherence of Iraq/Afghanistan era veterans for outpatient care for posttraumatic stress disorder. *Psychological Services, 6*, 175–183. http://dx.doi.org/10.1037/a0016662

Escudero, V., Friedlander, M. L., & Heatherington, L. (2011). Using the e-SOFTA for video training and research on alliance-related behavior. *Psychotherapy, 48*, 138–147. http://dx.doi.org/10.1037/a0022188

Fisher, M. A. (2016). *Confidentiality limits in psychotherapy: Ethics checklist for mental health professionals*. Washington, DC: American Psychological Association. http://dx.doi.org/10.1037/14860-000

Flückiger, C., Del Re, A. C., Wampold, B. E., & Horvath, A. O. (2018). The alliance in adult psychotherapy: A meta-analytic synthesis. *Psychotherapy, 55*, 316–340. http://dx.doi.org/10.1037/pst0000172

Flückiger, C., Del Re, A. C., Wampold, B. E., Symonds, D., & Horvath, A. O. (2012). How central is the alliance in psychotherapy? A multilevel longitudinal meta-analysis. *Journal of Counseling Psychology, 59*, 10–17. http://dx.doi.org/10.1037/a0025749

Foa, E. (1996). *Posttraumatic Diagnostic Scale manual*. Minneapolis, MN: National Computer Systems.

Garcia, H. A., McGeary, C. A., McGeary, D. D., Finley, E. P., & Peterson, A. L. (2014). Burnout in Veterans Health Administration mental health providers in posttraumatic stress clinics. *Psychological Services, 11*, 50–59. http://dx.doi.org/10.1037/a0035643

Gold, S. N. (2004). The relevance of trauma to general clinical practice. *Psychotherapy: Theory, Research, Practice, Training, 41*, 363–373. http://dx.doi.org/10.1037/0033-3204.41.4.363

Grumet, R., & Fitzpatrick, M. (2016). A case for integrating values clarification work into cognitive behavioral therapy for social anxiety disorder. *Journal of Psychotherapy Integration, 26*, 11–21. http://dx.doi.org/10.1037/a0039633

Gutner, C. A., Suvak, M. K., Sloan, D. M., & Resick, P. A. (2016). Does timing matter? Examining the impact of session timing on outcome. *Journal of Consulting and Clinical Psychology, 84*, 1108–1115. http://dx.doi.org/10.1037/ccp0000120

Hatfield, D. R., & Ogles, B. M. (2004). The use of outcome measures by psychologists in clinical practice. *Professional Psychology: Research and Practice, 35*, 485–491. http://dx.doi.org/10.1037/0735-7028.35.5.485

Herman, J. L. (1992). *Trauma and Recovery*. New York, NY: Basic Books.

Heron, R. L., Twomey, H. B., Jacobs, D. P., & Kaslow, N. J. (1997). Culturally competent interventions for abused and suicidal African American women. *Psychotherapy: Theory, Research, Practice, Training, 34*, 410–424. http://dx.doi.org/10.1037/h0087639

Hoffart, A., Øktedalen, T., Langkaas, T. F., & Wampold, B. E. (2013). Alliance and outcome in varying imagery procedures for PTSD: A study of within-person processes. *Journal of Counseling Psychology, 60*, 471–482. http://dx.doi.org/10.1037/a0033604

Holland, J. M., Lisman, R., & Currier, J. M. (2013). Mild traumatic brain injury, meaning made of trauma, and posttraumatic stress: A preliminary test of a novel hypothesis. *Rehabilitation Psychology, 58*, 280–286. http://dx.doi.org/10.1037/a0033399

Holmqvist, R., & Andersen, K. (2003). Therapists' reactions to treatment of survivors of political torture. *Professional Psychology: Research and Practice, 34*, 294–300. http://dx.doi.org/10.1037/0735-7028.34.3.294

Hook, J. N., Davis, D., Owen, J., & DeBlaere, C. (2017). *Cultural humility: Engaging diverse identities in therapy*. Washington, DC: American Psychological Association. http://dx.doi.org/10.1037/0000037-000

Hoyt, T., Rielage, J. K., & Williams, L. F. (2012). Military sexual trauma in men: Exploring treatment principles. *Traumatology, 18*, 29–40. http://dx.doi.org/10.1177/1534765611430724

Hundt, N. E., Harik, J. M., Barrera, T. L., Cully, J. A., & Stanley, M. A. (2016). Treatment decision-making for posttraumatic stress disorder: The impact of patient and therapist characteristics. *Psychological Trauma: Theory, Research, Practice, and Policy, 8*, 728–735. http://dx.doi.org/10.1037/tra0000102

Hundt, N. E., Mott, J. M., Cully, J. A., Beason-Smith, M., Grady, R. H., & Teng, E. (2014). Factors associated with low and high use of psychotherapy in veterans with PTSD. *Psychological Trauma: Theory, Research, Practice, and Policy, 6*, 731–738. http://dx.doi.org/10.1037/a0036534

Imel, Z. E., Laska, K., Jakupcak, M., & Simpson, T. L. (2013). Meta-analysis of dropout in treatments for posttraumatic stress disorder. *Journal of Consulting and Clinical Psychology, 81*, 394–404. http://dx.doi.org/10.1037/a0031474

Jensen-Doss, A., & Weisz, J. R. (2008). Diagnostic agreement predicts treatment process and outcomes in youth mental health clinics. *Journal of Consulting and Clinical Psychology, 76*, 711–722. http://dx.doi.org/10.1037/0022-006X.76.5.711

Johnson, D. M., & Zlotnick, C. (2009). HOPE for battered women with PTSD in domestic violence shelters. *Professional Psychology: Research and Practice, 40*, 234–241. http://dx.doi.org/10.1037/a0012519

Johnson, L. D., & Shaha, S. (1996). Improving quality in psychotherapy. *Psychotherapy: Theory, Research, Practice, Training, 33*, 225–236. http://dx.doi.org/10.1037/0033-3204.33.2.225

Johnson, W. B., Bertschinger, M., Snell, A. K., & Wilson, A. (2014). Secondary trauma and ethical obligations for military psychologists: Preserving compassion and competence in the crucible of combat. *Psychological Services, 11*, 68–74. http://dx.doi.org/10.1037/a0033913

Kang, S., Tucker, C. M., Wippold, G. M., Marsiske, M., & Wegener, P. H. (2016). Associations among perceived provider cultural sensitivity, trust in provider, and treatment adherence among predominately low-income Asian American patients. *Asian American Journal of Psychology, 7*, 295–304. http://dx.doi.org/10.1037/aap0000058

Kehle-Forbes, S. M., Meis, L. A., Spoont, M. R., & Polusny, M. A. (2016). Treatment initiation and dropout from prolonged exposure and cognitive processing therapy in a VA outpatient clinic. *Psychological Trauma: Theory, Research, Practice, and Policy, 8*, 107–114. http://dx.doi.org/10.1037/tra0000065

Keller, S. M., Zoellner, L. A., & Feeny, N. C. (2010). Understanding factors associated with early therapeutic alliance in PTSD treatment: Adherence, childhood sexual abuse history, and social support. *Journal of Consulting and Clinical Psychology, 78*, 974–979. http://dx.doi.org/10.1037/a0020758

Killian, K. D. (2008). Helping till it hurts? A multimethod study of compassion fatigue, burnout, and self-care in clinicians working with trauma survivors. *Traumatology, 14*, 32–44. http://dx.doi.org/10.1177/1534765608319083

Kilpatrick, D. G., Resnick, H. S., & Acierno, R. (2009). Should PTSD Criterion A be retained? *Journal of Traumatic Stress, 22*, 374–383. http://dx.doi.org/10.1002/jts.20436

Koo, K. H., Tiet, Q. Q., & Rosen, C. S. (2016). Relationships between racial/ethnic minority status, therapeutic alliance, and treatment expectancies among veterans with PTSD. *Psychological Services, 13*, 317–321. http://dx.doi.org/10.1037/ser0000029

Knapp, S. J., VandeCreek, L. D., & Fingerhut, R. (2017). *Practical ethics for psychologists: A positive approach* (3rd ed.). Washington, DC: American Psychological Association. http://dx.doi.org/10.1037/0000036-000

Lambert, M. J. (2010). *Prevention of treatment failure: The use of measuring, monitoring, and feedback in clinical practice*. Washington, DC: American Psychological Association. http://dx.doi.org/10.1037/12141-000

Lambert, M. J., & Hawkins, E. J. (2004). Measuring outcome in professional practice: Considerations in selecting and using brief outcome instruments. *Professional Psychology: Research and Practice, 35,* 492–499. http://dx.doi.org/10.1037/0735-7028.35.5.492

Lambert, M. J., Whipple, J. L., Hawkins, E. J., Vermeersch, D. A., Nielsen, S. L., & Smart, D. W. (2003). Is it time for clinicians to routinely track patient outcome? A meta-analysis. *Clinical Psychology: Science and Practice, 10,* 288–301. http://dx.doi.org/10.1093/clipsy.bpg025

Lester, K., Resick, P. A., Young-Xu, Y., & Artz, C. (2010). Impact of race on early treatment termination and outcomes in posttraumatic stress disorder treatment. *Journal of Consulting and Clinical Psychology, 78,* 480–489. http://dx.doi.org/10.1037/a0019551

Litz, B. T. (2014). Clinical heuristics and strategies for service members and veterans with war-related PTSD. *Psychoanalytic Psychology, 31,* 192–205. http://dx.doi.org/10.1037/a0036372

Long, J. R. (2001). Goal agreement and early therapeutic change. *Psychotherapy: Theory, Research, Practice, Training, 38,* 219–232. http://dx.doi.org/10.1037/0033-3204.38.2.219

Marich, J. (2010). Eye movement desensitization and reprocessing in addiction continuing care: A phenomenological study of women in recovery. *Psychology of Addictive Behaviors, 24,* 498–507. http://dx.doi.org/10.1037/a0018574

Marques, L., Dixon, L., Valentine, S. E., Borba, C. P., Simon, N. M., & Wiltsey Stirman, S. (2016). Providers' perspectives of factors influencing implementation of evidence-based treatments in a community mental health setting: A qualitative investigation of the training-practice gap. *Psychological Services, 13,* 322–331. http://dx.doi.org/10.1037/ser0000087

May, C. L., & Wisco, B. E. (2016). Defining trauma: How level of exposure and proximity affect risk for posttraumatic stress disorder. *Psychological Trauma: Theory, Research, Practice, and Policy, 8,* 233–240. http://dx.doi.org/10.1037/tra0000077

Miles, S. R., & Thompson, K. E. (2016). Childhood trauma and posttraumatic stress disorder in a real-world Veterans Affairs clinic: Examining treatment preferences and dropout. *Psychological Trauma: Theory, Research, Practice, and Policy, 8,* 464–467. http://dx.doi.org/10.1037/tra0000132

Miller, B., & Sprang, G. (2017). A components-based practice and supervision model for reducing compassion fatigue by affecting clinician experience. *Traumatology, 23,* 153–164. http://dx.doi.org/10.1037/trm0000058

Mueser, K. T., Rosenberg, S. D., & Rosenberg, H. J. (2009). Generalization training and termination. In K. T. Mueser, S. D. Rosenberg, & H. J. Rosenberg (Eds.), *Treatment of posttraumatic stress disorder in special populations: A cognitive restructuring program* (pp. 187–206). Washington, DC: American Psychological Association. http://dx.doi.org/10.1037/11889-009

Murdock, N. L., Edwards, C., & Murdock, T. B. (2010). Therapists' attributions for client premature termination: Are they self-serving? *Psychotherapy: Theory, Research, Practice, Training, 47,* 221–234. http://dx.doi.org/10.1037/a0019786

Myrick, A. C., & Green, E. J. (2014). Establishing safety and stabilization in traumatized youth: Clinical implications for play therapists. *International Journal of Play Therapy, 23,* 100–113. http://dx.doi.org/10.1037/a0036397

Newman, D. L., Moffitt, T. E., Caspi, A., & Silva, P. A. (1998). Comorbid mental disorders: Implications for treatment and sample selection. *Journal of Abnormal Psychology, 107,* 305–311. http://dx.doi.org/10.1037/0021-843X.107.2.305

Norcross, J. C., Zimmerman, B. E., Greenberg, R. P., & Swift, J. K. (2017). Do all therapists do that when saying goodbye? A study of commonalities in termination behaviors. *Psychotherapy, 54,* 66–75. http://dx.doi.org/10.1037/pst0000097

O'Brien, J. L., & Haaga, D. A. F. (2015). Empathic accuracy and compassion fatigue among therapist trainees. *Professional Psychology: Research and Practice, 46,* 414–420. http://dx.doi.org/10.1037/pro0000037

Olivera, J., Challú, L., Gómez Penedo, J. M., & Roussos, A. (2017). Client-therapist agreement in the termination process and its association with therapeutic relationship. *Psychotherapy, 54*, 88–101. http://dx.doi.org/10.1037/pst0000099

Ouimette, P., Moos, R. H., & Finney, J. W. (2003). PTSD treatment and 5-year remission among patients with substance use and posttraumatic stress disorders. *Journal of Consulting and Clinical Psychology, 71*, 410–414. http://dx.doi.org/10.1037/0022-006X.71.2.410

Owen, J., & Hilsenroth, M. J. (2014). Treatment adherence: The importance of therapist flexibility in relation to therapy outcomes. *Journal of Counseling Psychology, 61*, 280–288. http://dx.doi.org/10.1037/a0035753

Owen, J., Imel, Z., Adelson, J., & Rodolfa, E. (2012). 'No-show': Therapist racial/ethnic disparities in client unilateral termination. *Journal of Counseling Psychology, 59*, 314–320. http://dx.doi.org/10.1037/a0027091

Philips, B., & Wennberg, P. (2014). The importance of therapy motivation for patients with substance use disorders. *Psychotherapy, 51*, 555–562. http://dx.doi.org/10.1037/a0033360

Priebe, K., Kleindienst, N., Schropp, A., Dyer, A., Krüger-Gottschalk, A., Schmahl, C., . . . Bohus, M. (2018). Defining the index trauma in post-traumatic stress disorder patients with multiple trauma exposure: Impact on severity scores and treatment effects of using worst single incident versus multiple traumatic events. *European Journal of Psychotraumatology, 9*, 1486124. http://dx.doi.org/10.1080/20008198.2018.1486124

Reese, R. J., Norsworthy, L. A., & Rowlands, S. R. (2009). Does a continuous feedback system improve psychotherapy outcome? *Psychotherapy: Theory, Research, Practice, Training, 46*, 418–431. http://dx.doi.org/10.1037/a0017901

Reese, R. J., Toland, M. D., Slone, N. C., & Norsworthy, L. A. (2010). Effect of client feedback on couple psychotherapy outcomes. *Psychotherapy: Theory, Research, Practice, Training, 47*, 616–630. http://dx.doi.org/10.1037/a0021182

Renninger, S. M. (2013). Clinical application of meta-concepts that are essential to client change. *Psychotherapy, 50*, 302–306. http://dx.doi.org/10.1037/a0032154

Reynolds, C., Simms, J., Webb, K., Corry, M., McDermott, B., Ryan, M., . . . Dyer, K. F. W. (2017). Client factors that predict the therapeutic alliance in a chronic, complex trauma sample. *Traumatology, 23*, 294–302. http://dx.doi.org/10.1037/trm0000114

Rodolfa, E., Bent, R., Eisman, E., Nelson, P., Rehm, L., & Ritchie, P. (2005). A cube model for competency development: Implications for psychology educators and regulators. *Professional Psychology: Research and Practice, 36*, 347–354. http://dx.doi.org/10.1037/0735-7028.36.4.347

Rubin, N. J., Bebeau, M., Leigh, I. W., Lichtenberg, J. W., Nelson, P. D., Portnoy, S., . . . Kaslow, N. J. (2007). The competency movement within psychology: An historical perspective. *Professional Psychology: Research and Practice, 38*, 452–462. http://dx.doi.org/10.1037/0735-7028.38.5.452

Salcioglu, E., Urhan, S., Pirinccioglu, T., & Aydin, S. (2017). Anticipatory fear and helplessness predict PTSD and depression in domestic violence survivors. *Psychological Trauma: Theory, Research, Practice, and Policy, 9*, 117–125. http://dx.doi.org/10.1037/tra0000200

Schoenwald, S. K., & Garland, A. F. (2013). A review of treatment adherence measurement methods. *Psychological Assessment, 25*, 146–156. http://dx.doi.org/10.1037/a0029715

Slade, M., McCrone, P., Kuipers, E., Leese, M., Cahill, S., Parabiaghi, A., . . . Thornicroft, G. (2006). Use of standardised outcome measures in adult mental health services: Randomised controlled trial. *The British Journal of Psychiatry, 189*, 330–336. http://dx.doi.org/10.1192/bjp.bp.105.015412

Stamoulos, C., Trepanier, L., Bourkas, S., Bradley, S., Stelmaszczyk, K., Schwartzman, D., & Drapeau, M. (2016). Psychologists' perceptions of the importance of common factors in psychotherapy for successful treatment outcomes. *Journal of Psychotherapy Integration, 26,* 300–317. http://dx.doi.org/10.1037/a0040426

Swift, J. K., & Greenberg, R. P. (2014). A treatment by disorder meta-analysis of dropout from psychotherapy. *Journal of Psychotherapy Integration, 24,* 193–207. http://dx.doi.org/10.1037/a0037512

Swift, J. K., & Greenberg, R. P. (2015). *Premature termination in psychotherapy: Strategies for engaging clients and improving outcomes.* Washington, DC: American Psychological Association. http://dx.doi.org/10.1037/14469-000

Swift, J. K., Greenberg, R. P., Whipple, J. L., & Kominiak, N. (2012). Practice recommendations for reducing premature termination in therapy. *Professional Psychology: Research and Practice, 43,* 379–387. http://dx.doi.org/10.1037/a0028291

Teng, E. J., Bailey, S. D., Chaison, A. D., Petersen, N. J., Hamilton, J. D., & Dunn, N. J. (2008). Treating comorbid panic disorder in veterans with posttraumatic stress disorder. *Journal of Consulting and Clinical Psychology, 76,* 704–710. http://dx.doi.org/10.1037/0022-006X.76.4.710

Tummala-Narra, P., Kallivayalil, D., Singer, R., & Andreini, R. (2012). Relational experiences of complex trauma survivors in treatment: Preliminary findings from a naturalistic study. *Psychological Trauma: Theory, Research, Practice, and Policy, 4,* 640–648. http://dx.doi.org/10.1037/a0024929

Voss Horrell, S. C., Holohan, D. R., Didion, L. M., & Vance, G. T. (2011). Treating traumatized OEF/OIF veterans: How does trauma treatment affect the clinician? *Professional Psychology: Research and Practice, 42,* 79–86. http://dx.doi.org/10.1037/a0022297

Weathers, F. W., Litz, B. T., Keane, T. M., Palmieri, P. A., Marx, B. P., & Schnurr, P. P. (2013). *The PTSD Checklist for* DSM–5 *(PCL-5)* [Measurement instrument]. Retrieved from https://www.ptsd.va.gov/professional/assessment/adult-sr/ptsd-checklist.asp

Weiss, D. S., & Marmar, C. R. (1996). The Impact of Event Scale—Revised. In J. Wilson & T. M. Keane (Eds.), *Assessing psychological trauma and PTSD* (pp. 399–411). New York, NY: Guilford Press.

Wright, C. V., Beattie, S. G., Galper, D. I., Church, A. S., Bufka, L. F., Brabender, V. M., & Smith, B. L. (2017). Assessment practices of professional psychologists: Results of a national survey. *Professional Psychology: Research and Practice, 48,* 73–78. http://dx.doi.org/10.1037/pro0000086

Zilcha-Mano, S. (2017). Is the alliance really therapeutic? Revisiting this question in light of recent methodological advances. *American Psychologist, 72,* 311–325. http://dx.doi.org/10.1037/a0040435

3

Cognitive Behavior Therapy for PTSD

Dawn M. Johnson and Taylor L. Ceroni

The primary goals of cognitive behavior therapy (CBT) are to identify and challenge negative thoughts that are automatic and that developed around our view of ourselves and the world around us and to modify behavior (Taylor, 2006). Stemming from the theoretical framework of behavioral learning theories and cognitive theory, CBT posits that when an individual is able to identify automatic thoughts that were learned and ingrained from childhood or adverse life experiences, then the individual can develop rational responses to combat future automatic thoughts and change behavior (Beck, Rush, Shaw, & Emery, 1979). Although more modern versions of CBT focus on different disorders and techniques, at the core they all are composed of three main principles: (a) cognitions affect behavior, (b) cognitions can be assessed and changed over time, and (c) cognitive changes can lead to behavioral changes (Dobson, 2009).

For the first main principle of CBT, clients have to access and consider how their cognitions affect their responses to events that happen in their lifetimes. This process of assisting clients in gaining insight into how their cognitions affect their behaviors can be of great importance in their clinical treatment. The second CBT principle, that cognitions can be assessed and changed over time, and the third principle, that cognitive changes lead to behavioral changes, rely heavily on a clinician's ability to assess the reliability of an individual's reports of their cognitions and behaviors. Clinicians should also be administering continued cognitive assessments with supported evidence of behavior

This material is also the result of work supported with resources and the use of facilities at the Southeast Louisiana Veterans Health Care System in New Orleans, Louisiana. The contents do not represent the views of the VA or the United States Government.

http://dx.doi.org/10.1037/0000196-003

Casebook to the APA Clinical Practice Guideline for the Treatment of PTSD, edited by L. F. Bufka, C. V. Wright, and R. W. Halfond

(Dobson, 2009; Merluzzi, Glass, & Genest, 1981). Dobson (2009) further argued that the assessments of cognitive changes and of behavioral changes are equally important throughout the process of treatment but must also be independent of each other so that we can understand if the mechanism of change in an individual was actually a cognitive change or behavioral in nature. Thus, CBT is rooted in continual assessment by the therapist and client, and change is dependent on therapist and client effort. Of note, there are critics of traditional CBT (e.g., Gaudiano, 2006; Hayes, Luoma, Bond, Masuda, & Lillis, 2006; Jacobson et al., 2000; Longmore & Worrell, 2007) who argue that behavior has a greater role in treatment. This argument has led to many CBT treatments with larger behavioral components, such as dialectical behavioral Therapy (DBT; Linehan, Cochran, & Kehrer, 2001) and acceptance and commitment therapy (ACT; Hayes et al., 2006).

Dobson (2009) described three main types of cognitive behavior therapies: (a) coping-skills therapies, (b) problem-solving therapies, and (c) cognitive-restructuring methods. Each type of CBT can be applied to the client's presenting concerns, with some forms of treatment using an integration of all three types in treatment (Taylor, 2006). Coping-skills treatments use a skills-based approach to dealing with presenting concerns that are external to the client and may be perceived as stressful. Cognitive-restructuring treatments focus on maladaptive cognitions and how they relate to psychological distress internal to the client. The primary goal of cognitive-restructuring CBTs is to gain insight into these maladaptive thought patterns and ultimately change them through restructuring techniques. Problem-solving treatments use both coping skills and cognitive restructuring to better serve a wide range of a client's presenting concerns. This form of treatment emphasizes the collaboration between client and therapist for developing a solution to the reported problem (Dobson, 2009; Mahoney & Arnkoff, 1978).

Research finds CBT to be an effective treatment for many different psychological disorders. Hofmann, Asnaani, Vonk, Sawyer, and Fang (2012) conducted a review of meta-analyses on the efficacy of CBT for the treatment of various psychological disorders and found support for the use of CBT in the treatment of addiction and substance use disorders, schizophrenia and other psychotic disorders, depression and dysthymia, anxiety disorders, bipolar disorder, somatoform disorders, eating disorders, insomnia, and personality disorders, and in the treatment of anger and aggression as well as general stress. Hofmann et al. also found empirical support for CBT for posttraumatic stress disorder (PTSD) when compared to other treatments. Additionally, the historic empirical support discussed throughout this chapter on the efficacy of CBT for the treatment of PTSD has led to the development of *trauma-focused CBT treatments* (TF-CBTs), which primarily utilize methods that focus on processing the experience of a traumatic event or the meaning of the traumatic event (Ehring et al., 2014). TF-CBTs have been found to be effective in the treatment of PTSD (Bisson et al., 2007; Stewart & Chambless, 2009) as well as to significantly improve symptoms of PTSD (Bisson et al., 2007; Bradley, Greene, Russ, Dutra,

& Westen, 2005). Many TF-CBTs are considered the primary recommended treatments for PTSD resulting from some types of traumatic incidents, such as combat trauma (U.S. Department of Veterans Affairs & U.S. Department of Defense, 2010).

Several well-developed TF-CBTs are discussed elsewhere within this case-book: (a) cognitive processing therapy (e.g., Resick & Schnicke, 1992; Resick et al., 2017; see also Chapter 4, this volume), (b) prolonged exposure therapy (e.g., Foa et al., 1999; Foa et al., 2005; see also Chapter 6, this volume), and (c) narrative exposure therapy (e.g., Neuner, Schauer, Roth, & Elbert, 2002; see also Chapter 9, this volume). However, many other treatments that integrate core components of CBT but do not strictly follow the protocols for these other well-developed treatments have also been found to be effective in the treatment of PTSD. This chapter provides the rationale, research, applications, and a case study on the use of CBT for the treatment of PTSD.

TREATMENT RATIONALE

Ehlers and Clark (2000) described a cognitive model for PTSD that helps explain hypothesized mechanisms of change in the treatment of PTSD. This model is based on years of research on CBT for PTSD (e.g., Brewin, Dalgleish, & Joseph, 1996; Foa & Riggs, 1993; Foa, Rothbaum, Riggs, & Murdock, 1991; Foa, Steketee, & Rothbaum, 1989; Horowitz, 1997; Janoff-Bulman, 1992; Joseph, Williams, & Yule, 1997; Resick & Schnicke, 1992; van der Kolk & Fisler, 1995; van der Kolk & van der Hart, 1991). This cognitive model of PTSD has two key tenets: (a) distinct individual negative appraisals of the trauma and the trauma sequelae and (b) distinct differences in memory of the traumatic event and its link to other memories of life. These negative appraisals and negative memories about the trauma and the trauma sequelae can lead to an increase in an individual's sense of current threat, which may affect their PTSD symptoms and their understanding of their PTSD (Ehlers & Clark, 2000; McCann, Sakheim, & Abrahamson, 1988). Individuals who have an increased sense of threat, negative emotions, and maladaptive coping are more likely not to recover naturally and may develop an increase in PTSD symptoms (Ehlers & Clark, 2000). An important part of CBT for individuals with recent trauma is to assess their sense of current threat and develop healthy coping strategies to maintain and decrease their PTSD symptoms throughout the initial stages of CBT treatment while beginning to identify and challenge their automatic thought processes (Ehlers & Clark, 2000; Johnson, Zlotnick, & Perez, 2011).

McCann et al. (1988) also offered a model for understanding the unique differences in trauma survivors' posttraumatic reactions, which may influence the individual's response to treatments such as CBT. McCann et al. described five areas of dysfunction in trauma survivors: (a) safety, (b) trust, (c) power/control, (d) esteem, and (e) intimacy. Negative maladaptive beliefs about the self or others in any of these areas can lead trauma survivors to be at risk for future harm, be unable to trust themselves or others, engage in controlling behaviors or feel lack of control, possess beliefs that they are bad or caused their trauma, and be unable to self-soothe or feel lonely or empty. In the development of TF-CBTs, McCann et al.'s principles should be considered when challenging clients' beliefs about themselves, others, and the world as well as when creating coping skills.

RESEARCH SUPPORT

CBT has consistently been found to be effective in the treatment of PTSD (e.g., Butler, Chapman, Forman, & Beck, 2006; Fecteau & Nicki, 1999; Foa & Meadows, 1997; Hofmann et al., 2012). A variety of different CBTs have been developed to treat PTSD. These different forms of CBT utilize different techniques and modalities but are all attempting to change behavior through similar methods of change. Multiple studies have evaluated the efficacy of these different forms of CBT with different types of traumas (Blanchard et al., 2003; Bryant, Moulds, & Nixon, 2003; Cloitre, Koenen, Cohen, & Han, 2002; Cottraux et al., 2008; Fecteau & Nicki, 1999; Hinton et al., 2005; Hinton, Hofmann, Pollack, & Otto, 2009; Johnson, Johnson, Perez, Palmieri, & Zlotnick, 2016; Johnson et al., 2011; Kruse, Joksimovic, Cavka, Wöller, & Schmitz, 2009; Kubany, Hill, & Owens, 2003; Kubany et al., 2004; Litz, Engel, Bryant, & Papa, 2007; McDonagh et al., 2005; Spence et al., 2011; van Emmerik, Kamphuis, & Emmelkamp, 2008), and all found a significant reduction in PTSD symptoms.

CBT-Mixed Therapies for PTSD

In their systematic review of treatments for PTSD, Jonas et al. (2013) referred to therapies that incorporate core components of CBT "but don't quite fit cleanly into one of the other categories" (p. 4) as *CBT-mixed*. These interventions may include breathing retraining, cognitive restructuring, crisis and safety planning, guided meditation or imagery, in vivo exposure, imaginal exposure, mindfulness training, psychoeducation, relapse prevention relaxation training, self-monitoring, skills training, and stress management. The CBTs also vary in duration of treatment, techniques used, and mode of delivery.

For example, Blanchard et al. (2003) tested a mixed intervention form of CBT with a supportive therapy treatment and a wait-list condition. The CBT treatment consisted of eight to 12 visits that included PTSD education, writing a description of a motor vehicle accident and reading the account repeatedly, progressive muscle-relaxation training, other forms of relaxation, in vivo exposure to motor vehicle travel, and cognitive therapy aimed at changing self-defeating talk, cognitive fallacies, and behavioral activation for numbing symptoms of PTSD. Blanchard et al. found a greater reduction of PTSD symptoms after the completion of the CBT treatment than in the supportive therapy treatment or the wait-list condition. Comparatively, Kruse et al. (2009) used a CBT form of treatment in their study of trauma-focused psychotherapies for Bosnian war refugees, in which participants received 25 hours of manualized therapy in their native language. Therapy sessions occurred once a week for the first 3 months, then once every 2 weeks for the rest of the treatment. The therapy focused on skill training, interpersonal relationships, and affect regulation. Psychoeducation, cognitive restructuring, progressive muscle relaxation, skill building around regulation of affect, skills about self-perception and self-care, therapeutic relationship building, and development of feelings of safety were the seven elements of the treatment. The researchers compared participants receiving trauma-focused treatment with a group who received social support and medical treatment while also receiving counseling every 3 months at their outpatient clinic. This counseling focused on psychoeducation, information delivery, and assistance in paperwork for court-related issues. Overall, the researchers found a reduction in PTSD symptoms in participants in the CF-CBT group (Kruse et al., 2009). Although the treatments were different in their duration, mode of delivery, and techniques, the core components of CBT were used, and PTSD symptoms were reduced in trauma survivors. CBT interventions have also been offered via the internet (e.g., Litz et al., 2007; Spence et al., 2011).

CBT in Diverse Populations

TF-CBT has been applied and adapted for a wide range of adult populations, including veterans (e.g., Litz et al., 2007), survivors of motor vehicle accidents (e.g., Blanchard et al., 2003), interpersonal trauma survivors (e.g., sexual assault, Foa et al., 2005; child sexual abuse, Cloitre et al., 2002; and intimate partner violence, Johnson et al., 2011), and refugees (e.g., Kruse et al., 2009). Furthermore, CBT has been culturally adapted for non-Western countries and delivered in multiple languages (e.g., Hinton et al., 2005; Hinton, Hofmann, Rivera, Otto, & Pollack, 2011) and has been adapted to address various subgroups in the United States and other Western countries. TF-CBTs have also been evaluated in individuals with comorbid substance use disorders (e.g., Najavits, 2002), including female prisoners (e.g., Zlotnick, Najavits, Rohsenow, & Johnson, 2003). Although one criticism of empirically supported treatments (EST) is that manualized treatments are too structured and do not factor in individual differences, there is actually much flexibility for how a clinician implements a treatment, especially when considering the diversity of clients' identities (e.g., race, ethnicity, gender, sexual orientation, ability status, age, and religion). Hays (2009) argued that multiculturalism should be an important aspect of implementing CBT and that CBT specifically is an EST that works well with a multicultural lens in treatment. CBT focuses on individual differences, empowerment, and cognitions and behaviors that are specific and concrete, and it utilizes assessment during treatment. These aspects of CBT give the clinician flexibility to incorporate individual differences and be multiculturally sensitive when intervening (Hays, 2009).

Hinton and colleagues (2011) developed a culturally adapted CBT (CA-CBT) for Latina women with treatment-resistant PTSD. In their pilot study, they compared CA-CBT to applied muscle relaxation. The authors addressed concerns in CBT delivery with a Spanish-speaking population who may not speak English and may have culturally specific ideas about psychological distress and psychotherapy. Specifically, they adapted the CBT treatment to include Christian-type imagery in meditation, psychoeducation about cognitions about PTSD and symptoms of anxiety in an effort to not catastrophize symptoms, culturally appropriate examples, and culturally sensitive exposure techniques. Results indicated reductions in the CA-CBT group's PTSD symptoms pretreatment and posttreatment. These results indicate that CBT can be culturally adapted effectively for ethnic minorities with cultural sensitivity to the implementation of techniques in treatment.

CBT has also been adapted for refugee populations with multiple traumas and treatment-resistant PTSD. Hinton et al. (2009) explored the efficacy of a culturally adapted CBT for Cambodian refugees who were at least 6 years old when they witnessed the Cambodian genocide, were assessed as treatment resistant (i.e., had received supportive counseling and psychopharmacology interventions for at least one year but still met criteria for PTSD), and had comorbid orthostatic panic (i.e., panic triggered by rising from lying or sitting to standing). The experimental treatment consisted of 12 weekly sessions conducted by a Cambodian-speaking counselor; sessions included psychoeducation about PTSD and psychoeducation about a model of panic attacks that explains panic attacks as stemming from neck pain and orthostatic dizziness. The model provides an explanation for why trauma reminders and cognitions may lead to the production of panic, a common experience among Cambodian refugees. Muscle relaxation, breathing exercises, and relaxation techniques were also included. Culturally appropriate visualization, descriptions of relaxation as mindfulness, cognitive restructuring, exposure techniques, emotional processing for trauma recalls, awareness of neck and orthostatic panic, exposure with narration of trauma memories, and promotion of cognitive flexibility in techniques to be sensitive to individual differences in treatment were all utilized. Results of this culturally adapted mixed CBT suggested a reduction in PTSD symptoms, indicating that CBT is a useful treatment for Cambodian refugees who are treatment-resistant to supportive psychotherapy and psychopharmacology interventions.

CBT has also been used with women who have experienced interpersonal trauma (e.g., rape, sexual assault, intimate partner violence). Kubany and Watson (2002) adapted CBT for women survivors of intimate partner violence into a therapy known as *cognitive therapy for formerly battered women* (CTT-BW), which focuses on guilt and shame cognitions as well as on reducing symptoms of PTSD and low self-esteem. In a follow-up study, Kubany et al. (2003) explored CTT-BW in a sample of racially and ethnically diverse women, including White,

Asian, Japanese, Chinese, Filipino, Indonesian, Pacific Islander, African American, and Puerto Rican women. Results indicated that 94% of the women who completed treatment did not meet criteria for PTSD, and all racial and ethnic minority women who completed treatment no longer met criteria for PTSD. Additionally, Zoellner, Feeny, Fitzgibbons, and Foa (1999) explored differences between White women's and Black women's responses to CBT for PTSD-related symptoms following sexual and nonsexual assault. Results indicated no difference in treatment responses for White and African American women, suggesting that CBT may be an effective treatment for both populations. However, these studies on racial and ethnic differences in responses to CBT for PTSD had small sample sizes, which limit the generalizability of the findings. CBT may be a valuable treatment for diverse populations, but more research is needed to explore racial and ethnic differences in responses to CBT treatments for PTSD. Generally speaking, CBTs that maintain the core tenets of the original theory, even with mixed interventions and cultural adaptations, have overwhelming empirical support as leading treatments for PTSD and PTSD symptoms in diverse populations.

DESCRIPTION OF TREATMENT COMPONENTS

CBTs typically begin with a psychoeducational component that aims to educate clients about the cognitive model; automatic thoughts; and emotional, behavioral, and physiological reactions to situations that may trigger dysfunctional and maladaptive thoughts (Beck, 1995). There are 10 techniques that Beck discussed as important in CBT: (a) therapists should continually create case conceptualizations and revisions throughout treatment; (b) therapists should attempt to create strong therapeutic relationships with continual inquiring about feedback from clients about the therapeutic relationship; (c) therapists should foster collaboration and participation from clients throughout the therapeutic process; (d) ongoing guided discovery and empiricism should be the main components of the therapeutic relationship; (e) therapists should establish structured approaches in goal setting with clients based on the collection of problems; (f) a present-focused approach to problems should be the emphasis in the beginning of therapy; (g) therapy should include psychoeducation about the cognitive model and clients' problems to make clients an active part of their therapy and to promote relapse prevention; (h) therapists should discuss goal setting, structure of sessions, and time-limited nature of treatment; (i) therapists should use Socratic questioning to enable clients to identify, evaluate, and respond to maladaptive and dysfunctional thoughts; and (j) therapists may research and utilize techniques from other theoretical orientations they feel are appropriate in the treatment of their clients. Homework assignments based on these 10 techniques are designed to teach the clients about their thoughts, their behaviors, and how they developed these core beliefs; assignments assist in reducing overall psychological symptomatology. Initially, clients will take a psychoeducational approach in their learning about automatic thoughts through their homework assignments, then progress into evaluation of their intermediate and core beliefs, before finally focusing on relapse prevention and empowerment strategies to continue their treatment after CBT ends.

TREATMENT ILLUSTRATION: HOPE

One example of a CBT-mixed intervention is Helping to Overcome PTSD through Empowerment (HOPE). HOPE (Johnson, Johnson, et al., 2016; Johnson & Zlotnick, 2009; Johnson, Zlotnick, & Perez, 2011) integrates a CBT and empowerment approach and specifically targets PTSD in survivors of intimate partner violence (IPV) who seek refuge in domestic violence shelters. HOPE is based on Herman's (1992) multistage model of recovery. Herman identified three stages of recovery: (a) establishing safety, (b) remembrance and mourning, and (c) reconnection. IPV survivors who seek shelter are uprooted and in a state of crisis, facing continuous threats and ongoing revictimization. Thus, their most urgent clinical need is to establish physical and emotional safety. Consistently, HOPE adapts a first-stage, present-centered approach that emphasizes goals of safety, self-care, and protection. Although people of all genders can be victims of IPV and may seek shelter, HOPE was developed specifically for women who seek shelter, as women are the vast majority of shelter residents. However, HOPE can easily be adapted for men and for IPV survivors who do not seek shelter.

HOPE is a flexible manualized treatment that offers several different modules. The ordering of the modules and the emphasis placed on each module are determined by client needs and goals (see Exhibit 3.1 for a list of modules). HOPE also addresses the five schematic areas hypothesized by McCann et al. (1988), as discussed previously (i.e., safety, trust, power/control, esteem, and intimacy). Additionally, HOPE adopts a multicultural approach and provides space to address how the client's cultural background has influenced her experience of abuse. Finally, HOPE incorporates an empowerment approach (Worell & Remer, 2003), emphasizing choice and the client's specific goals throughout treatment. HOPE was initially offered exclusively in shelter, with residents being referred for ongoing treatment in the community if needed after being discharged from shelter. However, results of a randomized clinical trial evaluating the addition of HOPE to standard shelter services (Johnson et al., 2011) found that a majority of women left shelter prior to completing treatment, with many still meeting criteria for PTSD or subthreshold PTSD. Furthermore, most women had ongoing contact with their abusers after leaving shelter. Thus, HOPE was expanded to a 16-session intervention that continued for 3 months after leaving the shelter (Johnson et al., 2016). This expanded version of HOPE was associated with reduced IPV-related PTSD and depression severity as well as with increased empowerment and gain in personal and social resources relative to standard shelter services alone.

EXHIBIT 3.1

HOPE Modules

Establishing Safety and Empowerment
1. Goal Setting
2. Knowledge is Power: Psychoeducation re Abuse and PTSD
3. Safety Planning
4. Empowering Yourself
5. Establishing Trust in Relationships

Managing PTSD With Empowerment Tools
6. Rethinking Victim Thinking Into Survivor Thinking
7. Coping With Triggers
8. Safe Sleep
9. Self-Soothing and Relaxation

Improving Relationships
10. Establishing Boundaries
11. Establishing Safe and Health Relationships
12. Improving Relationships by Managing Anger

Post-Shelter Modules
1. Goal Setting
2. Safety Planning
3. Booster Sessions
4. Termination/Establishing Long-Term Support and Safety

Optional Modules
1. Crisis Management
2. PTSD and Substance Use
3. Grounding
4. Nightmares
5. Grief
6. Emotional Numbing
7. Co-Parenting With an Abuser

CASE ILLUSTRATION

The case presented here is a composite of multiple clients who completed this expanded version of HOPE.

Description of the Client

Mary is a 25-year-old biracial straight cisgender woman who lived with her abuser for the past 5 years. She dropped out of high school when she was pregnant with her first child and completed the requirements for her GED 4 years ago. She has since worked multiple part-time jobs (e.g., telemarketer, food server) but has not returned to work since the birth of her youngest child. Mary has two children (ages 2 and 4 years) with her abuser and one from a prior relationship (age 9 years). Mary came to shelter after her abuser punched and kicked her repeatedly, leaving her with multiple contusions on the face and stomach. She did not seek medical treatment for her injuries. Mary reported that this was the first abusive incident where she felt like her life was in danger, and that her fear prompted her to leave and seek shelter. This was Mary's second time in shelter; she had attempted to leave her abuser once before when she was pregnant with her youngest child and her abuser kicked her in the stomach. She reported that she returned to her abuser after staying in shelter for three days because she loved him and wanted her children to have both a mother and a father. Mary's immediate family lived in another state, and Mary reported few supports in the area. She had been in shelter for 2 weeks when she started HOPE. At this time her primary focus was to find employment and housing for herself and her three children. Her abuser was texting and calling her multiple times a day asking for forgiveness and for her to come home. At intake, Mary met full criteria for IPV-related PTSD, as well as major depressive disorder. Mary had a history of cocaine dependence, reporting that she had been clean for 5 years. She had been in shelter 2 weeks when she started HOPE.

General Structure of HOPE

All HOPE sessions begin with a brief check-in and agenda setting. Sessions are approximately 50 to 60 minutes in length and are held either weekly or biweekly, based on the client's needs and availability as well as length of time the client plans to stay in shelter (e.g., more frequently if the plan is a shorter shelter stay so that the client can participate in as many of the available 10 shelter sessions as possible). Each module begins with a quote related to the themes and content of the particular module. The therapist and client process the quote as a way of introducing the content of the session for the day. The content of each session and the order of presentation for the various HOPE modules across sessions are informed by the HOPE hierarchy. This hierarchy was designed to assist the therapist in determining which of the client's multitude of concerns to prioritize. Consistent with Herman's (1992) model, this hierarchy emphasized physical safety (e.g., revictimization or threat) and emotional safety (e.g., suicidal ideation, clinical deterioration) as well as PTSD symptoms that interfered with the client's safety and shelter goals (e.g., the module providing skills for safe sleep was prioritized if a client's lack of sleep was interfering with her ability to submit job applications and find housing). Specifically, the HOPE hierarchy prioritizes (a) immediate physical and emotional risks, (b) PTSD symptoms and behavioral and cognitive patterns that interfere with survivors' shelter and treatment goals, (c) PTSD symptoms and behavioral and cognitive patterns that interfere with or impact quality of life, and (d) post-shelter (or future) goals and safety. At the end of each session, the therapist processes the client's reaction to the session and collaboratively identifies "accomplishments" (i.e., tasks to accomplish or skills to use between sessions).

Early Sessions in HOPE

Typically, earlier sessions in HOPE focus on safety planning, engaging the client in the therapeutic process, and providing the client with the skills that empower her to make informed decisions about the abuse and to identify and address aspects of her situation where she has some control. In later sessions, the therapist tends to focus on traditional CBT skills that will help the client manage her PTSD and associated symptoms.

Mary met with her HOPE therapist weekly because she had no plans to leave shelter. The first HOPE session focused on establishing rapport, orienting and engaging the client to therapy, obtaining the client's narrative, and goal setting. Mary reported significant ambivalence about leaving her abuser, Tim. She denied any current safety concerns and felt that Tim expressed sufficient remorse and deserved a second chance. However, she also expressed that Tim had been apologetic in the past and this did not end the cycle of abuse. She expressed concern for her children—she believed that an intact family was important and wanted to provide her children something she did not experience as a child.

After providing a rationale for HOPE and gaining an understanding of some of Mary's concerns about therapy (e.g., difficulties trusting others, uncertainty if therapy could help), Mary was introduced to a core component of HOPE, the empowerment toolbox. The empowerment toolbox is a list of skills and tools for establishing safety and empowerment (e.g., "protect yourself," "take back your power"), managing symptoms (e.g., "rethink," "approach safe triggers"), and improving relationships (e.g., "give a little trust at a time," "ask for help"). The empowerment toolbox is incorporated throughout HOPE, with each HOPE module focusing on a series of specific tools or skills. Mary identified multiple skills that she was already using, including staying safe by coming to shelter, journaling about her feelings for Tim and the abuse she experienced, and asking for help by coming to therapy. To individualize her treatment and develop a treatment plan, she completed a goal-setting worksheet as her accomplishment before the second session.

Mary identified her primary goals as finding employment and housing for her and her children. She also identified goals of improving her self-esteem and staying safe. Mary reported being off cocaine for 5 years and noted that multiple women in shelter were using cocaine or other substances and had offered her drugs, including cocaine. She reported increased cravings for cocaine as a result. Thus, Mary also added maintaining her sobriety as a goal for therapy. Given her history of substance use and increased urges, the optional module on PTSD and substance use, which calls for the therapist to address substance use throughout multiple HOPE modules, was integrated into Mary's treatment plan.

A large component of HOPE includes working with the shelter staff to assure that the client is meeting her shelter and case management goals. As such, Mary, the therapist, and the shelter case manager had a brief meeting between the first and second sessions. This meeting allowed the therapist to educate the case manager about HOPE and allowed the shelter staff to educate the therapist on the case plan, including any barriers or difficulties that might affect Mary's ability to stay in shelter. Mary's case plan focused on obtaining employment and housing as well as finding subsidized child care for her three children. The shelter staff had no concerns about her progress.

Sessions 2 and 3 focused on providing psychoeducation about abuse and PTSD as well as about the interconnection between PTSD and substance use. The therapist and Mary also collaboratively established a safety plan. The safety plan focused on how to respond to the daily texts and emails from Tim (e.g., texting back that she needed space, asking him to respect this need, and agreeing only to communication with the children). Mary did not initially believe a civil protection order (CPO; i.e., a legal document that requires the abuser to stay a specified distance and cease all contact with the client) was necessary, but the therapist provided information on how to obtain one in case Mary ever felt otherwise. The bulk of the initial safety plan focused on how to safely manage Tim's visitations with the children. Mary identified a mutual friend who could pick up the children and bring them to Tim for occasional visits. This safety plan was updated as new threats to safety were identified in later sessions.

Sessions 2 and 3 of HOPE typically offer an opportunity to explore the client's cultural background and consider how the client's race or ethnicity affected her experience of abuse and symptoms of PTSD. Mary indicated that as a biracial woman, she seldom felt accepted by either White or Black people. She identified more with her Black race: Her mother, who raised her, was Black, and she had very little contact with her father, who was White. She described situations where Tim, who was Black, used her biracial identity to criticize her or put her down. It was during this time that Mary also explored how her race affected her experience in shelter. Mary reported that she did not feel accepted by either the Black or the White women in shelter and thus found it challenging to obtain support from other residents. Given the importance of support for IPV survivors and Mary's need to find alternative safe sources of support, related HOPE modules were prioritized and offered earlier in treatment. Furthermore, Mary's treatment plan was updated to include the goal of increasing her support network.

Sessions 4 and 5 incorporated modules on empowerment and trust. Mary identified multiple instances where Tim used his power to "take away" her power within the relationship. Given Mary's history of cocaine dependence, Mary also explored how her drug use affected her sense of power and control. Mary discussed feeling isolated from her family and noted that Tim seemed most triggered when she tried to assert her independence (e.g., wanting to go out for drinks with a girlfriend or travel to visit her family). Mary completed what is referred to in HOPE as the *circle of responsibility:* She identified who she perceived as responsible for the abuse and also identified a percentage that reflected each person's degree of responsibility. Like many HOPE clients, Mary initially assigned much of the blame to herself. The therapist used gentle challenges and Socratic questioning to help Mary evaluate her belief that she was to blame for the abuse. Mary eventually realized that although she was responsible for her decision to stay with Tim after other abusive incidents, that decision did not absolve Tim from his responsibility for the abuse. She also discussed how challenging she found it to trust anyone as a result of the abuse. Mary identified cognitions stemming from the abuse (e.g., "Never trust anybody," "Don't let people close to you or they will hurt you") that developed to protect her from future vulnerability but made it difficult to trust others, including other shelter residents.

Sessions Focusing on CBT Skills

Given that increasing Mary's support network was prioritized, Sessions 6 and 7 focused on assertiveness and asking for help as well as on developing safe and healthy relationships. Mary identified that she tended to silence herself and not ask for help from family or friends. She also indicated that church was a large part of her identity and that she had stopped going to church soon after she moved in with Tim, as church was not important to him. Mary evaluated her current relationships and identified multiple potential safe and supportive friends that she had shut out of her life as a result of the abuse. Mary was taught assertiveness skills, and the therapist and Mary role-played how to reconnect with these friends and ask for their support. Given Mary's history of cocaine dependence, these sessions also focused on helping Mary set boundaries around cocaine. For example, Mary role-played how to tell the shelter resident who had offered her cocaine that she was not interested and how to ask the resident to refrain from offering cocaine again.

During the Session 7 check-in, Mary reported to her therapist that Tim requested that they meet between Sessions 6 and 7 and that she agreed. Mary went to the house, and Tim began pleading with her to come home. Although she had some desire to reunite with Tim, she also believed things would not improve unless Tim received treatment. Mary tried to use the skills she was working on to establish a boundary and ask Tim to seek counseling for his anger and substance use (which she attributed as reasons for his abusive behavior). Tim refused, and the interaction eventually turned abusive: Tim threatened to kill Mary if she did not come home. He also threatened to take the children from her. Mary was able to leave without physical injury but felt more fear and confusion than ever before. Per the HOPE hierarchy, Session 7 thus focused on safety planning and crisis management.

As a result of this discussion, Mary decided to seek a CPO for herself and her children and to cease all communication with Tim. The therapist and shelter staff worked with Mary to obtain a CPO. Soon after Mary obtained the CPO, she got a job at a local fast-food restaurant. She reconnected with one of her friends, who offered her a place to stay. The friend's mother helped with child care of her grandchildren and was willing to help with Mary's children as well, at least for the short term. Given that Mary did not find the shelter to be an incredibly supportive setting, Mary left shelter and went to stay with her friend before Session 8 was scheduled.

Post-Shelter Sessions

Mary stayed in shelter for a total of 10 weeks, completing her first eight sessions over a 2-month period. Because she still had eight HOPE sessions remaining at the time she left shelter, she met with her HOPE therapist weekly for the first 6 weeks and then every other week for the last two sessions in an effort to titrate her off counseling.

Session 8 was Mary's first session after leaving shelter. As such, the next two sessions focused on updating Mary's goals and safety planning. Furthermore, as Mary no longer had a case manager from shelter, her case management plan was updated based on her new situation, living outside of shelter. The first 10 to 15 minutes of each post-shelter session focused on case management, with the remainder of the session focusing on the module for that session. Mary's therapy and case management goals remained the same. She saw her current living arrangement as temporary and still prioritized finding housing and subsidized child care. Her new job was going well, and there was the potential for her to move to full-time if needed. Mary continued to deny cocaine use and felt fewer urges to use since leaving shelter and no longer interacting with the residents who were using drugs.

Session 9 focused on updating Mary's safety plan. Because she had the CPO, she carried the document with her always and had 911 on speed dial on her phone in case she ran into Tim. She had no contact with Tim and moved to a location that was about 20 minutes from where Tim lived, so she thought she could hide her location from him. Tim had not tried to reach out to her since the CPO was issued and seemed to be honoring the terms of the CPO. Mary also developed a plan with her roommate and children for how to respond if Tim showed up at the house.

Sessions 10 and 11 focused on cognitive restructuring, or what is referred to in HOPE as *rethinking into survivor thinking*. Mary was taught the relationship between her thoughts, feelings, and behaviors. She received psychoeducation on how abuse and PTSD led to "victim thinking" and identified multiple "victim thoughts" stemming from her abuse and PTSD (e.g., "I should have been able to stop the abuse," "I should be over the abuse by now"). Mary was taught how victim thinking could also stem from her history of substance use and how these victim thoughts could increase her risk for relapse (e.g., "Cocaine will help me cope with everything I have to do"). Mary was taught to systematically challenge or rethink her victim thoughts and to identify new and healthier "survivor thoughts" (e.g., "I am not responsible for Tim's behavior," "I have the skills and tools to cope without cocaine"). These sessions also focused on helping Mary to identify triggers stemming from her abusive experiences, PTSD, or substance use and to identify empowerment tools to manage triggers. Mary was challenged to identify triggers that were objectively safe (e.g., taking the bus, as Tim had a car and never took the bus), which she should approach or move toward, as well as unsafe triggers that she should avoid (e.g., going to her favorite park in the neighborhood where she might run into Tim, who often went for runs in that park).

Sessions 12 and 13 focused on providing Mary with skills to improve her sleep, help her self-soothe to manage her PTSD symptoms and any urges to use cocaine, and provide her with the tools to manage and appropriately communicate anger stemming from her abuse and PTSD. Of particular relevance to Mary was the importance of self-soothing. Mary reported a tendency to focus on her children and never to prioritize her own needs. Mary's therapist worked with her to incorporate self-soothing activities for her (e.g., going to church, relaxation) and her children (e.g., reading books together, drawing together) as ways to self-soothe and manage symptoms. Mary was given a CD with a visualization exercise that she could use to relax outside of session.

Consistent with the HOPE model, Sessions 14 and 15 were booster sessions (i.e., sessions designed to reinforce skills used previously and help Mary apply the CBT skills to current life situations). These sessions involved Mary identifying which HOPE skills were most beneficial to her and which skills she needed to review so that she would be better equipped to use them in her day-to-day life. By this point, Mary had been living with her friend for 5 weeks and was finding the situation challenging. She was able to save up enough money for a deposit and found a two-bedroom apartment that she could afford if she worked full time. Mary was able to secure subsidized day care for her children while she was at work and thus felt she was ready to move out. However, Mary felt guilty for wanting to leave her friend who was so generous. As such, she chose to focus on assertiveness and setting boundaries, and she role-played with her therapist how best to tell her friend that she was moving out. Mary also identified that many of her victim thoughts were about not being worthy of happiness and beliefs that her needs were not as important as others' needs were. Thus, during these booster sessions Mary also spent time reviewing skills to systematically challenge her victim thoughts and identify healthier survivor thoughts.

Session 16 focused on termination and establishing long-term goals. Mary and her therapist processed Mary's progress in therapy and identified the skills that were most important for her to use moving forward. This session also focused on relapse prevention and development of a plan if her symptoms were to worsen or return. Mary reported that although Tim had not directly tried to contact her, one of Tim's friends had texted and called and made a plea for Tim's case. Mary discussed how she used her assertiveness skills to tell this friend that she was not interested and to request that he refrain from calling her. Mary reported that she still had feelings for Tim but would not be willing to go back to him without his first attending therapy. Mary expressed concern that Tim had not reached out to the children and expressed worry for her children, who missed their father. Generally, Mary reported feeling more in control of her life rather than feeling that her PTSD symptoms controlled her.

Although she still experienced some PTSD symptoms, she no longer met full criteria for PTSD, and her depression had significantly improved. Mary was also able to maintain her sobriety throughout treatment and follow-up. She acknowledged that she had a lot of work ahead of her to get back on her feet, but she indicated that she felt equipped to do so. She reported feeling that she could manage without therapy for the time being and that she had identified several options and locations where she could resume therapy if needed in the future.

Discussion of the Case

Mary is not a typical HOPE client. Mary completed all 16 sessions over a 5-month period, which is not possible for many clients given their many competing demands. However, her case demonstrates how CBT-mixed interventions can be helpful, especially when targeting a unique population such as IPV survivors who seek shelter. HOPE incorporates a variety of traditional CBT interventions (e.g., cognitive restructuring, skills training). However, for IPV survivors, safety planning and empowerment are also key interventions to address the abuse and PTSD stemming from years of chronic abuse. Additionally, like most HOPE clients who seek shelter, Mary was from a lower socioeconomic class, which often can limit a client's available options. Thus, it is integral for the HOPE therapist to be knowledgeable about local resources. Becoming knowledgeable often involves calling resources to determine the specifics regarding who qualifies for their services and what services they actually offer. Because many HOPE clients do not have access to case management through other facilities after leaving shelter, case management was an important part of Mary's treatment plan post-shelter.

Because Mary was followed through the research procedures evaluating HOPE, we know that she faced more abuse from Tim. However, she was empowered to utilize the necessary resources (e.g., her CPO, calling the police), and eventually Tim faced jail time for violating the CPO.

SUMMARY

Overall, CBT and CBT-mixed interventions have been found to be effective forms of treatment for PTSD with a diverse array of populations. CBT allows for the inclusion of a multicultural lens when evaluating and treating survivors of trauma and a unique flexibility for clinicians within manualized treatments. Therapists can seek training in CBT or CBT-mixed interventions in a number of ways, including continuing education workshops, conference workshops, and specialty organizations that offer online trainings (i.e., International Society for Traumatic Stress Studies).

CBT is also easily adaptable to a variety of trauma-specific clients, including, as we saw with HOPE, IPV survivors. HOPE is an example of a program that addresses multiculturalism and unique considerations of women who experience IPV, such as empowerment and safety planning against potential revictimization. The success of Mary's case, as well as the wealth of literature supporting the effectiveness of CBT in the treatment of PTSD, demonstrates that CBT can be used effectively with diverse populations of trauma survivors.

KEY IDEAS

- CBT-mixed therapies are flexible treatments that target a wide variety of trauma populations.

- CBT-mixed therapies are based on cognitive models of PTSD that link PTSD to negative appraisals of the trauma and trauma sequelae as well as to differences in how memories of traumatic events are processed.

- CBT-mixed therapies have strong research support in their efficacy for diverse trauma populations.

- HOPE is an example of a research-supported CBT-mixed treatment specifically for women survivors of IPV who seek shelter.

REFERENCES

Beck, A. T., Rush, A. J., Shaw, B. F., & Emery, G. (1979). *Cognitive therapy of depression*. New York, NY: Guilford Press.

Beck, J. S. (1995). *Cognitive therapy: Basics and beyond*. New York, NY: Guilford Press.

Bisson, J. I., Ehlers, A., Matthews, R., Pilling, S., Richards, D., & Turner, S. (2007). Psychological treatments for chronic post-traumatic stress disorder: Systematic review and meta-analysis. *The British Journal of Psychiatry, 190*, 97–104. http://dx.doi.org/10.1192/bjp.bp.106.021402

Blanchard, E. B., Hickling, E. J., Malta, L. S., Jaccard, J., Devineni, T., Veazey, C. H., & Galovski, T. E. (2003). Prediction of response to psychological treatment among motor vehicle accident survivors with PTSD. *Behavior Therapy, 34*, 351–363. http://dx.doi.org/10.1016/S0005-7894(03)80005-9

Bradley, R., Greene, J., Russ, E., Dutra, L., & Westen, D. (2005). A multidimensional meta-analysis of psychotherapy for PTSD. *The American Journal of Psychiatry, 162*, 214–227. http://dx.doi.org/10.1176/appi.ajp.162.2.214

Brewin, C. R., Dalgleish, T., & Joseph, S. (1996). A dual representation theory of posttraumatic stress disorder. *Psychological Review, 103*, 670–686. http://dx.doi.org/10.1037/0033-295X.103.4.670

Bryant, R. A., Moulds, M. L., & Nixon, R. V. (2003). Cognitive behaviour therapy of acute stress disorder: A four-year follow-up. *Behaviour Research and Therapy, 41*, 489–494. http://dx.doi.org/10.1016/S0005-7967(02)00179-1

Butler, A. C., Chapman, J. E., Forman, E. M., & Beck, A. T. (2006). The empirical status of cognitive-behavioral therapy: A review of meta-analyses. *Clinical Psychology Review, 26*, 17–31. http://dx.doi.org/10.1016/j.cpr.2005.07.003

Cloitre, M., Koenen, K. C., Cohen, L. R., & Han, H. (2002). Skills training in affective and interpersonal regulation followed by exposure: A phase-based treatment for

PTSD related to childhood abuse. *Journal of Consulting and Clinical Psychology, 70*, 1067–1074. http://dx.doi.org/10.1037/0022-006X.70.5.1067

Cottraux, J., Note, I., Yao, S. N., de Mey-Guillard, C., Bonasse, F., Djamoussian, D., . . . Chen, Y. (2008). Randomized controlled comparison of cognitive behavior therapy with Rogerian supportive therapy in chronic post-traumatic stress disorder: A 2-year follow-up. *Psychotherapy and Psychosomatics, 77*, 101–110. http://dx.doi.org/10.1159/000112887

Dobson, K. S. (Ed.). (2009). *Handbook of cognitive-behavioral therapies*. New York, NY: Guilford Press.

Ehlers, A., & Clark, D. M. (2000). A cognitive model of posttraumatic stress disorder. *Behaviour Research and Therapy, 38*, 319–345. http://dx.doi.org/10.1016/S0005-7967(99)00123-0

Ehring, T., Welborn, R., Morina, N., Wicherts, J. M., Freitag, J., & Emmelkamp, P. M. (2014). Meta-analysis of psychological treatments for posttraumatic stress disorder in adult survivors of childhood abuse. *Clinical Psychology Review, 34*, 645–657. http://dx.doi.org/10.1016/j.cpr.2014.10.004

Fecteau, G., & Nicki, R. (1999). Cognitive behavioural treatment of post traumatic stress disorder after motor vehicle accident. *Behavioural and Cognitive Psychotherapy, 27*, 201–214. http://dx.doi.org/10.1017/S135246589927302X

Foa, E. B., Dancu, C. V., Hembree, E. A., Jaycox, L. H., Meadows, E. A., & Street, G. P. (1999). A comparison of exposure therapy, stress inoculation training, and their combination for reducing posttraumatic stress disorder in female assault victims. *Journal of Consulting and Clinical Psychology, 67*, 194–200. http://dx.doi.org/10.1037/0022-006X.67.2.194

Foa, E. B., Hembree, E. A., Cahill, S. P., Rauch, S. A., Riggs, D. S., Feeny, N. C., & Yadin, E. (2005). Randomized trial of prolonged exposure for posttraumatic stress disorder with and without cognitive restructuring: Outcome at academic and community clinics. *Journal of Consulting and Clinical Psychology, 73*, 953–964. http://dx.doi.org/10.1037/0022-006X.73.5.953

Foa, E. B., & Meadows, E. A. (1997). Psychosocial treatments for posttraumatic stress disorder: A critical review. *Annual Review of Psychology, 48*, 449–480. http://dx.doi.org/10.1146/annurev.psych.48.1.449

Foa, E. B., & Riggs, D. S. (1993). Post-traumatic stress disorder in rape victims. In J. Oldham, M. B. Riba, & A. Tasman (Eds.), *American Psychiatric Press review of psychiatry* (Vol. 12, pp. 273–303). Washington, DC: American Psychiatric Press.

Foa, E. B., Rothbaum, B. O., Riggs, D. S., & Murdock, T. B. (1991). Treatment of posttraumatic stress disorder in rape victims: A comparison between cognitive-behavioral procedures and counseling. *Journal of Consulting and Clinical Psychology, 59*, 715–723. http://dx.doi.org/10.1037/0022-006X.59.5.715

Foa, E. B., Steketee, G., & Rothbaum, B. O. (1989). Behavioural/cognitive conceptual-izations of post-traumatic stress disorder. *Behavior Therapy, 20*, 155–176. http://dx.doi.org/10.1016/S0005-7894(89)80067-X

Gaudiano, B. A. (2006). The "third wave" behavior therapies in context: Review of Hayes et al.'s (2004) *Mindfulness and acceptance: Expanding the cognitive-behavioral tradition* and Hayes and Strosahl's (2004) *A practical guide to acceptance and commit-ment therapy. Cognitive and Behavioral Practice, 13*, 101–104.

Hayes, S. C., Luoma, J. B., Bond, F. W., Masuda, A., & Lillis, J. (2006). Acceptance and commitment therapy: Model, processes and outcomes. *Behaviour Research and Therapy, 44*, 1–25. http://dx.doi.org/10.1016/j.brat.2005.06.006

Hays, P. A. (2009). Integrating evidence-based practice, cognitive–behavior therapy, and multicultural therapy: Ten steps for culturally competent practice. *Professional Psychology: Research and Practice, 40*, 354–360. http://dx.doi.org/10.1037/a0016250

Herman, J. (1992). *Trauma and recovery*. New York, NY: Basic Books.

Hinton, D. E., Chhean, D., Pich, V., Safren, S. A., Hofmann, S. G., & Pollack, M. H. (2005). A randomized controlled trial of cognitive-behavior therapy for Cambodian refugees with treatment-resistant PTSD and panic attacks: A cross-over design. *Journal of Traumatic Stress, 18,* 617–629. http://dx.doi.org/10.1002/jts.20070

Hinton, D. E., Hofmann, S. G., Pollack, M. H., & Otto, M. W. (2009). Mechanisms of efficacy of CBT for Cambodian refugees with PTSD: Improvement in emotion regulation and orthostatic blood pressure response. *CNS Neuroscience & Therapeutics, 15,* 255–263. http://dx.doi.org/10.1111/j.1755-5949.2009.00100.x

Hinton, D. E., Hofmann, S. G., Rivera, E., Otto, M. W., & Pollack, M. H. (2011). Culturally adapted CBT (CA-CBT) for Latino women with treatment-resistant PTSD: A pilot study comparing CA-CBT to applied muscle relaxation. *Behaviour Research and Therapy, 49,* 275–280. http://dx.doi.org/10.1016/j.brat.2011.01.005

Hofmann, S. G., Asnaani, A., Vonk, I. J., Sawyer, A. T., & Fang, A. (2012). The efficacy of cognitive behavioral therapy: A review of meta-analyses. *Cognitive Therapy and Research, 36,* 427–440. http://dx.doi.org/10.1007/s10608-012-9476-1

Horowitz, M. J. (1997). *Stress response syndromes: PTSD, grief, and adjustment disorders* (3rd ed.). Northvale, NJ: Jason Aronson.

Jacobson, N. S., Dobson, K. S., Truax, P. A., Addis, M. E., Koerner, K., Gollan, J. K., . . . Prince, S. E. (2000). A component analysis of cognitive–behavioral treatment for depression. *Prevention & Treatment, 3*(1). http://dx.doi.org/10.1037/1522-3736.3.1.323a

Janoff-Bulman, R. (1992). *Shattered assumptions: Toward a new psychology of trauma.* New York, NY: The Free Press.

Johnson, D. M., Johnson, N. L., Perez, S. K., Palmieri, P. A., & Zlotnick, C. (2016). Comparison of adding treatment of PTSD during and after shelter stay to standard care in residents of battered women's shelters: Results of a randomized clinical trial. *Journal of Traumatic Stress, 29,* 365–373. http://dx.doi.org/10.1002/jts.22117

Johnson, D. M., & Zlotnick, C. (2009). HOPE for battered women with PTSD in domestic violence shelters. *Professional Psychology: Research and Practice, 40,* 234–241. http://dx.doi.org/10.1037/a0012519

Johnson, D. M., Zlotnick, C., & Perez, S. (2011). Cognitive behavioral treatment of PTSD in residents of battered women's shelters: Results of a randomized clinical trial. *Journal of Consulting and Clinical Psychology, 79,* 542–551. http://dx.doi.org/10.1037/a0023822

Jonas, D. E., Cusack, K., Forneris, C. A., Wilkins, T. M., Sonis, J., Middleton, J. C., . . . Gaynes, B. N. (2013). *Psychological and pharmacological treatments for adults with posttraumatic stress disorder (PTSD;* AHRQ Publication No. 13-EHC011-EF). Rockville, MD: Agency for Healthcare Research and Quality. http://dx.doi.org/10.1037/e553842013-001

Joseph, S., Williams, R., & Yule, W. (1997). *Understanding posttraumatic stress. A psychosocial perspective on PTSD and treatment.* Chichester, England: Wiley.

Kruse, J., Joksimovic, L., Cavka, M., Wöller, W., & Schmitz, N. (2009). Effects of trauma-focused psychotherapy upon war refugees. *Journal of Traumatic Stress, 22,* 585–592. http://dx.doi.org/10.1002/jts.20477

Kubany, E. S., Hill, E. E., & Owens, J. A. (2003). Cognitive trauma therapy for battered women with PTSD: Preliminary findings. *Journal of Traumatic Stress, 16,* 81–91. http://dx.doi.org/10.1023/A:1022019629803

Kubany, E. S., Hill, E. E., Owens, J. A., Iannce-Spencer, C., McCaig, M. A., Tremayne, K. J., & Williams, P. L. (2004). Cognitive trauma therapy for battered women with PTSD (CTT-BW). *Journal of Consulting and Clinical Psychology, 72,* 3–18. http://dx.doi.org/10.1037/0022-006X.72.1.3

Kubany, E. S., & Watson, S. B. (2002). Cognitive trauma therapy for formerly battered women with PTSD: Conceptual bases and treatment outlines. *Cognitive and Behavioral Practice, 9,* 111–127. http://dx.doi.org/10.1016/S1077-7229(02)80005-0

Linehan, M. M., Cochran, B. N., & Kehrer, C. A. (2001). Dialectical behavior therapy for borderline personality disorder. In D. H. Barlow (Ed.), *Clinical handbook of psychological disorders: A step-by-step treatment manual* (pp. 470–522). New York, NY: The Guilford Press.

Litz, B. T., Engel, C. C., Bryant, R. A., & Papa, A. (2007). A randomized, controlled proof-of-concept trial of an Internet-based, therapist-assisted self-management treatment for posttraumatic stress disorder. *The American Journal of Psychiatry, 164*, 1676–1684. http://dx.doi.org/10.1176/appi.ajp.2007.06122057

Longmore, R. J., & Worrell, M. (2007). Do we need to challenge thoughts in cognitive behavior therapy? *Clinical Psychology Review, 27*, 173–187. http://dx.doi.org/10.1016/j.cpr.2006.08.001

Mahoney, M. J., & Arnkoff, D. B. (1978). Cognitive and self-control therapies. In S. L. Garfield & A. E. Bergin (Eds.), *Handbook of psychotherapy and behavior change* (2nd ed., pp. 689–722). New York, NY: Wiley.

McCann, I. L., Sakheim, D. K., & Abrahamson, D. J. (1988). Trauma and victimization: A model of psychological adaptation. *The Counseling Psychologist, 16*, 531–594. http://dx.doi.org/10.1177/0011000088164002

McDonagh, A., Friedman, M., McHugo, G., Ford, J., Sengupta, A., Mueser, K., . . . Descamps, M. (2005). Randomized trial of cognitive-behavioral therapy for chronic posttraumatic stress disorder in adult female survivors of childhood sexual abuse. *Journal of Consulting and Clinical Psychology, 73*, 515–524. http://dx.doi.org/10.1037/0022-006X.73.3.515

Merluzzi, T. V., Glass, C. R., & Genest, M. (1981). *Cognitive assessment*. New York, NY: Guilford Press.

Najavits, L. M. (2002). *Seeking safety: A treatment manual for PTSD and substance abuse*. New York, NY: Guilford Press.

Neuner, F., Schauer, M., Roth, W. T., & Elbert, T. (2002). A narrative exposure treatment as intervention in a refugee camp: A case report. *Behavioural and Cognitive Psychotherapy, 30*, 205–209. http://dx.doi.org/10.1017/S1352465802002072

Resick, P. A., & Schnicke, M. K. (1992). Cognitive processing therapy for sexual assault victims. *Journal of Consulting and Clinical Psychology, 60*, 748–756. http://dx.doi.org/10.1037/0022-006X.60.5.748

Resick, P. A., Wachen, J. S., Dondanville, K. A., Pruiksma, K. E., Yarvis, J. S., Peterson, A. L., . . . STRONG STAR Consortium. (2017). Effect of group vs. individual cognitive processing therapy in active-duty military seeking treatment for posttraumatic stress disorder: A randomized clinical trial. *JAMA Psychiatry, 74*(1), 28–36. http://dx.doi.org/10.1001/jamapsychiatry.2016.2729

Spence, J., Titov, N., Dear, B. F., Johnston, L., Solley, K., Lorian, C., . . . Schwenke, G. (2011). Randomized controlled trial of Internet-delivered cognitive behavioral therapy for posttraumatic stress disorder. *Depression and Anxiety, 28*, 541–550. http://dx.doi.org/10.1002/da.20835

Stewart, R. E., & Chambless, D. L. (2009). Cognitive-behavioral therapy for adult anxiety disorders in clinical practice: A meta-analysis of effectiveness studies. *Journal of Consulting and Clinical Psychology, 77*, 595–606. http://dx.doi.org/10.1037/a0016032

Taylor, R. R. (2006). *Cognitive behavioral therapy for chronic illness and disability*. New York, NY: Springer Science & Business Media.

U.S. Department of Veterans Affairs, & U.S. Department of Defense. (2010). *VA/DoD clinical practice guidelines for the management of post-traumatic stress*. Washington, DC: U.S. Department of Veterans Affairs & U.S. Department of Defense.

van der Kolk, B. A., & Fisler, R. (1995). Dissociation and the fragmentary nature of traumatic memories: Overview and exploratory study. *Journal of Traumatic Stress, 8*, 505–525. http://dx.doi.org/10.1002/jts.2490080402

van der Kolk, B. A., & van der Hart, O. (1991). The intrusive past: The flexibility of memory and the engraving of trauma. *American Imago, 48*, 425–454.

van Emmerik, A. A., Kamphuis, J. H., & Emmelkamp, P. M. (2008). Treating acute stress disorder and posttraumatic stress disorder with cognitive behavioral therapy or structured writing therapy: A randomized controlled trial. *Psychotherapy and Psychosomatics, 77,* 93–100. http://dx.doi.org/10.1159/000112886

Worell, J., & Remer, P. (2003). *Feminist perspectives in therapy: Empowering diverse women.* New York, NY: Wiley.

Zlotnick, C., Najavits, L. M., Rohsenow, D. J., & Johnson, D. M. (2003). A cognitive-behavioral treatment for incarcerated women with substance abuse disorder and posttraumatic stress disorder: Findings from a pilot study. *Journal of Substance Abuse Treatment, 25,* 99–105. http://dx.doi.org/10.1016/S0740-5472(03)00106-5

Zoellner, L. A., Feeny, N. C., Fitzgibbons, L. A., & Foa, E. B. (1999). Response of African American and Caucasian women to cognitive behavioral therapy for PTSD. *Behavior Therapy, 30,* 581–595. http://dx.doi.org/10.1016/S0005-7894(99)80026-4

4

Cognitive Processing Therapy for PTSD

Kathleen M. Chard and Ellen T. Healy

Cognitive processing therapy (CPT; Resick & Schnicke, 1993) is a brief, cognitive behavioral treatment that has been found to be effective for the treatment of posttraumatic stress disorder (PTSD) and corollary symptoms. CPT has been listed in multiple practice guidelines as a best-practice intervention for symptoms resulting from traumatic events (Foa, Keane, Friedman, & Cohen, 2010; U.S. Department of Veterans Affairs & U.S. Department of Defense [VA/DoD], 2017), and research has supported its use with a variety of clients from many different countries (Resick, Monson, & Chard, 2017). In this chapter, we review several key areas related to CPT, including the treatment rationale, the research support, delivery options, developing competency in CPT, and an overview of the CPT treatment components, followed by a case illustration demonstrating the application of CPT.

TREATMENT RATIONALE

CPT can be delivered in seven to 15 sessions, using the core 12-session manual to guide content. The treatment has been found to be effective in addressing mental health symptoms resulting from a variety of traumatic events, including rape, assault, sexual abuse, and combat (Chard, 2005; Monson et al., 2006; Resick, Nishith, Weaver, Astin, & Feuer, 2002; Resick & Schnicke, 1992). CPT can be offered in individual, group, or combined group and individual

http://dx.doi.org/10.1037/0000196-004
Casebook to the APA Clinical Practice Guideline for the Treatment of PTSD, edited by
L. F. Bufka, C. V. Wright, and R. W. Halfond

formats depending on the population being served and the resources of the therapy site.

CPT is largely a cognitive therapy; it shares many of the same constructs and interventions as cognitive therapy (CT), developed by Aaron Beck (Beck, Rush, Shaw, & Emery, 1979). However, CPT extends beyond traditional CT in many ways. First, CPT incorporates the work of McCann and colleagues (McCann & Pearlman, 1990; McCann, Sakheim, & Abrahamson, 1988), who proposed a constructivist self-development theory of traumatic events. With their model, they suggested that individuals create their realities and that new experiences are incorporated based on an individual's existing view of "reality." Thus, individuals construct meaning from traumatic events based on their past experiences, their expectations, and their schemas about the world. These schemas can be directed inward or outward to the world and typically revolve around safety, trust, power and control, esteem, and intimacy.

Second, CPT incorporates the work of Hollon and Garber (1988), who described the process individuals go through when they are exposed to schema-discrepant information. They suggested that when an event happens, either new information is altered so that it can be assimilated into existing schemas, with no change to prior beliefs (e.g., "It could not have been a rape, because he is my best friend"), or existing beliefs (e.g., "Friends won't hurt you") are altered to incorporate, or accommodate, the new discrepant information (e.g., "Some friends will hurt you"). Extending from Hollon and Garber's work, CPT also includes the idea of overaccommodation, which entails an individual overgeneralizing new learning to the extreme and creating a new disruptive belief (e.g., "All men will hurt me"). CPT acknowledges that some disruptive beliefs are actually schema-congruent, especially for individuals with childhood trauma or chronic life histories with traumatic events.

Third, CPT is based on a biological model of stress, with therapy incorporating information about the hypothalamic–pituitary–adrenal axis (HPA axis) and the changes in the amygdala and prefrontal cortex in individuals with PTSD (Shin, Rauch, & Pitman, 2006). Researchers have found that individuals with PTSD have a highly active amygdala that is hypersensitive to perceived threat cues and a diminished prefrontal cortex response. In CPT, the goal is to help the client activate the prefrontal cortex by focusing on the meaning of the event, not the details of the event, and to better understand, and often challenge, the thought processes that are leading to the painful emotions the client is experiencing or avoiding (Resick, Monson, & Chard, 2017).

DIFFERENCES BETWEEN CPT AND OTHER TRAUMA THERAPIES

CPT is different from other trauma therapies in that there is no need for individuals to review their trauma account(s) in detail in the therapy sessions. This type of therapy can be a significant relief for those who fear talking about their trauma in session. The choice to include written trauma accounts is made at the onset of therapy. Furthermore, when completing weekly worksheet assignments, the client does not have to put explicit information about the trauma on the sheets, thus allowing the client to maintain control over the amount and frequency of trauma detail discussions.

Another difference between CPT and other trauma therapies is the focus on a greater range of trauma-related emotions. PTSD was considered an anxiety disorder until the publication of the fifth edition of the *Diagnostic and Statistical Manual of Mental Disorders* (*DSM–5*; American Psychiatric Association, 2013), and theory and interventions for many trauma therapies focus primarily on fear and anxiety. Theoretically, CPT is not built on anxiety/fear models, and thus the focus of the treatment is broader and allows for emotional reactions such as disgust, guilt, shame, or sadness in response to the traumatic event. In addition, CPT accounts for individuals whose trauma started very early in life and whose further trauma serves to confirm the beliefs they developed at the onset. Thus, CPT can easily address the needs of these individuals whose trauma-related beliefs (e.g., "Everyone will hurt me," "I am unlovable") are schema-congruent, often due to years of traumatic abuse from childhood into adulthood, and who are often labeled as having complex trauma.

RESEARCH SUPPORT

Across numerous samples and diverse international settings, the empirical support for CPT is strong, demonstrated in randomized controlled trials (RCTs) and in real-world clinical settings. Studies of CPT have examined differing trauma types ranging across civilian and military-related traumas in both men and women. In the RCTs, the majority of study participants endorsed experiencing multiple traumas, similar to clients seen in clinical settings. CPT has been examined in individual and group settings, for clients using telehealth, and when delivered with and without the written trauma account. The RCTs have demonstrated that CPT is equivalent to prolonged exposure and offers stronger outcomes than present-centered therapy, dialogical exposure therapy, and treatment as usual (e.g., Butollo, Karl, König, & Rosner, 2016; Monson et al., 2006; Resick et al., 2015). RCTs in the Democratic Republic of Congo, Australia, Germany, and Iraq have demonstrated diverse populations benefit from CPT (Bass et al., 2013; Bolton et al., 2014; Butollo et al., 2016; Forbes et al., 2012). Additionally, CPT was effective in treating refugees from war-torn countries (from Bosnia-Herzegovina and Afghanistan), both when an interpreter was used and when CPT was delivered in the client's native language (Schulz, Resick, Huber, & Griffin, 2006). Although major modifications have generally not been needed across cultures, attention to how translations affect the meanings of words and concepts is important. In some developing countries, for example in the Democratic Republic of Congo, more significant modifications were necessary (e.g., patients orally rehearsing and memorizing concepts) given the lack of literacy and access to paper. Translations of the CPT manual (and worksheets) have been developed in 12 languages, including Arabic, Chinese, Finnish, French, German, Hebrew, Japanese, Kurdish, and Spanish (Resick, Monson, & Chard, 2017).

Some of the RCTs that demonstrate CPT efficacy included racially diverse samples that were 40% to 60% non-White (e.g., Galovski, Blain, Mott, Elwood, & Houle, 2012; Resick, Wachen, et al., 2017; Surís, Link-Malcolm, Chard, Ahn, & North, 2013). The findings related to how racial or ethnic differences may affect engagement or outcome in CPT are mixed. An analysis of two RCTs suggested that Black women were more likely than White women to discontinue CPT prematurely, but there were no differences in PTSD measure outcomes (Lester, Artz, Resick, & Young-Xu, 2010). In another sample of Black and White females, race was not a predictor of symptom change, and there were no group differences in early termination (Holliday, Holder, Williamson, & Surís, 2017). In terms of qualitative differences in the CPT treatment course, Latino clients identified fewer stuck points than non-Latino clients, though the general content was similar across groups (Marques et al., 2016). This finding could have implications for a therapist's approach to finding stuck points with Latino clients. More research is needed to better understand how racial or ethnic differences affect treatment outcome and engagement.

The diversity of studies on CPT has helped to elucidate how patient characteristics such as sex, era of military service, and comorbidity may affect CPT outcome. With respect to sex differences, studies with mixed-sex samples have demonstrated that men and women largely respond similarly in CPT (e.g., Galovski, Blain, Chappuis, & Fletcher, 2013; Voelkel, Pukay-Martin, Walter, & Chard, 2015). A comparison of veterans from Operation Enduring Freedom (OEF) and Operation Iraqi Freedom (OIF) with Vietnam-era veterans suggested that recent veterans showed larger treatment gains, though they were also more likely to drop out of treatment (Chard, Schumm, Owens, & Cottingham, 2010). It is possible some dropped out when they achieved their treatment goals, although it is also possible other factors (e.g., competing work and family schedules) contributed to higher rates of dropout in the younger veterans. It is important to note, however, that despite the difference in gains, the Vietnam veterans still demonstrated significant and clinically meaningful treatment gains.

A question often raised is how well CPT works for those with more complex presentations and comorbid conditions. In particular, many clinicians are concerned that borderline personality disorder (BPD) may be contraindicated for trauma-focused treatment like CPT because of concerns about tolerability as well as treatment efficacy in this population, but the data do not support this concern. Individuals with comorbid BPD were not specifically excluded from any of the RCT samples, though BPD rates in these samples were not explicitly reported. A secondary analysis of Resick and colleagues' (2002) data indicated that 25% of the sample had a clinical level of borderline symptomatology and that the level of borderline personality characteristics did not predict treatment outcome (Clarke, Rizvi, & Resick, 2008). This finding was replicated by Walter, Bolte, Owens, and Chard (2012), who found no differences in PTSD treatment gains between those with and those without a personality disorder diagnosis including BPD.

CPT has been implemented with those who have experienced traumatic brain injury (TBI) with positive outcomes. Chard, Schumm, McIlvain, Bailey, and Parkinson (2011) found that individuals with mild TBI and those with moderate or severe TBI improved significantly in a CPT residential program. Individuals with TBI have done well in CPT both when the written trauma account was included (CPT+A) and when it was not (Walter, Dickstein, Barnes, & Chard, 2014).

Historically, clinicians believed that individuals with substance use disorders needed a period of sobriety and stability prior to engaging in trauma-focused treatment, but there is a solid consensus in recent years, supported in the VA/DoD (2017) Clinical Practice Guidelines, that PTSD and substance use disorders are often so inextricably linked that trauma treatment needs to be an integral part of treatment for those with comorbid substance use and PTSD. When the level of substance use requires medical detoxification, then that should be addressed first; otherwise, trauma intervention can occur. RCTs examining CPT excluded those who were dependent on substances and required detox, but other participants with substance use disorders were not excluded. One effectiveness study by Kaysen et al. (2014) showed no differences in outcomes among those with current or past histories of alcohol use disorders and those without.

Studies on CPT have also included analyses of treatment outcomes beyond PTSD. Findings consistently suggest that CPT leads to improvements in depression, suicidal ideation, health concerns, dissociation, physiological reactivity, occupational function and economic status, social and leisure involvement, family relationships, and intimacy and sexual concerns (e.g., Galovski, Monson, Bruce, & Resick, 2009; Gradus, Suvak, Wisco, Marx, & Resick, 2013; Griffin, Resick, & Galovski, 2012; Monson et al., 2012; Resick, Williams, Suvak, Monson, & Gradus, 2012). Thus, problems in these areas should not represent reasons to avoid providing CPT; rather, CPT should be considered because it may help address the cooccurring issues that often present with PTSD.

Although CPT was initially developed as a 12-session therapy, Galovski et al. (2012) explored whether outcomes could improve by tailoring the amount of therapy based on individual needs. In this study, the course of treatment was shortened if participants reached a significantly reduced symptom level prior to Session 12, and conversely, additional sessions were added if symptoms remained at Session 12. This flexible length yielded a higher rate of response (i.e., 92% no longer met criteria for a PTSD diagnosis posttreatment) than other studies that had provided only 12 sessions of CPT. This study demonstrated that CPT is not a one-size-fits-all treatment and that variable length depending on individual needs improves outcomes.

DELIVERY VARIATIONS OF CPT

Depending on needs of the client, therapists may choose to employ different versions of CPT, including CPT with the written trauma accounts (CPT+A) or without the accounts (CPT), group, individual, or a combination of group and individual. Resick and colleagues (2008) conducted a dismantling study to deconstruct CPT into its constituent components, cognitive therapy and narrative writing, compared with the full protocol. They found that cognitive processing therapy without the account was equally effective and perhaps more efficient than CPT+A. Written accounts may be particularly beneficial to those who have high levels of dissociation (Resick, Suvak, Johnides, Mitchell, & Iverson, 2012) or experiences of high-frequency abuse (Resick, Suvak, & Wells, 2014). In another study, Chard (2005) examined a group-plus-individual-format treatment with adult survivors of child sexual abuse and found it to be highly efficacious. This combined individual/group format has since been adopted by residential programs in the VA system and is particularly useful in brief, intensive programs. CPT can be delivered in inpatient, residential, and outpatient settings. Although CPT is typically delivered once or twice per week, there are some preliminary findings and ongoing studies examining CPT delivered in an intensive manner (over the course of 1 or 2 weeks; e.g., Bryan et al., 2018).

DEVELOPING COMPETENCY IN CPT

To achieve competency in providing CPT, clinicians are encouraged to participate in a CPT training workshop and then receive CPT consultation while seeing cases (see CPTforPTSD.com for more information). The 2- or 3-day workshop incorporates didactics, demonstrations, and experiential exercises. After clinicians attend a workshop, they should begin consultation right away to implement new learning with active PTSD cases. Consultation with a CPT expert provides an opportunity to continue the learning process and ensure that the therapy is implemented with fidelity. Consultation ensures the ongoing practice of the newly learned skills along with feedback, which is important for psychotherapy competency development (Kaslow, 2004). Given that delivering CPT with fidelity is important for ensuring treatment outcomes (Farmer, Mitchell, Parker-Guilbert, & Galovski, 2017; Holder, Holliday, Williams, Mullen, & Surís, 2018), consultants closely monitor consultation case progress to ensure adherence to the model as clinicians are learning.

Once a clinician has successfully completed the minimum number of CPT cases (typically two to four cases) while actively participating in CPT consultation (minimum of 20 group consultations), the clinician may be approved to be added to the CPT provider roster. The VA Healthcare System maintains a roster of all VA clinicians who have successfully completed CPT training; outside of the VA, the CPT developers keep a roster of community clinicians.

On the CPT developers' roster, clinicians may seek approval for quality-rated provider status by submitting tapes of CPT sessions for review. Once awarded, CPT provider status for community clinicians lasts for 3 years and must be renewed to ensure continued CPT fidelity.

DESCRIPTION OF TREATMENT COMPONENTS

As noted previously, the main goal of CPT is to reduce an individual's psychological distress caused by the symptoms of PTSD and related disorders. To facilitate this change, the therapist and the client work together in a "collaborative empiricism" framework in which the therapist teaches the client the skills necessary to achieve maximal improvement. We suggest that, prior to starting CPT, individuals be given an assessment to determine if they meet criteria for a diagnosis of PTSD. The first step is determining if the individual actually has experienced a traumatic event that meets diagnostic Criterion A. Although many life events can be stressful, some do not rise to the level of a traumatic event, and making that distinction is an important part of diagnosis for PTSD. It would be ideal if the assessor could use one of the gold standard interviews, such as the Clinician-Administered PTSD Scale (CAPS; Weathers, Marx, Friedman, & Schnurr, 2014), but it may not be feasible for the clinician to receive adequate training in the CAPS. Thus, we recommend using a self-report form such as the PTSD Checklist (PCL-5; Weathers et al., 2014), which also includes questions to assist in making a Criterion A determination. After the initial assessment using the monthly PCL-5, we recommend using the weekly PCL-5 to monitor ongoing symptom change through the therapy process. Prior to the start of treatment, clients should be given the option to write a narrative of their trauma as part of the therapy (CPT+A). They may choose not to have that component included (CPT); there is evidence that both variations (CPT/CPT+A) are effective (e.g., Resick, Galovski, et al., 2008; Resick, Nishith, et al., 2002; Resick, Wachen, et al., 2017). The delivery of CPT is divided into three phases: education, processing, and challenging.

First Phase: Education

In the first phase, which comprises the first three sessions, the client reviews the symptoms of PTSD and how their life has been affected by the disorder, the CPT treatment model including how PTSD develops biologically, and the connection between thoughts and feelings. The therapist introduces the concept of the *just world belief,* which is a commonly held belief that good things happen to good people and bad things happen to bad people. The just world belief is presented to demonstrate how our beliefs can affect our responses to traumatic events. The client is taught the ways in which the traumatic events can negatively affect their thinking, and the underlying concepts of *assimilation* (i.e., taking in the new information without changing preexisting beliefs), *overaccommodation* (i.e., changing beliefs about the self and the world to extremes), and *accommodation* (i.e., modifying preexisting beliefs to incorporate new information) are introduced to the client in lay language. For Session 2, the client is asked to write an impact statement, which explores the meaning(s) the client has made of the traumatic event and how the traumatic event(s) has affected the client's beliefs about self, others, and the world, especially in the areas of safety, trust, power and control, esteem, and intimacy. The client reads the impact statement in Session 2 and is taught to label thoughts that have become extreme or exaggerated as *stuck points*. In addition, the therapist uses the Stuck Point Help Sheet so the client can identify stuck points for review during the treatment. The Help Sheet describes stuck points as thoughts about oneself, others, or the world that prevent an individual from recovering from the traumatic event(s). The stuck points may be directly related to the traumatic event, or they may be overgeneralized negative thoughts that do not have a direct connection to the trauma. Often these thoughts become repetitive and can lead to recurring painful emotions that do not dissipate quickly, such as shame, blame, fear, and anger. At the end of Session 2, the A–B–C[1] Worksheet is introduced to demonstrate the connection between events, thoughts, and feelings and to facilitate the identification of additional stuck points. At this point in therapy, the therapist begins to incorporate gentle Socratic dialogue to facilitate the development of alternative, more accurate beliefs than the client's current way of thinking. The goal is not to show the client that the existing beliefs are wrong but to teach cognitive flexibility and the awareness that we can choose what to think depending on the facts of the situation. This practice teaches the client the art of cognitive flexibility that will be used during the remainder of the sessions.

Second Phase: Processing

In the second phase of treatment, processing, during Sessions 4 and 5 the therapist continues to use the A–B–C Worksheets and Socratic dialogue to help the client generate alternatives to their assimilated beliefs, particularly in the areas of blame, shame, and hindsight bias about the event. Next, the client is introduced to the Challenging Questions Sheet (CQS), a tool that helps the client to examine their thoughts and interpretations about the trauma by weighing the evidence for and against the stuck point, examining the full context of the situation(s) related to the belief, and determining whether the belief is based on facts or feelings. For example, a client may believe that the traumatic event (e.g., rape, combat-related death) is "all my fault." Using the CQS, the client can begin to see that one's rape or the death of a friend in combat was caused by someone else and that there was little they could have

---

[1]A–B–C refers to activating event, belief (thought), and consequence (emotional and behavioral).

done to prevent the end result given the situational variables, resources, and knowledge they had at the time. This process typically frees the client to feel the "natural" emotions associated with the treatment, such as grief, loss, or sadness. The client is asked to focus on the trauma-related beliefs first to avoid using these beliefs as evidence for later beliefs that developed from the trauma. For example, a client may state, "Because I let the rape happen, I am a bad person." If the client challenges "I let the rape happen" first, they will not use this belief as evidence for "I am a bad person."

Third Phase: Challenging

In the third and final phase of treatment, challenging, the therapist and client work together to help the client further examine the stuck points, including those about the trauma but also beliefs that have overgeneralized from the events (i.e., overaccommodated beliefs) over the course of Sessions 6 through 12. The goal of this phase is to generate healthier and more accurate beliefs in relation to the event(s), the self, others, and the world. Clients are introduced to the Patterns of Problematic Thinking Worksheet, which helps identify habitual and typically unproductive ways in which a person tends to respond to situations, such as jumping to conclusions, overgeneralizing from a single incident, and mind reading. As the client reviews the list of stuck points and begins to find typical patterns of responding, the client can become more aware of their reactions and can work to prevent these types of assumptions in their thinking in the future.

The remainder of the therapy uses the Challenging Beliefs Worksheet (CBW) to consolidate all prior worksheets in one form. The worksheet is typically introduced in Session 6. It allows the client to examine stuck points with all the tools the client has learned to this point. The client starts with a stuck point, identifies the feelings that stem from the stuck point, and then uses the challenging questions to examine the veracity of the thought. Next, the client determines which of the problematic thinking patterns are supporting the stuck point and then identifies an alternative thought. Finally, the client determines the emotions that coincide with the new belief. Thus, the CBW allows the therapist and client to identify the emotions that are linked to stuck points, challenge the accuracy of the assumptions behind the thoughts, and generate alternative beliefs, with related feelings, that are more reflective of all information relevant to the situation. Through examining the belief, seeing what problematic thinking patterns they are using, and then identifying new thoughts, the client is able to gauge how much relief they may feel if they look at the situation more realistically instead of through the lens of PTSD. The CBW can lead to modification of beliefs; for example, "I cannot trust anyone" may become "Although I cannot trust some people, I can trust many others." In other cases, the client will completely reverse the belief, for example changing "The trauma was my fault" to "There is nothing

I could have done to prevent the trauma" or changing "I am a bad person" to "There are a lot of people who think I am a great person."

At each session beginning with Session 7, clients are given a handout focused on a core area typically associated with PTSD: safety, trust, power and control, esteem, and intimacy. These handouts help clients conceptualize how PTSD may have affected their views in a much broader fashion than they previously had realized, and the handouts can help clients identify stuck points they may have overlooked in these five areas. Each module provides an explanation of the topic, describes how trauma can alter one's thinking in that area, and lists sample stuck points for the client to consider. For example, many clients do not realize how much PTSD has affected their sense of trust with self and others. They often report stuck points, such as "I cannot trust my own decisions" or "If I let other people get close to me, they will hurt me." Although some clients may resonate with one of the five areas more than others, clients typically find that spending time examining all five areas is helpful in ensuring that no overgeneralized stuck points are missed.

For Session 12, the client is asked to rewrite their impact statement to reflect what they now believe about the trauma(s), themselves, and the world. The client and the therapist then discuss the differences between the two statements to highlight the ways in which the client has changed in their thinking. In addition, the final impact statement may be used to generate future areas for work with additional worksheets at home or may help to identify a possible focus for future treatment, such as couples counseling, vocational rehabilitation, or relapse prevention.

Many clinicians are hesitant to start evidence-based PTSD treatments when a client has a comorbid symptom presentation because they have either an assumption that the other disorder must be treated first (as in the case of substance use) or a concern that the client is too fragile to handle trauma-focused treatment (e.g., has limited coping skills, a personality disorder, suicidal thoughts). To demonstrate how to conduct CPT with these complex symptom presentations, the following case examples illustrate the flexibility of CPT in working with the varied clients typically seen in a clinic. These examples are composites of patients typically seen in our treatment clinics. Tables 4.1 and 4.2 provide an overview of the CPT terminology and worksheets.

TABLE 4.1. CPT Terminology

CPT term	Definition
Stuck point	Problematic thoughts that keep a client from recovering
Assimilated stuck points	Thoughts about the trauma are understood through the lens of previously held beliefs. Often involves self-blame or attempts to "undo" the traumatic event
Overaccommodated stuck points	Thoughts that are changed dramatically as a result of a traumatic event. Often involves exaggerated or all-or-none thinking

TABLE 4.2. Description of CPT Worksheets

CPT worksheet	Description
ABC Worksheet	Worksheet to help identify the connection between events, thoughts, and feelings
Challenging Questions Worksheet	List of questions for clients to ask themselves to examine and challenge their thinking
Patterns of Problematic Thinking Worksheet	List of patterns of thinking to help clients recognize common tendencies in their thinking that may be problematic
Challenging Beliefs Worksheet	Worksheet to pull together the skills of identifying thoughts and emotions, challenging thinking, recognizing patterns, and developing new alternative beliefs

CASE ILLUSTRATION: SHAY

Shay is a 27-year-old African American woman who received our clinic contact information from the local emergency department when she visited them after experiencing a sexual assault in a parking lot when she was leaving work late one evening 6 months ago. Shay is a single parent with three children, and she also cares for her elderly mother. Shay was given the PCL-5, and her score of 55 was indicative of significant PTSD symptoms. She expressed significant reservations about her ability to do CPT because CPT has paper-and-pencil practice assignments and she "did not do well in school," although she did have her GED. She reported that she was diagnosed with a significant learning disability late in high school, but "by then it was too late to fix anything." She was working as the assistant manager of a local retail store and had been with the company for 8 years. Shay also was concerned about being able to make appointments because she had to juggle her work and her child care needs. We were able to create a flexible schedule for Shay with appointments before or after work, when her children were still at school, depending on her work schedule each week. In addition, we frequently had to provide last-minute appointment changes due to work obligations that required her to cover when an employee called in sick.

First Phase: Education

During the first therapy session, the therapist reviewed the CPT treatment rationale with Shay and began to discuss how and why people can become stuck in their recovery from a traumatic event. Shay was introduced to the concepts of natural emotions (i.e., emotions that most people would feel during a traumatic event, such as fear) and manufactured emotions (i.e., emotions that come from thoughts that are shaped by our experiences, such as guilt and shame). Shay stated that she was told by her parents at an early age that she was "too emotional" and that she "needed to get a hold of herself" so she tried not to react with emotions to events that happened in her life because "emotions are bad." The therapist used this discussion to segue into the information about stuck points and helped Shay begin to create her stuck point log. Shay was confused at first, suggesting that her "beliefs are not stuck points, but instead are facts." Her therapist gently asked her to consider putting them on the log and that they could look together at the evidence for the stuck points during the therapy. It would be Shay's choice which of the stuck points she wanted to edit, remove, or keep. Shay stated that she felt more comfortable knowing she had a choice. She was asked to write her impact statement for homework and expressed concern that she was not very good at writing and that her spelling was terrible. The therapist assured her that she would not be grading the document and that the only person that needed to know how to read it was Shay herself. She also told Shay about the CPT Coach application for smartphones and gave her the option of dictating her impact statement into the application if that was easier. Shay decided that using the phone app was a better way to keep her assignments with her so that she had them wherever she went. The therapist then inquired if Shay might have a stuck point about her reading and writing and Shay responded that "Only stupid people cannot read and write good." The therapist asked if this could be added to the log, and Shay agreed. Shay then said she would see how the week goes and that she would complete the assignment one way or the other.

Shay came in for her second session with a written impact statement. She expressed some trepidation about sharing it with her therapist, so the therapist asked her to read it out loud before showing it to her. The therapist praised Shay for her hard work completing the statement, and then they reviewed the document together to look for stuck points. They found several assimilated stuck points related to the trauma, including "I should have asked the security guard to walk me to my car" and "If I had not been looking at my phone he would not have been able to rape me." Shay was also able to identify several overaccommodated stuck points, including "I am damaged goods with three kids, so I am never going to get married," "I always make bad decisions," and "If I show emotion about the rape, it means I am weak." The initial stuck point log contained 13 stuck points, and the therapist reminded Shay to continue to build on it each week. The therapist then introduced the A–B–C Worksheet, and Shay again expressed some reservations about the writing, so the therapist suggested they use the sheet to address her concerns. In Column A the therapist wrote, "I have to do worksheets for homework." She then asked Shay what thoughts this generated that could be written in Column B. Shay responded, "I will mess it up because I am stupid." The therapist then asked her to identify emotions that results from this statement for Column C, and Shay responded, "Worthless and sad." The therapist then asked Shay to look at the bottom of the sheet where the client is asked if her thoughts in Column B are "realistic or helpful." Shay responded that "yes" her thoughts were realistic, so the therapist asked her for additional thoughts about this situation that might also be accurate, with the goal of creating cognitive flexibility rather than showing Shay that she was wrong.

The therapist asked Shay to focus on how well she did with the impact statement and if Shay could take that experience to create a new thought about completing the A–B–C Worksheet. She was able to say, "Maybe I will do better on this than I am thinking right now," and she remarked to the therapist that she is "always too hard on myself." The therapist asked Shay to take this sheet with her and to look at it again before she started her assignment that week.

Shay came to the next session stating that she could do some of the A–B–C Worksheets easily, but attempts to look at some of her experiences that week on other sheets were more difficult. The therapist asked to look at the most difficult one first, and they were able to work through it together. Shay completed two sheets on the rape. She stated that she realized she was putting all the blame for the rape on herself and none on her attacker but that she was having difficulty shaking the idea that she could have done something. The therapist assured her that this was normal, and she related that some stuck points require repeated challenges before they are finally altered in a way that works for the client. Shay was asked to complete another round of A–B–C Worksheets for homework.

Second Phase: Processing

In Session 4, the therapist introduced the Challenging Questions Worksheet, and Shay said that she was feeling more confident and was "actually excited to try this one at home." The therapist asked her to start with her stuck points related to the trauma, as it is important to address those before looking at the broader stuck points that developed afterward. Shay returned the following week, noting that she thought the worksheet was helpful but that some of the questions were confusing. The therapist reviewed the worksheets with Shay and helped her with the questions that she thought were harder to interpret. The therapist then introduced the Patterns of Problematic Thinking Worksheet, and Shay joked, "All of my thinking is problematic." She agreed to use the worksheet to identify which stuck points fit under which pattern.

Shay missed therapy the next week because of a last-minute work conflict and again the following week because her kids had the flu. The therapist talked to her each time and encouraged her to continue to do her worksheets, suggesting that she could go back to the Challenging Questions Worksheet if she wanted more practice. She reported that she would try, and she came in for Session 6 the following week. The therapist picked up where they left off by asking Shay to review her completed worksheets, starting with the ones that gave her the most trouble. The therapist then introduced the final worksheet, the CBW, and she showed Shay how it all comes together with the A–B–C Worksheet, Challenging Questions Worksheet, and Patterns of Problematic Thinking Worksheet all in one page. Shay expressed understanding and agreed to do six of the CBWs before the following week.

Third Phase: Challenging

Shay came in for Session 7 stating that she was feeling much better and that she was no longer blaming herself for the rape. She questioned whether she needed the rest of therapy. She and her therapist agreed to shorten the treatment by condensing the final modules so that safety and trust were covered in one session and both power and control and esteem were covered in the following session. Session 9 would cover intimacy; Shay would complete her final impact statement for homework, with therapy ending at Session 10. In her final session, Shay had a PCL of 8, clearly indicating that she no longer met criteria for PTSD. She reported a completely different outlook on the rape and changes in some of the negative self-talk about emotions that originated from her parents during her childhood. She said she was much more open and loving with her children and that she was considering going back to the local community college for some classes; she said she was "not as dumb as I thought I was."

CASE ILLUSTRATION: JOE

Joe is a White, male veteran of the wars in Iraq and Afghanistan who came to therapy stating that he was not engaging in any of his hobbies from high school, that he was feeling disconnected from his wife and kids, and that the only friends he talked with were some battle buddies to whom he occasionally sent text messages when he was having a bad day. He also noted that his work was suffering; he was worried he might lose his job. Joe indicated that his main coping mechanisms were smoking marijuana and drinking beer at night to help him go to sleep and all weekend to get through the days. At the initial assessment, Joe revealed a history of a moderate traumatic brain injury (TBI) due to multiple combat explosions during his three deployments to Iraq. He also reported some difficulties concentrating. This information was supported by a neuropsychological assessment.

   Joe's assessment revealed PTSD related to the death of a friend on a combat mission (PCL-5 of 63), and he noted that he had also experienced several other life-threatening situations throughout his various military deployments. Joe expressed some skepticism that CPT could help him, but he said he was "hopeful" and agreed to continue with the treatment. His therapist asked him to cut back on his alcohol and marijuana use and not to use before, during, or after session or while completing home practice assignments.

First Phase: Education

Joe first completed his impact statement. Examples of his stuck points included "I should have been able to prevent his death," "I have to be in control or bad things will happen," "If I let people get close to me they will die," and "My brain is too messed up for me to succeed at anything." Using the A–B–C Worksheets, Joe's therapist was able to begin gently challenging the stuck point that Joe could have prevented the trauma from happening, with Joe at one point stating, "Well, there should have been something I could have done, but I just cannot think of it."

Second Phase: Processing

Joe missed his fourth session and did not respond to calls for 2 weeks. When he came back in, he acknowledged that he had missed 6 days of work and that he had been drinking and smoking a great deal. The therapist and Joe then did an A–B–C Worksheet on what was going on in Joe's life and what he was thinking prior to his binge episode. Joe was able to use the sheet to see that he was greatly bothered by the realization that there was nothing he could have done to save his friend who died in combat, leading him to a new stuck point: "War is pointless." Joe noted that this thought really shook him, as he came from a long line of military service members.

Third Phase: Challenging

Joe's therapist introduced the Challenging Questions Worksheet, and he and Joe completed a practice sheet on "I should have been able to save my friend." The therapist also asked Joe to complete a sheet on his stuck point(s) about war. Joe struggled with some of the items on the Challenging Questions Worksheet, so his therapist used the abbreviated, 5-item version for individuals with cognitive impairment. Joe reported significant relief after completing the challenging questions: He was able to see that there was little evidence that he could have prevented his friend's death and recognized that he could not have saved him after he had been injured. Joe stated that he felt even more relief when he examined this same stuck point on the larger CBW, again using the five-item challenging questions. He was able to identify an alternative thought that "the enemy killed him, not me," and he was able to feel sadness over the loss of his friend (i.e., natural emotion) instead of the guilt (i.e., manufactured emotion) he had been feeling for years because of what he had been telling himself about the event. Treatment completed after 12 sessions, with Joe no longer meeting criteria for PTSD (PCL-5 = 11). In his final impact statement, Joe indicated that he was doing well at work and that his employer told him that he might be eligible for a promotion in the next few months if he maintains his current performance. Joe stated that he was no longer using marijuana (as of Session 11) because it impairs his concentration further, and he opted to start attending AA to maintain his sobriety. At 1-year follow-up, Joe had maintained his treatment gains and obtained a promotion; he and his wife were expecting another child.

CASE ILLUSTRATION: JULIE

Julie is a 35-year-old White woman who was referred to CPT by her primary care physician because she reported feeling triggered whenever she went in for a medical visit. Julie reported being molested by her stepfather from ages 10 to 15, and when she told her mother, her mother kicked her out of the house. At 18, she married her high school boyfriend, who was physically and emotionally abusive. They divorced when she was 30, after having three children. Julie is now living with her boyfriend; she says he is "controlling but not abusive." She indicated that she has little interaction with her ex-husband, as he does not see the children very often. At intake, Julie was diagnosed with PTSD (PCL-5 = 71) and BPD. She reported a prior history of self-injurious behavior, including cutting and taking very hot showers, and three prior suicide attempts using prescription pills in the past two years. The assessor completed a suicide risk plan, and Julie acknowledged current ideation but denied suicidal intent. She agreed to call her therapist or the Veterans Crisis Line if her symptoms worsened. Julie stated that she had tried "every therapy out there" and "there is nothing that can make her better." She was concerned that CPT could not help her because she had multiple traumas after years of abuse and that she would need months of sessions "to review all of my traumas with you." Throughout this discussion, Julie maintained poor eye contact and tended to keep her body turned away from the therapist. The therapist reminded Julie that reviewing the details of the traumatic events was not a part of CPT and that it was more important that they examine the "meaning she made" from the traumas, which typically manifests in stuck points or black-and-white assumptions she made about the trauma and her life after the traumatic events. Julie stated that because her doctor strongly recommended CPT, she agreed to attend sessions.

First Phase: Education

Julie was 30 minutes late to her initial assessment, and even though her therapist strongly encouraged her to be on time, Julie was 20 minutes late to her first and second therapy sessions. She stated that she "had a lot going on" and that it was difficult to keep track of everything in her life. In addition, she did not complete her assignment to write her impact statement. To address this, upon introduction of the A–B–C Worksheet for the Session 2 practice assignment, the therapist asked Julie to do a worksheet with "Have to do homework and attend my therapy sessions" in Column A. This is the first part of the A–B–C Worksheet, where the client is asked to identify something that happens; she will then work to identify her thoughts (Column B) and her related feelings (Column C).

Julie stated that her thought for Column B was "No one cares what happens to me" and her feelings for Column C were "angry and sad." The therapist used Socratic dialogue to help Julie with the remainder of the sheet and to help her challenge this belief herself, rather than the therapist providing the information for the challenge. The therapist asked, "Do you have any evidence that anyone does care about you?" and "What behaviors have people shown that demonstrate they might care about you?" Julie stated that her doctor might care about her or she would not have referred her for therapy and that her therapist might care or she would have terminated treatment when Julie was continually late. Julie acknowledged that she was testing the therapist by being late and not doing her assignments and that this was only hurting herself. Julie agreed to try working on her assignments that evening and to look at the worksheet they did in session for encouragement before she started.

Second Phase: Processing

Julie arrived for Session 3 on time. She stated that she had completed her impact statement and six A–B–C Worksheets, but then she coyly added, "You won't be happy with me, though." She proceeded to pull up her sleeve and started to remove a bandage that she said was covering cuts that she had made over the week. Her therapist asked her not to uncover them, stated that she was not a medical practitioner, and asked if Julie had seen a doctor or nurse. Julie responded, "They are not that bad. I just thought you might like to see what the therapy made me do." Instead of feeling a need to defend the treatment, the therapist used this situation as an opportunity to show Julie how the therapy can help her if she uses it in the moment when she is distressed. She asked if Julie had done an A–B–C Worksheet before or after her cutting. Because she had not, they completed one in session.

Julie had received a call from her ex-husband, who was refusing to pay child support for the month and was threatening to try to take full custody of their children. Julie noted that she immediately thought, "He still has control over me. I have no power, and he is going to hurt me and the kids," which led to strong emotions of fear, powerlessness, and anger. She said when she feels this way she typically cuts so that she can feel like she is powerful and in control again. The therapist asked if there was anything else that she could have said to herself after the call from her ex-husband, something that was more balanced or realistic based on their interactions over the past 5 years. Julie reported that she could survive without child support for a few months; she had done it before, and she could take him back to court if need be. She noted that he had not attempted to touch her since the divorce, and she remembered that her lawyer had told her he would never get full custody based on his abusive behavior in the past. When she thought about all these facts, she reported feeling calmer and more in control. The therapist pointed out the connection between Julie's thoughts, feelings, and subsequent cutting behavior and reminded Julie that if she can do a worksheet when confronted by a difficult situation, she is taking control and might be able to stop herself from feeling emotions that lead to her cutting behaviors.

Third Phase: Challenging

By Session 8, Julie had more than 50 stuck points on her log as she continued to add ones weekly. Julie at first assumed that this meant that she was very sick and that she was doing the therapy wrong, but the therapist assured her that all people are different and that challenging a stuck point will frequently negate more than one. Julie reported that she found the modules very helpful, especially the ones that focused on power and control and on esteem.

In Session 10, Julie came into therapy with her head up, making direct eye contact and with a huge smile on her face. The therapist asked about this dramatic change, and Julie said that she had challenged her stuck point that "I will always be a victim" using the CBW. She noted that by using the worksheet she could see that she did not ask to be abused as a child and that she had no idea that her high school boyfriend would become abusive as well. She also reported that her esteem was so low that when he did become abusive, she thought that she deserved it because she believed she had caused the child abuse. By breaking free of these thoughts, Julie could see that she had been taken advantage of by several people in her life and that those who were supposed to protect her (e.g., her mother) were probably too scared themselves to stand up to these abusive men. On the worksheet, Julie wrote that her new alternative thought was, "I am an adult now, and I have the ability to choose who I want in my life."

Julie and her therapist agreed to follow the protocol guidelines and flex the treatment by adding two sessions so that Julie could address more of her stuck points and because her scores on the PTSD Checklist had significantly reduced (PCL-5 = 25) but were not yet subthreshold for diagnosis. Julie also wanted to work on her stuck points about her relationship with her family (i.e., mother and sisters) and her current boyfriend. At Session 14, Julie left therapy no longer meeting criteria for PTSD (PCL-5 = 13) or for BPD. She reported a significant improvement in her close relationships. She had not cut herself since Session 3, and she believed she had skills to deal with difficult situations in her life. Julie returned for a check-in session two months later and reported continued improvement in symptoms. She stated, "I keep those sheets in my head and use them whenever I find myself getting upset."

SUMMARY

Although CPT was originally created as a group treatment for rape survivors, years of research and adaptation have resulted in a treatment manual that has been tested in all types of traumas and translated into many different languages. The cognitive distortions that trauma creates are specific to each individual, but the tools to help the client identify and resolve those distortions can be used across various trauma types and different populations. CPT provides therapists with a great deal of flexibility to meet the needs of their clients, including clients who need a simplified worksheet and more sessions, clients who quickly alter their cognitions and require fewer sessions, and clients who would like the support and interaction of group therapy, all while allowing clients to write or not write their trauma accounts. A basic understanding of cognitive behavioral theory is helpful before learning CPT, and online training materials are in production for those who would like to learn some of the skills before attending a workshop.

KEY IDEAS

- Cognitive processing therapy (CPT) is an evidence-based, trauma-focused psychotherapy for PTSD that typically consists of about 12 sessions and may be delivered individually or in groups.

- CPT is based on cognitive theory and posits that one's beliefs can disrupted by traumatic events in a way that can interrupt the normal recovery process from trauma.

- In CPT, the focus is on learning to identify, examine, and challenge thoughts to reach more accurate and balanced conclusions about the traumatic experience itself, as well as more balanced beliefs about oneself, others, and the world.

- CPT has been shown to be helpful for diverse populations who have experienced a wide range of traumas, including sexual and physical assault, combat trauma, and motor vehicle accidents, as well as for people who have experienced multiple traumas.

- CPT has been studied internationally, across different languages and cultures, with both veterans and civilians, and in group and individual formats. It has consistently demonstrated significant reductions in PTSD symptoms and increases in functioning.

REFERENCES

American Psychiatric Association. (2013). *Diagnostic and statistical manual of mental disorders* (5th ed.). Arlington, VA: Author.

Bass, J. K., Annan, J., McIvor Murray, S., Kaysen, D., Griffiths, S., Cetinoglu, T., . . . Bolton, P. A. (2013). Controlled trial of psychotherapy for Congolese survivors of sexual violence. *The New England Journal of Medicine, 368*, 2182–2191. http:// dx.doi.org/10.1056/NEJMoa1211853

Beck, A. T., Rush, A. J., Shaw, B. F., & Emery, G. (1979). *Cognitive therapy of depression.* New York, NY: Guilford Press.

Bolton, P., Bass, J. K., Zangana, G., Kamal, T., Murray, S., Kaysen, D., . . . Rosenblum, M. (2014). A randomized controlled trial of mental health interventions for survivors of systematic violence in Kurdistan, Northern Iraq. *BMC Psychiatry, 14*, 360. http:// dx.doi.org/10.1186/s12888-014-0360-2

Bryan, C. J., Leifker, F. R., Rozek, D. C., Bryan, A. O., Reynolds, M. L., Oakey, D. N., & Roberge, E. (2018). Examining the effectiveness of an intensive, 2-week treatment program for military personnel and veterans with PTSD: Results of a pilot, open-label, prospective cohort trial. *Journal of Clinical Psychology, 74*, 2070–2081. http://dx.doi.org/10.1002/jclp.22651

Butollo, W., Karl, R., König, J., & Rosner, R. (2016). A randomized controlled clinical trial of dialogical exposure therapy versus cognitive processing therapy for adult outpatients suffering from PTSD after Type I trauma in adulthood. *Psychotherapy and Psychosomatics, 85*, 16–26. http://dx.doi.org/10.1159/000440726

Chard, K. M. (2005). An evaluation of cognitive processing therapy for the treatment of posttraumatic stress disorder related to childhood sexual abuse. *Journal of Consulting and Clinical Psychology, 73*, 965–971. http://dx.doi.org/10.1037/0022-006X.73.5.965

Chard, K. M., Schumm, J. A., McIlvain, S. M., Bailey, G. W., & Parkinson, R. B. (2011). Exploring the efficacy of a residential treatment program incorporating cognitive processing therapy–cognitive for veterans with PTSD and traumatic brain injury. *Journal of Traumatic Stress, 24*, 347–351. http://dx.doi.org/10.1002/jts.20644

Chard, K. M., Schumm, J. A., Owens, G. P., & Cottingham, S. M. (2010). A comparison of OEF and OIF veterans and Vietnam veterans receiving cognitive processing therapy. *Journal of Traumatic Stress, 23*, 25–32. http://dx.doi.org/10.1002/jts.20500

Clarke, S. B., Rizvi, S. L., & Resick, P. A. (2008). Borderline personality characteristics and treatment outcome in cognitive-behavioral treatments for PTSD in female rape victims. *Behavior Therapy, 39*, 72–78. http://dx.doi.org/10.1016/j.beth.2007.05.002

Farmer, C. C., Mitchell, K. S., Parker-Guilbert, K., & Galovski, T. E. (2017). Fidelity to the cognitive processing therapy protocol: Evaluation of critical elements. *Behavior Therapy, 48*, 195–206. http://dx.doi.org/10.1016/j.beth.2016.02.009

Foa, E., Keane, T., Friedman, M., & Cohen, J. (2010). *Effective treatments for PTSD* (2nd ed.). New York, NY: Guilford Press.

Forbes, D., Lloyd, D., Nixon, R. D. V., Elliott, P., Varker, T., Perry, D., . . . Creamer, M. (2012). A multisite randomized controlled effectiveness trial of cognitive processing therapy for military-related posttraumatic stress disorder. *Journal of Anxiety Disorders, 26*, 442–452. http://dx.doi.org/10.1016/j.janxdis.2012.01.006

Galovski, T. E., Blain, L. M., Chappuis, C., & Fletcher, T. (2013). Sex differences in recovery from PTSD in male and female interpersonal assault survivors. *Behaviour Research and Therapy, 51*, 247–255. http://dx.doi.org/10.1016/j.brat.2013.02.002

Galovski, T. E., Blain, L. M., Mott, J. M., Elwood, L., & Houle, T. (2012). Manualized therapy for PTSD: Flexing the structure of cognitive processing therapy. *Journal of Consulting and Clinical Psychology, 80*, 968–981. http://dx.doi.org/10.1037/a0030600

Galovski, T. E., Monson, C., Bruce, S. E., & Resick, P. A. (2009). Does cognitive-behavioral therapy for PTSD improve perceived health and sleep impairment? *Journal of Traumatic Stress, 22*, 197–204. http://dx.doi.org/10.1002/jts.20418

Gradus, J. L., Suvak, M. K., Wisco, B. E., Marx, B. P., & Resick, P. A. (2013). Treatment of posttraumatic stress disorder reduces suicidal ideation. *Depression and Anxiety, 30*, 1046–1053. http://dx.doi.org/10.1002/da.22117

Griffin, M. G., Resick, P. A., & Galovski, T. E. (2012). Does physiologic response to loud tones change following cognitive-behavioral treatment for posttraumatic stress disorder? *Journal of Traumatic Stress, 25*, 25–32. http://dx.doi.org/10.1002/jts.21667

Holder, N., Holliday, R., Williams, R., Mullen, K., & Surís, A. (2018). A preliminary examination of the role of psychotherapist fidelity on outcomes of cognitive processing therapy during an RCT for military sexual trauma-related PTSD. *Cognitive Behaviour Therapy, 47*, 76–89. http://dx.doi.org/10.1080/16506073.2017.1357750

Holliday, R. P., Holder, N. D., Williamson, M. L. C., & Surís, A. (2017). Therapeutic response to cognitive processing therapy in White and Black female veterans with military sexual trauma-related PTSD. *Cognitive Behaviour Therapy, 46*, 432–446. http://dx.doi.org/10.1080/16506073.2017.1312511

Hollon, S. D., & Garber, J. (1988). Cognitive therapy. In L. Y. Abramson (Ed.), *Social cognition and clinical psychology: A synthesis* (pp. 204–253). New York: Guilford Press.

Kaslow, N. J. (2004). Competencies in professional psychology. *American Psychologist*, *59*, 774–781. http://dx.doi.org/10.1037/0003-066X.59.8.774

Kaysen, D., Schumm, J., Pedersen, E. R., Seim, R. W., Bedard-Gilligan, M., & Chard, K. (2014). Cognitive processing therapy for veterans with comorbid PTSD and alcohol use disorders. *Addictive Behaviors*, *39*, 420–427. http://dx.doi.org/10.1016/j.addbeh.2013.08.016

Lester, K., Artz, C., Resick, P. A., & Young-Xu, Y. (2010). Impact of race on early treatment termination and outcomes in posttraumatic stress disorder treatment. *Journal of Consulting and Clinical Psychology*, *78*, 480–489. http://dx.doi.org/10.1037/a0019551

Marques, L., Eustis, E. H., Dixon, L., Valentine, S. E., Borba, C. P. C., Simon, N., . . . Wiltsey-Stirman, S. (2016). Delivering cognitive processing therapy in a community health setting: The influence of Latino culture and community violence on post-traumatic cognitions. *Psychological Trauma: Theory, Research, Practice, and Policy*, *8*, 98–106. http://dx.doi.org/10.1037/tra0000044

McCann, I. L., & Pearlman, L. A. (1990). *Psychological trauma and the adult survivor: Theory, therapy, and transformation*. New York, NY: Brunner/Mazel.

McCann, I. L., Sakheim, D. K., & Abrahamson, D. J. (1988). Trauma and victimization: A model of psychological adaptation. *The Counseling Psychologist*, *16*, 531–594. http://dx.doi.org/10.1177/0011000088164002

Monson, C. M., Macdonald, A., Vorstenbosch, V., Shnaider, P., Goldstein, E. S. R., Ferrier-Auerbach, A. G., & Mocciola, K. E. (2012). Changes in social adjustment with cognitive processing therapy: Effects of treatment and association with PTSD symptom change. *Journal of Traumatic Stress*, *25*, 519–526. http://dx.doi.org/10.1002/jts.21735

Monson, C. M., Schnurr, P. P., Resick, P. A., Friedman, M. J., Young-Xu, Y., & Stevens, S. P. (2006). Cognitive processing therapy for veterans with military-related post-traumatic stress disorder. *Journal of Consulting and Clinical Psychology*, *74*, 898–907. http://dx.doi.org/10.1037/0022-006X.74.5.898

Resick, P. A., Galovski, T. E., Uhlmansiek, M. O., Scher, C. D., Clum, G. A., & Young-Xu, Y. (2008). A randomized clinical trial to dismantle components of cognitive processing therapy for posttraumatic stress disorder in female victims of interpersonal violence. *Journal of Consulting and Clinical Psychology*, *76*, 243–258. http://dx.doi.org/10.1037/0022-006X.76.2.243

Resick, P. A., Monson, C. M., & Chard, K. M. (2017). *Cognitive processing therapy for PTSD: A comprehensive manual*. New York, NY: Guilford Press.

Resick, P. A., Nishith, P., Weaver, T. L., Astin, M. C., & Feuer, C. A. (2002). A comparison of cognitive-processing therapy with prolonged exposure and a waiting condition for the treatment of chronic posttraumatic stress disorder in female rape victims. *Journal of Consulting and Clinical Psychology*, *70*, 867–879. http://dx.doi.org/10.1037/0022-006X.70.4.867

Resick, P. A., & Schnicke, M. K. (1992). Cognitive processing therapy for sexual assault victims. *Journal of Consulting and Clinical Psychology*, *60*, 748–756. http://dx.doi.org/10.1037/0022-006X.60.5.748

Resick, P. A., & Schnicke, M. K. (1993). *Cognitive processing therapy for rape victims: A treatment manual*. Newbury Park, CA: Sage.

Resick, P. A., Suvak, M. K., Johnides, B. D., Mitchell, K. S., & Iverson, K. M. (2012). The impact of dissociation on PTSD treatment with cognitive processing therapy. *Depression and Anxiety*, *29*, 718–730. http://dx.doi.org/10.1002/da.21938

Resick, P. A., Suvak, M. K., & Wells, S. Y. (2014). The impact of childhood abuse among women with assault-related PTSD receiving short-term cognitive-behavioral therapy. *Journal of Traumatic Stress*, *27*, 558–567. http://dx.doi.org/10.1002/jts.21951

Resick, P. A., Wachen, J. S., Dondanville, K. A., Pruiksma, K. E., Yarvis, J. S., Peterson, A. L., . . . STRONG STAR Consortium. (2017). Effect of group vs individual cognitive processing therapy in active-duty military seeking treatment for posttraumatic stress disorder: A randomized clinical trial. *JAMA Psychiatry, 74*, 28–36. http://dx.doi.org/10.1001/jamapsychiatry.2016.2729

Resick, P. A., Wachen, J. S., Mintz, J., Young-McCaughan, S., Roache, J. D., Borah, A. M., . . . Peterson, A. L. (2015). A randomized clinical trial of group cognitive processing therapy compared with group present-centered therapy for PTSD among active duty military personnel. *Journal of Consulting and Clinical Psychology, 83*, 1058–1068. http://dx.doi.org/10.1037/ccp0000016

Resick, P. A., Williams, L. F., Suvak, M. K., Monson, C. M., & Gradus, J. L. (2012). Long-term outcomes of cognitive-behavioral treatments for posttraumatic stress disorder among female rape survivors. *Journal of Consulting and Clinical Psychology, 80*, 201–210. http://dx.doi.org/10.1037/a0026602

Schulz, P. M., Resick, P. A., Huber, L. C., & Griffin, M. G. (2006). The effectiveness of cognitive processing therapy for PTSD with refugees in a community setting. *Cognitive and Behavioral Practice, 13*, 322–331. http://dx.doi.org/10.1016/j.cbpra.2006.04.011

Shin, L. M., Rauch, S. L., & Pitman, R. K. (2006). Amygdala, medial prefrontal cortex, and hippocampal function in PTSD. *Annals of the New York Academy of Sciences, 1071*, 67–79. http://dx.doi.org/10.1196/annals.1364.007

Surís, A., Link-Malcolm, J., Chard, K., Ahn, C., & North, C. (2013). A randomized clinical trial of cognitive processing therapy for veterans with PTSD related to military sexual trauma. *Journal of Traumatic Stress, 26*, 28–37. http://dx.doi.org/10.1002/jts.21765

U.S. Department of Veterans Affairs, & U.S. Department of Defense. (2017). *VA/DoD clinical practice guideline for the management of posttraumatic stress disorder and acute stress disorder.* Washington, DC: Author. Retrieved from https://www.healthquality.va.gov/guidelines/MH/ptsd/VADoDPTSDCPGFinal012418.pdf

Voelkel, E., Pukay-Martin, N. D., Walter, K. H., & Chard, K. M. (2015). Effectiveness of cognitive processing therapy for male and female U.S. veterans with and without military sexual trauma. *Journal of Traumatic Stress, 28*, 174–182. http://dx.doi.org/10.1002/jts.22006

Walter, K. H., Bolte, T. A., Owens, G. P., & Chard, K. M. (2012). The impact of personality disorders on treatment outcome for veterans in a posttraumatic stress disorder residential treatment program. *Cognitive Therapy and Research, 36*, 576–584. http://dx.doi.org/10.1007/s10608-011-9393-8

Walter, K. H., Dickstein, B. D., Barnes, S. M., & Chard, K. M. (2014). Comparing effectiveness of CPT to CPT-C among U.S. veterans in an interdisciplinary residential PTSD/TBI treatment program. *Journal of Traumatic Stress, 27*, 438–445. http://dx.doi.org/10.1002/jts.21934

Weathers, F. W., Marx, B. P., Friedman, M. J., & Schnurr, P. P. (2014). Posttraumatic stress disorder in *DSM–5*: New criteria, new measures, and implications for assessment. *Psychological Injury and Law, 7*, 93–107. http://dx.doi.org/10.1007/s12207-014-9191-1

5

Cognitive Therapy for PTSD

Anke Ehlers and Jennifer Wild

Cognitive therapy is rooted in the idea that clients' symptoms, emotions, and behavior are understandable, arising from perceptions they hold of themselves and the world and what they make of these perceptions. To help clients change their unhelpful cognitions, therapists need to "get into the client's head" to understand how their clients perceive and interpret the world around them, which often involves eliciting the thoughts they have of themselves and the beliefs that motivate their behavior. Cognitive therapy for posttraumatic stress disorder (CT-PTSD) is a trauma-focused treatment. It builds on clinical observations that while traumatic events are highly threatening and distressing for everyone, people differ greatly in what they find most troubling about their trauma and what it means to them.

TREATMENT RATIONALE: EHLERS AND CLARK'S (2000) MODEL

CT-PTSD builds on Ehlers and Clark's (2000) model of PTSD. This model suggests that PTSD develops when individuals process the traumatic experience in a way that gives rise to a sense of serious current threat, which is accompanied

The development and evaluation of the treatment program described in this chapter was funded by the Wellcome Trust (Grant 069777). We gratefully acknowledge the contributions of David M. Clark, Ann Hackmann, Melanie Fennell, Freda McManus, and Nick Grey. Anke Ehlers is supported by a Wellcome Trust Principal Research Fellowship (200796), the NIHR Oxford Health Biomedical Research Centre, and a NIHR Senior Investigator Award.

http://dx.doi.org/10.1037/0000196-005
Casebook to the APA Clinical Practice Guideline for the Treatment of PTSD, edited by L. F. Bufka, C. V. Wright, and R. W. Halfond

by high arousal and strong negative emotions such as guilt, shame, anger, or fear. The sense of current threat is driven by two key processes (see Figure 5.1).

First, negative appraisals (i.e., personal meanings) of the trauma and often its sequelae (e.g., reactions of other people, initial PTSD symptoms, physical consequences of the trauma) that extend beyond what most people would find distressing about the situation induce a sense of current threat (external or internal). People with PTSD typically experience a range of negative emotions, which depend on the type of appraisal (Ehlers & Clark, 2000). Perceived external threat can result from appraisals about imminent danger (e.g., "Nowhere is safe," "I cannot trust anyone"), leading to excessive fear; appraisals about the unfairness of the trauma or its aftermath (e.g., "I will never be able to accept that the perpetrator got away with it") lead to persistent anger. Perceived internal threat results from negative appraisals of what the trauma means for the individual's view of themselves. Appraisals about one's reactions, emotions, or behavior during the trauma may lead to shame (e.g., "My actions were despicable," "I am a bad person") or guilt (e.g., "It was my fault"). A common negative appraisal about the consequences of the trauma is perceived permanent change of the self or one's life (e.g., "I have permanently changed for the worse"), which can lead to sadness and hopelessness (Dunmore, Clark, & Ehlers, 2001; Ehlers & Clark, 2000; Kleim, Ehlers, & Glucksman, 2012).

The second source of perceived current threat are characteristics of trauma memories. According to Ehlers and Clark (2000), the worst moments of the

FIGURE 5.1. Treatment Goals in Cognitive Therapy for PTSD (CT-PTSD)

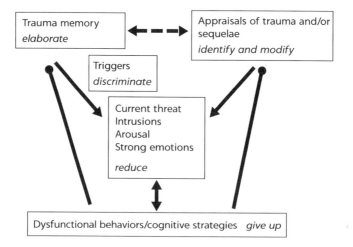

Treatment goals in cognitive therapy for PTSD (CT-PTSD; Ehlers & Clark, 2000). Pointed arrows stand for "leads to." Round arrows stand for "prevents a change in." Dashed arrows stand for "influences." From "Trauma-Focused Cognitive Behavior Therapy for Posttraumatic Stress Disorder and Acute Stress Disorder," by A. Ehlers, in G. Simos and S. G. Hofmann (Eds.), *CBT for Anxiety Disorders: A Practitioner Book* (p. 166), 2013, New York, NY: Wiley. Copyright 2013 by Wiley. Reprinted with permission.

trauma memories are poorly elaborated and poorly integrated within the context of the trauma and also within relevant previous and subsequent experiences and information. The effect is that people with PTSD remember these parts of the trauma in a disjointed way. When they recall the worst moments, they typically do so without much contextual information; in particular, it is difficult for them to access information that could correct the impressions they had or predictions they made at the time (e.g., "I am going to die and my children will be alone"). In other words, they do not naturally update their memory for these moments with what they know now (e.g., "I survived and am still looking after my children"). This disjointed, decontextualized recall has the effect of inducing a sense of threat similar to the threat they experienced during these moments and making them relive the same emotions and high arousal as though the trauma were reoccurring now rather than being a memory from the past (Ehlers, Hackmann, & Michael, 2004).

Ehlers and Clark (2000) also noted that sensory cues in the present that overlap with sensory features of the trauma (e.g., similar sounds, colors, smells, shapes, movements, bodily sensations) can easily trigger intrusive trauma memories. They suggested that during trauma, the brain is attuned to perceptual features of the experience (i.e., data-driven processing), leading to strong perceptual priming, which lowers the threshold for spotting similar perceptual patterns in the environment. Through learned associations, the stimuli become associated with strong affective responses, which can generalize to other similar stimuli. Both processes (i.e., perceptual priming and associative learning) are thought to lead to easy detection of similar stimuli in the individual's environment and poor discrimination from those encountered during the trauma. The easy detection and poor recall has the effect that in people with PTSD, reexperiencing is easily triggered by a wide range of cues (in particular, those that share common perceptual features).

According to Ehlers and Clark's (2000) model, the symptoms are maintained because people with PTSD use understandable but unhelpful cognitive strategies and behaviors to control the perceived current threat. These correspond in meaningful ways to the problematic appraisals they may have about their trauma, symptoms, or future safety. The strategies include rumination, effortful suppression of memories, avoidance of reminders, safety behaviors (i.e., excessive precautions), and substance use. These cognitive strategies and behaviors prevent change in the unhelpful appraisals or nature of a person's trauma memories and may increase symptoms, thereby keeping the sense of current threat going and maintaining PTSD.

Figure 5.1 illustrates the three factors (i.e., appraisals, memory characteristics, cognitive strategies and behaviors) that maintain a sense of current threat and PTSD symptoms, according to Ehlers and Clark's (2000) model. CT-PTSD uses the theoretical framework of this model and targets these three factors. The model suggests three treatment goals:

1. Modify threatening appraisals (i.e., personal meanings) of the trauma and its sequelae.

2. Reduce reexperiencing by elaboration of the trauma memories and discrimination of triggers.

3. Reduce cognitive strategies and behaviors that maintain the sense of current threat.

Therapist and client collaboratively develop an individualized version of the model, which serves as the case formulation to be tested and revised in therapy (described later in the chapter). Treatment is tailored to the individual formulation and focuses on reducing the client's distressing symptoms and emotions by changing appraisals and maintaining cognitive strategies and behaviors that are directly relevant to his or her problems and addressing the relevant moments in memory and the memory triggers. The relative weight given to different treatment procedures differs from client to client, depending on the formulation.

RESEARCH SUPPORT

The role of the cognitive factors proposed in Ehlers and Clark's (2000) model of PTSD has been empirically supported in many studies. Prospective studies of people who had experienced interpersonal violence or accidents showed that negative appraisals, trauma memory features, and maintaining behaviors and cognitive strategies assessed soon after the trauma predicted PTSD at 6 to 12 months after the event. In addition, they predicted chronic PTSD over and above what could be predicted from early symptoms (e.g., Beierl, Böllinghaus, Clark, Glucksman, & Ehlers, 2019; Dunmore et al., 2001; Ehlers et al., 1998; Ehring et al., 2008; Halligan, Michael, Clark, & Ehlers, 2003; Kleim, Ehlers, & Glucksman, 2012). A path analysis testing Ehlers and Clark's model in 700 emergency department attendees who had been injured in an assault or traffic collision found an excellent fit of the data to the model. A 2-year prospective study of emergency workers showed that measures of appraisals, memory, and unhelpful cognitive processes such as rumination taken at baseline predicted the likelihood of developing PTSD after subsequent trauma exposure (Wild et al., 2016). Experimental studies with traumatized participants and healthy volunteers (see Ehlers, Ehring, & Kleim, 2012, for a review) provided evidence for the memory processes thought to underlie reexperiencing symptoms. For example, several studies supported the hypothesis that trauma memories are more disjointed than memories of other negative events (e.g., Sachschal, Woodward, Wichelmann, Haag, & Ehlers, 2019), that this difference is greater in people with PTSD than traumatized people without PTSD (e.g., Kleim, Wallott, & Ehlers, 2008), and that degree of trauma memory disjointedness predicts intrusive memories (Sachschal et al., 2019) and PTSD (Beierl et al., 2019). Other studies with traumatized participants and healthy volunteers supported the role of enhanced perceptual priming for trauma-related stimuli in understanding triggers of reexperiencing (e.g., Ehlers, Michael,

Chen, Payne, & Shan, 2006; Kleim, Ehring, & Ehlers, 2012; Sündermann, Hauschildt, & Ehlers, 2013).

Several randomized controlled trials (RCTs) evaluated the efficacy of CT-PTSD in adults (Ehlers, Clark, Hackmann, McManus, & Fennell, 2005; Ehlers, Clark, Hackmann, McManus, Fennell, et al., 2003; Ehlers, Hackmann, Grey, et al., 2014; Ehlers, Wild, et al., 2019). With the exception of Ehlers et al. (2003), which focused on acute PTSD after road traffic collisions, these studies included clients with chronic PTSD who had experienced a range of different traumas (e.g., interpersonal violence, accidents, natural disasters, terrorist acts, war zone experiences, traumatic death of others), and a high proportion had comorbid disorders. Very low dropout rates (3% on average) and high client satisfaction scores showed that CT-PTSD was highly acceptable to clients. Intent-to-treat analyses showed very large improvements in PTSD symptoms with effect sizes of around 2.5, and over 70% of clients recovered from PTSD. RCTs with children found similarly high effect sizes in symptom improvement and low dropout rates (Meiser-Stedman et al., 2017; Smith et al., 2007). In addition, the studies showed large changes in disability, depression, anxiety, and quality of life. The results were replicated in outreach open trials (Brewin et al., 2010; Gillespie, Duffy, Hackmann, & Clark, 2002) that treated consecutive samples of clients who developed PTSD after the London and Omagh bombings. Hardly any clients showed PTSD symptom deterioration with treatment, and the percentage was smaller than in clients waiting for treatment (Ehlers et al., 2014). This suggests that CT-PTSD is an efficacious and safe treatment.

Three studies investigated the efficacy of CT-PTSD in routine clinical services (Duffy, Gillespie, & Clark, 2007; Ehlers, Grey, Warnock-Parkes, et al., 2020; Ehlers, Grey, Wild, et al., 2013). The clinical samples comprised an ethnically diverse range of clients with a wide range of traumas and educational and socioeconomic backgrounds. Many showed complicating factors such as very severe depression, emotionally unstable personality disorder, living currently in danger, serious social problems, or multiple traumatic events and losses. Therapists included trainees as well as experienced therapists. The studies showed very good treatment outcomes, with large intent-to-treat effect sizes of 1.25 and higher for pre- to post-treatment changes in PTSD symptoms and remission rates of around 60%. Dropout rates of around 15% were below the average for trials of trauma-focused cognitive-behavior therapy for PTSD of 23% (Bisson, Roberts, Andrew, Cooper, & Lewis, 2013). Symptom deterioration was very rare. Kleim et al. (2013) used growth curve modeling to investigate whether changes in negative appraisals drive symptom change in CT-PTSD, as predicted by Ehlers and Clark's (2000) model. Results supported this hypothesis: Changes in negative appraisals predicted changes in symptoms in the subsequent treatment session, and not vice versa. Overall, the empirical evaluations of CT-PTSD showed encouraging results and support CT-PTSD as an evidenced-based treatment for PTSD following a wide range of traumas. A meta-analysis showed similar findings for 11 of 15 studies investigating process of change during a range of trauma-focused CBT programs (Brown, Belli, Asnaani, & Foa, 2019).

DESCRIPTION OF TREATMENT COMPONENTS

The following section (adapted from Ehlers & Wild, 2015) describes the general therapeutic style and treatment procedures in CT-PTSD.

Therapeutic Style

The therapeutic style in cognitive therapy is collaborative and centers on guided discovery. Client and therapist work together like a team of detectives who set out to test how well the client's perceptions and ideas match reality. Together, they consider the client's cognitions like hypotheses, exploring and evaluating the evidence the client has for and against them. The aim is to collaboratively generate a less threatening alternative interpretation. Socratic questioning is essential in this process of guided discovery[1] and involves the therapist gently asking questions that help the client to consider their problems from different perspectives, drawing their attention to information that is relevant yet likely outside their current focus and helping them to reevaluate a previous conclusion or construct a new idea (Padesky, 1993). For example, clients who believe that they are likely to experience another trauma consider the alternative hypothesis that the perceived "nowness" of their intrusive memories gives them the impression that another trauma is likely to occur but is not evidence of an impending trauma. Generating an alternative interpretation (i.e., insight) is usually not sufficient to generate a lasting emotional shift. Therefore, the cognitive therapist will emphasize experiential learning and plan behavioral experiments to test the client's appraisals, which they will carry out in or out of the office. Behavioral experiments are very important for helping the client to experience new evidence against their threatening interpretations. These experiments are often the most compelling tests of client's unhelpful appraisals.

CT-PTSD follows these general principles, with some modifications. Because many clients with PTSD feel they can no longer trust people, therapists need to take extra care to establish good therapeutic relationships and make sure the client feels safe in the therapeutic setting (as subtle trauma reminders can make the client feel unsafe in many situations). Because CT-PTSD focuses on changing cognitions that induce a sense of current threat after trauma, careful assessment of the relevant appraisals is necessary. Clients may have unhelpful beliefs (e.g., perfectionism) that are not relevant to their sense of current threat and thus do not need to be addressed in treating their PTSD unless they hinder the client's engagement and progress in therapy or are important for maintaining comorbid problems that would interfere with the treatment of PTSD.

---

[1]A video on guided discovery including Socratic questioning in CT-PTSD is available online (https://oxcadatresources.com).

Importantly, the main problematic appraisals that induce a sense of current threat and that need to be addressed in therapy are usually linked to the worst moments during the trauma. The nature of memory recall and cognitive avoidance influences what clients with PTSD remember about their traumas, which in turn may influence their problematic appraisals. In addition, disjointed recall makes it difficult to assess the problematic meanings by simply talking about the trauma. It also has the effect that insights from cognitive restructuring may be insufficient to produce a large shift in affect. Thus, work on appraisals of the trauma is closely integrated with work on the trauma memory in CT-PTSD.

Monitoring Progress in Treatment

The effects of interventions are assessed with weekly measures of PTSD symptoms. It is also useful to regularly assess the three cognitive factors targeted in treatment, using measures such as a short version of the Posttraumatic Cognitions Inventory (Foa, Ehlers, Clark, Tolin, & Orsillo, 1999; short version: Kleim et al., 2013), Memory Questionnaire (Halligan et al., 2003), Response to Intrusions Questionnaire and Safety Behaviours Questionnaire (Dunmore et al., 2001; Ehring, Ehlers, & Glucksman, 2008),[2] and measures of depression and anxiety. Changes in appraisals in the sessions are tracked with regular belief ratings: Clients are asked to rate their degree of conviction in the appraisals on a percentage scale from 0% (*not at all*) to 100% (*completely*). Changes in trauma memories are tracked by ratings of their nowness (i.e., the extent to which the memory appears to happen in the here and now rather than in the past, from 0 [*not at all*] to 100 [*completely*] and ratings of the individual's distress).

Developing an Individual Case Formulation and Treatment Rationale

In the first treatment session, the therapist and client discuss the client's symptoms and treatment goals and start developing an individualized case formulation. The therapist normalizes the PTSD symptoms as common reactions to an extremely stressful event and explains that many of the symptoms are signs that the memory for the trauma is not fully processed yet.

The therapist asks the client to give a brief account of the trauma and starts exploring its personal meanings (e.g., "What was the worst thing about the trauma?" "What were the worst moments and what did they mean to you?"). The Posttraumatic Cognitions Inventory (Foa et al., 1999) can help with identifying cognitive themes (i.e., appraisals such as negative view of the self, self-blame, permanent change, and overgeneralized sense of danger) that will need to be addressed in treatment. The therapist also asks the client about

---

[2]Questionnaires are available online (https://oxcadatresources.com).

the content of his or her intrusive memories and what they mean to the client. This question is important because intrusions point to moments that are essential for understanding the sense of current threat; they are often the moments that clients reexperience yet omit from their trauma narratives.

To identify problematic strategies that contribute to the maintenance of PTSD, the therapist asks the client what strategies he or she has used to cope with the distressing memories. Suppression of memories, avoidance, safety behaviors (i.e., excessive precautions), and numbing of emotions (including substance use) are commonly mentioned, as is rumination (i.e., dwelling on the memories). The Response to Intrusions Questionnaire (which measures suppression, rumination, and numbing; e.g., Ehring et al., 2008) and Safety Behaviours Questionnaire[3] (which assesses excessive precautions; Dunmore et al., 2001) can help to identify strategies that need to be reduced in therapy. The therapist then uses a thought-suppression experiment (i.e., asking the client to try hard not to think about an image such as a green rabbit or a black and white cat sitting on the therapist's shoulder) to demonstrate that suppressing mental images has paradoxical effects. Usually clients find that, despite trying hard not to think of the image, it popped into their mind. After discussing this experience, the therapist encourages the client to try to experiment with letting intrusive memories come and go during the next week. An exception to this homework assignment is made with clients who spend much of their time ruminating about the trauma, as they first need to learn the distinction between intrusive memories (e.g., an image of the assailant threatening them with a knife) and rumination (e.g., dwelling on how the attack could have been prevented).

The therapist then uses the information gathered so far to develop an individual case formulation with the client. This formulation contains the following core messages in individualized form, using the client's words as much as possible (adapted from Ehlers, 2013):

- Many of the client's current symptoms are caused by problems in the trauma memory. Therapy will help the client to get the trauma memory in a shape in which it no longer pops up as frequent unwanted memories. It will feel like a memory of the past rather than something that is happening now.

- The memory of the trauma and what happened in its aftermath influences the client's current view of their self and the world. The client perceives a threat from the outside world, a threat to their view of themselves, or both. In therapy, the therapist and client will discuss whether these conclusions are fair representations of reality and will consider the possibility that the trauma memory colors their perception of reality.

- Some of the strategies that the client has used to control the symptoms and threat are understandable but counterproductive and maintain the

---

[3]Available online (https://oxcadatresources.com).

difficulties the client is having. In therapy, the client will experiment with replacing these strategies with other behaviors that may be more helpful.

The graphic presentation of the treatment model shown in Figure 5.1 is usually not presented to the client, as it is quite complex. Instead, different parts of the model, such as the vicious cycle between intrusive memories and memory suppression or the relationship between beliefs about future danger, safety behaviors, and hypervigilance, may be drawn for the client to illustrate particular maintenance cycles that the client is trying to change.

Modifying Personal Meanings (Appraisals) of the Trauma and Its Sequelae

Problematic appraisals that are important in maintaining the sense of current threat are addressed from the first session.

Reclaiming/Rebuilding Your Life Assignments

People with PTSD often feel that they have permanently changed for the worse and have become a different person since the trauma (e.g., Dunmore et al., 2001). This sense of permanent change is closely related to having given up activities and relationships that used to be important to the client. This withdrawal from previously important activities in the client's life usually goes beyond avoidance of reminders of the traumatic event. Some activities may not have been possible in the immediate aftermath of the event, and the client has not taken them up again. Giving up these significant activities maintains the perception of permanent change by providing confirmation that the client has become a different person and that his or her life is less worthwhile since the trauma.

Reclaiming/rebuilding your life assignments are discussed in every treatment session. The aim of the initial discussion in the first session is to map the areas where clients would like to reclaim or rebuild their lives. Therapist and client then agree on an achievable first step in one of these areas and develop the first homework assignment. The therapist refers to the client's treatment goals, which usually include an improvement in the ability to work or study and in their relationships. This intervention helps to instill hope that the client will be able to improve their quality of life. It also helps the therapist to get an idea of the client's life and personality before the trauma so that they can build on previous strengths and interests. If clients have lost much of their former lives since the trauma (e.g., loss of significant other or home, life-changing injuries, the trauma occurred when they were very young), it is best to refer to "(re)building your life" as these clients may say they can never get back what was lost, that they never had a life, or their former life was not one they wish to reclaim. This intervention has some similarities with behavioral activation (Jacobson, Martell, & Dimidjian, 2001) but focuses on meaningful and pleasant activities that were lost since the trauma to help clients retrieve specific memories of their former selves and address their sense of permanent change (Kleim & Ehlers, 2008).

Changing Meanings of Trauma by Updating Trauma Memories

CT-PTSD uses a special procedure to access and shift problematic meanings (i.e., appraisals) of the trauma, called the *updating trauma memories* procedure. This involves three steps.

Step 1: Identifying Threatening Personal Meanings. To access the personal meanings of the trauma that generate a sense of current threat, the moments during the trauma that create the greatest distress and sense of nowness during recall (i.e., *hot spots*; Foa & Rothbaum, 1998) are identified through imaginal reliving (Foa & Rothbaum, 1998) or narrative writing (Resick & Schnicke, 1993) and through discussion of the content of intrusive memories (see Exhibit 5.1 for other possibilities).

The personal meanings of these moments are explored through careful questioning (e.g., "What was the worst thing about this?" "What did you think was going to happen?" "What did this mean to you at the time?" "What does this mean to you now?" "What would it mean if what you feared most did happen?"). It is important to ask direct questions about clients' worst expected outcomes, including their fears about dying, to elicit the underlying meanings, as this guides what information is needed to update their trauma memory.

Imaginal reliving and narrative writing each has its strengths when working with trauma memories, and the relative weight given to each in CT-PTSD depends on the client's level of engagement with the trauma memory and the length of the event. In *imaginal reliving* (Foa & Rothbaum, 1998), clients visualize the traumatic event (usually with their eyes closed), starting with the first perception that something was wrong and ending at a point when they were safe again (e.g., the assailant left; being told in hospital that they were not paralyzed). Clients describe (usually in the present tense) what is happening in the visualized event moment by moment, including what they are feeling and thinking. This technique is powerful in facilitating emotional

---

EXHIBIT 5.1

Accessing Personal Meanings of the Trauma That Lead to a Sense of Current Threat

1. Access hot spots in memory (i.e., the moments during the trauma that create the greatest distress and sense of nowness during recall).

2. Discuss the content of intrusive memories and determine which moments of the trauma they represent (often omitted when talking about trauma). Include these moments in imaginal reliving or narrative writing.

3. Explore personal meanings of these moments.

engagement with the memory and accessing details of the memory, including emotions and sensory components. In CT-PTSD, the therapist will usually guide imaginal reliving of the traumatic event two or three times to access the hot spots with sufficient detail to assess their problematic meanings and then will move on to the steps of updating their meaning. This is different from prolonged exposure therapy, in which more sessions are devoted to reliving the traumatic event (Foa & Rothbaum, 1998). Identifying hot spots and their meanings may take longer if clients suppress their reactions or skip over difficult moments because, for example, they are ashamed about what happened.

An alternative method of accessing the personal meanings of the event is *narrative writing* (Resick & Schnicke, 1993). This method is used when the traumatic event lasted a long time and reliving the whole event would not be possible. The narrative covers the entire traumatic time period and helps to identify the moments or events with the greatest emotional significance so that their meaning can be explored further. Narrative writing is also particularly suitable if clients dissociate and lose contact with the present situation or show very strong physical reactions when remembering the trauma (e.g., clients who were unconscious during parts of the trauma may feel very faint). Writing a narrative on a whiteboard or computer screen with the support of the therapist can help introduce the necessary distance for the client to take in that they are looking back at the trauma rather than reliving it. Narrative writing is also especially helpful when the client is not clear about aspects of what happened or the order of events because the therapist can interweave a discussion about the different ways the event may have unfolded. Reconstructing the event with diagrams and models and a visit to the site of the trauma (which provides many retrieval cues) can also help in such instances. The narrative is useful for considering the event as a whole and for identifying information from different moments that have implications for the problematic meanings of the trauma and for updating the memory (see Steps 2 and 3). After completing therapy, clients at times find it helpful to refer back to their updated narrative when memories are triggered, such as around anniversaries of the trauma.

In our clinic, the majority of clients start with a few imaginal relivings in Session 2, and the information generated during reliving is then used to write a narrative. The remaining clients only write a narrative with the help of the therapist and do not do reliving for the reasons stated previously.

Step 2: Identifying Updating Information. Once a hot spot and its meaning is identified, the next step is to discover information that does not fit with the problematic meanings (i.e., updating information). It is important to remember that some of the updating information may be about what happened in the trauma or afterward. It can be something that the client is already aware of but has not yet linked to the meaning of this particular moment in memory, or it may be something the client remembers only during imaginal reliving or narrative writing. Examples include knowledge that the outcome of the traumatic event was better than expected (e.g., the client did not die, is not paralyzed), information that explained the client's or other people's behavior (e.g., the client complied with the perpetrator's instructions because he had threatened to kill him; other people did not help because they were in shock), and the realization that an impression or perception during the trauma was not true (e.g., the perpetrator had a toy gun rather than a real gun). Information and explanations from reliable sources or experts (e.g., cars are built in a way that makes explosions after accidents very unlikely; certain distressing procedures in hospital were done to save the client's life) can also be valuable in identifying updating information.

For other appraisals (e.g., "I am a bad person," "It was my fault," "My actions were disgraceful," "I attract disaster"), guided discovery to generate an alternative perspective is necessary. Cognitive therapy techniques such as Socratic questioning, systematic discussion of evidence for and against the appraisals, behavioral experiments, discussing hindsight bias, pie charts, or surveys are helpful. Imagery techniques can also be helpful in widening the client's awareness of other factors that contributed to the event or in considering the value of alternative actions. For example, assault survivors who blame themselves for not fighting back during the trauma may visualize what would have happened if they had. This experience usually leads them to realize that they may have escalated the violence further and the assailant may have hurt them even more (see Exhibit 5.2).

Step 3: Active Incorporation of the Updating Information Into the Hot Spots.
Once the therapist and client have worked together to identify updating information that the client finds compelling, it is actively incorporated into the relevant hot spot. This can be done as soon as the updating information has been identified for that particular hot spot, for example, in the same session as the first reliving. Clients are asked to bring this hot spot to mind through imaginal reliving or reading the corresponding part of the narrative and then to remind themselves, prompted by the therapist, of the updating information (a) verbally (e.g., "I know now that . . ."), (b) by imagery (e.g., visualizing how one's wounds have healed, visualizing the perpetrator in prison, looking

---

EXHIBIT 5.2

Changing Personal Meanings of Hot Spots in Memory

1. *Identify updating information:* Identify information that does not fit with the meanings by considering what happened during the course of the event, information from reliable sources, or by considering a wider range of interpretations in cognitive restructuring.

2. *Updating:* Link the new information with the relevant moments in memory; client holds the moment in mind while reminding himself or herself of updating information. Reminders can be verbal, movements, touch, sounds, smells, tastes, and images.

at a recent photo of the family or of oneself, visualizing the person who died in the trauma in a peaceful place where they are no longer suffering), (c) by performing movements or actions that are incompatible with the original meaning of this moment (e.g., moving about or jumping up and down for hot spots that involved predictions about dying or being paralyzed), or (d) through incompatible sensations (e.g., touching a healed arm). To summarize the updating process, the therapist and client create an updated written narrative that includes the new meanings for each hot spot and highlights them in a different font or color (e.g., "I know now that it was not my fault").

Changing Appraisals of Trauma Sequelae

For some clients, a main source of current threat comes from threatening appraisals of the aftermath of the traumatic event. For example, some clients believe that intrusive memories are signs that they are going crazy (e.g., Ehlers, Mayou, & Bryant, 1998). Their failed attempts to control the intrusions are seen as further confirmation of their appraisals. Others interpret some people's responses after the event as signs that no one cares for them or understands them or that other people see them as inferior (e.g., Dunmore et al., 2001). Such appraisals are modified through education about the symptoms of PTSD, Socratic questioning, providing new information, and behavioral experiments.

Memory Work to Reduce Reexperiencing

Memory work focuses on elaboration and updating trauma memories and discrimination training with trauma triggers.

Imaginal Reliving and Narrative Writing

The updating trauma memories procedure described previously helps to elaborate the trauma memory. Retrieving the memory and talking about it helps make it appear less vivid and intrusive. Clients may describe that some of the sensory impressions from the trauma fade away (e.g., colors or taste fading). When the hot spots have been successfully updated, clients usually experience a large reduction in reexperiencing symptoms and improvement in sleep (Woodward et al., 2017).

Identification and Discrimination of Triggers of Reexperiencing Symptoms

Clients with PTSD often report that intrusive memories and other reexperiencing symptoms occur "out of the blue" in a wide range of situations. Careful detective work with the therapist usually identifies sensory triggers that clients have not been aware of (e.g., particular colors, sounds, smells, tastes, touch, body posture or movement). To identify these subtle triggers, client and therapist carefully analyze where and when reexperiencing symptoms occur. Systematic observation by the client and the therapist in the session and through homework is usually necessary to identify all triggers. Once a trigger has been identified, the next aim is to weaken the link between the trigger and the trauma memory. This involves several steps.

First, the client learns to distinguish between "then" and "now," that is, to focus on how the present triggers and their context (i.e., now) are different from the trauma (i.e., then). This leads them to realize that there are more differences than similarities and that they are responding to a memory, not current reality. Second, intrusions are intentionally triggered in therapy so that the client can learn to apply the then-versus-now discrimination. For example, traffic accident survivors may listen to sounds, such as brakes screeching, collisions, glass breaking, or sirens, that remind them of their car accidents. People who were attacked with a knife may look at a range of metal objects. People who were shot may listen to the sounds of gunfire generated on a computer. Survivors of bombings or fires may look at smoke produced by a smoke machine. People who saw a lot of blood during the trauma may look at red fluids. The then-versus-now discrimination can be facilitated by carrying out actions that were not possible during the trauma (e.g., movements that were not possible in the trauma, touching objects or looking at photos that remind them of their present life). Third, clients apply these strategies in their natural environments. When reexperiencing symptoms occur, clients remind themselves that they are responding to memories. They focus their attention on how the present situation is different from the trauma and may carry out actions that were not possible during the trauma.

Site Visit

A visit to the site of the trauma completes the memory work. This visit is done in person where possible or via Google Street View if not possible (e.g., if the trauma happened in another country). Visiting the site can help correct remaining problematic appraisals because the site provides many retrieval cues and helps access further information to update the appraisals. The site visit also helps complete the stimulus discrimination work. Clients realize that the site now is very different from then, which helps place the trauma in the past.

Imagery Work

If reexperiencing symptoms persist after successful updating of the client's hot spots and discrimination of triggers, imagery transformation techniques can be useful. The client transforms the trauma image into a new image that signifies that the trauma is over. For example, with the help of the therapist, a client may transform their image of impact in a car accident to an image of a recent birthday celebration with their children to signify that the client is safe now, their trauma is in the past and their fears that their children would lose a parent did not happen. Transformed images can provide compelling evidence that the intrusions are a product of the client's mind rather than perceptions of current reality. Image transformation is also particularly helpful with intrusions that represent images of things that did not actually happen during the trauma (e.g., transforming images of the future that represented their worst fears such as images of a client's children growing up sad and alone or images of people's reactions at their funeral).

Dropping Unhelpful Cognitive Strategies and Behaviors

The first step in addressing cognitive strategies and behaviors that maintain PTSD is usually to discuss their problematic consequences. Sometimes these consequences can be demonstrated directly by a behavioral experiment. For example, the effects of selective attention to danger cues can be demonstrated by asking the client to attend to possible signs of danger unrelated to the trauma. An assault survivor may be asked to stand by a busy road for a few minutes and attend to signs of potentially risky driving. Clients find that this exercise makes them more aware of a range of possible dangers. They then reflect on what this means for their own efforts to scan for signs of danger, typically specific to their trauma, and consider the possibility that the world may not be as dangerous as they assumed. They discuss with the therapist the alternative hypothesis that their intrusive trauma memories lead to the impression that they are in danger. This discussion leads to further behavioral experiments in which they test their appraisals. For example, a person may test "If I do not look carefully for people who look like the assailant, I will be attacked again" by walking to a local shop whilst dropping their hypervigilance and any safety behaviors. They are encouraged to use the then-versus-now discrimination to deal with any reexperiencing symptoms that may be triggered during the experiment. Clients usually predict a very high chance of being attacked and are surprised to find that no one attacked them. Note that the focus of the discussion is whether the prediction was correct rather than on anxiety levels.

In other instances, a discussion of advantages and disadvantages of the strategy is a helpful start. For example, when discussing rumination with the therapist, a client may generate the perceived advantage that dwelling on questions like "Why did it happen me?" and "If I had done X, could I have prevented the trauma from happening or influenced the outcome?" will help to prevent another trauma. The client may then reflect on the fact that the rumination has not generated any answers, makes him or her feel worse, wastes a lot of time, and prevents him or her from moving on with life. This process motivates clients to experiment with moving to other activities when they notice the first signs of rumination.

Blueprint

Toward the end of therapy, client and therapist collaboratively develop a summary of what the client has learned in treatment and how to apply what they learned to any setbacks. Questions asked in the blueprint are "How did my problems develop?" "What kept my problems going?" "What did I learn during treatment that helped?" "What were my most unhelpful thoughts?" "What are the helpful alternatives or updated thoughts?" "How will I continue to build on what I have learned?" and "How will I deal with any setbacks in the future?" Prompts help the client remember details.

FLEXIBLE ORDER OF INTERVENTIONS AND DURATION OF TREATMENT

CT-PTSD allows for flexibility in the order in which the core treatment procedures are delivered, depending on the individual formulation and client preference. The memory updating procedure usually has a fast and profound effect on symptoms (Woodward et al., 2017) and is generally conducted in the first few sessions, if possible. For patients with severe dissociative symptoms, training in trigger discrimination is conducted first, and narrative writing is preferred over imaginal reliving. In addition, for certain cognitive patterns, the memory work is prepared through discussion of the client's appraisals and cognitive processing at the time of the trauma. For example, if clients believe they are to blame for a trauma, and their shame or guilt prevents them from being able to describe it fully to the therapist, therapy would start with addressing these appraisals. If a client experienced mental defeat (i.e., the perceived loss of all autonomy) during an interpersonal trauma, therapy would start with discussing the traumatic situation from a wider perspective to raise the client's awareness that the perpetrators intended to control and manipulate their feelings and thoughts at the time but are no longer exerting control.

CT-PTSD usually involves up to 12 weekly sessions of 60 to 90 minutes, and up to three optional monthly booster sessions if clients currently reexperience a small number of traumas. The mean number of sessions is around 10. When multiple traumas need to be addressed in treatment, more sessions are offered, usually up to 20. For sessions that include work on the trauma memory—imaginal reliving, updating memories, or the site visit—the therapist needs to allow sufficient time for the memory to be processed, usually around 90 minutes. The client needs sufficient time to refocus on current reality and his or her further plans for the day before going home after these sessions. Studies have shown that the content of treatment can be effectively delivered in a range of treatment formats, such as a 7-day intensive version of the treatment (delivered over 7 consecutive working days, with 2 to 4 hours of treatment per day, plus a few booster sessions; Ehlers et al., 2014) and a self-study assisted brief treatment (Ehlers, Wild, et al., 2019).

ADDRESSING COMPLEXITY

Complexity in the client's presentation can be included in the individual case formulation (see also Ehlers & Murray, 2020). For example, comorbid conditions such as depression, social anxiety disorder, panic disorder, or substance misuse are common in PTSD. The cognitions and unhelpful coping strategies linked to comorbid symptoms are incorporated into the individual case formulation and addressed in cognitive therapy. An example is given in the case illustration.

Many clients with PTSD have experienced more than one trauma, but not all traumas are necessarily linked to their current PTSD and need to be addressed in therapy. To determine which traumas to focus on, the therapist and client discuss which traumas still bother the client (i.e., are reexperienced or are linked to personal meanings that trouble the client at present). This discussion also provides a first assessment of problematic meanings that link several traumas. For example, repeated trauma may lead to generalized negative appraisals such as "There is something about me that attracts disaster" or "I deserve bad things to happen to me." Client and therapist discuss which trauma to start with, usually a trauma that the client currently finds the most distressing or a trauma during which an important problematic meaning originated. A timeline of the events can be helpful in this discussion. The therapist also notes whether elements from other traumas come up when the client relives the identified trauma, as these may have influenced its personal meanings. Once the hot spots from the identified trauma have been updated, the therapist checks whether the reexperiencing of other traumas that carry related meanings has decreased. The remaining traumas that are still reexperienced or relevant for problematic appraisals are then addressed in turn.

For clients displaying complex features of PTSD, other problems may need to be addressed as an initial priority, particularly if reexperiencing symptoms and coping strategies are currently placing a client at risk. This could be through severe dissociative episodes, excessive use of substances, self-harm, or risky sexual behavior, for example, which would require immediate attention. In addition, a comorbid condition that is a clinical priority and would interfere with the successful or safe delivery of CT-PTSD, such as severe depression with acute suicidal intent or acute psychosis, would require prior treatment. In some cases, it may be necessary to prioritize other problems or events for a few sessions during treatment if they become the client's primary problem.

CULTURE, PERSONAL MEANINGS, AND THERAPY

In our experience, cultural beliefs may influence an individual's personal meanings of trauma and their attempts to deal with trauma memories in helpful and unhelpful ways. As cognitive therapy uses an individual case formulation, treatment is tailored to the individual's preexisting beliefs, including their cultural beliefs (see the treatment manual[4] and case illustration that follows; Schnyder et al., 2016). For example, cultures differ in their

---

[4]Available online (https://oxcadatresources.com).

views about what happens after death, and these beliefs are taken into account when working on appraisals with clients who were bereaved by the trauma. Outcome data for a consecutive sample of 330 PTSD clients treated at a National Health Service outpatient clinic serving a multicultural area in London suggested that ethnic background did not predict treatment outcome with CT-PTSD (Ehlers et al., 2013). The results were replicated in a second study (Ehlers, Grey, et al., 2020).

If possible, CT-PTSD aims to change the threatening appraisals of the trauma within the client's general belief system. The aim is to see the traumatic meanings in a new light by considering a wider range of information than was available during the trauma. When treating clients from a cultural background with which the therapist is not familiar, obtaining relevant information from respected individuals in the client's community can be very helpful in identifying updating information that is consistent with the client's cultural beliefs. Sometimes a reflection on rigidly held cultural beliefs is needed to overcome the effects of trauma, ideally supported by people from the client's cultural background who have more nuanced views. Participation in cultural practices can also help overcome threatening meanings; for example, cultural practices after the death of a significant other may help the client feel connected to others and realize that the deceased is no longer suffering. Rebuilding social activities is an important element of treatment for most people with chronic PTSD (see "Reclaiming/Rebuilding Your Life Assignments") and may be especially important if they feel disconnected from others or their culture or they believe that they have failed in their social roles.

Engagement with trauma memories is an essential part of treatment. Cultural beliefs may contribute to a reluctance to disclose details of the event or shame about the trauma. Other ways of accessing the memories may be needed at the start of therapy, as for other clients who are initially uncomfortable talking about the trauma with the therapist. Alternative ways to start engaging with trauma memories include writing in private about the event and its meaning, communicating remotely with the therapist (e.g., via Internet-delivered treatment), or using other ways of accessing the painful memories such as drawing or visiting places that evoke memories.

CASE ILLUSTRATION

Suvik, a 31-year-old man of Sri Lankan ancestry who had lived in the United Kingdom for 14 years, was visiting an island in Thailand at the age of 23 when the Asian tsunami struck. For 30 consecutive hours in the aftermath of the disaster, he helped to search and rescue tourists and local Thai people. He had no medical training to deal with dead and dying people. He saved numerous people yet saw many more injured and many dead. Suvik returned to the United Kingdom in the month following the tsunami, experiencing unwanted memories, flashbacks, and low mood. He sought medical help and was treated with medication for depression. His PTSD diagnosis was missed for many years. He lost his job as a teacher and lost his romantic relationship. Eventually, 8 years after his return home to the United Kingdom from the tsunami, he was referred for assessment for PTSD.

The assessment showed that Suvik was suffering from PTSD, major depression, panic disorder, and social anxiety disorder, all of which had developed after his initial event, the tsunami. He used cannabis to try to block the memories but did not meet criteria for dependence. He agreed he would not use on the days of his treatment sessions. His goals for treatment were (a) to be able to live with the memories of the tsunami without having them disrupt his day, (b) to stop dwelling about how he failed to save a man, (c) to go to the gym again, and (d) to be able to concentrate enough that he could reapply for work.

Case Formulation

The cognitive assessment revealed the following factors that contributed to Suvik's sense of current threat.

Appraisals

Suvik blamed himself for a young man's death. He believed that he should have been able to save him, that it was his fault that the man died, and that he was a failure (100%). He also believed that loved ones could die at any time and that his mum and dad would die unexpectedly and soon (90%). He believed the level of guilt he felt and the frequent uncontrollable memories that came to mind meant that he was "losing it" and that he would never recover and hold down a job again (90%). The following sections describe further appraisals that were identified by discussing Suvik's intrusive memories and hot spots.

Trauma Memories

Suvik's main reexperiencing symptoms included images of a young man who had let go of his hand when he had tried to pull him to safety. The image meant that he was responsible for the man dying and that he was a failure for being unable to convince him to be pulled to safety. The second intrusive image was the mutilated thigh of a young woman. He had seen the woman just before the second wave engulfed the island. The image became a warning sign that something terrible was about to happen. The image meant that it was the end, he would die. When the image came to mind, Suvik's heart raced, and he felt chest pain. He believed he would have a heart attack and die, and he often had panic attacks. The third image was a young woman whose shins were severely injured. The image meant that he could not cope and that he made things worse. At the time, the untrained tourists and locals who were helping the injured were asked to look after them overnight with whatever medical supplies they had traveled with. Suvik decided to pour iodine on the woman's shins and then believed that he had made them worse and that her legs would be amputated as a result of his inexperience. The fourth image was a dead pregnant teenager. The image meant that life was unfair, that tragedy could strike at any time, and that he should have died, not a young girl with a baby. When Suvik described his four worst memories of the tsunami in the first session, he was distraught and tearful. He remembered what happened but was unsure of why the man let go of his hand and of how helpful he had been to the woman with the mutilated thigh and the woman with the mutilated shins. He believed that his inexperience caused them to suffer and that they were still suffering. Suvik's intrusive images were triggered by hearing or seeing accidents, hospitals, or injured people on television; seeing similar-looking people; seeing pictures of distressed people; children screaming; and hearing foreign accents. Often the images came out of the blue, suggesting there were triggers he had not spotted yet.

Maintaining Cognitive Strategies and Behaviors

A range of cognitive strategies and behaviors maintained Suvik's PTSD and low mood: suppression of memories, rumination and self-criticism, safety behaviors and hypervigilance, withdrawal from social life and other activities, and cannabis use.

When images of the trauma came to mind, Suvik tried hard to push them away. He told himself not to think about the memories, which kept them on his mind. The images were distressing, and when they lingered, he would turn to cannabis to numb himself, which made it impossible for him to access information that could help to update the memories and their meanings. Or, he would criticize himself for his inexperience in rescue work and for causing people to suffer. Self-criticism often triggered periods of rumination, and vice versa, during which he questioned why the young man let go of his hand, why people younger than he had to suffer, and why life was unfair. The self-criticism and rumination kept him feeling low, maintained his belief that he was a failure, and prevented him from identifying all that he did that was heroic and helpful at the time.

Suvik took unnecessary precautions (i.e., safety behaviors) to keep himself and his parents in Sri Lanka safe. He called them several times a day to check where they were and that nothing bad had happened. He avoided leaving the house to protect himself from an unexpected accident. When images came to mind and his heart raced, he took steps to calm himself, such as smoking cannabis, which he believed would prevent a heart attack. He was hyper-vigilant at home, double-locking his doors, and he overchecked weather reports to make sure there were no storms en route to the United Kingdom or to Sri Lanka where his parents and extended family lived.

After the tsunami, Suvik lost confidence and felt nervous teaching his class. He had been teaching English as a second language, and he avoided teaching as much as possible to avoid speaking to groups of people and to avoid hearing accents, which triggered trauma memories. He believed people could see his nerves and that he was a failure. He eventually lost his job. He felt detached from others and unsafe when he was outside his flat; as a result, he stopped going out with friends. He also stopped weight lifting and running, since he had to leave the house to do these activities.

Comorbid Conditions

The assessment suggested that many of the appraisals and cognitive strategies and behaviors maintaining Suvik's PTSD symptoms were also maintaining his depression, panic disorder, and social anxiety. His appraisals that he was a failure and that he caused people to suffer, his rumination, his self-criticism, and his withdrawal from friends and activities he used to enjoy, including exercise, maintained his depression. His appraisals that he would have a heart attack, that he needed to stop physical activity and rest, and that cannabis would prevent a heart attack maintained his panic disorder. His appraisals that he was a failure and that other people could see his nerves as well as his avoidance of speaking to groups of people maintained his social anxiety.

Treatment

Suvik attended 12 sessions, each lasting between 60 and 90 minutes.

Work on Appraisals

Some of Suvik's appraisals concerned interpretation of symptoms: "I'm losing it" and "I'll never recover and hold down a job again." These appraisals were addressed with normalizing information and reclaiming your life assignments. In Session 1, the therapist normalized Suvik's PTSD symptoms: "Intrusive, distressing memories are normal after trauma. They are a sign that we need to work on the trauma memory to help you process it and put it in the past, which will make the memories less intrusive." She also gave information about the nature of trauma memories: "Trauma memories often feel like they are happening now and give you a sense that there is immediate danger. For example, one of your trauma memories is seeing the mutilated leg of a woman you helped. This brings back the feeling of danger because just after you saw her, the second wave engulfed the island and you were at risk of losing your life. This feeling that you are in danger now when the memory comes to mind is coming from the trauma memory."

Reclaiming your life assignments were also introduced in Session 1 and discussed in every session. Examples of the activities Suvik built up over the course of therapy included (a) weight lifting at home for 7 minutes twice a week, then 20 minutes, then at the gym once a week with a friend and once a week by himself; (b) running at home 7 minutes twice a week, then 20 minutes, then running at the gym twice a week, then outdoors and running a 10K race by the end of treatment; (c) researching available local courses on social media and enrolling in one; (d) seeing an advisor about job options; and (e) booking a holiday. These activities helped to reduce the strength of Suvik's belief that he would never recover or hold down a job again as well as to increase his social contact, which improved his mood.

Suvik's other appraisals, such as "I am a failure," were linked to particular moments during the trauma and addressed with the updating memories procedure. His appraisal that he and his parents would die soon and his excessive precautions were also addressed with behavioral experiments (described later in this chapter).

Updating Hot Spots and Work on Appraisals Linked to Them

Because the trauma was prolonged, narrative writing was used as part of the updating memories procedure to identify hot spots and to reconstruct what had happened. Suvik wrote the entire account of his trauma for homework over 3 weeks. To access more details of the hot spots and to identify updating information, Suvik described them in imaginal reliving whilst the therapist wrote the details in narrative format. The worst moments corresponded with intrusive memories.

In Session 2, Suvik described in imaginal reliving the moment when the young man let go of his hand and the receding wave carried him to his death. He did not understand why the man let go of his hand, and he blamed himself for being unable to save the man. Suvik remembered that the man was shouting for his girlfriend, who had been swept away a moment before. The man was crying that he wanted to save her. He let go of Suvik's hand and was swept away in her direction. They both died. To identify updating information, the therapist (with permission) conducted an informal survey with friends and colleagues, describing the situation of the young man and asking people to indicate what they thought they would have done in similar circumstances: try to save their loved one or save themselves. The therapist also asked Suvik what he thought he would have done. They discussed the results of the survey in Session 3. He responded, like all the people who completed the survey, that he would have gone after his girlfriend to try to save her. The therapist and Suvik constructed a pie chart to look at all the contributing reasons for the man's death. Suvik was asked to apportion responsibility to each factor as a percentage before apportioning responsibility for his own actions. Suvik concluded that he was not responsible for the man's death, that he had tried to save him, and that the tsunami and the man's loyalty and care for his girlfriend were the main reasons he died. This updating information was then linked to the hot spot in reliving and in the updated narrative.

In Session 4, Suvik described in imaginal reliving the moment in the trauma when he saw the woman with the mutilated thigh. It was just before the second wave engulfed the island, and he believed they would both die. The therapist elicited the worst meaning of dying, and Suvik revealed it meant he would not see his parents again and they would suffer as a result. He identified the updating information that he spoke to his parents regularly, had seen them on eight occasions in Sri Lanka since the tsunami, and they were in good health, and he added this information to his narrative. While visualizing the hot spot, he looked at a photo with his parents taken on a recent visit to the family home in Sri Lanka, which was evidence that his worst fears linked to this moment did not happen: He survived the tsunami, his parents did not lose him, and they were not suffering or about to die.

He thought the worst thing about dying for the woman was that her life would be unfulfilled. To access updating information, the therapist asked what Suvik knew now about the woman and whether or not she had survived. Suvik knew the woman had survived without permanent injury and was living in California. The therapist suggested that Suvik write to her by email to discover how she was today. The woman replied that she believed she would not be alive today, had it not been for Suvik. She described his actions as heroic, and she also described her own progress, writing that she had returned to California after the tsunami and married her childhood sweetheart and that they had a baby girl together. Suvik updated his narrative with this information. When the image of the woman's mutilated thigh popped to mind, he transformed the image to one that captured the information he had now: She was living a fulfilling life. He pictured her with husband and baby.

Sessions 4 and 5 addressed Suvik's appraisal "I caused people to suffer" (90%). Suvik felt guilty that he had limited medical knowledge whilst helping severely injured people. He frequently had intrusive images of a woman with exposed tendons on her shins, which he had treated by dousing in iodine. The therapist helped Suvik to access updating information. Together they researched the benefits of iodine and its uses. Suvik realized that pouring iodine on the wounds was instrumental in stopping them from becoming infected. He also wrote to ask the woman about the outcome of her recovery. The woman's reply reminded Suvik of all that he did that had been helpful for her. She mentioned that he had liaised with the British Embassy in Bangkok once she had been airlifted to hospital. She also said that he called her insurance company and her parents and that he spoke to the consultant and emphasized that they save her legs. She wrote that she had received excellent medical care in Bangkok and retained the use of her legs because of Suvik's actions. Suvik updated the hot spot with this information. Suvik was asked to complete homework, writing all the steps he had taken to help people in the aftermath of the tsunami, referring to the emails he had received. This process helped to refocus his attention to a more balanced view of the past as well as to reduce his feelings of guilt. When images of the injured woman came to mind, Suvik focused on what he had done that was helpful and the woman's kind words, and then he pictured her walking, all of which reduced the strength of his belief that he caused people to suffer to 0%.

In imaginal reliving during Session 5, Suvik described the moment he found the young pregnant Thai woman. At the time of the trauma, Suvik sobbed uncontrollably when he saw this woman. He was overcome with sorrow for the life that she and her baby would never experience. This moment meant to him that life was unfair (80%) and that tragedy could strike at any time, cutting short the life of your loved ones (90%). To access updating information, Suvik and the therapist reviewed this moment in detail, along with the beliefs linked to Suvik's Buddhist culture, beliefs also held by many Thai people. Buddhists believe in reincarnation—that when people die in any circumstance, it is the soul's choice to move onto a better experience. They believe that suffering is impermanent.

Suvik and his therapist accessed Google Street View images to see the island today, to see that it had moved on in line with Buddhist beliefs that suffering is impermanent, and to see Thai people and how they may reflect the impermanence of suffering linked to the tsunami. Suvik predicted that the island would still be devastated and that if there were Thai people in the images, they would look distraught. In Google Street View, he saw how the island had been rebuilt. The images showed many Thai people smiling and looking peaceful. Suvik updated his narrative to include information that the Thai woman and her baby were no longer suffering, that they had been reincarnated into better circumstances, and that their families were comforted with this knowledge.

To address the belief that "tragedy could strike at any time, cutting short the life of your loved ones" (90%), the therapist used Socratic questioning, asking Suvik to consider his loved ones: Who was alive? Who had been struck by tragedy? Suvik's parents were alive, and whilst Sri Lanka had been affected by the tsunami, his parents had not been. Suvik's grandparents were no longer living, they had died from age-related illnesses. Suvik and the therapist then researched the probability of a similar tsunami striking Thailand and the surrounding region and discovered that the likelihood was low. Suvik concluded that although tragedy does occur, such as the tsunami, these events are relatively rare, meaning that loved ones are more likely to lead full lives than to lead lives cut short by tragedy. As Suvik updated his narrative with the new information, he re-rated his belief as 10%.

Memory Work to Reduce Reexperiencing

Imaginal reliving, writing a narrative, transforming images, and visiting the island by Google Street View helped Suvik identify hot spots and update the meanings linked to each one. He learned that he had done everything possible to save the young man who let go of his hand and that it had been the tsunami and the young man's decision to try to save his girlfriend that contributed to his death. He learned through updating the memories that his actions were nothing short of heroic and the very people he helped saw them as such, that they were no longer suffering, and that Suvik was in no way at fault for helping them with his limited medical knowledge. No one had been harmed and no one was worse off because of his help.

In Sessions 6 and 7, Suvik explored with his therapist triggers for his intrusive memories. Through observation and attention to sensory similarities between possible triggers and the trauma, he spotted a range of triggers he had not noticed before. Examples included activities that made his heart race (e.g., running) because his heart had been racing at the time, photos of holiday destinations with sunshine and sea, blood, and pregnant women. The therapist helped Suvik to discriminate between current triggers and the trauma in the past, focusing on their differences. In-session work included running up and down stairs whilst focusing on where he was, how it was different from the time of the trauma, and how his heart racing signified fitness rather than danger; looking at images of blood on the computer; looking at holiday destinations on the computer; going out with the therapist and looking at pregnant women; and focusing on how the images on the computer and people today were different from the trauma.

In Session 8, the therapist again guided Suvik to revisit the island on Google Street View to practice then-versus-now discrimination, focusing on the differences between the island during the tsunami and its aftermath versus the island today. Then-versus-now practice with Google Street View was instrumental in helping Suvik to consolidate what he had learned in Session 5—that the island had been rebuilt, that the Thai people had moved on and were no longer suffering, and that it was a safe place to visit. Following the session, Suvik booked a trip to the island to take place within a month of therapy ending.

Work on Maintaining Cognitive Strategies and Behaviors

Therapy addressed Suvik's maintaining strategies as early as Session 1, beginning with suppression in response to memories. The therapist asked Suvik to think about anything he wanted for 60 seconds, except a bunny rabbit with a green bow and floppy ears. Suvik discovered that suppressing the rabbit only made it come to mind more often and that the same was most likely true for the memories he was trying to suppress, which helped him to experiment with dropping suppression as a strategy.

To address Suvik's rumination and self-criticism, the therapist elicited recent examples of times that he had ruminated and criticized himself. The memory of the woman who had the severely injured shins triggered episodes of rumination. When the memory came to mind, Suvik would question why he had poured so much iodine on her wounds and whether or not he had caused her to suffer. He then criticized himself for failing to have basic medical knowledge or first aid training. The therapist set up a behavioral experiment to test the effect of ruminative thinking versus concrete thinking on his mood. Suvik discovered that thinking in a ruminative way made him feel low and led to no plan or action. He spotted that his triggers for rumination were seeing injured people in news stories (which triggered the memory of the woman with the injured shins), being alone at home, and lying in bed at night. With the help of his therapist, he learned to spot when he was ruminating and to use the awareness as a cue to break the cycle by reminding himself of updating information and new imagery and by becoming active with weight lifting when possible. He also spotted his self-critical thoughts and, in response, reread the electronic letters the two women had sent as well as the list of helpful steps he had taken to help people in the aftermath of the tsunami. He then practiced self-compassion, speaking to himself with the same kindness that he would extend to a friend in similar circumstances.

Safety Behaviors and Hypervigilance

Suvik's safety behaviors, hypervigilance, and avoidance were addressed by considering the hypothesis that his trauma memories made him feel as if his parents were in danger. He experimented with reducing his checking behaviors (e.g., repeatedly calling his parents), using a series of behavioral experiments incorporating stimulus discrimination in session and for homework. He learned that his parents' safety was unrelated to his telephone calls or the past trauma and that focusing on the differences between their life in Sri Lanka today and their life at the time of the tsunami helped to reduce his anxiety about their safety. He experimented with checking weather reports one day and not the next, and he discovered that checking the reports made him feel more rather than less anxious, which helped him to stop checking altogether. He continued to double-lock his doors at home, but he stopped checking whether or not they were locked since he learned that checking kept his mind focused on danger, which made him more anxious.

Suvik experimented with overexercising for a moment when he noticed his heart was racing and believed he would have a heart attack. He did not have a heart attack in response, which helped him to discover that a fast-beating heart was not a sign of impending death. The experiment also helped him to realize that he did not need to smoke cannabis when he noticed his racing heart, and he was able to experiment with cannabis-free days. Over a period of a few weeks, with reduced cannabis use, he noticed that his sleep improved, and it was easier for him to recall updating information in response to intrusive memories. Self-criticism had also been a trigger for using cannabis use; he reminded himself of his updating information when self-critical thoughts came to mind and practiced self-compassion, seeing self-criticism and the urge to smoke as a sign that he needed to take more care of himself.

By focusing on the appreciation of the people he had helped, Suvik developed the confidence to enroll in a social media course during follow-up, and he experimented with asking questions in the course, focusing his attention on how people responded to him rather than on how he was feeling. The experiments helped Suvik to see that people responded to him in a kind and friendly manner and that no one judged him now or in the past, which made him feel much more comfortable in social situations.

Discussion of the Case

After normalizing the symptoms of PTSD and establishing the client's goals for therapy, the therapist and the client collaboratively developed an individualized case formulation, that is, an individualized version of Ehlers and Clark's (2000) cognitive model of PTSD, which served as the framework for tailoring therapy treatment procedures to the formulation.

From the first session, reclaiming your life assignments were agreed to address the client's perceived permanent change after trauma. These assignments involved reclaiming or (re)building activities and social contacts. Other appraisals of trauma sequelae (e.g., reactions of other people after the trauma) were addressed with information and cognitive therapy techniques, including behavioral experiments. Trauma memory characteristics and appraisals (i.e., personal meanings) of the trauma were addressed with the updating trauma memories procedure: first accessing memories of the worst moments during the trauma (i.e., hot spots) and their threatening meanings, then identifying information that updates these meanings for each hot spot, and finally linking the new information to the hot spot in memory by holding both simultaneously in mind. The easy triggering of reexperiencing symptoms was addressed with discrimination training with triggers of reexperiencing. This training involved systematically spotting idiosyncratic triggers (i.e., often subtle sensory cues) and learning to discriminate between then (i.e., cue in the traumatic situation) and now (i.e., cue in a new, safe context). Strategies for changing unhelpful cognitive strategies and behaviors such as rumination, hypervigilance for threat, thought suppression, and excessive precautions (i.e., safety behaviors) included behavioral experiments in which the client contrasted using the unhelpful strategies with reducing them. A blueprint summarized what the client learned in therapy and what he planned to do if he experienced a setback. Comorbidity was addressed alongside the trauma-focused work by addressing appraisals and maintaining behaviors.

At the end of treatment, Suvik no longer suffered from PTSD, depression, panic disorder, or social anxiety disorder. He occasionally felt sad when he thought about the devastation the Thai people and tourists endured as a result of the tsunami. However, reminding himself of Buddhist beliefs about suffering, life, and death and returning to Thailand within a month of treatment ending helped Suvik to experience firsthand that the Thai people had moved on, they were no longer suffering, their deceased loved ones were no longer suffering, and the island was once again flourishing. One year after treatment ended, Suvik had successfully completed a course on building an online presence and implemented those strategies to his benefit.

SUMMARY

This chapter described Ehlers and Clark's (2000) cognitive model of PTSD and the corresponding treatment approach, CT-PTSD. CT-PTSD aims to change negative personal meanings (i.e., appraisals) of the trauma or its sequelae, characteristics of the trauma memory (e.g., disjointedness, nowness), and unhelpful cognitive strategies and behaviors that maintain PTSD. Core techniques include an individualized case formulation, reclaiming/rebuilding your life assignments, updating the worst moments of the trauma with information that makes them less threatening in the present, discrimination training of trauma triggers, guided discovery and behavioral experiments to change excessively negative appraisals and cognitive strategies and behaviors that maintain a sense of internal or external threat, a site visit, and a blueprint. The individualized approach makes CT-PTSD applicable to a wide range of traumas and cultural backgrounds. Therapists delivering CT-PTSD should have professional training in CBT, have read the treatment manual, and have attended at least a 2-day workshop on the procedures of CT-PTSD, followed by supervision of at least two cases by an experienced CT-PTSD supervisor. A manual including case examples and videos illustrating core treatment procedures is available free of charge (see https://oxcadatresources.com).

KEY IDEAS

- A course of CT-PTSD usually involves between 12 and 20 treatment sessions, depending on the number of traumas that are reexperienced. For sessions that include memory work, 90-minute sessions should be allowed.

- The treatment is based on Ehlers and Clark's (2000) model of PTSD.

- Treatment focuses on changing excessively negative personal meanings of the trauma and its consequences, reducing reexperiencing through updating memories and trigger discrimination, and changing behaviors and cognitive strategies that maintain PTSD.

- The treatment is designed for all types of trauma.

- An individual case formulation guides therapy, with treatment procedures and the order in which they are delivered tailored to the formulation. CT-PTSD can therefore be applied to a wide variety of presentations, traumas, and cultural backgrounds and can incorporate comorbid conditions and the effects of multiple traumas.

REFERENCES

Beierl, E. T., Böllinghaus, I., Clark, D. M., Glucksman, E., & Ehlers, A. (2019). Cognitive paths from trauma to posttraumatic stress disorder: A prospective study of Ehlers and Clark's model in survivors of assaults or road traffic collisions. *Psychological Medicine.* Advance online publication. http://dx.doi.org/10.1017/S0033291719002253

Bisson, J. I., Roberts, N. P., Andrew, M., Cooper, R., & Lewis, C. (2013). Psychological therapies for chronic post-traumatic stress disorder (PTSD) in adults. *Cochrane Database of Systematic Reviews.* http://dx.doi.org/10.1002/14651858.CD003388.pub4

Brewin, C. R., Fuchkan, N., Huntley, Z., Robertson, M., Thompson, M., Scragg, P., . . . Ehlers, A. (2010). Outreach and screening following the 2005 London bombings: Usage and outcomes. *Psychological Medicine, 40,* 2049–2057. http://dx.doi.org/10.1017/S0033291710000206

Brown, L. A., Belli, G. M., Asnaani, A., & Foa, E. B. (2019). A review of the role of negative cognitions about oneself, others, and the world in the treatment of PTSD.

Cognitive Therapy and Research, *43*, 143–173. http://dx.doi.org/10.1007/s10608-018-9938-1

Duffy, M., Gillespie, K., & Clark, D. M. (2007). Post-traumatic stress disorder in the context of terrorism and other civil conflict in Northern Ireland: Randomised controlled trial. *BMJ: British Medical Journal*, *334*, 1147–1150. http://dx.doi.org/10.1136/bmj.39021.846852.BE

Dunmore, E., Clark, D. M., & Ehlers, A. (2001). A prospective investigation of the role of cognitive factors in persistent posttraumatic stress disorder (PTSD) after physical or sexual assault. *Behaviour Research and Therapy*, *39*, 1063–1084. http://dx.doi.org/10.1016/S0005-7967(00)00088-7

Ehlers, A. (2013). Trauma-focused cognitive behavior therapy for posttraumatic stress disorder and acute stress disorder. In G. Simos & S. G. Hofmann (Eds.), *CBT for anxiety disorders: A practitioner book* (pp. 161–188). New York, NY: Wiley. http://dx.doi.org/10.1002/9781118330043.ch7

Ehlers, A., & Clark, D. M. (2000). A cognitive model of posttraumatic stress disorder. *Behaviour Research and Therapy*, *38*, 319–345. http://dx.doi.org/10.1016/S0005-7967(99)00123-0

Ehlers, A., Clark, D. M., Hackmann, A., McManus, F., & Fennell, M. (2005). Cognitive therapy for post-traumatic stress disorder: Development and evaluation. *Behaviour Research and Therapy*, *43*, 413–431. http://dx.doi.org/10.1016/j.brat.2004.03.006

Ehlers, A., Clark, D. M., Hackmann, A., McManus, F., Fennell, M., Herbert, C., & Mayou, R. (2003). A randomized controlled trial of cognitive therapy, a self-help booklet, and repeated assessments as early interventions for posttraumatic stress disorder. *Archives of General Psychiatry*, *60*, 1024–1032. http://dx.doi.org/10.1001/archpsyc.60.10.1024

Ehlers, A., Ehring, T., & Kleim, B. (2012). Information processing in posttraumatic stress disorder. In J. G. Beck & D. M. Sloan (Eds.), *The Oxford handbook of traumatic disorders* (pp. 191–218). New York, NY: Oxford University Press.

Ehlers, A., Grey, N., Warnock-Parkes, E., Wild, J., Stott, R., Cullen, D., . . . Clark, D. M. (2020). *Effectiveness of cognitive therapy for PTSD in routine clinical care: Second phase implementation*. Manuscript submitted for publication.

Ehlers, A., Grey, N., Wild, J., Stott, R., Liness, S., Deale, A., . . . Clark, D. M. (2013). Implementation of cognitive therapy for PTSD in routine clinical care: Effectiveness and moderators of outcome in a consecutive sample. *Behaviour Research and Therapy*, *51*, 742–752. http://dx.doi.org/10.1016/j.brat.2013.08.006

Ehlers, A., Hackmann, A., Grey, N., Wild, J., Liness, S., Albert, I., . . . Clark, D. M. (2014). A randomized controlled trial of 7-day intensive and standard weekly cognitive therapy for PTSD and emotion-focused supportive therapy. *The American Journal of Psychiatry*, *171*, 294–304. http://dx.doi.org/10.1176/appi.ajp.2013.13040552

Ehlers, A., Hackmann, A., & Michael, T. (2004). Intrusive re-experiencing in post-traumatic stress disorder: Phenomenology, theory, and therapy. *Memory*, *12*, 403–415. http://dx.doi.org/10.1080/09658210444000025

Ehlers, A., Mayou, R. A., & Bryant, B. (1998). Psychological predictors of chronic posttraumatic stress disorder after motor vehicle accidents. *Journal of Abnormal Psychology*, *107*, 508–519. http://dx.doi.org/10.1037/0021-843X.107.3.508

Ehlers, A., Michael, T., Chen, Y. P., Payne, E., & Shan, S. (2006). Enhanced perceptual priming for neutral stimuli in a traumatic context: A pathway to intrusive memories? *Memory*, *14*, 316–328. http://dx.doi.org/10.1080/09658210500305876

Ehlers, A., & Murray, H. L. (2020). Cognitive therapy for complex traumatic stress disorders. In C. A. Courtois & J. D. Ford (Eds.), *Treating complex traumatic stress disorders (adults): Scientific foundations and therapeutic models* (2nd ed.). New York, NY: Guilford Press.

Ehlers, A., & Wild, J. (2015). Cognitive therapy for PTSD: Updating memories and meanings of trauma. In U. Schnyder & M. Cloitre (Eds.), *Evidence based treatments for trauma-related psychological disorders* (pp. 161–187). Cham, Switzerland: Springer. http://dx.doi.org/10.1007/978-3-319-07109-1_9

Ehlers, A., Wild, J., Stott, R., Warnock-Parkes, E., Grey, N., & Clark, D. M. (2019). *Efficient use of therapist time in the treatment of posttraumatic stress disorder: A randomized clinical trial of brief self-study assisted and standard weekly cognitive therapy for PTSD.* Manuscript submitted for publication.

Ehring, T., Ehlers, A., & Glucksman, E. (2008). Do cognitive models help in predicting the severity of posttraumatic stress disorder, phobia, and depression after motor vehicle accidents? A prospective longitudinal study. *Journal of Consulting and Clinical Psychology, 76*(2), 219–230. http://dx.doi.org/10.1037/0022-006X.76.2.219

Foa, E. B., Ehlers, A., Clark, D. M., Tolin, D., & Orsillo, S. (1999). The Post-Traumatic Cognitions Inventory (PTCI): Development and validation. *Psychological Assessment, 11*, 303–314. http://dx.doi.org/10.1037/1040-3590.11.3.303

Foa, E. B., & Rothbaum, B. O. (1998). *Treating the trauma of rape: Cognitive-behavior therapy for PTSD.* New York, NY: Guilford Press.

Gillespie, K., Duffy, M., Hackmann, A., & Clark, D. M. (2002). Community based cognitive therapy in the treatment of posttraumatic stress disorder following the Omagh bomb. *Behaviour Research and Therapy, 40*, 345–357. http://dx.doi.org/10.1016/S0005-7967(02)00004-9

Halligan, S. L., Michael, T., Clark, D. M., & Ehlers, A. (2003). Posttraumatic stress disorder following assault: The role of cognitive processing, trauma memory, and appraisals. *Journal of Consulting and Clinical Psychology, 71*, 419–431. http://dx.doi.org/10.1037/0022-006X.71.3.419

Jacobson, N. S., Martell, C. R., & Dimidjian, S. (2001). Behavioral activation for depression: Returning to contextual roots. *Clinical Psychology: Science and Practice, 8*, 255–270. http://dx.doi.org/10.1093/clipsy.8.3.255

Kleim, B., & Ehlers, A. (2008). Reduced autobiographical memory specificity predicts depression and posttraumatic stress disorder after recent trauma. *Journal of Consulting and Clinical Psychology, 76*, 231–242. http://dx.doi.org/10.1037/0022-006X.76.2.231

Kleim, B., Ehlers, A., & Glucksman, E. (2012). Investigating cognitive pathways to psychopathology: Predicting depression and posttraumatic stress disorder from early responses after assault. *Psychological Trauma: Theory, Research, Practice, and Policy, 4*, 527–537. http://dx.doi.org/10.1037/a0027006

Kleim, B., Ehring, T., & Ehlers, A. (2012). Perceptual processing advantages for trauma-related visual cues in post-traumatic stress disorder. *Psychological Medicine, 42*, 173–181. http://dx.doi.org/10.1017/S0033291711001048

Kleim, B., Grey, N., Wild, J., Nussbeck, F. W., Stott, R., Hackmann, A., . . . Ehlers, A. (2013). Cognitive change predicts symptom reduction with cognitive therapy for posttraumatic stress disorder. *Journal of Consulting and Clinical Psychology, 81*, 383–393. http://dx.doi.org/10.1037/a0031290

Kleim, B., Wallott, F., & Ehlers, A. (2008). Are trauma memories disjointed from other autobiographical memories in posttraumatic stress disorder? An experimental investigation. *Behavioural and Cognitive Psychotherapy, 36*, 221–234. http://dx.doi.org/10.1017/S1352465807004080

Meiser-Stedman, R., Smith, P., McKinnon, A., Dixon, C., Trickey, D., Ehlers, A., & Dalgleish, T. (2017). Cognitive therapy versus wait list as an early intervention for posttraumatic stress disorder in children and adolescents: A randomized controlled trial addressing preliminary efficacy and mechanisms of action. *Journal of Child Psychology and Psychiatry, 58*, 623–633. http://dx.doi.org/10.1111/jcpp.12673

Padesky, C. A. (1993, September). *Socratic questioning: Changing minds or guiding discovery?* Invited keynote address presented at the 1993 European Congress of Behaviour and Cognitive Therapies, London, England. Retrieved from https://padesky.com/newpad/wp-content/uploads/2012/11/socquest.pdf

Resick, P. A., & Schnicke, M. K. (1993). *Cognitive processing therapy for rape victims.* Newbury Park, CA: Sage.

Sachschal, J., Woodward, E., Wichelmann, J., Haag, K., & Ehlers, A. (2019). Differential effects of poor recall and memory disjointedness on trauma symptoms. *Clinical Psychological Science.* http://dx.doi.org/10.1177/2167702619847195

Schnyder, U., Bryant, R. A., Ehlers, A., Foa, E. B., Hasan, A., Mwiti, G., . . . Yule, W. (2016). Culture-sensitive psychotraumatology. *European Journal of Psychotraumatology, 7.* http://dx.doi.org/10.3402/ejpt.v7.31179

Smith, P., Yule, W., Perrin, S., Tranah, T., Dalgleish, T., & Clark, D. M. (2007). Cognitive-behavioral therapy for PTSD in children and adolescents: A preliminary randomized controlled trial. *Journal of the American Academy of Child & Adolescent Psychiatry, 46,* 1051–1061. http://dx.doi.org/10.1097/CHI.0b013e318067e288

Sündermann, O., Hauschildt, M., & Ehlers, A. (2013). Perceptual processing during trauma, priming and the development of intrusive memories. *Journal of Behavior Therapy and Experimental Psychiatry, 44,* 213–220. http://dx.doi.org/10.1016/j.jbtep.2012.10.001

Wild, J., Smith, K. V., Thompson, E., Béar, F., Lommen, M. J., & Ehlers, A. (2016). A prospective study of pre-trauma risk factors for post-traumatic stress disorder and depression. *Psychological Medicine, 46,* 2571–2582. http://dx.doi.org/10.1017/S0033291716000532

Woodward, E., Hackmann, A., Wild, J., Grey, N., Clark, D. M., & Ehlers, A. (2017). Effects of psychotherapies for posttraumatic stress disorder on sleep disturbances: Results from a randomized clinical trial. *Behaviour Research and Therapy, 97,* 75–85. http://dx.doi.org/10.1016/j.brat.2017.07.001

6

Prolonged Exposure for PTSD

Thea Gallagher, Julie Petersen, and Edna B. Foa

Prolonged exposure (PE) is an effective, evidence-based, cognitive behavior intervention for individuals with posttraumatic stress disorder (PTSD; Foa, Hembree, & Rothbaum, 2007; van Minnen, Harned, Zoellner, & Mills, 2012). PE combines elements of assessment, psychoeducation, and exposure to provide a comprehensive treatment package for PTSD (Foa et al., 2007). In this chapter, we review the treatment rationale and the wide variety of research support for PE, including a detailed breakdown of treatment components. We also present case examples to illustrate PE in action.

TREATMENT RATIONALE

PE is based in emotional processing theory (EPT), which suggests that emotions such as fear are represented in a cognitive network; this network includes information related to the fear stimuli, fear responses, and meanings behind the fear and related responses (Foa & Kozak, 1986). EPT further posits that any input related to the fear structure can ultimately activate the entire cognitive network. For example, a combat veteran may interpret a loud noise as a dangerous and feared stimulus, even if it is only fireworks. The fear structure can subsequently become pathologically activated, particularly if the client is no longer in a place where the fear structure is adaptive (such as a combat zone). Thus, researchers posit that clients with PTSD may have different fear

http://dx.doi.org/10.1037/0000196-006
Casebook to the APA Clinical Practice Guideline for the Treatment of PTSD, edited by
L. F. Bufka, C. V. Wright, and R. W. Halfond

networks than those without PTSD, as these fear networks are less adaptive, activating more easily and intensely (Foa & Cahill, 2001; Foa, Steketee, & Rothbaum, 1989).

To conquer and adjust this maladaptive fear structure in clients with PTSD, EPT requires that a client activate it repeatedly while receiving corrective and disconfirming information; in this way, the fear structure can be appropriately relearned over time (Cahill & Foa, 2007). However, because clients with PTSD commonly avoid trauma reminders, they do not have opportunities to incorporate corrective information into the fear structure, thus perpetuating PTSD symptoms. The confrontation of trauma-related constructs can result in habituation—the client's trauma-related anxiety and fear decrease over time and with repeated exposures. PE allows for the client to activate and correct the fear structure through the confrontation of trauma-related memories, thoughts, and situations (Foa, Huppert, & Cahill, 2006; McLean & Foa, 2011).

RESEARCH SUPPORT

McLean and Foa (2011) showed that PE is very effective for reducing PTSD symptoms. However, PE does not improve only PTSD; research has demonstrated that PE reduces other secondary treatment outcomes such as depression (Foa, Dancu, et al., 1999; Foa et al., 2005; Powers, Halpern, Ferenschak, Gillihan, & Foa, 2010), guilt (Resick, Nishith, Weaver, Astin, & Feuer, 2002), and anger (Cahill, Rauch, Hembree, & Foa, 2003). Furthermore, PE reduces a variety of other psychological symptoms, including psychosis (van den Berg et al., 2015), anxiety sensitivity (Feske, 2008), and dissociation (Rothbaum, Astin, & Marsteller, 2005). PE also has long-lasting effects: Improvement has been maintained up to 10 years after treatment (Resick, Williams, Suvak, Monson, & Gradus, 2012).

SPECIFIC APPLICATIONS OF PE

Broadly speaking, McLean and Foa's (2011) review of PE demonstrates that it reduces PTSD symptoms in a wide range of trauma types (e.g., sexual assaults, physical assaults, motor vehicle accidents, combat). In particular, PE has been researched extensively in sexual assault victims. Studies examining the effectiveness in treating female rape and sexual assault victims found that PE successfully reduces PTSD symptoms (Foa & Rauch, 2004; Resick et al., 2002; Rothbaum et al., 2005). PE has even been successfully used for adolescent (ages 13–18 years) female sexual assault survivors, which suggests that clinicians can use PE with a broad age range (Foa, McLean, Capaldi, & Rosenfield, 2013). Combat-related PTSD in military populations has also been a focus of much PE research. Many studies have demonstrated effectiveness in using PE to treat veterans with PTSD (Nacasch et al., 2011; Schnurr et al., 2007; Tuerk et al., 2011). Further research shows that PE is also effective for active-duty military members (Reger et al., 2016). Finally, PE has even been used successfully to treat veterans with mild traumatic brain injury (Sripada et al., 2013).

Beyond combat and sexual assault, PE has been utilized in many other populations and settings. PE has been used effectively to treat clients at academic, community, and residential clinics (Feske, 2008; Foa et al., 2005; Henslee & Coffey, 2010). More specifically, Feske (2008) found that a sample of primarily low-income, minority women who received PE showed greater improvement in their PTSD symptoms than those who received treatment as usual. Williams and colleagues (2014) adapted PE for use with African American populations by adding more rapport-building sessions as well as advice for clinicians on how to be more candid with clients about experiences with racism and discrimination. PE has also been studied as a treatment for Japanese clients with PTSD; a small randomized controlled trial found that PE resulted in a greater symptom reduction than treatment as usual (Asukai, Saito, Tsuruta, Kishimoto, & Nishikawa, 2010). Additionally, the PE protocol was merged with dialectical behavioral therapy (DBT) to create a joint DBT–PE protocol for clients with borderline personality disorder (Harned, Korslund, & Linehan, 2014). PE has been used as a treatment for people living with HIV and PTSD (Pacella et al., 2012), as well as for clients with comorbid substance abuse, such as alcohol or nicotine dependence (Foa, Asnaani, et al., 2017; Foa, Yusko, et al., 2013). PE has also been successfully implemented as a treatment for PTSD in a residential substance use treatment facility, accounting for the constraints of residential living via twice weekly 60-minute sessions, facility-provided audio recording devices, and use of the internet and residential staff for creative in vivo exposures (Berenz, Rowe, Schumacher, Stasiewicz, & Coffey, 2012; Henslee & Coffey, 2010).

DESCRIPTION OF TREATMENT COMPONENTS

PE typically consists of eight to 15 treatment sessions that last 90 minutes, delivered once or twice a week. The overall aim of PE is to assist PTSD clients in repeatedly and safely facing trauma-related memories, situations, and reminders (Foa, Hembree, & Rothbaum, 2007). PE consists of two main components, imaginal and in vivo exposure. *Imaginal exposure* is the repeated revisitation and recounting of the trauma memory, followed by processing of the revisitation experience. *In vivo exposure* is the repeated exposure to safe situations or activities that the client was avoiding because the situations reminded them of the trauma.

Session-by-Session Overview

Assessment

Before beginning the PE treatment protocol, the therapist must assess whether PE is appropriate for the client. Safety is a priority, so PE is not recommended for clients who are experiencing current and serious suicidal, homicidal, or self-harming behaviors. These behaviors should be stabilized before a client enters treatment. Similarly, clients who are at high risk for experiencing another trauma (e.g., living with an abusive partner) should not be treated with PE—attempting to teach a client habituation to real threats of harm would be dangerous. Thus, the therapist should first work with the client to help them enter a safer environment, if possible, before starting PE. Additionally, PE is not recommended for clients with insufficient memory of the trauma because of the narrative component of imaginal exposures. Clients must be able to tell the trauma as a story with a beginning, middle, and end. If a client is unable to tell the trauma as a story, another treatment may be more appropriate.

To assess for these complicating factors, the clinician should take a detailed trauma history and assess for PTSD and its severity. One of the myriad methods to assess PTSD diagnosis and severity is the Posttraumatic Symptom Scale—Interview for *DSM–5* (PSSI-5; Foa, McLean, Zang, Zhong, Rauch, et al., 2016). The PSSI-5 assists a therapist in determining the most currently distressing trauma as well as the type and frequency of symptoms the client has experienced in the past month. For example, the PSSI-5 includes questions such as "Have you had unwanted distressing memories about the trauma?" and "Have you been jumpier or more easily startled?" (Foa, McLean, Zang, Zhong, Rauch, et al., 2016). The maximum score on the PSSI-5 is 80, and the cutoff for a probable diagnosis of PTSD is 23 (Foa, McLean, Zang, Zhong, Rauch, et al., 2016).

It is also recommended that therapists use self-report measures to receive a more complete perspective on the client's symptoms. Although many empirically supported self-report measures are available, we recommend the PTSD Diagnostic Scale for *DSM–5* (PDS-5; Foa, McLean, Zang, Zhong, Powers, et al., 2016) and the Posttraumatic Cognitions Inventory (PTCI; Foa, Ehlers, Clark, Tolin, & Orsillo, 1999). The PDS-5 allows the client to rate questions, similar to those on the PSSI-5, from his or her own perspective. The PTCI is useful for evaluating clients' cognitions regarding the trauma: Clients rate statements that examine self-blame and negative cognitions about the world and self (Foa, Ehlers, et al., 1999). For example, the PTCI includes statements such as "The event happened because of the way I acted" and "The world is a dangerous place." Information about cognitions may be especially useful, as studies have found changes in PTSD-related cognitions to be a mechanism of PE, contributing to symptom reduction (McLean, Su, & Foa, 2015; Zalta et al., 2014). It may also be helpful to give self-report measures with every session to track client progress.

Finally, assessment should also include a comprehensive overview for any other possible comorbid psychiatric diagnoses and their severity. It should be determined whether PTSD is the primary issue or if another disorder, such as substance abuse or depression, needs to be stabilized or addressed before focusing on PTSD symptoms with PE. This is important because primary depression or substance abuse may interfere with the client's ability to engage fully with exposures and may limit new learning, which is the goal of PE. If an individual with primary PTSD can safely abstain from substances or can engage in harm reduction (e.g., drinking or smoking marijuana in moderation outside of session), there is reason to believe that individual would benefit from PE. Clients with primary PTSD and moderate to severe depression connected to the trauma memory might also benefit from PE, depending on their level of functioning and ability to engage with in vivo exposures, in spite of anhedonia.

Session 1

The first session begins with an overview of PE and its components—it is assumed that assessment has taken place before the official first session of PE. The therapist presents the rationale for PE and explains how PE reduces PTSD symptoms. The therapist then collects information about the client's trauma through a trauma interview, working specifically to identify the most distressing trauma memory. It may be hard for clients to identify the one "most distressing" memory. Thus, it helps to be creative and curious when asking clients to identify a memory to use in PE; for example, a therapist might ask the client which memory stands out as the most haunting or which memory most frequently comes up in nightmares or intrusive thoughts. Next, the therapist teaches the client breathing retraining. Breathing retraining involves exhaling slowly and deeply after a normal inhale, drawing out a word such as *ca-a-a-a-alm* (or any other relaxing word of the client's choice) during the exhale. Finally, the therapist assigns homework for the next session, typically to review treatment rationale worksheets and to practice the new breathing technique.

Session 2

Session 2 focuses primarily on the client's trauma and reactions to the trauma. The therapist discusses different common reactions to trauma (e.g., anxiety, fear, nightmares) with the client, helping the client to identify and describe the experiences. After that, the rationale for in vivo exposure is presented. Subsequently, the client and therapist work together to create a hierarchy of situations or places that the client is avoiding. For example, clients who have been in a car accident may avoid driving, being in cars, or the site of the accident; in vivo exposures therefore may include driving short distances or going past the site of the accident. Another example is a female client who was sexually assaulted by a male and has been avoiding men since—a beginning in vivo exposure may be to talk briefly with a male store clerk or waiter. With the fear hierarchy in place, the first in vivo exposure is assigned for homework.

Session 3

Session 3 begins with a review of the first in vivo exposure assignment, followed by the introduction of imaginal exposure. The therapist presents the imaginal exposure rationale to the client. Then, the client begins the first imaginal exposure, revisiting and recounting the trauma memory for approximately 45 to 60 minutes. To understand and make note of the distress levels the client is experiencing, the therapist should ask for a 1-to-100 rating of subjective units of distress (SUDS) while the client recounts the trauma. Asking for SUDS ratings allows both the client and the therapist to note when distress increases and decreases throughout the imaginal exposure. The imaginal exposure should be recorded so that the client can relisten to the narrative as part of homework. The last 15 to 20 minutes of the session are used for "processing," which includes discussion of the trauma memory and revisitation experience. During the imaginal exposure, it is common for clients to experience new observations or perspectives—these should be discussed during the processing period. Processing can also be used to review the change in distress or habituation observed as well as thoughts and feelings present during or after the imaginal that may be contributing to the maintenance of PTSD symptoms. The processing period can also be used to decrease the distress created by the imaginal exposure through further encouragement, support, or use of breathing retraining. The client should not leave the session greatly distressed.

Sessions 4 and 5
Sessions 4 and 5 consist of repeated imaginal exposure and processing.

Sessions 6 Through 9
As in Sessions 4 and 5, imaginal exposure is conducted in Sessions 6 through 9. However, during these later sessions, the client and therapist select "hot spots" to target and focus on. Hot spots are the parts of the trauma or memory that are most distressing to the client. It is important to introduce hot spots after the client has had the chance to habituate to the rest of the memory. If the client has difficulty selecting a hot spot, it may be useful simply to select the part of the memory with the highest SUDS ratings. Once a hot spot has been sufficiently repeated and habituated to, it is important to remember that there may be other hot spots to explore and repeat.

Session 10
At the last session, the client recounts the entire memory for a final time. Typically, this takes about 20 to 30 minutes, as the imaginal exposures tend to become shorter with continued repetition. The therapist and client then discuss the client's change and progress over the course of therapy. It is important to highlight how the client's distress or anxiety in response to the memory and other trauma reminders has changed over the course of treatment. The session ends with a focus on relapse prevention, treatment completion, and how the client can continue to apply skills from therapy in life.

CASE ILLUSTRATIONS

To demonstrate the application of PE, two detailed case examples are provided here. The first case example shows the use of PE in addressing PTSD symptoms in a woman who was raped on a first date. The second case example illustrates how PE was used to treat PTSD symptoms in a male veteran. Each case example is accompanied by discussion about how PE was specifically used and adapted for each client.

Ms. E

Ms. E is a 29-year-old White woman who was raped by a man on a first date. After the rape, she developed PTSD symptoms, such as hypervigilance, avoidance, and isolation, and symptoms of depression. The initial evaluation found that Ms. E had moderate PTSD, with a PSSI-5 score of 60. No other diagnoses were given at the time of the evaluation, and there was no reported history of prior psychiatric disorders or trauma.

Ms. E used an online dating website where she messaged back and forth with a White man for about one week. She had been using this dating application for about six months and had been on approximately 12 prior first dates. During the date, Ms. E had a "lovely time," and after dinner and 2 hours of "fulfilling" discussion, she invited her date back to her apartment. After he came up to her apartment, they began kissing, and the man began to display aggressive behaviors. He ripped her clothes off and used his strength to push her onto the couch and then violently rape her. Ms. E initially fought him by trying to push him away and screamed for him to stop numerous times. When she realized that he was not stopping, she became afraid for her life, and she froze and waited for it to be over. After her assailant was finished raping her, he called her a "whore" and a "slut" and told her that she "wanted it." He left her apartment shortly after.

Ms. E stated that she incurred physical injuries as a result of this event: She was bleeding and was physically sore for more than a week. After the rape, the client took a shower and tried to forget what happened. She did not tell anyone and proceeded with her daily life. She noticed an increase in anxiety and fear when she went to check the dating website about one week later, and as a result of these feelings of discomfort, she closed her dating profiles. The client began to notice an increase in anxiety while in crowds, bars, and parking garages, and she began to structure her life around avoiding these places. After avoiding these places for a few months, she also noticed increased fear in the gym and her apartment. She began avoiding many social situations, as she was not able to engage socially without significant anxiety and distress. The catalyst for seeking treatment was the fear that she might lose important friendships—as well as lose the opportunity to date people, get married, and start a family one day—if she continued to isolate herself.

When she came to the clinic for treatment, Ms. E had been feeling depressed and lonely for 3 months; those were the months that she had not been able to date and had spent more time alone in her apartment rather than with friends or colleagues. The client was able to go to work as a schoolteacher but was unable to do much outside of work. She had noticed that she was becoming increasingly avoidant of crowds, spent most of her time alone in her apartment, and was avoiding TV, movies, or news for fear that sexual assault and rape might be referenced. Ms. E stated that her fears had continued to increase since the rape, and her domains of avoidance were also extending to crowded places or any reminders of that night. She was experiencing frequent intrusive thoughts about the details of the rape as well as the physical pain she felt and was experiencing intense emotional distress when reminded of it. Ms. E was also avoiding any thoughts or situations that triggered memories of the rape, and she was continuing to experience flashbacks from that night. She reported having nightmares about the event, accompanied by significant sleep difficulties, such as difficulty falling asleep and waking up in the middle of the night.

Ms. E had no prior trauma history, nor had she had any prior psychiatric or psychological treatment history. She stated that she would drink socially but denied any prior or present alcohol or drug abuse at the time of her initial evaluation and stated that she had not been drinking alcohol since the rape. She decided to seek help after 3 months of suffering.

In formulating the treatment plan for Ms. E, the therapist took into account the index trauma (i.e., the rape) with the goal of helping Ms. E return to socializing, dating, and activities involving groups, all of which she was completely avoiding. Imaginal exposure focused on the rape. The imaginal exposure began with her assailant kissing her, followed by his ripping her clothes off, throwing her onto the couch, and raping her, and ended with his calling her a "whore" and a "slut," telling her she "wanted it," and then exiting her apartment building. Her in vivo exposure hierarchy included items such as going to crowded places, going to the gym, going to parking garages during the day and then at night, and progressed to looking at pictures of men that looked like him, watching *Law & Order: Special Victims Unit* episodes, going on dates, and reading news articles about sexual assault.

During the imaginal processing, it became clear that Ms. E had felt helpless during the rape and yet held herself responsible. She had always considered herself a strong woman with "street smarts," and she was considered by many to be competent and successful in many areas. She commented several times, "I should have known better" and "I should have seen this coming." She also felt guilt and shame because she had had a few drinks and "invited a rapist into her home." She stated that she blamed herself for not preventing the rape and not being a "better judge of character," and she expressed anger and frustration toward herself and her inability to "get over it and get back to her life."

Ms. E showed appropriate emotional engagement with the trauma memory during her imaginal exposures. She initially reported high distress (SUDS levels in the 80–95 range), but she experienced progressive habituation of distress and anxiety between and during sessions (SUDS of 20–30 at treatment end). Her affect was congruent with her SUDS ratings. She engaged in productive processing following her imaginal exposure work where she verbalized feelings of guilt, shame, fear, and responsibility. She was able to process through these themes, and she developed new insights, such as "There was no way for me to know this man was going to rape me." During her sessions she eventually realized, "I can't completely control my environment" and "I can't always keep bad things from happening to me." She also was able to conclude that "it is hard for me to understand that people do bad things to hurt others." The client began to accept that the rape was a terrible event that was out of her control and that she did her best to fight back and make smart decisions during the crisis. She also came to realize that the world can sometimes be dangerous and that some people want to hurt others, but this is not always the case.

There was quite a significant shift during treatment in her negative views of herself, the future, and the world, which had developed after the rape. The shift in these thoughts was evidenced by significant decrease in her self-report PSSI-5 scores over time. She was able to see that she used to view the world more positively and began to return to that way of thinking.

Ms. E was highly motivated, worked hard in her therapy sessions, was compliant with homework assignments and utilized the skills she learned in treatment between sessions. The treatment produced a significant reduction in Ms. E's PTSD symptoms, and she began to engage socially, even returning to online dating as she was doing before the trauma. By the end of treatment, she had plans to begin volunteering at a rape crisis center. Assessments were conducted before, during, and after treatment, up to a year following therapy. Ms. E's PTSD severity decreased by 80% from pre- to post-treatment, and a year after treatment, the severity was reduced by 90%. These measures indicated that she continued to maintain her treatment gains. Two years after treatment, the therapist received an email from the client, informing her she was engaged to be married. She indicated that this was a sign to her that she had successfully moved forward in her life despite such a tragedy.

Mr. G

Mr. G, a 30-year-old Latino man, was referred to our PTSD program by his psychiatrist. Mr. G's trauma history consisted of experiencing multiple "shockwave detonations" when he was on tour in Iraq 3 years prior. He stated that during these events he believed that he would die. The client reported that his problems began 2 years after his return from Iraq when he experienced a "vivid flashback" while he was at school. After that he realized that he had other symptoms of PTSD. He struggled with shame about having a "mental disorder" and tried to ignore his symptoms for an extended period. However, he desired to resolve these issues before beginning to write his dissertation. He was experiencing frequent intrusive thoughts and images of Iraq and these detonations, intense emotional distress when reminded of his tour, avoidance of thoughts and situations that triggered memories, nightly sleep disturbance, and apathy toward his studies. In addition, he was experiencing fear and worry about his safety and future. He wanted to resolve these problems and fears "before it affects my entire life."

Mr. G endorsed symptoms of hypervigilance, avoidance, depression, anxiety, and guilt and shame. The client reported that his most avoided memories were of shockwaves of detonations in Iraq where he feared for his life. Even though he was accepted into a PhD program (his lifelong dream), he noticed an increase in negative views about his own competence and self-worth. He felt particularly unworthy when compared to other veterans because it "wasn't as bad" for him, as he was an engineer and not "on the front lines." He stated that he primarily felt guilty for surviving and worked to avoid any veteran related events; he felt as though "invisible weights" were on him all the time. He also believed that he had to pay a price for being in the military and that he "bears the scar." To help manage anxiety and these negative feelings, he reported using marijuana three times a day, but he agreed to reduce his use for treatment purposes. He reported that he was specifically using marijuana to avoid his feelings and thoughts about his trauma and his life.

The initial evaluation showed that Mr. G had moderately severe PTSD with a PSSI-5 score of 70. His history included one episode of major depression, beginning after he came out as gay at age 20 and lasting at least one year. In addition, Mr. G had struggled with cannabis abuse and dependence, which developed shortly after he returned from Iraq (3 years prior). No other diagnoses were given. Mr. G stated that he sought out a psychiatrist 6 months ago and was prescribed an SSRI for his depression. He stated that he had noticed a minor decrease in depressive symptoms and anxiety. He reported no prior psychiatric treatment or psychiatric hospitalizations.

It was clear early in treatment that Mr. G was feeling guilty about having PTSD because he never experienced combat in Iraq. He had beliefs that he was weak, damaged, and "bad." He commented several times, "I didn't have it as bad as many other vets have had it." Mr. G also had strong negative feelings about his time in the military, which he felt guilty about. He reported, "I feel damaged and weak, and when people thank me for my service, I try to move the conversation along, because I don't deserve their praise." Although he thought he should feel pride about being in the military, he reported negative feelings toward his experience, and that was difficult for him to reconcile. He also described struggling with loneliness during his tour: "I wasn't allowed to talk about being gay, and I wasn't allowed to express my feelings of fear to anyone, because that's not what you do in the army." These feelings and thoughts were prominent in his imaginal exposure from the outset.

Imaginal exposure focused on one particularly strong detonation that shook the furniture because this was the most distressing and most frequently reexperienced traumatic memory. His in vivo exposure hierarchy included items such as going to restaurants and keeping his back to the door, sitting at the front of class (his back toward most of the room), watching the Ken Burns *The Vietnam War* television series, interacting with other veterans at events, and engaging in more social activities (for exposure and behavioral activation purposes). Mr. G was motivated but skeptical about getting better because he lacked confidence in himself. He committed to doing the work in therapy, completed his homework assignments weekly, and practiced the skills between sessions.

Mr. G showed initial emotional underengagement with the traumatic memory during his imaginal exposures. He stated that he was nervous about feeling emotions, as he had spent much of the last few years trying to avoid feeling anything about his time in Iraq. At Session 5, the therapist asked many questions about Mr. G's sensory experience, and he was able to engage with his emotions and became tearful. He reported initially low distress (SUDS) levels for Sessions 3 and 4, but by Session 5 he endorsed more accurate SUDS ratings and then showed continued habituation of anxiety within and between subsequent sessions. His affect during exposure initially was flat and incongruent with the self-report measures he had completed. Successful emotional processing of the traumatic experiences was seen beginning in Session 5 onward. After his fifth imaginal exposure, he said, "I've been listening to myself continue to say that I was afraid for my life and I believed I wouldn't leave Iraq alive, and I'm beginning to realize that my fear was just as valid as someone in combat. I truly believed I was going to die!" He reported in the next session that for the first time, he felt he had "permission" to feel fear and sadness about what he had experienced.

This acceptance was enhanced by his recall of a few aspects of the traumatic events that he had not reflected on before. For example, his distress about "feeling weak" was validated by his own realization that he lived in terror and fear for many months with no way to process this. He also began to realize that he brought the fear of death home from Iraq with him. After the imaginal exposure in the seventh session, he spontaneously said, "You know, I'm beginning to realize that I'm not in Iraq anymore and I am safe, and I want to live the life I dreamed about living." This was quite a significant change in his thinking about his safety, his future, and his competence. He was able to say that he learned from his time in Iraq but will likely always have conflicting feelings about war in general.

The treatment produced a significant reduction in Mr. G's PTSD symptoms and in his depression and anxiety. Assessments were conducted before and immediately after therapy, and no follow-up assessments have been conducted to date, as the client recently completed PE. Mr. G's PTSD severity decreased by 70% from pre- to post-treatment. Comparable decreases in depression and anxiety were noted.

Toward the end of treatment, it became clear that the client's cannabis dependence was out of his control, and he decided to enroll in a 30-day rehabilitation program for his substance abuse after completing PE. He stated that he would not have been able to go to rehab if he had not engaged in PE for his PTSD and learned that he could face distressing memories and experience painful emotions. He indicated that he now felt he had the courage to tackle this problem. Although he believed that he no longer used marijuana to avoid his feelings, the cravings to use at night were too difficult for him to resist. Mr. G stated he would reach out to the center following rehab to complete follow-up measures and to discuss maintenance of his treatment gains.

Two months later, Mr. G reached out to the clinician for a follow-up visit. The client was able to successfully stop his cannabis use with the help of the drug and alcohol treatment facility. He stated that the work he did in his PE sessions helped him to realize that he was capable of feeling strong and uncomfortable emotions, which was important in his drug and alcohol treatment. He indicated that learning to tolerate both emotional and physical distress was crucial in his work at rehab, and the work of PE had given him measurable confidence in his ability to handle this discomfort. The client stated that he is now able to live his life enjoying the things that he used to enjoy and is excited about the next phase of his graduate education.

SUMMARY

As seen in Mr. G's and Ms. E's case examples—and through extensive research—PE is a potent treatment for PTSD. Through in vivo and imaginal exposures, PE helps clients face their trauma(s), process what happened to them, and return to normalcy. PE helped Ms. E and Mr. G overcome intrusive thoughts, avoidance, and flashbacks, and it can improve a variety of other, non-PTSD symptoms. It is important to remember that PE is shown to be effective for ameliorating the effects of a variety of traumas, not just combat or sexual assault. Finally, it has been used successfully with a wide range of populations and cultures (Asukai et al., 2010; Williams et al., 2014). In sum, PE is an effective cognitive behavior therapy that can be used for a wide range of traumas, symptoms, and people.

KEY POINTS

- PE is a cognitive behavior therapy consisting of 90-minute sessions once or twice a week. The sessions involve in vivo and imaginal exposures as well as processing of these experiences.

- The theory behind PE (i.e., EPT) suggests that clients with PTSD may have fear networks that activate more easily and intensely than those in clients without PTSD. PE addresses this by giving the client the opportunity to reengage with the trauma memory, thereby receiving corrective information.

- In vivo exposure hierarchies should focus on situations and activities that the client has been avoiding since the trauma.

- Imaginal exposures should be a complete story of the traumatic event; hot spots should focus on the currently most distressing part of the traumatic memory.

- PE can be used for a variety of trauma types and helps clients with a wide range of psychological symptoms, not just PTSD.

- PE has been used successfully with clients from diverse backgrounds, ages, and comorbidities.

REFERENCES

Asukai, N., Saito, A., Tsuruta, N., Kishimoto, J., & Nishikawa, T. (2010). Efficacy of exposure therapy for Japanese patients with posttraumatic stress disorder due to mixed traumatic events: A randomized controlled study. *Journal of Traumatic Stress, 23,* 744–750. http://dx.doi.org/10.1002/jts.20589

Berenz, E. C., Rowe, L., Schumacher, J. A., Stasiewicz, P. R., & Coffey, S. F. (2012). Prolonged exposure therapy for posttraumatic stress disorder among individuals in a residential substance use treatment program: A case series. *Professional Psychology: Research and Practice, 43,* 154–161. http://dx.doi.org/10.1037/a0026138

Cahill, S. P., & Foa, E. B. (2007). Psychological theories of PTSD. In M. J. Friedman, T. M. Keane, & P. A. Resick (Eds.), *Handbook of PTSD: Science and practice* (2nd ed., pp. 55–77). New York, NY: Guilford Press.

Cahill, S. P., Rauch, S. A., Hembree, E. A., & Foa, E. B. (2003). Effect of cognitive-behavioral treatments for PTSD on anger. *Journal of Cognitive Psychotherapy, 17,* 113–131. http://dx.doi.org/10.1891/jcop.17.2.113.57434

Feske, U. (2008). Treating low-income and minority women with posttraumatic stress disorder: A pilot study comparing prolonged exposure and treatment as usual conducted by community therapists. *Journal of Interpersonal Violence, 23,* 1027–1040. http://dx.doi.org/10.1177/0886260507313967

Foa, E. B., Asnaani, A., Rosenfield, D., Zandberg, L. J., Gariti, P., & Imms, P. (2017). Concurrent varenicline and prolonged exposure for patients with nicotine dependence and PTSD: A randomized controlled trial. *Journal of Consulting and Clinical Psychology, 85,* 862–872. http://dx.doi.org/10.1037/ccp0000213

Foa, E. B., & Cahill, S. P. (2001). Psychological therapies: Emotional processing. In N. J. Smelser & P. B. Bates (Eds.), *International encyclopedia of the social and behavioral sciences* (pp. 12363–12369). Oxford, England: Elsevier. http://dx.doi.org/10.1016/B0-08-043076-7/01338-3

Foa, E. B., Dancu, C. V., Hembree, E. A., Jaycox, L. H., Meadows, E. A., & Street, G. P. (1999). A comparison of exposure therapy, stress inoculation training, and their combination for reducing posttraumatic stress disorder in female assault victims. *Journal of Consulting and Clinical Psychology, 67,* 194–200. http://dx.doi.org/10.1037/0022-006X.67.2.194

Foa, E. B., Ehlers, A., Clark, D. M., Tolin, D. F., & Orsillo, S. M. (1999). The Posttraumatic Cognitions Inventory (PTCI): Development and validation. *Psychological Assessment, 11,* 303–314. http://dx.doi.org/10.1037/1040-3590.11.3.303

Foa, E. B., Hembree, E. A., Cahill, S. P., Rauch, S. A., Riggs, D. S., Feeny, N. C., & Yadin, E. (2005). Randomized trial of prolonged exposure for posttraumatic stress disorder with and without cognitive restructuring: Outcome at academic and community clinics. *Journal of Consulting and Clinical Psychology, 73*, 953–964. http://dx.doi.org/10.1037/0022-006X.73.5.953

Foa, E. B., Hembree, E. A., & Rothbaum, B. O. (2007). *Prolonged exposure therapy for PTSD: Emotional processing of traumatic experiences: Therapist guide.* New York, NY: Oxford University Press. http://dx.doi.org/10.1093/med:psych/9780195308501.001.0001

Foa, E. B., Huppert, J. D., & Cahill, S. P. (2006). Emotional processing theory: An update. In B. O. Rothbaum (Ed.), *Pathological anxiety: Emotional processing in etiology and treatment* (pp. 3–24). New York, NY: Guilford Press.

Foa, E. B., & Kozak, M. J. (1986). Emotional processing of fear: Exposure to corrective information. *Psychological Bulletin, 99*, 20–35. http://dx.doi.org/10.1037/0033-2909.99.1.20

Foa, E. B., McLean, C. P., Capaldi, S., & Rosenfield, D. (2013). Prolonged exposure vs. supportive counseling for sexual abuse-related PTSD in adolescent girls: A randomized clinical trial. *JAMA, 310*, 2650–2657. http://dx.doi.org/10.1001/jama.2013.282829

Foa, E. B., McLean, C. P., Zang, Y., Zhong, J., Powers, M. B., Kauffman, B. Y., . . . Knowles, K. (2016). Psychometric properties of the Posttraumatic Diagnostic Scale for *DSM–5* (PDS-5). *Psychological Assessment, 28*, 1166–1171. http://dx.doi.org/10.1037/pas0000258

Foa, E. B., McLean, C. P., Zang, Y., Zhong, J., Rauch, S., Porter, K., . . . Kauffman, B. Y. (2016). Psychometric properties of the Posttraumatic Stress Disorder Symptom Scale Interview for *DSM–5* (PSSI-5). *Psychological Assessment, 28*, 1159–1165. http://dx.doi.org/10.1037/pas0000259

Foa, E. B., & Rauch, S. A. M. (2004). Cognitive changes during prolonged exposure versus prolonged exposure plus cognitive restructuring in female assault survivors with posttraumatic stress disorder. *Journal of Consulting and Clinical Psychology, 72*, 879–884. http://dx.doi.org/10.1037/0022-006X.72.5.879

Foa, E. B., Steketee, G., & Rothbaum, B. O. (1989). Behavioral/cognitive conceptualizations of post-traumatic stress disorder. *Behavior Therapy, 20*, 155–176. http://dx.doi.org/10.1016/S0005-7894(89)80067-X

Foa, E. B., Yusko, D. A., McLean, C. P., Suvak, M. K., Bux, D. A., Jr., Oslin, D., . . . Volpicelli, J. (2013). Concurrent naltrexone and prolonged exposure therapy for patients with comorbid alcohol dependence and PTSD: A randomized clinical trial. *JAMA, 310*, 488–495. http://dx.doi.org/10.1001/jama.2013.8268

Harned, M. S., Korslund, K. E., & Linehan, M. M. (2014). A pilot randomized controlled trial of dialectical behavior therapy with and without the dialectical behavior therapy prolonged exposure protocol for suicidal and self-injuring women with borderline personality disorder and PTSD. *Behaviour Research and Therapy, 55*, 7–17. http://dx.doi.org/10.1016/j.brat.2014.01.008

Henslee, A. M., & Coffey, S. F. (2010). Exposure therapy for posttraumatic stress disorder in a residential substance use treatment facility. *Professional Psychology: Research and Practice, 41*, 34–40. http://dx.doi.org/10.1037/a0018235

McLean, C. P., & Foa, E. B. (2011). Prolonged exposure therapy for post-traumatic stress disorder: A review of evidence and dissemination. *Expert Review of Neurotherapeutics, 11*, 1151–1163. http://dx.doi.org/10.1586/ern.11.94

McLean, C. P., Su, Y. J., & Foa, E. B. (2015). Mechanisms of symptom reduction in a combined treatment for comorbid posttraumatic stress disorder and alcohol dependence. *Journal of Consulting and Clinical Psychology, 83*, 655–661. http://dx.doi.org/10.1037/ccp0000024

Nacasch, N., Foa, E. B., Huppert, J. D., Tzur, D., Fostick, L., Dinstein, Y., . . . Zohar, J. (2011). Prolonged exposure therapy for combat- and terror-related posttraumatic stress disorder: A randomized control comparison with treatment as usual. *The Journal of Clinical Psychiatry, 72*, 1174–1180. http://dx.doi.org/10.4088/JCP.09m05682blu

Pacella, M. L., Armelie, A., Boarts, J., Wagner, G., Jones, T., Feeny, N., & Delahanty, D. L. (2012). The impact of prolonged exposure on PTSD symptoms and associated psychopathology in people living with HIV: A randomized test of concept. *AIDS and Behavior, 16*, 1327–1340. http://dx.doi.org/10.1007/s10461-011-0076-y

Powers, M. B., Halpern, J. M., Ferenschak, M. P., Gillihan, S. J., & Foa, E. B. (2010). A meta-analytic review of prolonged exposure for posttraumatic stress disorder. *Clinical Psychology Review, 30*, 635–641. http://dx.doi.org/10.1016/j.cpr.2010.04.007

Reger, G. M., Koenen-Woods, P., Zetocha, K., Smolenski, D. J., Holloway, K. M., Rothbaum, B. O., . . . Gahm, G. A. (2016). Randomized controlled trial of prolonged exposure using imaginal exposure vs. virtual reality exposure in active duty soldiers with deployment-related posttraumatic stress disorder (PTSD). *Journal of Consulting and Clinical Psychology, 84*, 946–959. http://dx.doi.org/10.1037/ccp0000134

Resick, P. A., Nishith, P., Weaver, T. L., Astin, M. C., & Feuer, C. A. (2002). A comparison of cognitive-processing therapy with prolonged exposure and a waiting condition for the treatment of chronic posttraumatic stress disorder in female rape victims. *Journal of Consulting and Clinical Psychology, 70*, 867–879. http://dx.doi.org/10.1037/0022-006X.70.4.867

Resick, P. A., Williams, L. F., Suvak, M. K., Monson, C. M., & Gradus, J. L. (2012). Long-term outcomes of cognitive-behavioral treatments for posttraumatic stress disorder among female rape survivors. *Journal of Consulting and Clinical Psychology, 80*, 201–210. http://dx.doi.org/10.1037/a0026602

Rothbaum, B. O., Astin, M. C., & Marsteller, F. (2005). Prolonged exposure versus eye movement desensitization and reprocessing (EMDR) for PTSD rape victims. *Journal of Traumatic Stress, 18*, 607–616. http://dx.doi.org/10.1002/jts.20069

Schnurr, P. P., Friedman, M. J., Engel, C. C., Foa, E. B., Shea, M. T., Chow, B. K., . . . Bernardy, N. (2007). Cognitive behavioral therapy for posttraumatic stress disorder in women: A randomized controlled trial. *JAMA, 297*, 820–830. http://dx.doi.org/10.1001/jama.297.8.820

Sripada, R. K., Rauch, S. A., Tuerk, P. W., Smith, E., Defever, A. M., Mayer, R. A., . . . Venners, M. (2013). Mild traumatic brain injury and treatment response in prolonged exposure for PTSD. *Journal of Traumatic Stress, 26*, 369–375. http://dx.doi.org/10.1002/jts.21813

Tuerk, P. W., Yoder, M., Grubaugh, A., Myrick, H., Hamner, M., & Acierno, R. (2011). Prolonged exposure therapy for combat-related posttraumatic stress disorder: An examination of treatment effectiveness for veterans of the wars in Afghanistan and Iraq. *Journal of Anxiety Disorders, 25*, 397–403. http://dx.doi.org/10.1016/j.janxdis.2010.11.002

van den Berg, D. P. G., de Bont, P. A. J. M., van der Vleugel, B. M., de Roos, C., de Jongh, A., Van Minnen, A., & van der Gaag, M. (2015). Prolonged exposure vs eye movement desensitization and reprocessing vs waiting list for posttraumatic stress disorder in patients with a psychotic disorder: A randomized clinical trial. *JAMA Psychiatry, 72*, 259–267. http://dx.doi.org/10.1001/jamapsychiatry.2014.2637

van Minnen, A., Harned, M. S., Zoellner, L., & Mills, K. (2012). Examining potential contraindications for prolonged exposure therapy for PTSD. *European Journal of Psychotraumatology, 3*, 18805. http://dx.doi.org/10.3402/ejpt.v3i0.18805

Williams, M. T., Malcoun, E., Sawyer, B. A., Davis, D. M., Bahojb Nouri, L., & Bruce, S. L. (2014). Cultural adaptations of prolonged exposure therapy for treatment and prevention of posttraumatic stress disorder in African Americans. *Behavioral Sciences, 4*, 102–124. http://dx.doi.org/10.3390/bs4020102

Zalta, A. K., Gillihan, S. J., Fisher, A. J., Mintz, J., McLean, C. P., Yehuda, R., & Foa, E. B. (2014). Change in negative cognitions associated with PTSD predicts symptom reduction in prolonged exposure. *Journal of Consulting and Clinical Psychology, 82*, 171–175. http://dx.doi.org/10.1037/a0034735

7

Brief Eclectic Psychotherapy for PTSD

Berthold P. R. Gersons, Mirjam J. Nijdam, Geert E. Smid, and Marie-Louise Meewisse

Brief eclectic psychotherapy for PTSD (BEPP) is a 16-session, manualized treatment specially designed for the treatment of posttraumatic stress disorder (PTSD; Gersons, Meewisse, Nijdam, & Olff, 2011). When first developed in the 1980s and 1990s, BEPP was used and evaluated for treating police officers with PTSD in the Netherlands (Gersons, Carlier, Lamberts, & van der Kolk, 2000). When it proved to be effective in this population, the application of the treatment gradually broadened to other patient populations with PTSD and to other countries. The protocol was translated into several languages.[1] Further studies have demonstrated the treatment to be efficacious in patients with PTSD resulting from various trauma backgrounds (Lindauer et al., 2005; Schnyder, Müller, Maercker, & Wittmann, 2011) and have shown that the treatment is as effective as eye-movement desensitization and reprocessing therapy (EMDR) and has effect sizes similar to trauma-focused cognitive behavior therapy (CBT; Nijdam, Gersons, Reitsma, de Jongh, & Olff, 2012).

We gratefully acknowledge Anouk van Berlo and Marthe Hoofwijk for providing two of the case illustrations. All described cases have been disguised to protect the privacy of the individuals or had the oral or written agreement of the patients to use their treatment stories for education of colleagues.

[1]Dutch, English, German, Spanish, Italian, Polish, Lithuanian, Georgian, and Korean; all are available online (http://www.traumatreatment.eu).

http://dx.doi.org/10.1037/0000196-007
Casebook to the APA Clinical Practice Guideline for the Treatment of PTSD, edited by
L. F. Bufka, C. V. Wright, and R. W. Halfond

TREATMENT RATIONALE

What distinguishes BEPP from other trauma-focused treatments is that it focuses on the acknowledgment of the array of intense emotions that the person experiences in relation to the trauma. Its aim is for individuals to learn life-changing lessons from the trauma, rather than focusing only on symptom decrease. Moreover, in BEPP, trauma is often framed as a loss of trust in others or the loss of the belief that the world is a safe place. Such framing helps to understand how the traumatic experiences have shaped one's beliefs, and it will be the start of rebuilding realistic trust in the world and in others. BEPP is considered eclectic because it combines insights and interventions from cognitive-behavioral, grief, and psychodynamic approaches, including psychoeducation, imaginal exposure, writing letters and bringing memorabilia, making meaning of what has happened, and a farewell ritual (see Figure 7.1).

RESEARCH SUPPORT

BEPP can be applied and adapted for specific patient populations, and several studies have demonstrated its efficacy. Four randomized controlled trials (RCTs) have been conducted, three in the Netherlands and one in Switzerland. The first RCT (Gersons et al., 2000), conducted with 42 police officers, showed a significant difference between BEPP and a waiting-list control condition in favor of BEPP. The treatment had a large-sized effect on clinician-rated PTSD (Cohen's $d = 1.30$) and led to significant improvements in the return to work, agoraphobia, and self-reported symptoms, with no dropout from treatment.

FIGURE 7.1. Brief Eclectic Psychotherapy for PTSD

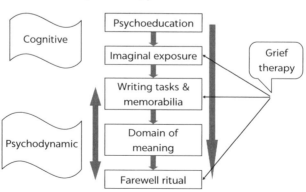

An overview of the combined theoretical orientations for Brief Eclectic Psychotherapy for PTSD. Data from Gersons, Carlier, Lamberts, and van der Kolk (2000).

Lindauer and colleagues (2005) conducted the second RCT with 24 patients from a psychiatric outpatient clinic; each had experienced interpersonal violence (including rape), accident, or disaster. The study showed a significant difference between the group who received BEPP and the group on the waiting list, with a large-sized treatment effect on clinician-assessed PTSD (Cohen's $d = 1.62$). Five patients dropped out of BEPP during the course of the trial. BEPP also led to significant decreases in general anxiety symptoms but not in depressive symptoms, sick leave, or problems in the relationship with a partner. In studies by Lindauer et al. (2008), after BEPP, individuals showed significant alterations in the right middle frontal gyrus, left superior temporal gyrus, and superior and middle frontal gyrus, brain regions associated with PTSD. Symptom decrease during BEPP was positively related to changes in the latter two areas.

Schnyder et al. (2011) did an RCT as an independent replication in a Swiss psychiatric outpatient clinic; they compared BEPP with a minimal attention intervention in 30 patients who enrolled in treatment after serious accidents, sexual and nonsexual assaults, war, disaster, and childhood trauma. Results indicated significant between-group differences on clinician-assessed PTSD, self-reported depressive and general anxiety symptoms, and posttraumatic growth. Treatment effects for all outcomes, except posttraumatic growth, were stable at 6-month follow-up.

The fourth RCT was a comparison of BEPP and EMDR in 140 patients of a psychiatric outpatient clinic; participants had experienced sexual or nonsexual assault, accidents, disaster, and war (Nijdam et al., 2012). More than half the patients from this culturally diverse sample had experienced previous traumatic experiences, and 19% met criteria for prolonged interpersonal trauma in their youth. BEPP and EMDR were found to be equally effective in this trial, but the speed of change was different. EMDR led to a faster drop in symptoms as compared with BEPP, which resulted in more gradual symptom decrease. Large-sized effects were found for both self-reported PTSD (Cohen's $d = 1.55$ for BEPP) and clinician-rated PTSD (Cohen's $d = 1.95$ for BEPP). Dropout rates for the treatments were not significantly different (i.e., around 30%). Large-sized effects on self-reported depressive and general anxiety symptoms were found for both treatments, along with small- to medium-sized effects on measures of neuropsychological functioning (Nijdam, Martens, Reitsma, Gersons, & Olff, 2018). Medium- to large-sized effects on posttraumatic growth were found for BEPP and EMDR (Nijdam, van der Meer, et al., 2018). Positive effects on comorbid disorders were shown as well.

In summary, research shows that BEPP is efficacious in the treatment of PTSD and comorbidity, and BEPP has been recommended in several treatment guidelines and books on evidence-based treatments (American Psychological Association, 2017; National Institute for Health and Care Excellence, 2005; Schnyder & Cloitre, 2015).

SPECIAL TOPICS

Differences Between BEPP and Other Trauma-Focused Treatments

Systematic reviews show similar efficacy and dropout rates for trauma-focused treatments (e.g., Bradley, Greene, Russ, Dutra, & Westen, 2005; Cusack et al., 2016). The diversity of symptoms and patient preferences among individuals who have experienced trauma suggests tailoring of treatment is necessary (Cloitre, 2015). Although the efficacy of CBT is most clearly documented by the largest number of RCTs, all trauma-focused approaches have specific merits and limitations. Eight founders of specific evidence-based treatments for PTSD (Schnyder et al., 2015) agreed that the commonalities among the many trauma-focused treatments are much greater than the differences. However, BEPP has some specific differences in comparison to other evidence-based treatments for PTSD, and these can be helpful in deciding on treatment to best meet patients' needs.

An important focus of BEPP is the much wider interest in the patient's lifespan, which is also seen in narrative exposure therapy (NET). Whereas in NET the focus is specifically on positive and negative events, the focus in BEPP is on lessons learned during the lifespan that relate to views on trauma, expectancies of others, and self-image. In the meaning and integration phase of the treatment, BEPP focuses on the significance of the trauma in the context of earlier life experiences. Intense emotions are not to be dissolved as quickly as possible in BEPP because they reflect how the person has been moved or affected by the traumatic event. Emotions other than fear (e.g., grief, helplessness, anger, guilt, regret, self-blame, self-compassion, shame) are also important. Acknowledgment of the full emotional sequelae of traumatic events is essential. It is comparable with the process of mourning after the loss of a loved one. It takes time to process the trauma, its significance, and the connected range of strong emotions.

BEPP originates from a background in which grief, mourning, and attachment (Bowlby, 1980; Parkes, 1972) and neoanalytic theory (Horowitz, 1986) are important. Central in BEPP is the notion that emotions such as sorrow and anger are part and parcel of adapting from the life before trauma to the life after trauma. The events need to be processed—as with mourning, a person needs to feel emotions to understand their impact before being able to leave the event behind and focus again on the future.

Imaginal exposure in BEPP consists of a detailed sensory and emotional revisiting of consecutive parts of the trauma story over the course of several sessions. As imaginal exposure in BEPP is meant not for diminishing anxiety but for experiencing and expressing emotions, it is not repeated to achieve habituation. The primary aim is to fully experience, in the here and now, the grief and sadness over what has happened in the past.

BEPP exposure, exposure in CBT, and returning to a target image in EMDR all result in symptom reduction. However, the path toward that outcome is clearly different. In CBT and EMDR, patients experience relief that the story is not so vivid, frightening, or distressing anymore. In BEPP, the distress or fear is seen as a secondary emotion, that is, as fear of other emotions such as grief, shame, or anger. Often those who study BEPP call it an "exposure of feelings." After a slow discharge of these emotions, fear diminishes and self-compassion develops. Patients experience a deep satisfaction of having "mourned" what happened.

Both BEPP and NET use exposure and have the goal of integrating traumatic events into the personal life history of patients. NET has been developed in Africa for populations living with ongoing trauma and in areas where war, rape, killings, armed raids, and burning of villages commonly occur. NET, therefore, focuses much more on surviving and building resilience by systematically paying attention to and making a written report of all major good and bad experiences in someone's life (Schauer, Neuner, & Elbert, 2012). The intended result is to integrate all relevant life experiences in a balanced life view, which we also see as an important objective in BEPP.

In various trauma-focused treatments such as cognitive processing therapy and NET, writing about traumatic experiences takes place to aid the processing of the trauma. In BEPP, writing assignments are used to let the patient express suppressed emotions and intentions as well as unmet needs. Usually, patients write letters to the people they feel are responsible for the trauma or to those who let them down in the aftermath. Frequently, patients express their anger; following the loss of a loved one, they may express regret and take the opportunity to say what they were not able to say during life. Drawing can also be helpful for these purposes. As in NET, the writing in BEPP gives insight to one's life and the personal aspects of someone's experiences. It also enables a better understanding between therapist and patient. Some treatments for PTSD focus specifically on diminishing certain symptoms, such as unrealistic expectations, negative cognitions, excessive fear, or vividness of intrusions. The focus of BEPP is not only to reduce symptoms but also to acknowledge the difficult period one has experienced, accept emotions, express oneself, and develop self-compassion and self-acceptance.

In contrast to other trauma therapies, in BEPP the partner or someone close to the patient is involved in the treatment. They participate at the start in the psychoeducation session, and often during this phase they are invited to participate in a session to evaluate the patient's progress. Patients are actively encouraged to let loved ones participate in their farewell rituals.

BEPP in Different Populations

BEPP is extensively used for the treatment of PTSD in police officers (Gersons, Meewisse, & Nijdam, 2015; Smid, van der Meer, Olff, & Nijdam, 2018) and other first responders. The detailed case illustration of the BEPP treatment of a paramedic, later in this chapter, shows its applicability with this population. Other patient groups in which BEPP has been applied include refugees, veterans, patients with complex trauma, and patients with traumatic grief (i.e., comorbid PTSD and persistent complex bereavement disorder [PCBD] following the loss of a loved one under violent circumstances). BEPP has been used with men and women as well as with people of different nationalities and across a range of ages; however, systematic analyses comparing various groups have not been conducted. BEPP has been applied in many clinical settings (e.g., inpatient, day clinic, outpatient and ambulatory settings, private practice) in many countries.

The BEPP framework allows integration of grief-focused exposure techniques, resulting in a treatment known as brief eclectic psychotherapy for traumatic grief (BEP-TG; Smid et al., 2015). The loss of loved ones may lead to separation distress, comprising feelings of yearning and longing for the deceased, preoccupation with the deceased person or the circumstances of the death, emotional pain, guilt, anger, and distrust (Boelen & Smid, 2017). Losses of loved ones may therefore lead to manifestations of psychopathology other than PTSD. PCBD is a disorder of grief newly included in the "Emerging Measures and Models" section of the fifth edition of the *Diagnostic and Statistical Manual of Mental Disorders* (*DSM–5*; American Psychiatric Association, 2013). Prolonged grief disorder (PGD) is a disorder with similar symptoms, recently included in the 11th edition of the International Classification of Diseases (ICD-11; Boelen & Smid, 2017). Per *DSM–5*, nonviolent or nonaccidental losses of loved ones do not qualify as traumatic events potentially leading to PTSD. This highlights the need for clinicians to focus diagnostic assessments on grief symptoms consistent with PCBD and PGD and to consider specifically targeting grief-related psychopathology in the presence of these diagnoses. The feasibility of BEP-TG as part of a 1-year treatment program for patients with extreme PTSD as well as PCBD or PGD following multiple and traumatic losses has recently been documented (de Heus et al., 2017).

Competencies to Practice BEPP

The focus on the intense emotions originating from the traumatic experience is the most important ingredient of BEPP treatment. Therefore, a therapist must be able to win the patient's trust to "travel back together" to the traumatic events and often to review gruesome details. BEPP therapists need to be compassionate and good listeners as they pinpoint painful aspects without rushing the patient's story. Often, beginning therapists feel pressure to reach goals in the treatment rather than trusting the patient's pace.

The attitude and tasks of the therapist will be different during the various modules of BEPP. In the psychoeducation sessions, the therapist's attitude resembles the attitude of a teacher. The therapist starts by welcoming the patient and his or her partner or friend. The therapist then explains that the goal of this session is for the patient and the partner to understand how the traumatic event has caused the development of the PTSD symptoms, why symptoms did not resolve naturally, and how BEPP treatment is organized to regain control, diminish the symptoms, and find meaning. The therapist is in an active mode and shows his or her expertise regarding the development of symptoms and dysfunction as a result of experiencing a trauma.

The therapist starts the following session by again explaining the goal of imaginal exposure as a way of going through the traumatic story to feel past and current emotions related to the traumatic event. During imaginal exposure, the role of the therapist changes from an explanatory one to that of a compassionate and active listener. The therapist should nonverbally show patience, interest, and comfort. It is key to pinpoint *hot spots* (i.e., the moments of the traumatic event with the greatest emotional impact) and to slow down the pace, without saying more than necessary, as this might distract the patient's attention.

When therapists have difficulty tolerating the intensity of imaginal exposure, various avoidance mechanisms and barriers can occur. The simplest one is just to keep talking about other important issues and "forget" to start the exposure. Sometimes the patient is afraid of the exposure and, consciously or not, continues to share other important concerns with the therapist, thus avoiding the intense exposure. Patients usually are sensitive to the therapist's reactions and will observe if the therapist is able to handle their emotions. When a therapist isn't able to regulate their own emotions, becomes frightened, or starts to sweat or cry, the patient may stop and may feel guilty for burdening the therapist. On the other hand, if a therapist has a blank face and shows no compassion, it can be difficult for something therapeutic to happen. Patient and therapist may go through the whole story with courage but with little release of emotions. The therapist must strike the balance between emotionally empathizing with the patient and the story and being overwhelmed by his or her own reaction.

The next phase is called *domain of meaning*. In this phase, the treatment is no longer focused on a reduction of symptoms but rather is focused on meaning. The patient is able to learn from the devastating experiences to go on with life. The often-used slogan to describe this phase is "becoming sadder but wiser." During the domain of meaning phase, the approach is slightly different from the exposure phase. The traumatic event itself is now in the background. The focus is on how one's view of the world and of oneself has been changed by the traumatic experience. In the domain of meaning phase, it is important for the therapist to listen as the patient looks back at how the event has influenced his or her life. The personal history is always important in how the event affects one's ideas, thoughts, and activities.

In BEPP, the therapist is interested in how the patient's history, childhood experiences with love and trust, and any experiences of abuse and violence form the basis for how the patient reacts to a traumatic event and how it changes the patient's view of self and of the world. However, the here and now (i.e., the reality of work, income, house, family, relations) is also part of the discussions in the sessions because all these important aspects of life are often affected by the trauma.

Planning the farewell ritual requires the therapist to think creatively, together with the patient and partner. In the BEPP treatment, emotional stories are shared; often these stories have not been told to anyone before. This experience creates a strong positive bond between patient and therapist. The farewell ritual aims to help the patient leave the therapist and the traumatic story behind, and it also helps the therapist to end the treatment and let the patient leave therapy. The farewell ritual, therefore, is an event for the patient with relatives or friends, without the therapist. To make the farewell ritual work, creative thinking is needed. For example, a patient wanted to burn photos of his traumatic event on his barbecue together with his family. If he were to do this, he would associate his barbecue with the traumatic event. The therapist suggested finding an alternative outside the home for the ritual. The patient was responsive to this suggestion and decided to go to a beach, dig a hole with his children, and burn the photos. After burning the photos, he would play with the children on the beach. Another well-chosen farewell ritual was conducted by a woman who lost a child during delivery. She wrote a letter to the baby, then she went with her husband and their two other children to the woods, tied the letter to a balloon, and released the balloon. Afterward, they picnicked in the woods to celebrate the end of the treatment with a good result. The therapist's limited contribution was explaining the value of a farewell ritual and giving some examples.

To become a BEPP therapist, it is essential to participate in clinical training to become a psychotherapist. It is helpful when the therapist received training in different schools of psychotherapy, such as CBT, psychodynamic psycho-therapy, and family therapy. Therapists with this background can then partici-pate in a two-and-a-half day BEPP training program in a group of eight to 15 participants, with a follow-up training session 6 months later. The ratio-nale of each intervention in the BEPP protocol is explained and illustrated with video material of real-life BEPP therapy sessions, and participants practice with role-playing. Participants are motivated to apply BEPP and bring video clips of the sessions for feedback. A short written exam is also part of the training. Individual or group supervision, available in person or via videoconferencing, is necessary to become an experienced BEPP therapist.

Future Developments

In previous studies, several treatment outcome predictors have been identified for BEPP. Future studies either to replicate or to contrast these findings would be most welcome, as treatment predictors sometimes vary in different patient groups and depend on the outcome measure used. Predictors have been found in several domains, including treatment-related variables, neuropsychological performance, and neuroendocrine functioning. Nijdam, de Vries, Gersons, and Olff (2015) found that pretreatment verbal memory performance is an important predictor of treatment success in BEPP. The more difficulty patients have with learning and retrieving verbal information, the more limited the symptom reduction is during treatment. Compared to unsuccessful treatments, successful BEPP treatments are characterized by more frequent revisiting of hot spots and more hot spot characteristics (such as an audible change in affect; Nijdam, Baas, Olff, & Gersons, 2013). A more sensitive neuroendocrine stress system, measured by the body's response to a small amount of dexamethasone, seems an important predictor for PTSD symptom decrease in BEPP treatment as well (Nijdam, van Amsterdam, Gersons, & Olff, 2015). Police officers who reported experiencing more injury and maltreatment events and more private traumatic events showed larger PTSD symptom reduction during BEPP (Smid et al., 2018). In contrast, police officers with more losses of loved ones showed a more limited PTSD symptom decrease over the course of BEPP.

In addition, further studies into the efficacy of BEPP in various patient groups are warranted (e.g., patients with prolonged childhood trauma, refugees, patients with a combination of PTSD and persistent complex bereavement disorder). One direction is the development of a BEPP treatment protocol specifically for children (8–12 years) and adolescents (12–18 years). Although the protocol is still being developed (de Kok, Roland, Knipschild, & Nijdam, 2018), parents and children both play important roles. We propose that parents and young children begin the psychoeducation session together and that they start and end the exposure sessions together. We are constructing a workbook with drawings for the children to do homework assignments guided by cartoon images. For adolescents, involvement of same-age peers is especially important in the patient's treatment. We are planning a digital workbook for adolescents to work on important aspects of letter writing and meaning making. After the development of the treatment protocol and workbooks, we plan to pilot test the treatment in this target population.

DESCRIPTION OF TREATMENT COMPONENTS

Psychoeducation

BEPP starts with psychoeducation about the origins of the symptoms and the rationale of the treatment. The aim of the psychoeducation session is to help the patient understand why the PTSD symptoms occur and to learn about what the treatment entails. Insights from neurobiological research in PTSD, such as the bodily response to danger and threat, are explained to the patient in a comprehensive way. The therapist illustrates how these response patterns persist when one develops avoidant strategies to ease discomfort and fears rejection of important others at a time that one needs social support. Fight and flight responses are automatically initiated by the brain when an individual is confronted with danger. Pathways in the brain are activated to assess danger (LeDoux, 1996), and information about external stimuli, such as sounds and smells, reach the amygdala very fast. The amygdala functions like an alarm center, from which responses such as fleeing or fighting are rapidly initiated in case of danger. A much more precise but much slower cortical pathway involving the prefrontal cortex gives a clearer picture of whether the situation is dangerous and which response should be given. When a person experiences a traumatic event, limbic structures such as the amygdala are thought to be excessively activated, whereas emotion regulation through the prefrontal cortex is insufficiently activated. If this system is not properly reset because the patient experiences continuous avoidant reactions, a prolonged sense of danger may result, and initial PTSD symptoms will be maintained. With this information, psychoeducation serves as a first step in regaining control.

Case Example

A woman from Afghanistan[2] fled the country with her husband and children because her brother had been killed in front of their house. In addition to this traumatic event, she had experienced the many wars the country had faced over past decades. She started to suffer from PTSD symptoms after she found her deceased brother. She came in for the psychoeducation session with her husband. Both of them understood for the first time how her irritability and sleeping problems originated from a constant sense of being in danger, resulting from the traumatic events she had experienced in Afghanistan. At the end of the session, a sense of trust in the therapist was established as a result of these explanations.

Imaginal Exposure, Memorabilia, and Letter Writing

When someone experiences a traumatic event such as a disaster, terrorist attack, sexual assault, or sudden loss of a loved one, she or he experiences a variety of emotions. These emotions and the symptoms that may or may not arise, including stages of healthy and pathological processing, were described in detail by Horowitz (1986), who has informed the BEPP approach. Horowitz's central hypothesis was that the ability to tolerate extreme emotions is the key to healthy processing of a trauma. When a person suppresses emotions, panic and exhaustion disrupt his or her daily life. If the suppression goes on, it will lead to strong avoidance and eventually to more chronic psychosomatic, psychological, and social withdrawal responses. The person needs to integrate the new information inherent in the traumatic event on the one hand; on the other hand, the person wards off the information because it provokes a high emotional response. This, according to Horowitz, leads to the repetitive alternation between reexperiencing and avoidance.

In BEPP, it is essential to address the trauma story fully and in detail, letting out the sadness, anger, and grief about what has happened. Accepting that trauma brings about intense emotions is the core of the imaginal exposure in BEPP; it restarts healthy processing of what has happened. The discharge of emotions also reduces anxiety in the present, as the trauma can be placed more in the past. An element that helps to make the imaginal exposure vivid is

---

[2]This case example is a composite sketch of clients we have seen.

that the person is asked to bring memorabilia, objects that are strong emotional reminders of the traumatic event.

One intense emotion connected to trauma is anger, which can be suppressed or misplaced and acted out in daily life—constantly being angry at everything and everyone. Anger is addressed in BEPP by writing a letter to someone or to an organization the person sees as responsible for the trauma. The letter is an uncensored one that is not meant to be sent but gives room to the intense emotion and leads it back to its origin. If the mourning of lost persons is coupled with the traumatic event, the letter is often written to the deceased person to express what the client did not have the opportunity to convey.

Case Example

When enrolling for treatment, a young veteran with PTSD[3] was not sure to which event(s) his symptoms were related. His complaints of nightmares and physical reactions to reminders of deployment appeared to be related to an incident with an improvised explosive device (IED) during his mission in Afghanistan: His best friend was killed when their vehicle drove over the IED. This incident was the focus of the imaginal exposure, and he felt deep sadness over the friend he lost. He wrote a letter to his friend to express his feelings of powerlessness and his feelings that he had not been able to do something about it. At the end of the treatment, he went to the graveyard together with his wife and placed the letter on his friend's grave.

Meaning Making and Farewell Ritual

After the imaginal exposure and letter writing, symptoms of PTSD typically decrease, and the person often notices increased capacity to deliberately process the event(s) that happened and to concentrate on daily life. Many people expect that they will be the same person after they have recovered from a traumatic event, but crisis theory importantly illustrates how a person can change in response to life events or crises (Caplan, 1961). Traumatic events imply a loss of control over what happens to someone in life. Cognitive assumptions about the world as safe, people as trustworthy, and the idea that "bad things happen to other people, not to me" are shattered and prove to be an illusion (Janoff-Bulman, 1992). The world itself has not changed, but the person views the world and other people with a different perspective.

It is an enormous challenge for the person to cope with these changed expectations and the accompanying emotions. Some people do not really leave behind the belief that they are unable to return to their old selves, and the negative changes resulting from the trauma and its aftermath are most prominent, resulting in a decreased level of functioning. For others, the positive changes that result from the struggle with trauma lead to an increased appreciation for life even though it is fragile and can take unexpected turns, possibly

---

[3]This case example is a composite sketch of clients we have seen.

resulting in greater well-being (Helgeson, Reynolds, & Tomich, 2006) and better health (Barskova & Oesterreich, 2009). This outcome is termed *posttraumatic growth* (Tedeschi, Park, & Calhoun, 1998). These positive and negative changes in a person's views about the world after the trauma are extensively discussed during the meaning-making phase of BEPP (Gersons & Schnyder, 2013). The objective of this phase of treatment is to obtain a new equilibrium in how the individual relates to himself or herself, others, the world, and the future.

A common phenomenon at the end of various trauma treatments is that individuals find it difficult, after a period of disturbed life, to say goodbye to the therapist by whom they felt so acknowledged. To help people leave behind the disturbed or interrupted period of life that was greatly influenced by the trauma, therapy ends with a *farewell ritual* (Gersons, 1988). This is a symbolic way to go on after trauma and, together with family or other important people, to celebrate fully participating in life again. This ritual serves to mark a new start in life.

Case Example

A man living in the Netherlands[4] suffered from PTSD symptoms after he had witnessed his mother being killed by a bomb attack in their native Iraq. He had been reluctant to go back to the country to see his relatives and the spot where the bombing had taken place because he was concerned about what it would do to him. After he had talked through the bomb attack in great detail in the imaginal exposure and had experienced, during treatment, the physical pain in his chest and sadness about the loss of his mother, he went on vacation to Iraq with his wife and children and was able to enjoy connecting with his relatives. He went back to the place of the bombing and the grave of his mother feeling sad but also relieved that he had been able to do it.

CASE ILLUSTRATION: MR. D

History

Mr. D[5] is a young paramedic. In 2005, after taking a patient to a general hospital, his ambulance coincidentally passed a meadow along the highway where a large passenger aircraft had just crashed. This airplane had landed on the meadow instead of the landing strip and had broken into two parts. Mr. D and his colleague, the driver, halted the ambulance near the highway, and he went toward the plane in the meadow. First, he looked through the window into the cockpit. He could see that the three pilots were dead. Through other windows, he saw that many people were unconscious or dead. He had the impression that one man was waving to him, but at that moment he was unable to enter the plane. When more rescue workers had reached the disaster

---

[4]This case example is a composite sketch of clients we have seen.
[5]This case illustration is a composite sketch of clients we have seen.

area, he was the first one who entered the plane. He saw dead people, including the man who had waved at him; the man's head was now hanging down, as he had since died. Other ambulance colleagues, in the beginning, refused to go into the plane because they did not want to be confronted by the dreadful images. Speaking about this part of the story made Mr. D cry, and his body trembled as he recalled the images of dead people, the moaning of sufferers, and the otherwise strange silence surrounding this catastrophe.

This event coincided with threatening experiences he and his partner underwent. A stone was thrown through a window of their home, and the tires of their car were punctured. The sickness of a friend and a conflict with his boss were also important stressors. Although Mr. D had been experiencing conflict with his boss for some time, he did not understand why this conflict was occurring.

Some months after the plane crash, Mr. D started to suffer from a tense abdomen, heart palpitations, tiredness, being easily irritated, and being forgetful. He experienced recurrent distressing intrusions of entering the plane during the daytime and in nightmares. He stayed at home more and more, afraid to go out, and he had suicidal thoughts. His affect was diminished, and he had unexpected startle reactions.

Referral

Mr. D went to the occupational physician who, in consultation with Mr. D's general practitioner, referred Mr. D to a specialized trauma treatment center. He was diagnosed with PTSD complicated by other psychosocial problems, and it was recommended that he participate in BEPP.

Treatment

In the first session, Mr. D, with his partner present, was invited to tell again, briefly, his distressing experiences at the plane crash and with the people he saw in the plane. He was also invited to describe the threatening experiences. After he described the traumatic event and the circumstances around it, he was asked to describe the symptoms he was suffering from. The therapist explained how these symptoms were connected with the traumatic experiences.

Typically in BEPP, the therapist explains that the memory of such drastic events is very precise and impressive, in contrast to memories from ordinary moments in our life, which fade away much more easily. The traumatic memories are so strong and intrusive because they relate to danger and death and are important for survival. In PTSD, the memory of the traumatic event has all the details and even the smells as if it just happened, as if it were yesterday. The intensity of the memories instills much fear in the person and often evokes the feeling that the event will happen again. In the psychoeducation session, this fear is described as mostly irrational—it feels as if it will happen again, but that is very unlikely. The brain is kept in a state of alarm without the need to still be alarmed. In the BEPP model, the person fears the strong emotions, such as sadness and anger, that are connected to the traumatic event. To get relief from these strong emotions, it helps to go back in memory to the traumatic events. This is the imaginal exposure process in BEPP; it is not a pleasurable experience but is an essential one to let the suppressed sorrow and pain come out. Feeling once again how awful the experience was helps the person to develop self-compassion instead of self-blame. The therapist illustrates how the state of alarm makes it difficult to concentrate on ordinary daily tasks and how it may result in quick irritation. After this phase of the treatment, the person is told that the symptoms of PTSD will diminish.

In BEPP, after the connection is made between the symptoms and the traumatic experiences, the therapist explains the different aspects of the treatment as part of the psychoeducation session. The imaginal exposure in the next sessions is necessary to express the emotions until the tension and fear disappears. Bringing memorabilia of the event, such as photos of the crashed plane and newspaper articles, is essential to relive the traumatic event in its fullness. Writing letters allows the patient to express suppressed anger toward people or organizations that the person blames for the traumatic event.

Mr. D responded to these explanations with much agreement. He was looking forward to the next sessions; he was looking forward to writing an angry letter to the perpetrators who had threatened him and his partner and who had thrown a stone through his window and another angry letter to his boss, with whom he had ongoing work conflict. In BEPP, the letters are not meant to be sent but are used to discharge the intense emotions.

The treatment continued with the domain of meaning phase. The therapist explained that traumatic experiences not only lead to fear, sorrow, and anger but also confront us with the frailty of life and often of our personal life. How do we experience the world and ourselves after such crucial experiences? Do we still trust others? People often experience that life is not guaranteed but a treasure to be aware of and to take care of.

At the end of the psychoeducation session, the partner was asked to tell his part of the story, describing how things had changed and why life is more difficult for both of them. Mr. D had tears in his eyes but was also thankful because he and his partner now understood how the experiences had affected their lives. He expressed that he was looking forward to the next session.

The next session was the first imaginal exposure. The imaginal exposure sessions always take place without the partner. The therapist explained the goal of the exposure again: to access the strong emotions of sorrow and anger and to let these come out. Mr. D was instructed to start with a short relaxation exercise aimed at facilitating his focus on the memories of the traumatic event. In BEPP, exposure is not limited to selected images of the event but concerns a slow imaginal revisiting of the traumatic experiences from beginning to end, in parts over several sessions. This is done in the present tense and in the first person, with the eyes closed. The exposure is successful when the tears or intense feelings of sadness or anger have been expressed. These intense emotions are connected to the hot spots of the traumatic event, which are the worst moments experienced by the person.

Mr. D started the exposure by telling how he and his driver had just left the general hospital where they had taken a patient. They are in a good mood on their way to return to their station. He looks out of the window and sees a huge airplane in the grass. When he told this, he became tense in his chair and pressed his hands on the armrests. He returned to his memory and described getting out of the ambulance and walking into the meadow and seeing the broken plane with no other persons present at that moment. He looks through a window and totally forgets that getting so close to the broken plane can be dangerous because of the risk of explosions. Looking in the cockpit, he sees the dead pilots. Through another window, he sees blood on the window and someone waving at him. Mr. D then became extremely sad and opened his eyes, marking the end of the first exposure session. It is typical during BEPP exposure that the person remembers new details while going over the event so slowly, just as Mr. D remembered the blood on the window. After he opened his eyes, he and the therapist discussed the exposure, and Mr. D was informed about the agenda for the next session. He left this session very tired but also happy about having cried about the event.

In the next session, Mr. D. and the therapist discussed the first exposure. Mr. D reported that he suffered from a headache and felt extremely sad afterward. The therapist explained that accessing this feeling of sadness was the aim of the exposure. Mr. D said he now could tolerate how sad this experience was for him, but he also told the therapist that he was happy he could tell and reexperience what happened and that he felt a bit relieved after having cried.

In the second exposure session, Mr. D started at the moment that more rescue workers arrive at the disaster site. The front door is opened, and he is the first one who enters the plane. He sees the man who waved to him now with his head hanging, dead. He started to sob when he told this memory. He also reported the picture of a flight attendant who lost her feet. The memory of the strange smell in the plane and the moaning of people came back. Again, Mr. D was experiencing strong emotions. After Mr. D opened his eyes at the end of the exposure session, the therapist suggested that Mr. D's intention to enter the wrecked plane as soon as possible was prompted by a desire to rescue the man who waved to him. Mr. D agreed with this viewpoint. Discussing the letter-writing part of the treatment, he decided that he wanted to write a farewell letter to this man. Writing angry letters was also discussed, and Mr. D was asked to look for memorabilia of the plane crash to bring along to the next session.

In the third exposure session, Mr. D described how he, together with other rescue workers and medical personnel, brought out passengers who were in very bad conditions, with broken legs and bones sticking out. As he told this, he was notably still impressed by the memories but not so sad and tense. He had written a letter to the man who waved to him and later died. In this letter, he expressed how sorry he felt for this man and his sorrow that he could not open the door to enter and rescue him. Perhaps the man could have survived the crash if this had been possible. While discussing this letter, he realized how fragile life can be. This man was just a passenger and because of a wrong landing of the plane, he died.

The fourth exposure session was devoted to describing Mr. D's departure from the disaster site to go to his workstation and then home. He is exhausted when he comes home, but it is still very difficult to sleep. He had brought newspaper articles about the crash to the session, along with angry letters he had written, at home between sessions, to the offenders who had threatened him and his partner and to his boss. During the session, the therapist encouraged him to read these letters out loud and feel how angry he was.

By the fifth session, the exposure part of the treatment ended because Mr. D felt no need to go back to the traumatic experience and said he was sleeping well without having nightmares. Treatment naturally transitioned to the domain of meaning phase, in which patients start to focus on the sequelae of the traumatic event for their sense of self and often for how it relates to their childhood experiences; in this phase they focus less on their emotions. Mr. D became interested in the fact that he neglected the serious danger of explosion when approaching the plane; before treatment, he never thought about this aspect of the event. In the sessions, he realized that choosing his profession as a paramedic on an ambulance was connected with his desire to want to help other people as much as possible, regardless of possible harm to himself. He realized that thankfulness from the people he helped was what he most desired. He now understood why he often spent more time than other paramedics attending to the families of patients. His boss criticized him for these delays, which resulted in conflict. He described how, in his childhood, he had longed for more appreciation from his parents and brother. Coming out as gay as an adult led to less appreciation from his family. His heterosexual brother became the favorite son, and he felt not much more than tolerated. He realized how helping others in his work was motivated partly to compensate for what he lacked from his family.

As this phase of treatment ended, he felt much more capable of fighting for his job, as his boss wanted to fire him. Looking back at his actions related to the crashed plane, he realized how much he had neglected his own safety and his own reactions to such a disastrous event. He reflected on the fact that in many other work situations he paid attention only to what was needed for patients. He did not realize what these events meant for himself or how emotional it often was. With more appreciation of his own emotions, he realized he wanted to pay much more attention to his own safety and his emotions and to avoid "hero behavior" in work situations. This new understanding and self-compassion helped him approach his boss to resolve their conflicts.

One of the last sessions took place together with his partner again. The results of the treatment were discussed and also confirmed by the partner. They were both happy that Mr. D no longer had nightmares and that he felt really relieved. The therapist explained that the farewell ritual was a means to end the treatment, to leave behind the trauma and to return to one's usual life again. The first action in a farewell ritual is emotional, letting things go, and the next step is the positive celebration of ending the treatment. Its intention is to ritually leave behind the traumatic event and its effect on the person, to step into the here and now, and to face the future in a positive way. They decided to plan a farewell ritual to burn the angry letters and to celebrate with a dinner, marking that they had left behind the PTSD and the sad events.

Half a year later, Mr. D returned to the therapist for an evaluation session. He noted that he was satisfied with his job as a paramedic and now was also taking care of his own reactions and limitations. He spoke about the plane crash with emotion but did not have PTSD symptoms anymore. This was also confirmed by the routine independent evaluation at the treatment institute where the therapist was employed.

CASE ILLUSTRATION: MR. M

This case illustrates the application of BEP-TG with a military veteran. Mr. M[6] is a 55-year-old Dutch military veteran who is married and the father of two children. During his first mission abroad (when he was 17 years old), he experienced many traumatic events and lost one of his closest comrades on site because of an accident. He first came to treatment 33 years later. He suffered from intrusive memories of his deployment experiences, his sleep was disrupted, and he couldn't stand loud noises. His wife reported sudden outbursts of anger. Mr. M obsessively kept himself busy and drank too much alcohol. Mr. M was diagnosed with PTSD, and several trauma-focused treatments were tried, but they had limited effects. As treatment proceeded, it became clear that the loss of his comrade on site was still causing the most symptoms. Mr. M experienced frequent moments of intense grief over the loss but could not bear the emotions that came along with this. A diagnosis of PCBD was made in addition to PTSD, and Mr. M was referred for treatment with BEP-TG. At the beginning of treatment, Mr. M brought his wife along, and the therapist shared information about his symptoms as well as about the treatment ahead. After the initial session, Mr. M began disclosing personal information about the trauma to his friends and family.

During therapy, he talked about his meaningful friendship with his comrade and another young man during training and deployment. While this evoked

---

[6]We gratefully acknowledge Marthe Hoofwijk for providing the case illustration. Permission to use this case illustration was granted by the client and is on file.

some feelings of sadness, avoidance persisted in other behavioral areas. Mr. M hadn't visited his comrade's grave and had avoided his own father's grave for years. Therapy was then focused on being able to visit the grave-yard and tolerating the associated emotions. A 7-point anxiety hierarchy was made: The bottom three steps involved visiting his father's grave, and the top four steps involved visiting his comrade's grave. Mr. M's initial approach was to work through the steps quickly to avoid his feelings, the way he usually did outside of therapy. After this tendency was identified and discussed in therapy, he had the nerve to slow down and allow his emotions to emerge.

When visiting his comrade's grave for the first time in 35 years, he felt overwhelmed with sadness, even with his wife present. Both the visit and his ability to access his emotions felt like great victories to him, although he wondered why this loss had hit him so hard. Mr. M started writing a letter to his deceased comrade. Reading it out loud during therapy sessions evoked deep feelings of sadness, which he was able to tolerate and release because he felt safe enough to do so with the therapist.

In the final phase of treatment, Mr. M decided to arrange a small ceremony at his comrade's grave as a farewell ritual. His plan was to gather some close others at the cemetery and read his letter out loud. Then he would place a small keepsake at the grave. As the end of therapy approached, he felt as if the loss of his comrade had become a part of his life that he could accept as tragic but real and not to be suppressed. There were hardly any moments of agitation anymore. His wife confirmed this and was glad that she had a deeper understanding of what he had been through.

CASE ILLUSTRATION: MR. Z

This case illustrates the application of BEP-TG with a refugee with PTSD and traumatic grief. It illustrates the use of interpreters and drawings and also shows how the imaginal conversation with the deceased (Shear, Frank, Houck, & Reynolds, 2005) can be integrated into the finding-meaning phase of therapy.

Mr. Z[7] is a 36-year-old refugee from Iraq who had fled with his family to the Netherlands. Two years later, he received a telephone call in which he learned that his younger brother had died in an attack on his parental home by the Islamic State. It was unclear whether the other relatives were still alive. Mr. Z developed nightmares about how this attack had happened. He felt guilty and yearned for his brother. He was often angry at his wife and

---

[7]We gratefully acknowledge Anouk van Berlo for providing the case illustration. Permission to use this case illustration was granted by the client and is on file.

children. He started suffering physical pains and was treated for a somatization disorder, with limited results. Following his referral to a specialized trauma treatment facility, Mr. Z was diagnosed with PCBD as well as PTSD. He had high scores on the Traumatic Grief Inventory (TGI = 66) and the Clinician-Administered PTSD Scale for *DSM–5* (CAPS-5 = 33).

Mr. Z was offered BEP-TG. Information about the treatment was provided to Mr. Z and his wife. Mr. Z viewed the painful memories and grief that he would confront during the treatment as "a lion" from whom he had to win the battle. He requested an interpreter on speaker phone during all the sessions (which were in person). Grief-focused exposure centered on the decision to flee, saying goodbye to his family, and the moment he heard that his brother was dead.

Mr. Z drew his parental home and described how he imagined the attack had taken place. At first he found it difficult to express his feelings of sadness but succeeded in doing so over the sessions. His somatic pains temporarily increased, and he felt strong anger at the Taliban. Mr. Z narrated a letter during the next session. Because he did not know how to write, he dictated to the interpreter, and the therapist wrote. The letter started with revenge fantasies. As the therapist normalized Mr. Z's anger, he felt free to express his aggressive thoughts in the letter. He felt able to hand over the judgment of the perpetrators to Allah.

The only mementos Mr. Z possessed were a picture of his heavily wounded brother and a family portrait. He had only dared to cast a quick glimpse at these pictures. Upon request, he brought the pictures to therapy, and the therapist asked him to choose which photo to see first. The photo of the wounded brother evoked a lot of sorrow. He fully accepted that his brother was dead and wrote a letter to him, saying that he felt sure he was now in a good place. He still felt very guilty, not only because he had fled the country and missed the attack but also because he had not been able to bury his brother. Therefore, Mr. Z had an imaginary conversation in which he asked his brother for forgiveness and then answered on behalf of his brother. In this conversation, he imagined that his brother forgave him and hoped that Mr. Z would find his parents so that he could take care of them. For Mr. Z, this conversation felt like saying goodbye.

Mr. Z was then able to think about the future. He noted that he would like to give his children the same warm family as his own. To search for his missing family, Mr. Z wanted to find contacts that could help him. As a farewell ritual, he buried the letters and, together with his wife, held a short ceremony with burning candles. Afterward, with the candles still burning, they had a meal together with their children. When Mr. Z returned to therapy, he said he felt lighter, as if he had finally been able to bury his brother. For the final session, his wife was invited. She said he was less irritable, was now able to listen to family members, and had developed a positive bond with his family. Mr. Z reflected on the therapy, noting "I won the fight with the lion."

He showed a strong decline in symptoms of PCBD (TGI = 39) as well as symptoms of PTSD (CAPS-5 = 13).

DISCUSSION OF CASES

The cases of Mr. D, Mr. M, and Mr. Z illustrate the intensity and complexity of emotions involved in traumatic events and traumatic loss, including fear, sadness, guilt, shame, anger, and sometimes yearning or disgust. BEPP addresses not only fear of the memories but also fear of the associated, overwhelming emotions through its different components.

When a patient starts sharing a horrific story during the exposure, with moments of intense silence and often hesitation to go on, the therapist may feel the fear. The therapist also starts to imagine the scene and begins to experience overwhelming feelings, such as the drive to survive, the fear of dying or becoming powerless, and anger about what has happened. The compassionate, emotional involvement of the therapist can acknowledge moral dilemmas and help the patient express frightening feelings when reliving them during exposure. The compassion breaks through the intense loneliness of the traumatic experience.

It is obvious that the compassionate involvement of the therapist is a demanding task; however, in the end, it is also very rewarding to have been of help to the patient by tolerating the intense emotions and the vivid imagination of what occurred. It is also very demanding for the patient to go through such an exposure, but when performed effectively, it is clearly valued in the end.

SUMMARY

BEPP has been recognized as one evidence-based treatment for individuals with PTSD. In our experience, patients favor this treatment when there is a need to learn from a trauma that changed the way someone views life. Often, losses are involved that make it impossible to go on with life as previously lived, and patients value the attention to their changed perspective and finding meaning. Clinicians interested in reducing symptoms and helping patients understand their traumatic experiences often resonate with BEPP as a treatment option. Recent research has also contributed to the knowledge base on treatment outcome predictors and neurobiological as well as neuropsychological effects (Nijdam et al., 2013; Nijdam, de Vries, et al., 2015; Nijdam, van Amsterdam, et al., 2015; Smid et al., 2018). Other efforts are currently underway, such as the further testing of the BEP-TG protocol and the development of BEPP for children and adolescents. We believe that it is essential for BEPP that research continues and that we find out more about treatment effects in various cultures and traumatized populations. New research will lead to more insights about BEPP, which will benefit optimal treatment matching with the patients' needs in the future.

KEY IDEAS

- BEPP is an intense, emotional treatment of 16 sessions for patients with PTSD to recover and learn from trauma and life.

- BEPP is based on grief and crisis theory and on cognitive elements.

- The first part of the therapy is focused on psychoeducation with one's partner. Later sessions involve imaginal exposure, letter writing and use of memorabilia, and meaning making of how the trauma has affected one's view of self and the world. Therapy ends with a farewell ritual with one's partner.

- BEPP helps individuals who have experienced simple and complex trauma and have PTSD.

- BEPP has been applied with adults, police officers, veterans, refugees, individuals after abuse, and people experiencing other traumas.

REFERENCES

American Psychiatric Association. (2013). *Diagnostic and statistical manual of mental disorders* (5th ed.). Arlington, VA: Author.

American Psychological Association. (2017). *Clinical practice guideline for the treatment of PTSD.* http://dx.doi.org/10.1037/e514052017-001

Barskova, T., & Oesterreich, R. (2009). Post-traumatic growth in people living with a serious medical condition and its relations to physical and mental health: A systematic review. *Disability and Rehabilitation, 31,* 1709–1733. http://dx.doi.org/10.1080/09638280902738441

Boelen, P. A., & Smid, G. E. (2017). Disturbed grief: Prolonged grief disorder and persistent complex bereavement disorder. *British Medical Journal, 357,* j2016. Advance online publication. http://dx.doi.org/10.1136/bmj.j2016

Bowlby, J. (1980). *Loss: Sadness and depression, Vol. 3.* New York, NY: Basic Books.

Bradley, R., Greene, J., Russ, E., Dutra, L., & Westen, D. (2005). A multidimensional meta-analysis of psychotherapy for PTSD. *The American Journal of Psychiatry, 162,* 214–227. http://dx.doi.org/10.1176/appi.ajp.162.2.214

Caplan, G. (1961). *An approach to community mental health.* London, England: Tavistock.

Cloitre, M. (2015). The "one size fits all" approach to trauma treatment: Should we be satisfied? *European Journal of Psychotraumatology, 6*(1), 27344. http://dx.doi.org/10.3402/ejpt.v6.27344

Cusack, K., Jonas, D. E., Forneris, C. A., Wines, C., Sonis, J., Middleton, J. C., . . . Gaynes, B. N. (2016). Psychological treatments for adults with posttraumatic stress disorder: A systematic review and meta-analysis. *Clinical Psychology Review, 43,* 128–141. http://dx.doi.org/10.1016/j.cpr.2015.10.003

de Heus, A., Hengst, S. M. C., de la Rie, S. M., Djelantik, A. A. A. M. J., Boelen, P. A., & Smid, G. E. (2017). Day patient treatment for traumatic grief: Preliminary evaluation of a one-year treatment programme for patients with multiple and traumatic losses. *European Journal of Psychotraumatology, 8*(1), 1375335. http://dx.doi.org/10.1080/20008198.2017.1375335

de Kok, M., Roland, S., Knipschild, R., & Nijdam, M. J. (2018). *Treatment protocol: Brief eclectic psychotherapy for children and adolescents.* Manuscript in preparation.

Gersons, B. P. R. (1988). Adaptive defense mechanisms in post-traumatic stress disorders and leave-taking rituals. In O. van der Hart (Ed.), *Coping with loss: The therapeutic use of leave-taking rituals* (pp. 135–149). New York, NY: Irvington.

Gersons, B. P. R., Carlier, I. V. E., Lamberts, R. D., & van der Kolk, B. A. (2000). Randomized clinical trial of brief eclectic psychotherapy for police officers with post-traumatic stress disorder. *Journal of Traumatic Stress, 13*, 333–347. http://dx.doi.org/10.1023/A:1007793803627

Gersons, B. P. R., Meewisse, M. L., & Nijdam, M. J. (2015). Brief eclectic psychotherapy for PTSD. In U. Schnyder & M. Cloitre (Eds.), *Evidence based treatments for trauma-related psychological disorders* (pp. 255–276). Cham, Switzerland: Springer.

Gersons, B. P. R., Meewisse, M. L., Nijdam, M. J., & Olff, M. (2011). *Protocol: Brief eclectic psychotherapy for posttraumatic stress disorder (BEPP)* (3rd ed.; J. Maul-Phillips, Trans.). Amsterdam, The Netherlands: Academic Medical Centre, University of Amsterdam.

Gersons, B. P. R., & Schnyder, U. (2013). Learning from traumatic experiences with brief eclectic psychotherapy for PTSD. *European Journal of Psychotraumatology, 4*(1), 21369. http://dx.doi.org/10.3402/ejpt.v4i0.21369

Helgeson, V. S., Reynolds, K. A., & Tomich, P. L. (2006). A meta-analytic review of benefit finding and growth. *Journal of Consulting and Clinical Psychology, 74*, 797–816. http://dx.doi.org/10.1037/0022-006X.74.5.797

Horowitz, M. J. (1986). *Stress response syndromes* (2nd ed.). Northvale, NJ: J. Aronson.

Janoff-Bulman, R. (1992). *Shattered assumptions: Towards a new psychology of trauma.* New York, NY: Simon & Schuster.

LeDoux, J. E. (1996). *The emotional brain: The mysterious underpinnings of emotional life.* New York, NY: Simon & Schuster.

Lindauer, R. J. L., Booij, J., Habraken, J. B. A., van Meijel, E. P. M., Uylings, H. B. M., Olff, M., . . . Gersons, B. P. R. (2008). Effects of psychotherapy on regional cerebral blood flow during trauma imagery in patients with post-traumatic stress disorder: A randomized clinical trial. *Psychological Medicine, 38*, 543–554. http://dx.doi.org/10.1017/S0033291707001432

Lindauer, R. J. L., Gersons, B. P. R., van Meijel, E. P. M., Blom, K., Carlier, I. V. E., Vrijlandt, I., & Olff, M. (2005). Effects of brief eclectic psychotherapy in patients with posttraumatic stress disorder: Randomized clinical trial. *Journal of Traumatic Stress, 18*, 205–212. http://dx.doi.org/10.1002/jts.20029

National Institute for Health and Care Excellence. (2005). *Post-traumatic stress disorder: management.* London, England: Author.

Nijdam, M. J., Baas, M. A., Olff, M., & Gersons, B. P. (2013). Hotspots in trauma memories and their relationship to successful trauma-focused psychotherapy: A pilot study. *Journal of Traumatic Stress, 26*(1), 38–44. http://dx.doi.org/10.1002/jts.21771

Nijdam, M. J., de Vries, G. J., Gersons, B. P. R., & Olff, M. (2015). Response to psychotherapy for posttraumatic stress disorder: The role of pretreatment verbal memory performance. *The Journal of Clinical Psychiatry, 76*, e1023–e1028. http://dx.doi.org/10.4088/JCP.14m09438

Nijdam, M. J., Gersons, B. P. R., Reitsma, J. B., de Jongh, A., & Olff, M. (2012). Brief eclectic psychotherapy v. eye movement desensitisation and reprocessing therapy for post-traumatic stress disorder: Randomised controlled trial. *The British Journal of Psychiatry, 200*, 224–231. http://dx.doi.org/10.1192/bjp.bp.111.099234

Nijdam, M. J., Martens, I. J. M., Reitsma, J. B., Gersons, B. P. R., & Olff, M. (2018). Neurocognitive functioning over the course of trauma-focused psychotherapy for PTSD: Changes in verbal memory and executive functioning. *British Journal of Clinical Psychology, 57*, 436–452. http://dx.doi.org/10.1111/bjc.12183

Nijdam, M. J., van Amsterdam, J. G. C., Gersons, B. P. R., & Olff, M. (2015). Dexamethasone-suppressed cortisol awakening response predicts treatment outcome in posttraumatic stress disorder. *Journal of Affective Disorders, 184,* 205–208. http://dx.doi.org/10.1016/j.jad.2015.05.058

Nijdam, M. J., van der Meer, C. A. I., van Zuiden, M., Dashtgard, P., Medema, D., Qing, Y., . . . Olff, M. (2018). Turning wounds into wisdom: Posttraumatic growth over the course of two types of trauma-focused psychotherapy in patients with PTSD. *Journal of Affective Disorders, 227,* 424–431. http://dx.doi.org/10.1016/j.jad.2017.11.031

Parkes, C. M. (1972). *Bereavement: Studies of grief in adult life.* Madison, CT: International Universities Press.

Schauer, M., Neuner, F., & Elbert, T. (2012). *Narrative exposure therapy: A short-term treatment for traumatic stress disorders* (2nd ed.). Boston, MA: Hogrefe.

Schnyder, U., & Cloitre, M. (Eds.). (2015). *Evidence based treatments for trauma-related psychological disorders: A practical guide for clinicians.* Cham, Switzerland: Springer. http://dx.doi.org/10.1007/978-3-319-07109-1

Schnyder, U., Ehlers, A., Elbert, T., Foa, E. B., Gersons, B. P. R., Resick, P. A., . . . Cloitre, M. (2015). Psychotherapies for PTSD: What do they have in common? *European Journal of Psychotraumatology, 6*(1). http://dx.doi.org/10.3402/ejpt.v6.28186

Schnyder, U., Müller, J., Maercker, A., & Wittmann, L. (2011). Brief eclectic psychotherapy for PTSD: A randomized controlled trial [Letter]. *The Journal of Clinical Psychiatry, 72,* 564–566. http://dx.doi.org/10.4088/JCP.10l06247blu

Shear, K., Frank, E., Houck, P. R., & Reynolds, C. F., III. (2005). Treatment of complicated grief: A randomized controlled trial. *JAMA, 293,* 2601–2608. http://dx.doi.org/10.1001/jama.293.21.2601

Smid, G. E., Kleber, R. J., de la Rie, S. M., Bos, J. B. A., Gersons, B. P. R., & Boelen, P. A. (2015). Brief eclectic psychotherapy for traumatic grief (BEP-TG): Toward integrated treatment of symptoms related to traumatic loss. *European Journal of Psychotraumatology, 6*(1). http://dx.doi.org/10.3402/ejpt.v6.27324

Smid, G. E., van der Meer, C. A. I., Olff, M., & Nijdam, M. J. (2018). Predictors of outcome and residual symptoms following trauma-focused psychotherapy in police officers with posttraumatic stress disorder. *Journal of Traumatic Stress, 31,* 764–774. http://dx.doi.org/10.1002/jts.22328

Tedeschi, R. G., Park, C. L., & Calhoun, L. G. (Eds.). (1998). *Posttraumatic growth: Positive transformations in the aftermath or crisis.* Mahwah, NJ: Erlbaum. http://dx.doi.org/10.4324/9781410603401

8

Eye-Movement Desensitization and Reprocessing Therapy for PTSD

Louise Maxfield, Roger M. Solomon, and E. C. Hurley

Eye-movement desensitization and reprocessing (EMDR) therapy (Shapiro, 1995, 2018) is a comprehensive psychotherapy intervention with empirically validated efficacy in the treatment of posttraumatic stress disorder (PTSD). EMDR therapy differs from most other trauma-focused treatment in that its therapeutic effects are achieved without extended exposure to the disturbing memory, detailed descriptions of the trauma, challenges to dysfunctional beliefs, or homework assignments (World Health Organization [WHO], 2013). Rather than focusing on changing the client's thoughts, feelings, or behaviors, EMDR therapy focuses on processing the memory. It is a client-friendly technique, with clients typically reporting, during therapy sessions, reductions in physiological arousal (Schubert, Lee, & Drummond, 2016), changes to negative beliefs (Gauhar, 2016), and decreases in negative emotions (Kim, Bae, & Chon Park, 2008). EMDR also contains a unique element: the use of bilateral stimulation (BLS), such as eye movements, taps, or tones, during brief 30-second "sets" while the client focuses on aspects of the traumatic memory.

EMDR therapy was developed by Francine Shapiro in 1987 (Shapiro, 1989) for the treatment of PTSD. It has been used with clients of all ages, from children as young as 2 years with age-appropriate modifications (e.g., Hensel, 2009) to older adults (e.g., Amano & Toichi, 2014), with individuals of all sexual orientations (e.g., Reicherzer, 2011), and with individuals from diverse cultures (Maxfield, 2014). EMDR therapy is effective for PTSD arising from all kinds of trauma, including trauma resulting from motor vehicle accidents, military

http://dx.doi.org/10.1037/0000196-008
Casebook to the APA Clinical Practice Guideline for the Treatment of PTSD, edited by
L. F. Bufka, C. V. Wright, and R. W. Halfond

combat, and sexual violence (e.g., Rothbaum, Astin, & Marsteller, 2005). It is also used for many other disorders (Maxfield, 2019) that are comorbid with PTSD or that begin following a distressing life event, such as panic disorder (Horst et al., 2017), obsessive–compulsive disorder (Marsden, Lovell, Blore, Ali, & Delgadillo, 2018), and major depressive disorder (Ostacoli et al., 2018). In a comparison of EMDR with prolonged exposure (PE), de Bont et al. (2019) found that patients with psychosis tolerated both EMDR and PE; results showed a decrease not only in PTSD symptoms but also in some psychotic symptoms.

EMDR therapy has been widely used internationally—in North and South America, Europe, Africa, the Middle East, Asia, Latin America, and the Caribbean (Maxfield, 2014). Although EMDR's standard procedures have proven robust, various cultural adaptations are occasionally recommended and easily achieved (see Nickerson, 2016). For example, Allon (2015) described adaptations made when successfully providing group EMDR for women in the Democratic Republic of Congo who had been sexually assaulted during the ongoing civil war, some of whom had no understanding of numbers, could not read or write, or had no experience with metacognitive tasks.

Although treatment is usually provided individually on a once-weekly basis, research has shown that EMDR can be effectively provided in an intensive manner (e.g., twice daily for 4 or 5 days a week for 1 or 2 weeks). Bongaerts, van Minnen, and de Jongh (2017) reported significant improvement for Dutch civilians with complex PTSD who received EMDR twice daily for 10 days. Hurley (2018) used intensive treatment successfully for American combat veterans and military personnel with previously unremitting PTSD. An uncontrolled study comparing the outcome results of EMDR therapy offered to veterans in weekly or daily intensive formats showed that both groups achieved statistically significant effects that were maintained at one-year follow-up (Hurley, 2018).

EMDR therapy can also be provided in a group format, using modified protocols (Jarero & Artigas, 2016; Lehnung, Shapiro, Schreiber, & Hofmann, 2017). Group treatment may be provided in agency or private practice settings for small groups of clients, and studies report significant improvement for patients with ongoing traumatic stress, such as individuals with cancer (Jarero, Givaudan, & Osorio, 2018; Roberts, 2018) and Chinese immigrant women distressed after divorce (Wong, 2018). EMDR group treatment is often provided to groups of children or adults following a disaster (e.g., Maslovaric et al., 2017) and to transient refugees (e.g., Acarturk et al., 2015). In such settings, one or two sessions provide rapid, efficient treatment and allow for screening and identification of clients who require more intensive individual treatment.

TREATMENT RATIONALE

EMDR therapy is guided by Shapiro's (2007) adaptive information processing model, which considers symptoms of PTSD and most other disorders the result of past disturbing experiences that continue to cause distress because the memories were not adequately processed. These inadequately processed memories, containing the disturbing emotions, thoughts, beliefs, and sensations, are stored in isolation, unable to link into the wider memory network. Presenting symptoms occur when these maladaptively stored memories are triggered and perceptions of the current situation are automatically interpreted through the lens of the past.

POSSIBLE MECHANISMS OF ACTION

Research studies have investigated potential mechanisms for the full EMDR protocol to determine the components that contribute to its effectiveness. Many other studies have examined the specific effects of EMDR's eye movement component to discover the ways in which eye movements achieve these effects.

Hypothesized Mechanisms for the Full EMDR Eight-Phase Treatment Package

EMDR therapy is a comprehensive treatment approach, guided by Shapiro's (2018) adaptive information processing model and incorporating the use of eye movements and other forms of BLS. EMDR procedures also integrate elements of many effective psychotherapeutic approaches (Norcross & Shapiro, 2002), including experiential therapies, psychodynamic orientations, CBT strategies, mindfulness, and somatic treatment; like those approaches, EMDR also emphasizes the therapeutic alliance. All these elements are understood to contribute, in some way, to EMDR's outcomes.

A review of EMDR's mechanisms of action showed that 87 studies have investigated the various mechanisms, with 45 looking at the mechanisms within EMDR's full eight-phase treatment program (Landin-Romero, Moreno-Alcazar, Pagani, & Amann, 2018). Landin-Romero et al. concluded, "multiple mechanisms may work to produce treatment gains in EMDR; hence, an integrative model may be necessary in order to capture its myriad effects" (p. 18).

Nevertheless, although it is not possible to specify which treatment elements create or moderate which effects, the predicted outcomes are evident. For example, the adaptive information processing model (Shapiro, 2018) specifies that when clients briefly focus on the trauma memory and simultaneously experience BLS, adaptively stored information can link into the memory networks holding the maladaptive information. This integration of memories into existing adaptive memory networks is thought to change the way that the memory is stored in the brain permanently, through the process of *memory reconsolidation* (Elsey & Kindt, 2017).

Several studies, using various types of brain scans, have shown that EMDR therapy produces measurable and consistent pre–post changes, with a return to normalized function at post-treatment. Studies have also found highly significant shifts in brain activation, from limbic regions with high emotional valence to cortical regions with higher cognitive and associative valence (Pagani, Högberg, Fernandez, & Siracusano, 2013). Hence the memory was stored in a new way, consistent with predictions from the adaptive information processing model.

These findings may also be consistent with the theory of memory reconsolidation (Elsey & Kindt, 2017), one of EMDR's possible mechanisms of action. When a memory is accessed and updated with new contradictory information, the original memory may be transformed and reconsolidated (i.e., stored in a neurologically different form, such as when moving from implicit subcortical to an explicit cortical status). This differs from trauma-focused CBT (TF-CBT) where the underlying mechanisms are hypothesized to be habituation and extinction, which are thought to create a new memory while leaving the original one intact. Craske, Hermans, and Vansteenwegen (2006) suggested that extinction does not eliminate or replace previous associations. Rather, it results in new learning that competes with the old information.

Hypothesized Mechanisms for the Eye Movement Component

The EMDR component that has generated the most interest, and the most research, is eye movement. Eye movements originally were the subject of controversy, and an early meta-analysis showed marginal significance for eye movements only when comparing EMDR-with-eye-movements to EMDR-with-eyes-fixed in studies with clinical participants (Davidson & Parker, 2001). However, in the last 20 years, much more research, using better methodology, has been conducted. A more recent meta-analysis of 26 controlled trials demonstrated that the eye movement component of EMDR therapy, in and of itself, has a significant therapeutic effect (Lee & Cuijpers, 2013). There are now more than 42 studies that have focused on the effects of eye movements (cf. Landin-Romero et al., 2018). The results show that eye movements have several significant robust effects that are thought to contribute to therapeutic outcome. These include the reduction of memory vividness and related emotion, physiological de-arousal, and increased cognitive flexibility.

One mechanism of action is that the eye movements used in EMDR therapy interfere with working memory. The working memory system has a limited capacity, and when taxed by the competing tasks of holding a memory in mind while moving the eyes, it experiences a degradation of performance, resulting in the targeted memory losing its quality and power. Lee and Cuijpers's (2013) meta-analysis showed that eye movement conditions, across multiple studies, produced a large effect size for reduction of memory vividness and a moderate effect size for the reduction of associated emotion, supporting the working memory model explanation (Van den Hout & Engelhard, 2012) for the mechanism of eye movements in EMDR.

Another mechanism with some research support is that the eye movements elicit an orienting response that activates the parasympathetic nervous system. For example, research conducted by Schubert et al. (2016) demonstrated that

EMDR therapy resulted in de-arousal effects such as an immediate significant decrease in heart rate and an increase in skin conductance, consistent with an orienting response. In addition, researchers have postulated that eye movements may stimulate the same neurological processes that take place during rapid eye movement (REM) sleep (Stickgold, 2002). It is thought that the increased cognitive flexibility shown with EMDR (e.g., Kuiken, Bears, Miall, & Smith, 2001) may be similar to the loose associations in dreams. Though this hypothesis is theoretically plausible given the role of REM in memory consolidation, more research is warranted to verify it.

Finally, recent brain and animal studies are revealing evidence for the effects of eye movements on frightening memories. De Voogd et al. (2018) found that eye movements suppressed fear-related amygdala activity during recall of a traumatic memory. Similar results were found in an animal study (Baek et al., 2019; Holmes, 2019): When alternating BLS was combined with exposure to trauma cues, there was significant sustained inhibition of the amygdala, with long-lasting fear reduction. The neural pathway involved greater activity of the superior colliculus (i.e., the area of the brain that directs attention and processes visual information) and the mediodorsal thalamus, with a resulting decrease in amygdala activity. The effects were significantly greater for the exposure-plus-alternating-BLS condition (i.e., lights moving in a sequential line, back and forth) than for all other conditions (exposure/extinction alone, exposure combined with continual lights, and exposure with all lights flashing on and off simultaneously).

RESEARCH SUPPORT

More than 30 randomized controlled trials (RCTs) have validated the efficacy of EMDR therapy for adults with PTSD, and seven RCTs did so for traumatized children (de Jongh, Amann, Hofmann, Farrell, & Lee, 2019; Wilson et al., 2018). EMDR therapy has been designated internationally as effective in the practice guidelines of organizations and agencies such as the World Health Organization (WHO, 2013). The U.S. Department of Veterans Affairs and the U.S. Department of Defense (VA/DoD; 2017) and many other organizations have given EMDR their highest level of recommendation because of research demonstrating its efficacy.

Several meta-analyses of the results of RCTs investigating treatment of PTSD have shown that EMDR is significantly superior to no-treatment and standard-care conditions, with large effect sizes indicating important clinical effects at posttreatment and follow-up (e.g., ISTSS Guidelines Committee, 2018). Meta-analyses comparing EMDR therapy and TF-CBT showed very little difference between the two treatments, noting that each produced similar outcomes (e.g., Bisson, Roberts, Andrew, Cooper, & Lewis, 2013). More recently, Chen, Zhang, Hu, and Liang's (2015) meta-analysis included 11 RCTs that directly compared EMDR and CBT. Chen et al. reported a possible advantage for EMDR, as it was better in reducing intrusion and arousal symptoms than CBT; the treatments did not differ in their effects on avoidant symptoms.

EMDR therapy may be more efficient than TF-CBT. In an RCT for children with PTSD, De Roos et al. (2017) used a stopwatch in EMDR and TF-CBT sessions and found that children who received EMDR therapy lost their PTSD diagnosis significantly faster than those receiving CBT (2 hours and 20 minutes vs. 3 hours and 47 minutes). An RCT for adults with PTSD compared the efficiency of 12 EMDR sessions with that of 12 PE sessions (Stanbury, Drummond, Laugharne, Kullack, & Lee, 2020). Although both treatments effectively reduced symptoms with no difference in symptom reduction, EMDR was significantly more efficient than PE on all measures: EMDR used fewer hours of exposure to traumatic memories to achieve the same results; EMDR produced lower scores of subjective disturbance at the end of the first session; fewer EMDR sessions were needed to bring the target memory to near zero distress levels; and EMDR participants processed more traumatic memories over the course of the treatment than PE participants did.

EMDR therapy also appears effective in the treatment of complex trauma (i.e., traumatic events that are interpersonal, long-term, repeated, and severe; American Psychiatric Association, 2013, p. 276). A meta-analysis by Chen et al. (2018) included six RCTs to study the effects of EMDR therapy for participants with complex childhood trauma. Although EMDR effectively reduced symptoms, the studies were highly heterogeneous. For example, the number of treatment sessions ranged from two to 12. Whether lengthy stabilization prior to providing to trauma-focused treatment is needed for this population is a current controversy, but recent research suggests that clients with PTSD from complex trauma may benefit from EMDR and TF-CBT with minimal stabilization (de Jongh, Bicanic, et al., 2019). This is an area of ongoing research; however, it is strongly recommended in EMDR therapy training that screening for dissociative disorder be conducted and that appropriate preparation be provided before doing memory work. Furthermore, it is recommended that clinicians have specialized training in dissociative disorders before utilizing EMDR therapy.

Although preliminary research indicates that EMDR therapy shows the same effectiveness with military personnel as with civilians, more research is needed to investigate its efficacy with this population. Carlson, Chemtob, Rusnak, Hedlund, and Muraoka (1998) conducted the only Department of Veterans Affairs RCT of EMDR therapy using a full course of treatment (12 sessions) with combat veterans. Results showed a reduction in symptoms of PTSD in 77.7% of participants, with effects maintained at follow-up. McLay et al. (2016), using archival data from active-duty military mental health clinics, also found that service members who received EMDR therapy showed significantly greater improvement on the PTSD measure, in fewer sessions, than those who received an alternative treatment modality. Numerous published case studies (e.g., Russell, 2006, 2008; Wesson & Gould, 2009) have further demonstrated the effectiveness of EMDR therapy in treating military personnel and veterans.

SPECIAL TOPICS

Basic EMDR therapy training is typically provided in two parts (usually 3-day parts), with 5 hours of consultation after each part. It is also recommended that the clinician have 15 to 20 client sessions between Parts 1 and 2. After completion of the basic training, advanced training on a variety of topics and clinical populations is available. For example, advanced training includes utilization of EMDR therapy with children and for patients experiencing substance abuse and addiction, grief and mourning, complex trauma, and medical issues.

Many modified EMDR protocols have been developed, some for clients with disorders other than PTSD and some for special populations. For example, there are several effective protocols for early intervention that reduce or eliminate stress in the first few months posttrauma, with the goal of preventing the development of PTSD (see Shapiro, 2018, for a summary).

EMDR treatment has an optional approach, the *blind to therapist technique* (Blore & Holmshaw, 2009), which can be used when a client does not want to disclose any details of the event. This option is particularly appreciated by individuals who are hesitant to recount events related to moral injury or sexual trauma and by military personnel whose disturbing memories may involve classified or secret missions. In this adaptation, the technique uses the standard EMDR protocol but reduces the conversational load for the client, who responds to each turn with one of two words, one indicating change and one indicating no change. The EMDR therapist and client mutually agree on two words, one word to mean "change" and the other "no change." The client processes the details internally, and when the therapist asks for brief feedback, the client uses the appropriate word to indicate whether change has occurred. The EMDR processing continues as long as change is reported. When "no change" is reported twice, the therapist checks to see if the subjective level of disturbance is resolved.

DESCRIPTION OF TREATMENT COMPONENTS
WITH CASE EXAMPLE

EMDR therapy is an eight-phase, three-pronged protocol (Shapiro, 2018). The three prongs are past, present, and future. With current problems resulting from maladaptively stored memories, relevant past memories are identified and processed. Then, present triggers (e.g., people, place, situations that evoke symptoms) are processed. A future template for adaptive behavior is provided for each present trigger. After the therapist ensures that the client has the necessary skills, the client imagines dealing with the present trigger, or a similar one, in an adaptive way. Any tension or blocks are identified and further processed.

The following case example outlines and illustrates the eight phases of treatment. Jan[1] sought EMDR therapy at the age of 32, when her PTSD symptoms were worsening. Jan had previously seen different therapists over a period of 9 years, beginning at age 23, when she sought therapy to deal with her failing marriage and childhood sexual abuse. However, she never resolved issues related to the sexual abuse, and she continued to be plagued by flashbacks and occasional nightmares. In past therapy sessions, she had often relived the worst part of the abuse at a bodily level, and although she could calm herself, she could not get past the trauma.

Jan was now divorced, with two children, working as a nurse, and functioning well in her job. She practiced yoga and was a certified yoga instructor. Although Jan had a few friends she socialized with, she was reluctant to go to parties or be in a room with large groups of people. She felt defective and worthless, and she ate lunch alone rather than going to the lunchroom where others gathered. Recently, during exercise when her heart rate increased, she had flashbacks of the abuse. She also had feelings of guilt because she had enjoyed the offender's attention, and even though she could intellectually understand how hungry she was for attention and that he took advantage of this, she believed that she participated in her own abuse.

In summarizing the abuse, Jan related that she had been sexually abused at age 6 by a gardener, once or twice a week over a 2-month period. Prior to the first abuse, the gardener had been very friendly, and Jan had looked forward to his visits. The abuse occurred in a small backyard shed, and the gardener's big dog was sometimes present. He told Jan not to tell or the dog would hurt her and her siblings. Jan was vulnerable to the gardener's attention because, as she described, her mother was emotionally distant and unresponsive and her father was absent most of her childhood (i.e., working away from home). As a result, Jan felt invisible and unseen.

Phase 1: History-Taking and Treatment Planning

In addition to obtaining a full history and conducting appropriate assessment, the therapist works together with the client to identify targets for treatment. Targets include past memories, present triggers, and future challenges related to the presenting problem(s).

---

[1]The client gave informed consent and permission for the use of her personal information in this chapter. The name Jan is a pseudonym, and some minor details were changed to protect her confidentiality.

Phase 2: Preparation

The therapist explains EMDR and teaches affect regulation and coping strategies as appropriate for the client. Jan's first two sessions were spent taking a
history, reinforcing affect regulation skills, and explaining EMDR therapy.
After the years of therapy, Jan had good affect regulation skills and practiced
mindfulness meditation. She was taught a safe/calm place exercise, which
worked well for her.

Phase 3: Assessment

This phase activates the memory being targeted in the session. Following
the therapist's directions, the client identifies the image associated with the
incident, a self-referencing negative cognition (NC), and a preferred positive
cognition (PC). The client then rates the validity of the PC when it is paired with
the memory, using the Validity of Cognition (VOC) Scale, with 1 = *completely
false* and 7 = *completely true* (Shapiro, 1995, 2018). Next, the client identifies
the associated affect and rates the level of disturbance, using the Subjective
Units of Disturbance (SUD) Scale, with 0 = *no disturbance* and 10 = *worst possible*.
The client then indicates the body location of this disturbance.

   The first memory to be targeted was Jan's worst memory of an oral
molestation when she was 6. In this phase, Jan identified the components
of the memory. The image had to do with the perpetrator's genitals coming
toward her. The NC was "It's my fault." The PC was "I am innocent," with
a VOC score of 1. The emotions were fear and guilt, with a SUD score of 10,
and sensations were experienced in her throat.

Phase 4: Desensitization

During this phase, the client focuses on the memory while engaging in
eye movements or other bilateral stimulation (BLS). After each set of BLS
(typically lasting about 30 seconds, with about 30 "passes" or left–right–left
movements), the client reports whatever new material was elicited during
the set. This new material may include a shift in images, thoughts, emotions,
sensations, or other memories. Usually the associated material becomes the
focus of the next BLS set, although the therapist, using standardized procedures (Shapiro, 2018), may choose another focus. The desensitization process
continues until the client reports a SUD score of 0 or 1, or a higher rating that
is appropriate to the situation (e.g., when Jan later processed a painful late-
term miscarriage, the SUD score remained at 2, which would not go lower
because "a child had died"; this score was determined to be appropriate to
the situation). The processing of a memory may take place in one session or
over several sessions, depending on the nature of the client and the clinical
situation.

   Jan experienced strong emotions during the initial sets of eye movements
and was teary, with irregular breathing. The clinician checked in with her,

and Jan said it was okay and she wanted to continue. Eight minutes into the processing of the memory, she started to relive the incident at a body level. After another 10 minutes of processing, she said she felt "so small and helpless." The therapist thought about offering a *cognitive interweave*, a strategy that is provided when processing is stuck or blocked or when the emotional intensity is too much. In a cognitive interweave, the therapist provides information, offers a statement, or asks a question that will help link adaptive information. For example, a question such as "Are you aware that you are now in (city) and are an adult now?" can help a client realize the situation is over and they survived. Because Jan was very present and had dual awareness (i.e., one foot in the present, one foot in the past), further sets of BLS were provided, without the therapist intervening. At this point, the client started to have an adult perspective:

CLIENT: There was nobody I could trust. . . . Now I understand—the gardener saw me . . . at home I was invisible. . . . Now I understand why I feel guilty. I hated what he did to me, but at least he saw me. I was confused. I did not participate in the abuse—he did this to me, it's not my fault.

THERAPIST: Okay, let's go with that. You're doing fine (35 repetitions of eye movements). Take a breath, let it go. What do you get now?

CLIENT: Now I can view as way far away, and I understand he saw me where nobody in my family did, and that does not mean I wanted to be abused. He did it, not me.

After about another 10 minutes of EMDR processing, Jan stated that the incident "felt over," and her body calmed. The image of the gardener was "way over there," and although she never knew what happened to him, she said "he is probably now shriveled up somewhere as an old man and no longer dangerous . . . and hopefully he got what was coming to him." With further processing, the memory had a SUD score of 0.

Phase 5: Installation

This phase strengthens the preferred PC and uses standardized procedures, involving the BLS while focusing on the cognition and the traumatic incident, to increase validity on the VOC Scale to a 7. Jan stated that her PC, "I'm innocent," now had a VOC score of 7. Further sets of BLS were administered to "install" and strengthen this belief in relationship to the traumatic incident.

Phase 6: Body Scan

The client is asked to evaluate his or her body while thinking of the incident and the positive cognition and to identify any residual somatic distress. If the client reports any disturbance, standardized procedures involving the BLS are used to process it. Jan was asked to close her eyes and think of the event and the words "I'm innocent" while scanning her body for distress. She reported feeling calm.

Phase 7: Closure

This phase is used to end the session. If the targeted memory was not fully processed in the session, specific instructions and techniques are used to provide containment and ensure safety until the next session.

Jan felt calm. She said she was particularly positively affected by her new understanding that the abuse was not her fault, now realizing that as a little girl she got everything confused. She also felt safe in the present, with the incident over and in the past.

Phase 8: Reevaluation

This phase is used to begin the next session. The therapist evaluates the client's current psychological state, whether treatment effects have maintained, and what memories may have emerged since the last session. The therapist works with the client to identify targets for the current session.

Subsequent EMDR Sessions

Jan's symptoms abated significantly. Getting in touch with and understanding the attachment issues from childhood enabled her to integrate the trauma within the context of her life. During four sessions, Jan processed other memories of abuse by the gardener. Over the next year, further sessions were provided to deal with her sense of isolation, how alone she felt after the abuse, the impact of the abuse on the family relationships, and her sense of worth. All sessions used standard EMDR procedures, focusing on early memories related to these issues, and resulted in increased self-esteem and interpersonal confidence. The processing of present triggers regarding socializing with other people, and future templates for adaptive coping, were also provided.

Discussion of the Case

This case shows the importance of processing not only past traumatic memories but also present triggers that stimulate the problem and the importance of laying down a foundation for adaptive behavior through use of future templates. It describes EMDR treatment with a woman who has a history of complex trauma, illustrating a history of sexual abuse complicated by significant attachment issues. The family dynamics resulted in the client feeling invisible, making her vulnerable to the attention of the gardener who abused her. In addition to the horror of the abuse, the client experienced feelings of guilt and self-blame. Previous talk therapy, on and off for years, had addressed the abuse and its impact on Jan and had taught her containment and affect regulation skills. However, she was still traumatized by the event and was experiencing significant symptoms. Although more time for stabilization (i.e., Phase 2, preparation) may be needed with some clients suffering from complex trauma or dissociative disorders, Jan had learned affect regulation and grounding skills in her previous therapy sessions and was able to begin processing the traumatizing events after two sessions.

Throughout the intensity of the sessions, Jan always maintained dual awareness, and processing occurred with minimal input from the therapist. Other clients may require the therapist to slow down the processing with shorter sets of eye movements (e.g., 8–12 repetitions vs. the usual 20–30 repetitions), provide grounding or reassurance in between sets, or offer cognitive interweaves to facilitate processing and working through intense affect.

CASE ILLUSTRATION

Steve[2] was a 24-year-old Asian American Operation Iraqi Freedom veteran who was referred for EMDR therapy after having been treated with other psychotherapy modalities by seven other psychologists and psychiatrists without success. He had been diagnosed with PTSD on return from his deployment to Iraq. By the time he presented for EMDR therapy he was reporting nightmares three or four times weekly. When speaking of an attack on a base by an insurgent driving a vehicle loaded with a bomb (i.e., a vehicle-born explosive device [VBED]), his hands shook uncontrollably. He was easily triggered by sounds.

In the 5- and 10-day daily intensive treatment programs, only a few hours transpire between sessions. Two sessions are provided daily: The most disturbing aspects of the memory are treated in the morning, with an afternoon follow-up for completing the eight phases of EMDR therapy. Steve needed an average of two sessions to complete the reprocessing of each targeted memory in Phases 3 through 8. In such cases, this schedule allows for the assessment phase (Phase 3) and reprocessing of the disturbing aspects of memory (Phase 4, desensitization) to be conducted in the morning session, resulting in substantial reduction of the SUD score. The afternoon sessions provided time to ensure reduction of the SUD score to 0 and the completion of Phases 5 through 7. In Phase 5, the positive self-referencing belief (i.e., PC) was enhanced as much as possible, usually to a VOC score of 7. The body scan (Phase 6) was then completed, ensuring the somatically expressed body sensations, associated with the disturbing memory, were resolved. Each session was closed (Phase 7) by monitoring Steve's ability to provide appropriate

---

[2]Steve gave informed consent and permission for the use of his personal information in this chapter. Some minor details were changed to protect his confidentiality.

self-regulation. Phase 8, reevaluation, was utilized at the beginning of each subsequent session to evaluate the current state of the memory and to identify any aspects of the disturbing memory yet to be processed. Complete treatment of each targeted memory ensured Steve had a SUD score of 0, a VOC score of 7, and a clear body scan with no body tensions or other physical sensations related to the target memory.

Monday, Sessions 1 and 2

On arrival for treatment, Steve provided a history of his life experiences, including his achievements and successes as well as challenging, disturbing events in his life. Toward the end of the Vietnam War, Steve's parents had escaped Vietnam through Thailand as part of the refugee immigration of "boat people" from Southeast Asia to the United States. Steve described his family as hardworking immigrants bent on making a new home in America. He was the youngest of three children born and raised in an inner city in the northeastern United States. Although Steve's mother still could not speak English, Steve knew life as an American. However, growing up, Steve was assaulted by inner-city gangs daily because of his Asian ethnicity. The assaults left him with a continuing sense of vulnerability accompanied by hypervigilance. His ongoing anxiety and fear of the unexpected kept him on edge. His military combat experiences further enhanced his anxiety.

Steve's traumatic experiences included (a) having to fight his way to school each day and back home each evening, (b) the VBED on the base, (c) subsequent panic attacks following the VBED mass casualty, and (d) his base being attacked with rockets and mortars. During history taking, Steve reflected that much of his life had been spent with a sense of "being under attack."

Steve processed his disturbing memories well, with each traumatic memory requiring one or two sessions. Because Steve had frequently experienced panic attacks, his treatment plan included treating the earliest event, his childhood fights going and coming from school, then the worst event (i.e., the VBED mass casualty and being constantly under rocket and mortar attacks), and his recent panic attacks. His 5-day treatment sessions included the following (see Table 8.1).

Tuesday, Sessions 3 and 4

Steve stated that the terror he felt during the childhood assaults by inner-city gangs was like the terror he experienced during the VBED attack. A discussion of these assaults revealed a core belief that danger was waiting around the next corner, and a desire for community, acceptance, and approval. Steve's childhood memory was viewed as an early touchstone memory that created the initial sense of vulnerability to being attacked. His sense of vulnerability was accompanied with a sense of being helplessly overwhelmed. These feelings appeared to facilitate the development of panic attacks. The touchstone

TABLE 8.1. Summary of Steve's 5-Day Treatment

Time of day	Session phase
Monday morning	History taking (Phase 1)
Monday afternoon	Complete history-taking and preparation (Phases 1 and 2)
Tuesday morning	Treat childhood memory: Gang attack walking to school (Phases 3 and 4)
Tuesday afternoon	Complete childhood memory (Phases 4–7)
Wednesday morning	VBED [vehicle-born explosive device] attack on the base with mass casualties (Phases 3 and 4)
Wednesday afternoon	Complete VBED mass casualties (Phases 4–8)
Thursday morning	Panic attack (Phases 3 and 4)
Thursday afternoon	Panic attack (Phases 4–8)
Friday morning	Rocketing of base (Phases 3–8)
Friday afternoon	Future template on returning home and debrief

memory of the gang fights, with the negative belief "I am overwhelmed," was reprocessed in two sessions, during which Steve's original SUD score of 8 reduced to 0 and his VOC score increased to 7. As Steve recognized body sensations of tightness in his chest and back of the neck, the body scan process (i.e., Phase 6) cleared the body tension within 10 minutes. At the end of the day, Steve reported no distress related to this memory. His positive desired belief "I am taking care of myself" was enhanced as strongly as possible (i.e., score of 7).

Wednesday, Sessions 5 and 6

Treatment of the most distressing memory, the VBED causing mass casualties on the base, was conducted in Sessions 5 and 6. With the success of the previous day, Steve reported a positive attitude, being more hopeful toward his treatment while acknowledging his anxiety toward the unknown as he addressed the memory that had haunted him since his deployment. When asked the assessment questions (i.e., Phase 3), Steve readily accessed the mental picture, "The IAs [Iraqi Army soldiers] yelling, and there was a lot of blood, a shitload of blood and body parts." However, when questioned about a negative cognition about himself in the situation, Steve found it difficult to identify one because he saw himself helping. With the therapist's assistance, he was able to identify "I'm going to be killed" as an appropriate NC. The PC was "I'm okay with it," meaning he would prefer to believe "I am okay even though it happened!"

THERAPIST: So, when you think of that incident, how true do those words, *I'm okay with it*, feel to you in the gut if 1 is *totally false* and 7 is *totally true*?

CLIENT: (*Shakes head as if saying "no"*) It's like a 1. It's false—I don't feel it; I don't feel it.

THERAPIST: So, what emotion do you feel when you think of it?

CLIENT: Sad. Mad. Sad and mad.

THERAPIST: And, as you think about it, how upsetting is it to you now on a scale of 0 to 10, with 0 meaning *no disturbance at all* and 10 being *the highest disturbance a person could imagine?*

CLIENT: I'd give it about a 9.

THERAPIST: And where do you feel that in your body?

CLIENT: My chest . . . I feel my heart pumping too!

THERAPIST: I want you to bring up the memory of that incident, and the words *I am going to be killed.* Notice where you feel it in your body and follow my fingers.

CLIENT: Still feeling it in my chest. I can see "Doc" calling me, calling me to the MEDIC tent—to come and help him.

THERAPIST: Okay, let's go with that. You're doing fine. (*35 repetitions of eye movements*) Take a breath, let it go. What do you get now?

CLIENT: Feeling it in my hands, feeling like—it grabbed me!

THERAPIST: Okay, go with that. (*35 repetitions of eye movements*) Take a breath, let it go. What do you get now?

CLIENT: Seeing everything. Starting to see everything. Feeling my hands placing things down. Placing stretchers down. I'm seeing everything. (*Breathing heavily*)

THERAPIST: Go with that. (*35 repetitions of eye movements*) Take a breath, let it go. What do you get now?

CLIENT: I feel my stomach. Like, I am getting nauseated. Just the smell; like just looking at it (in my mind). (*Pause*) Can I get something to drink, Doc? (*Speaking to the therapist as he reaches for a bottle of green tea he brought with him to the session and takes a drink. Because this occurred near the beginning of the session, the brief response did not interrupt the treatment, and the ability to identify his personal needs and respond provided a sense of his being in control of his treatment process and enhanced his sense of safety.*)

THERAPIST: You are doing fine. This is part of the memory, go with that. (*35 repetitions of eye movements*) Take a breath, let it go. What do you get now?

CLIENT: My hands; using my hands a lot taking things back and forth.

THERAPIST: Go with that. (*35 repetitions of eye movements*) Take a breath, let it go. What do you get now?

CLIENT: I'm talking to my NCOIC [noncommissioned officer in charge].

THERAPIST: Go with that. (*35 repetitions of eye movements*) Take a breath, let it go. What do you get now?

CLIENT: Talking to my NCOIC and feeling really sad. This is really going to the depth with things. Like I am actually looking at it really in depth. Like how I felt; the things he said to me. I remember him telling me, "You did enough. Just take the day off." This is really in depth, Doc [in my memory]. (*Client's breathing is more settled now; he is calmer*)

CLIENT: (*12 minutes into the session*) I remember getting ready for bed that night and thinking about what happened. Thinking today was a crazy day but also an exciting day.

His memory processing began to focus on the bonding among soldiers who shared the intensity as he recalled their sharing food at the dining area. "I can remember eating quesadillas and later chili-mac and mash potatoes, even though it has been 4 years since the incident." The Wednesday morning session ended with a SUD score of 0. The VOC score increased to 7, followed by a clear body scan. The client successfully completed the targeted memory that had disturbed him since its occurrence 4 years previously. At the end of the session, Steve reported feeling lighter and calmer.

Thursday, Sessions 7 and 8

The next two sessions focused on Steve's panic attack following the VBED mass casualty. He had accompanied a civil affairs team into a nearby village when he began to feel overwhelmed, worried that a suicide bomber could easily be among the crowd. Steve began thinking he would die. Feeling overwhelmed, with his heart racing and having difficulty breathing, he had to exit the marketplace quickly to calm down. Afterward, he avoided the marketplace and any place where crowds of Iraqis would be located. For the sake of doing his duty, he worked to manage his anxiety when on assigned combat missions with other soldiers.

The morning session consisted of Phase 3 (assessment) and Phase 4 (desensitization). Steve's negative cognition was "I am going to die," with a SUD score of 9; his PC, "I am okay now," was rated 4. During the reprocessing, he reported his hands felt clammy and his upper torso, arms, and hands felt sweaty as he recalled the distressing event. By the end of the morning session, the sweaty and clammy body feelings had cleared out. Steve experienced a decrease in his SUD score from 9 to 0 during the morning session. He was calm and composed as the session ended just before lunch.

The Thursday afternoon session allowed Steve to finish the incomplete session from the morning. A reevaluation (Phase 8) indicated Steve's SUD score remained at 0. Treatment resumed with Phase 5 (Installation), and the

VOC score for "I am okay now" increased from 4 to 7 during the enhancement of the installation. During the body scan (Phase 6), Steve reported no disturbance.

Friday, Session 9

Session 9 successfully treated Steve's memory of a rocket attack on the base. The attack left him feeling vulnerable, with an enhanced NC, "I'm going to be killed." His PC, which he would prefer to believe, if possible, was "I am okay now." As he identified his PC, he stated, "But I know a part of me is not okay." As he reprocessed the memory of the attack, Steve described feeling the ground shake as the rockets hit inside his compound. His respiration became more intense at this point. Offering assurance (i.e., a cognitive interweave), the therapist stated, "It's a memory of something from the past; it's over now." As the reprocessing continued, Steve's SUD score dropped from 7 to 0. His breathing adjusted as he became calmer. As Steve moved into the installation phase (Phase 5), his positive cognition continued to strengthen as his VOC score increased from 2 to 7. Next, while completing the body scan, Steve noted a tightness in his chest during the processing. With additional sets of eye movement (i.e., 30–35 passes), the sensations shifted in body location and dissipated. His somatic sensations dissipated as the disturbing memory was reprocessed.

The session closed with Steve reporting a sense of calmness and a relaxed body. His level of disturbance declined, and he reported feeling fatigued by the end of the session. The therapist suggested his tiredness was a natural feeling once his body adjusted to a relaxed state with less adrenaline being produced.

Friday, Session 10: Final Session With Terminal Reevaluation and Future Template

The 10th session provided a terminal reevaluation of the overall 5-day treatment plan, ensuring that each targeted memory maintained a SUD score of 0 with a VOC score of 7. The reevaluation indicated each SUD score and VOC score remained consistent. The future template—the third prong of EMDR treatment, which includes past events, present triggers, and the anticipated future—was incorporated to the client's positive cognition, "I am okay as I am," and focused on his anticipated adjustments on returning to his home social network. His VOC score began at 5 and strengthened to 7 within 15 minutes. A challenge, or anticipated difficulty, was introduced in which the client viewed himself facing financial stressors on his return home. After four sets with 35 repetitions each, his positive thoughts included "I have the ability to earn extra income should I face economic challenges." A terminal reevaluation was conducted before concluding treatment, ensuring all the disturbing memories treated during the 5 days had maintained a SUD score of 0 and a VOC score of 7. Results were maintained.

Discussion of the Case

Steve had been diagnosed with PTSD by his referring Warrior Transition Unit (WTU). On arrival for his 5-day treatment, two instruments were used to evaluate his PTSD: the PTSD Checklist—Military version (PCL–M) and the Impact of Events Scale—Revised (IES–R). The PCL–M, developed by the Department of Veterans Affairs (Kimerling, 2009), is a widely recognized measure based on the fourth edition of the *Diagnostic and Statistical Manual of Mental Disorders* (*DSM–IV*). The IES–R, a 22-item screening tool for PTSD, has an endorsement of clinical utility, and the cutoff score for the IES–R is recognized to be 34 for PTSD (Morina, Ehring, & Priebe, 2013). While recognizing the current PCL is the PCL–5 (Weathers et al., 2013), PCL–M cutoff scores range from 45 (U.S. Department of Veterans Affairs, National Center for PTSD, 2012) to 60 (Beck et al., 2008). Creamer, Bell, and Failla (2003) compared the PCL with the IES–R. They used the PCL cutoff score of 50 to identify PTSD+ cases while noting a total score of 33 on the IES–R yielded a diagnostic sensitivity of .91 with a specificity of .82. Research suggests a 5- to 10-point change in outcome scores is reliable (i.e., not due to chance) and a 10- to 20-point change is clinically meaningful (U.S. Department of Veterans Affairs, National Center for PTSD, 2012).

Outcome measures for Steve's 5-day intensive EMDR treatment (two sessions each day for 5 days) indicated that his PCL–M score dropped from 57 to 20. His IES–R score changed from 44 to 3. At 3-year follow-up, his IES–R was 12. Steve noted his hands no longer shook when he recalled the VBED incident. No panic attacks were experienced after the 5-day EMDR therapy treatment.

Steve's case demonstrates how a particular life theme can run through many stressful life events, such as the daily gang attacks on his way to and from his inner-city school, with a basic sense of vulnerability represented by beliefs such as "I am outnumbered," "I am overwhelmed" and "I'm going to die." It also illustrates the relationship between an unprocessed disturbing memory, PTSD symptoms, and a panic attack. Treating the early disturbing memory of those inner-city fights first allowed the resolution of the early touchstone memory, which appeared to have set the scene for an ongoing sense of vulnerability. Rapid processing of the VBED memory resolved Steve's distress associated with that event, with a decrease in his SUD score from 9 to 0. Within 12 minutes, the nausea associated with the memory of gathering body parts was resolved, and he described the day as being "a crazy day but also an exciting day."

This case is also notable for how EMDR processing elicited a depth of memory, in which Steve remembered many details of the events. According to the adaptive information processing theory, the theoretical model underlying EMDR therapy, the stimulation of the target memory using eye movement allowed the client to access additional memory networks. This process allowed Steve to recall other, previously forgotten experiences that occurred during the disturbing day, including praise from his commanding officer and camaraderie and bonding with his fellow soldiers. These experiences were very important to Steve, and as those memories were integrated into that of the disturbing event, the memory was transformed so that it was no longer distressing. The panic attack and rocket attacks were treated in chronological sequence and were resolved, with the SUD score diminishing to 0, the VOC score increasing to 7 (i.e., the strongest possible belief that the positive cognition was true), and the body scan showing no somatic sensations associated with the disturbing targeted memory.

This case exemplifies how EMDR therapy can be provided on a daily basis. Further research is recommended to compare the treatment efficacy of EMDR provided in weekly sessions with that of EMDR administered in intensive daily formats.

SUMMARY

EMDR therapy is an evidence-based psychological approach that focuses on the role of the brain's information processing system. According to the adaptive information processing model that guides EMDR therapy, inappropriately processed memories of disturbing experiences are conceptualized as resulting in the presenting symptoms of PTSD and other psychological disorders, except for those caused by organic deficit, injury, or substance use (Shapiro, 2007). EMDR is an eight-phase, three-pronged protocol that resolves distressing memories of past experiences and current triggers and lays down a positive future template for adaptive behavior. The clinical effects have been shown to occur rapidly, without the use of detailed descriptions or homework, and can be provided in extended sessions, on consecutive days, and in group applications. EMDR therapy has been utilized with a wide range of clinical populations, with positive outcomes for women and men, individuals with different trauma types, and individuals from various ethnic and racial backgrounds and having unique personal characteristics. Future rigorous research is needed to extend the existing research base investigating EMDR treatment of PTSD and other psychological disorders.

KEY IDEAS

- Eye-movement desensitization and reprocessing (EMDR) therapy is a comprehensive psychotherapy intervention with empirically validated efficacy for PTSD treatment.

- EMDR therapy uses a standardized protocol, consisting of eight phases, to address past distressing memories, current triggers, and future challenges.

- The focus of therapeutic work is on changing the memory, not the symptoms.

- A unique element in EMDR is bilateral stimulation—usually horizontal eye movements. Research suggests that bilateral stimulation makes memories less vivid and less emotional, facilitates physiological relaxation, and increases cognitive flexibility.

- EMDR sessions are usually 60 to 90 minutes long. Clients with a single trauma benefit from two to five sessions; clients with multiple traumatic events often require 12 or more sessions. Treatment is typically provided in one session once per week, although some clients receive intensive treatment of 10 sessions per week for 1 or 2 weeks.

- Research has shown that EMDR therapy successfully and rapidly reduces symptoms of PTSD as well as associated depression and anxiety.

REFERENCES

Acarturk, C., Konuk, E., Cetinkaya, M., Senay, I., Sijbrandij, M., Cuijpers, P., & Aker, T. (2015). EMDR for Syrian refugees with posttraumatic stress disorder symptoms: Results of a pilot randomized controlled trial. *European Journal of Psychotraumatology, 6*. http://dx.doi.org/10.3402/ejpt.v6.27414

Allon, M. (2015). EMDR group therapy with women who were sexually assaulted in the Congo. *Journal of EMDR Practice and Research, 9*, 28–34. http://dx.doi.org/10.1891/1933-3196.9.1.28

Amano, T., & Toichi, M. (2014). Effectiveness of the on-the-spot-EMDR method for the treatment of behavioral symptoms in patients with severe dementia. *Journal of EMDR Practice and Research, 8*, 50–65. http://dx.doi.org/10.1891/1933-3196.8.2.50

American Psychiatric Association. (2013). *Diagnostic and statistical manual of mental disorders* (5th ed.). Washington, DC: Author.

Baek, J., Lee, S., Cho, T., Kim, S.-W., Kim, M., Yoon, Y., . . . Shin, H.-S. (2019). Neural circuits underlying a psychotherapeutic regimen for fear disorders. *Nature, 566*, 339–343. http://dx.doi.org/10.1038/s41586-019-0931-y

Beck, J. G., Grant, D. M., Read, J. P., Clapp, J. D., Coffey, S. F., Miller, L. M., & Palyo, S. A. (2008). The Impact of Event Scale–Revised: Psychometric properties in a sample of motor vehicle accident survivors. *Journal of Anxiety Disorders, 22*, 187–198. http://dx.doi.org/10.1016/j.janxdis.2007.02.007

Bisson, J. I., Roberts, N. P., Andrew, M., Cooper, R., & Lewis, C. (2013). Psychological therapies for chronic post-traumatic stress disorder (PTSD) in adults. *Cochrane Database of Systematic Reviews.* http://dx.doi.org/10.1002/14651858.CD003388.pub4

Blore, D., & Holmshaw, M. (2009). EMDR "blind to therapist protocol." In M. Luber (Ed.), *Eye movement desensitization and reprocessing (EMDR) scripted protocols: Basics and special situations* (pp. 233–240). New York, NY: Springer. http://dx.doi.org/10.1891/9780826122384.0025

Bongaerts, H., van Minnen, A., & de Jongh, A. (2017). Intensive EMDR to treat patients with complex posttraumatic stress disorder: A case series. *Journal of EMDR Practice and Research, 11*, 84–95. http://dx.doi.org/10.1891/1933-3196.11.2.84

Carlson, J. G., Chemtob, C. M., Rusnak, K., Hedlund, N. L., & Muraoka, M. Y. (1998). Eye movement desensitization and reprocessing (EDMR) treatment for combat-related posttraumatic stress disorder. *Journal of Traumatic Stress, 11*, 3–24. http://dx.doi.org/10.1023/A:1024448814268

Chen, L., Zhang, G., Hu, M., & Liang, X. (2015). Eye movement desensitization and reprocessing versus cognitive-behavioral therapy for adult posttraumatic stress disorder: Systematic review and meta-analysis. *Journal of Nervous and Mental Disease, 203*, 443–451. http://dx.doi.org/10.1097/NMD.0000000000000306

Chen, R., Gillespie, A., Zhao, Y., Xi, Y., Ren, Y., & McLean, L. (2018). The efficacy of eye movement desensitization and reprocessing in children and adults who have experienced complex childhood trauma: A systematic review of randomized controlled trials. *Frontiers in Psychology, 9.* http://dx.doi.org/10.3389/fpsyg.2018.00534

Craske, M. G., Hermans, D., & Vansteenwegen, D. (Eds.). (2006). *Fear and learning: From basic processes to clinical implications.* Washington, DC: American Psychological Association.

Creamer, M., Bell, R., & Failla, S. (2003). Psychometric properties of the Impact of Event Scale—Revised. *Behaviour Research and Therapy, 41*, 1489–1496. http://dx.doi.org/10.1016/j.brat.2003.07.010

Davidson, P. R., & Parker, K. C. H. (2001). Eye movement desensitization and reprocessing (EMDR): A meta-analysis. *Journal of Consulting and Clinical Psychology, 69*, 305–316.

de Bont, P. A. J. M., Van der Vleugel, B. M., Van den Berg, D. P. G., De Roos, C., Smit, F., de Jongh, A., . . . Van Minnen, A. (2019). Health–economic benefits of treating trauma in psychosis. *European Journal of Psychotraumatology, 10.* http://dx.doi.org/10.1080/20008198.2018.1565032

de Jongh, A., Amann, B. L., Hofmann, A., Farrell, D., & Lee, C. W. (2019). Status of EMDR therapy in the treatment of posttraumatic stress disorder 30 years after its introduction. *Journal of EMDR Practice and Research, 13*, 261–269. http://dx.doi.org/10.1891/1933-3196.13.4.261

de Jongh, A., Bicanic, I., Matthijssen, S., Amann, B. L., Hofmann, A., Farrell, D., . . . Maxfield, L. (2019). The current status of EMDR therapy involving the treatment of complex PTSD. *Journal of EMDR Practice and Research, 13*, 284–290. http://dx.doi.org/10.1891/1933-3196.13.4.284

De Roos, C., Van der Oord, S., Zijlstra, B., Lucassen, S., Perring, S., Emmelkamp, P., & de Jongh, A. (2017). Comparison of EMDR therapy, cognitive behavioral writing therapy and wait-list in pediatric PTSD following single-incident trauma: A multi-center randomized clinical trial. *Journal of Child Psychology and Psychiatry, and Allied Disciplines, 58*, 1219–1228.

De Voogd, L. D., Kanen, J. W., Neville, D. A., Roelofs, K., Fernández, G., & Hermans, E. J. (2018). Eye-movement intervention enhances extinction via amygdala deactivation. *The Journal of Neuroscience, 38*, 8694–8706. http://dx.doi.org/10.1523/JNEUROSCI.0703-18.2018

Elsey, J. W., & Kindt, M. (2017). Tackling maladaptive memories through reconsolidation: From neural to clinical science. *Neurobiology of Learning and Memory, 142*(Part A), 108–117. http://dx.doi.org/10.1016/j.nlm.2017.03.007

Gauhar, Y. W. M. (2016). The efficacy of EMDR in the treatment of depression. *Journal of EMDR Practice and Research, 10*, 59–69. http://dx.doi.org/10.1891/1933-3196.10.2.59

Hensel, T. (2009). EMDR with children and adolescents after single-incident trauma: An intervention study. *Journal of EMDR Practice and Research, 3*, 2–9. http://dx.doi.org/10.1891/1933-3196.3.1.2

Holmes, A. (2019, February). Biological clues to an enigmatic treatment for traumatic stress. *Nature, 566*, 335–336. Retrieved from: https://www.nature.com/articles/d41586-019-00294-8

Horst, F., Den Oudsten, B., Zijlstra, W., de Jongh, A., Lobbestael, J., & De Vries, J. (2017). Cognitive behavioral therapy vs. eye movement desensitization and reprocessing for treating panic disorder: A randomized controlled trial. *Frontiers in Psychology*, *8*. http://dx.doi.org/10.3389/fpsyg.2017.01409

Hurley, E. C. (2018). Effective treatment of veterans with PTSD: Comparison between intensive daily and weekly EMDR approaches. *Frontiers in Psychology*, *9*. http://dx.doi.org/10.3389/fpsyg.2018.01458

ISTSS Guidelines Committee. (2018). *Posttraumatic stress disorder prevention and treatment guidelines: Methodology and recommendations*. Oakbrook Terrace, IL: Author. Retrieved from http://www.istss.org/treating-trauma/new-istssprevention-and-treatment-guidelines.aspx

Jarero, I., & Artigas, L. (2016). EMDR integrative group treatment protocol for adolescents (14–17 years) and adults living with ongoing traumatic stress. In M. Luber (Ed.), *Eye movement desensitization and reprocessing (EMDR) therapy scripted protocols and summary sheets: Treating trauma- and stressor-related conditions* (pp. 169–180). New York, NY: Springer.

Jarero, I., Givaudan, M., & Osorio, A. (2018). Randomized controlled trial on the provision of the EMDR Integrated Group Treatment Protocol adapted for ongoing traumatic stress to female patients with cancer-related posttraumatic stress disorder symptoms. *Journal of EMDR Practice and Research*, *12*, 94–104. http://dx.doi.org/10.1891/1933-3196.12.3.94

Kim, E., Bae, H., & Chon Park, Y. (2008). Validity of the subjective units of disturbance scale in EMDR. *Journal of EMDR Practice and Research*, *2*, 57–62. http://dx.doi.org/10.1891/1933-3196.2.1.57

Kimerling, R. (2009). *Examining the diagnostic and clinical utility of the PTSD Checklist*. Retrieved from U.S. Department of Veterans Affairs website: https://www.hsrd.research.va.gov/research/abstracts.cfm?Project_ID=2141698713

Kuiken, D., Bears, M., Miall, D., & Smith, L. (2001). Eye movement desensitization reprocessing facilitates attentional orienting. *Imagination, Cognition and Personality*, *21*, 3–20. http://dx.doi.org/10.2190/L8JX-PGLC-B72R-KD7X

Landin-Romero, R., Moreno-Alcazar, A., Pagani, M., & Amann, B. L. (2018). How does eye movement desensitization and reprocessing therapy work? A systematic review on suggested mechanisms of action. *Frontiers in Psychology*, *9*. http://dx.doi.org/10.3389/fpsyg.2018.01395

Lee, C. W., & Cuijpers, P. (2013). A meta-analysis of the contribution of eye movements in processing emotional memories. *Journal of Behavior Therapy and Experimental Psychiatry*, *44*, 231–239. http://dx.doi.org/10.1016/j.jbtep.2012.11.001

Lehnung, M., Shapiro, E., Schreiber, M., & Hofmann, A. (2017). Evaluating the EMDR Group Traumatic Episode Protocol with refugees: A field study. *Journal of EMDR Practice and Research*, *11*, 129–138. http://dx.doi.org/10.1891/1933-3196.11.3.129

Marsden, Z., Lovell, K., Blore, D., Ali, S., & Delgadillo, J. (2018). A randomized controlled trial comparing EMDR and CBT for obsessive-compulsive disorder. *Clinical Psychology & Psychotherapy*, *25*, e10–e18. http://dx.doi.org/10.1002/cpp.2120

Maslovaric, G., Zaccagnino, M., Mezzaluna, C., Perilli, S., Trivellato, D., Longo, V., & Civilotti, C. (2017). The effectiveness of Eye Movement Desensitization and Reprocessing Integrative Group Protocol with adolescent survivors of the Central Italy earthquake. *Frontiers in Psychology*, *8*. http://dx.doi.org/10.3389/fpsyg.2017.01826

Maxfield, L. (2014). Commemorating EMDR's 25th anniversary by highlighting EMDR humanitarian projects. *Journal of EMDR Practice and Research*, *8*, 179–180. http://dx.doi.org/10.1891/1933-3196.8.4.179

Maxfield, L. (2019). A clinician's guide to the efficacy of EMDR therapy. *Journal of EMDR Practice and Research*, *13*, 239–246. http://dx.doi.org/10.1891/1933-3196.13.4.239

McLay, R. N., Webb-Murphy, J. A., Fesperman, S. F., Delaney, E. M., Gerard, S. K., Roesch, S. C., . . . Johnston, S. L. (2016). Outcomes from eye movement desensitization and reprocessing in active-duty service members with posttraumatic stress disorder. *Psychological Trauma: Theory, Research, Practice and Policy, 8,* 702–708. http://dx.doi.org/10.1037/tra0000120

Morina, N., Ehring, T., & Priebe, S. (2013). Diagnostic utility of the Impact of Event Scale–Revised in two samples of survivors of war. *PLoS One, 8.* http://dx.doi.org/10.1371/journal.pone.0083916

Nickerson, M. (Ed.). (2016). *Cultural competence and healing culturally based trauma with EMDR therapy.* New York, NY: Springer. http://dx.doi.org/10.1891/9780826142870

Norcross, J. C., & Shapiro, F. (2002). Integration and EMDR. In F. Shapiro (Ed.), *EMDR and the paradigm prism: Experts of diverse orientations explore an integrated treatment* (pp. 341–356). Washington, DC: American Psychological Association.

Ostacoli, L., Carletto, S., Cavallo, M., Baldomir-Gago, P., Di Lorenzo, G., Fernandez, I., . . . Hofmann, A. (2018). Comparison of eye movement desensitization reprocessing and cognitive behavioral therapy as adjunctive treatments for recurrent depression: The European Depression EMDR Network (EDEN) randomized controlled trial. *Frontiers in Psychology, 9.* http://dx.doi.org/10.3389/fpsyg.2018.00074

Pagani, M., Högberg, G., Fernandez, I., & Siracusano, A. (2013). Correlates of EMDR therapy in functional and structural neuroimaging: A critical summary of recent findings. *Journal of EMDR Practice and Research, 7,* 29–38. http://dx.doi.org/10.1891/1933-3196.7.1.29

Reicherzer, S. (2011). Eye movement desensitization and reprocessing in counseling a male couple. *Journal of EMDR Practice and Research, 5,* 111–120. http://dx.doi.org/10.1891/1933-3196.5.3.111

Roberts, A. K. P. (2018). The effects of the EMDR Group Traumatic Episode Protocol with cancer survivors. *Journal of EMDR Practice and Research, 12,* 105–117. http://dx.doi.org/10.1891/1933-3196.12.3.105

Rothbaum, B. O., Astin, M. C., & Marsteller, F. (2005). Prolonged exposure versus eye movement desensitization and reprocessing (EMDR) for PTSD rape victims. *Journal of Traumatic Stress, 18,* 607–616. http://dx.doi.org/10.1002/jts.20069

Russell, M. (2006). Treating combat-related stress disorders: A multiple case study utilizing eye movement desensitization and reprocessing (EMDR) with battlefield casualties from the Iraqi war. *Military Psychology, 18,* 1–18. http://dx.doi.org/10.1207/s15327876mp1801_1

Russell, M. (2008). Treating traumatic amputation-related phantom limb pain: A case study utilizing eye movement desensitization and reprocessing (EMDR) within the armed services. *Clinical Case Studies, 7,* 136–153. http://dx.doi.org/10.1177/1534650107306292

Schubert, S. J., Lee, C. W., & Drummond, P. D. (2016). Eye movements matter, but why? Psychophysiological correlates of EMDR therapy to treat trauma in Timor-Leste. *Journal of EMDR Practice and Research, 10,* 70–81. http://dx.doi.org/10.1891/1933-3196.10.2.70

Shapiro, F. (1989). Efficacy of the eye movement desensitization procedure in the treatment of traumatic memories. *Journal of Traumatic Stress, 2,* 199–223. http://dx.doi.org/10.1002/jts.2490020207

Shapiro, F. (1995). *Eye movement desensitization and reprocessing: Basic principles, protocols, and procedures.* New York, NY: Guilford Press.

Shapiro, F. (2007). EMDR, adaptive information processing, and case conceptualization. *Journal of EMDR Practice and Research, 1,* 68–87. http://dx.doi.org/10.1891/1933-3196.1.2.68

Shapiro, F. (2018). *Eye movement desensitization and reprocessing: Basic principles, protocols, and procedures* (3rd ed.). New York, NY: Guilford Press.

Stanbury, T. M. M., Drummond, P. D., Laugharne, J., Kullack, C., & Lee, C. W. (2020). Comparative efficiency of EMDR and prolonged exposure in treating posttraumatic stress disorder: A randomized trial. *Journal of EMDR Practice and Research, 14,* 1–11. http://dx.doi.org/10.1891/1933-3196.14.1.1

Stickgold, R. (2002). EMDR: A putative neurobiological mechanism of action. *Journal of Clinical Psychology, 58*, 61–75. http://dx.doi.org/10.1002/jclp.1129

U.S. Department of Veterans Affairs, National Center for PTSD. (2012). Using the PTSD checklist (PCL). Retrieved from https://sph.umd.edu/sites/default/files/files/PTSDChecklistScoring.pdf

U.S. Department of Veterans Affairs, & U.S. Department of Defense. (2017). *VA/DoD clinical practice guideline for the management of posttraumatic stress disorder and acute stress disorder*. Washington, DC: Authors. Retrieved from https://www.healthquality.va.gov/guidelines/MH/ptsd/VADoDPTSDCPGFinal082917.pdf

Van den Hout, M. A., & Engelhard, I. M. (2012). How does EMDR work? *Journal of Experimental Psychopathology, 3*, 724–738. http://dx.doi.org/10.5127/jep.028212

Weathers, F. W., Litz, B. T., Keane, T. M., Palmieri, P. A., Marx, B. P., & Schnurr, P. P. (2013). The PTSD Checklist for *DSM–5* (PCL–5). Retrieved from https://www.ptsd.va.gov/professional/assessment/adult-sr/ptsd-checklist.asp

Wesson, M., & Gould, M. (2009). Intervening early with EMDR on military operations: A case study. *Journal of EMDR Practice and Research, 3*, 91–97. http://dx.doi.org/10.1891/1933-3196.3.2.91

Wilson, G., Farrell, D., Barron, I., Hutchins, J., Whybrow, D., & Kiernan, M. D. (2018). The use of eye-movement desensitization reprocessing (EMDR) therapy in treating post-traumatic stress disorder—A systematic narrative review. *Frontiers in Psychology, 9*, 923. http://dx.doi.org/10.3389/fpsyg.2018.00923

Wong, S.-L. (2018). EMDR-based divorce recovery group: A case study. *Journal of EMDR Practice and Research, 12*, 58–70. http://dx.doi.org/10.1891/1933-3196.12.2.58

World Health Organization. (2013). *Guidelines for the management of conditions that are specifically related to stress*. Geneva, Switzerland: Author.

Narrative Exposure Therapy for PTSD

Frank Neuner, Thomas Elbert, and Maggie Schauer

Narrative exposure therapy (NET) is a trauma-focused psychotherapy that shares many commonalities with other evidence-based treatments for posttraumatic stress disorder (PTSD). Like other trauma-focused procedures, its aim is to change the structure of trauma-related memories, cognitions, and emotions related to the traumatic events (Schnyder et al., 2015). Although there is evidence that targeting coping skills or problems in the present life of the client may be beneficial, trauma-focused procedures are recommended as first-line treatment for individuals with PTSD (Bisson et al., 2007; Ehlers et al., 2010), including traumatized refugees (ter Heide, Mooren, & Kleber, 2016) and refugee children (Eberle-Sejari, Nocon, & Rosner, 2015).

In NET, the client, empathically guided by the therapist, creates a written autobiography containing major emotional memories from birth to the present. This process occurs within a predetermined number of sessions, each about 90 minutes in duration. The focus of NET is on reconstructing the fragmented memories of traumatic experiences into coherent narrations that are connected to the temporal and spatial context of the lifetime periods. At the end of treatment, a copy of the final consistent life narration is handed over to the client, and the therapist keeps one copy that may, depending on the wishes of the client, be used for human rights purposes. A large number of clients with trauma, in particular victims of wars and persecution, have witnessed and experienced atrocities such as torture and attacks on civilians. The detailed and vivid descriptions of such experiences in the context of personal life stories are valuable documents for human rights work.

http://dx.doi.org/10.1037/0000196-009
Casebook to the APA Clinical Practice Guideline for the Treatment of PTSD, edited by
L. F. Bufka, C. V. Wright, and R. W. Halfond

However, NET differs from other trauma-focused psychotherapy methods in some fundamental ways. NET was originally developed and tested with a global perspective as a brief and economic procedure for application in resource-poor settings in conflict areas around the world. In war-affected populations, PTSD prevalence rates reach up to 50% (Fazel, Reed, Panter-Brick, & Stein, 2012; Fazel, Wheeler, & Danesh, 2005; Karunakara et al., 2004; Miller, Elbert, & Rockstroh, 2005). The clinical presentations of survivors are typically complex and may include symptoms of depression, difficulties in self-regulation, violent behavior, interpersonal problems, somatization, dissociation, self-harm, and substance use disorders.

Part of the pragmatism involved in NET is that the procedure can be applied across contexts and cultures with limited adaptations. This principle is based on the assumption that, with some cultural particularities in the expression of symptoms, trauma reactions are universal phenomena as they result from innate neurobiological processes involved in the memories of threat and stress. At the same time, sharing one's histories is a personal and cultural practice that helps the survivor to cope with life events and to foster interpersonal closeness. While diagnostic instruments need to be adapted carefully for each language, only minor modifications in the NET procedure are required when this approach is implemented across cultures. Rather than focusing on the differences between cultures, the NET approach acknowledges that, in every culture, survivors hold a wide variety of values and attitudes and come from varying economic and educational backgrounds. Accordingly, any treatment approach has to be adjusted to the individual needs of each client rather than according to clichés and stereotypes that are commonly ascribed to any given culture (Schnyder et al., 2016).

Within the family of exposure-based trauma-focused approaches, the unique feature of NET is the *life-span approach*. Most trauma-focused treatments require the client to identify the event that he or she experienced as most traumatic, often referred to as the *index trauma*. However, victims of wars and persecution have typically experienced a series of traumatic events rather than a single traumatic stressor; thus, whole periods of life may have traumatized a survivor. A key assumption of NET is that the distorted memory representation of the accumulation of aversive events and conditions over the life-span, rather than a single index trauma memory, maintains posttraumatic stress symptoms. Recent research has confirmed that, in addition to war events, traumatic events within families as well as adverse conditions in communities predict trauma-related symptoms and dysfunction in war-affected populations (Catani, 2010; Nandi, Crombach, Bambonye, Elbert, & Weierstall, 2015; Olema, Catani, Ertl, Saile, & Neuner, 2014; Saile, Ertl, Neuner, & Catani, 2016; Saile, Neuner, Ertl, & Catani, 2013). The life-span approach seeks to integrate a course of aversive and traumatic memories into a meaningful autobiographic memory representation, which is a key requisite of identity and self-acceptance.

Furthermore, rather than taking a socially and politically neutral position, NET is directly connected to advocacy for the survivors of severe human rights violations. Because they have fragmented autobiographic representations, avoidance behavior, and feelings of shame, as well as trauma-related feelings of helplessness and inferiority, victims of violence often have difficulties expressing themselves and talking about their experiences. This speechlessness of trauma is a double-sided phenomenon, as the society and public are also ignorant regarding the stories of trauma survivors. From this perspective, NET can provide comprehensible documentations of individual life stories that facilitate feelings of empathy for the victims and contribute to the social recognition of the suffering. For the victims, regaining access to their biographies and communicating their histories to others can empower them to stand up for their rights as victims of violence. At the request of the survivor, the resulting testimonies can be used by agencies for human rights work and documentary purposes.

TREATMENT RATIONALE

Current research indicates that the re-creation of a context for dysfunctional associative stimulus–response connections is the key mechanism for unlearning fear (Craske et al., 2008; Craske, Treanor, Conway, Zbozinek, & Vervliet, 2014) and for the treatment of PTSD (Ehlers & Clark, 2000; Neuner, Catani, et al., 2008). Based on this principle, the aim of NET is to reestablish a consistent autobiographical context of the traumatic events and to reconnect the context to the threat structure—in colloquial terms, to tie cold memories around hot memories, defined by their sensory representations. Therefore, the client, with the assistance of the therapist, constructs a chronological narrative of her or his life story with a focus on the traumatic experiences. Within a predefined period, usually about four to fourteen 90-minute sessions, the fragmented reports of the traumatic experiences will be transformed into a coherent narrative that is documented in written form. This procedure involves the reconstruction of a meaningful narrative for the client that is compatible with realistic and adaptive self-representations. For survivors of domestic or organized violence, the testimony can be recorded and used for human rights purposes.

Trauma-Related Disorders Are Disorders of Memory

Current neuropsychological theories of PTSD share the assumption that the disorder is caused and maintained by memory processes (Brewin, 2014; Brewin, Dalgleish, & Joseph, 1996; Ehlers & Clark, 2000). Emotional experiences are represented in episodic memory, which consists of associative networks (also referred to as *situationally accessible memory*, *hot memory*, *fear structure*, or *s-rep*) that are tied to verbally coded contextual information (similar concepts have been referred to as *verbally accessible memory*, *cold memory*, or *c-rep*; Brewin, 2014; Brewin et al., 1996; Metcalfe & Jacobs, 1996). Neurocognitive processes that occur due to extreme stress during traumatic events cause a dissociation of the associative memories from their context, and that dissociation finally results in PTSD symptoms.

The Threat Networks

Threat networks are associative representations of traumatic experiences that contain typical stimulus and response elements of the traumatic experiences. The idea of threat networks is based on Lang, Davis, and Ohman's (2000) construct of *fear structures* as well as Foa and Kozak's (1986) model of *fear networks*, but the content of threat networks includes emotional and behavioral response patterns other than fear. Instead, threat networks represent vivid memories of traumatic events as associative networks of the sensory, cognitive, emotional, and physiological details of the traumatic situations. The sensory elements contain stimuli of the situation that signaled threat (e.g., a gun or injury) as well as neutral and everyday stimuli that happened to be present during the traumatic event. In cases of multiple traumatization, processes of stimulus generalization lead to the inclusion of visually or conceptually similar stimuli or the formation of prototypical or generic stimuli (e.g., an angry face or aggressive tone in cases of child maltreatment, the vision of naked bodies or the smell of body fluids in cases of sexual violence). In threat networks, these stimulus elements are tied to response items that represent the cognitive, physiological, and emotional reactions during the traumatic event.

The typical reaction to a threatening event is fear, which includes an increase in physiological activity such as heart rate acceleration, elevation of blood pressure, vasoconstriction, and multiple other changes that prepare the organism for a flight reaction. However, extreme threat can provoke defensive reactions that involve a consecutive sequence of reactions beyond fear (Bracha, 2004), including phases of physiological and behavioral up- as well as down-regulations (Schauer & Elbert, 2010).

Although emotional networks that tie stimulus and response characteristics of an experience are commonly considered part of human memory, threat networks differ from normal emotional memory representations in two ways. First, they grow with each additional experience of a traumatic stressor and thus become unusually large. Because more items are coded in the structure, the likelihood that the network is activated by reminder cues increases. Second, the single items are tied more closely together. As a consequence, a widespread activation of the threat network can occur from the activation of single elements of the association through an environmental stimulus or internal cue. Such an intense activation results in experiences of intrusive reliving and flashbacks. Depending on the peritraumatic experience, threat networks may include the full cascade of defensive reactions, such as alarm (fight–flight) responses, stages of tonic immobility, or shut-down reactions, with a decrease of sympathetic and an increase in parasympathetic arousal. From this perspective, dissociative reactions or aggressive dominance behaviors are conditioned in the same way as fear responses and may be reactivated by reminders of the situation.

Context Memory

Associative learning is not restricted to learning stimulus and response elements; it also involves coding the temporal and spatial context of the event. Current clinical theories of fear conditioning share an assumption that unlearning a fear through extinction learning leaves the original stimulus–fear association intact but modifies contextual information that is tied to the event representation (Kindt, 2014). Depending on the context, the identical conditioned stimulus can signal threat in one environment but safety in a different surrounding. In animal studies, a conditioned stimulus (e.g., the noise of a bell) can trigger a conditioned fear reaction in one cage but not in a different cage. In human memory, context memory is not restricted to environmental cues but rather involves the coding of the temporal and spatial information in autobiographic memory. This type of cognitive memory, which has also been referred to as the *conceptual frame* (Conway & Pleydell-Pearce, 2000) of the event, represents the location of the event within the biography of the person (i.e., information about *lifetime periods*) as well as the chronological sequence of single events (i.e., information about so-called *single events* or *general events*). Autobiographic memory is the basis for a narrative account of event and, because of the tight connection to self-representations, provides information about the meaning of the event in a life-span perspective (Conway & Pleydell-Pearce, 2000).

Disconnection of Threat Structure From Context Memory

Stress hormones have a substantial impact on the coding and consolidation of human memory. High levels of adrenaline, noradrenaline, and cortisol cause opposing effects for declarative and nondeclarative memory processes, resulting in augmented associative but fragmented contextual representations (Cohen, Liberzon, & Richter-Levin, 2009). As a consequence, traumatic experiences are represented in excessive threat structures that are only loosely tied to autobiographic information. Weak context information impairs the inhibitory control over the association (Kindt, 2014). The key assumption of the memory theory is that the dissociation of the associative network from context memory causes PTSD symptoms. The lack of accompanying temporal and spatial context information results in a "here and now" sensation of the recollection of the traumatic event. It feels as if the event is happening again, and the memory activation involves the perception of current threat. At the same time, the disorganized autobiographic memory results in disorganized narrations of the traumatic events (Jelinek, Randjbar, Seifert, Kellner, & Moritz, 2009), which contribute to the maintenance of PTSD symptoms (Brewin, 2014; Ehring, Ehlers, & Glucksman, 2008; Halligan, Michael, Clark, & Ehlers, 2003). Because autobiographic memory and self-representations are intricately connected (Conway & Pleydell-Pearce, 2000), the weak contextual memory of the traumatic event involves an inconsistency in the representation of the meaning of the event. Self-representations about a person's safety, trust, intimacy, responsibility, or even the whole identity are poorly elaborated and integrated.

RESEARCH SUPPORT

Results from more than a dozen randomized controlled trials in adults (up to 75 years) and children and adolescents (from 7 years on) have demonstrated that, within a limited number of sessions, NET is effective in reducing PTSD symptoms. Improvements typically continue during follow-up and have been observed even one year after treatment (Morath, Gola, et al., 2014; Morath, Moreno-Villanueva, et al., 2014; Robjant & Fazel, 2010).

NET is constructed to counter the impact of multiple and complex traumatic stress experiences that have occurred across an entire lifetime. NET provides a well-supported treatment option to survivors of repeated torture, persecution, and civil war, including refugees (Hensel-Dittmann et al., 2011; Neuner et al., 2010). Trauma types include experiencing and witnessing war events such as combat, aerial bombings, massacres, political incarceration and torture, sexual violence including rape but also events that occurred outside the context of war, including family violence and child sexual abuse. NET has effectively been applied in situations that remain insecure, such as with refugees who continue to live close to war zones (e.g., in Uganda) and experience threats and violence.

A number of reviews have identified NET as an evidence-based treatment, especially for survivors of violence (Crumlish & O'Rourke, 2010; McPherson, 2012; Robjant & Fazel, 2010; ter Heide et al., 2016). Several effectiveness studies have been conducted fully independent of the developers of NET (e.g., Hijazi, 2012; Hijazi et al., 2014; Zang, Hunt, & Cox, 2013) in a variety of countries, such as China (Zang et al., 2013), Rwanda (Jacob, Neuner, Maedl, Schaal, & Elbert, 2014), Sri Lanka (Köbach, Schaal, Hecker, & Elbert, 2017), Uganda (Ertl, Pfeiffer, Schauer, Elbert, & Neuner, 2011; Karunakara et al., 2004; Saile et al., 2013, 2016), and the United States (Hijazi, 2012; Hijazi et al., 2014). Well-established centers for torture victims and refugees, including Centrum 45 in the Netherlands and the Center for Victims of Torture in Minnesota, regularly use NET in their clinical practice in their clinics and abroad. Manuals have appeared in print in Dutch, English, Farsi, French, Italian, Korean, Slovakian, and Japanese and are also available from the authors in Spanish and Arabic.

Evidence for the effect of NET includes changes of biological markers such as oscillatory neural activity measured with magnetencephalograph. In addition, Adenauer et al. (2011) observed that NET caused an increase in activity associated with cortical top-down regulation of attention toward aversive pictures. Morath, Gola, et al. (2014) showed that symptom improvements caused by NET were mirrored in an increase in the originally reduced proportion of regulatory T cells in the NET group at a 1-year follow-up. Moreover, completion of NET was associated with increased levels of damaged DNA in traumatized survivors returning to a normal level (Morath, Moreno-Villanueva, et al., 2014). These biological findings are consistent with the observation that NET reduces the frequencies of self-reported cough, diarrhea, and fever among refugees (Neuner, Onyut, et al., 2008).

Two decisive strengths of NET are its low dropout rate and its high potential for dissemination, including its provision by lay counselors in low-income countries and in war and crisis regions (Catani et al., 2009; Ertl et al., 2011; Jacob et al., 2014; Köbach et al., 2017; Neuner, Onyut et al., 2008). Across trials, qualification levels of lay therapists included those with bachelor's degrees in psychology, schoolteachers, and fellow refugees without substantial psychosocial background. However, it needs to be emphasized that this type of so-called task shifting requires that the interventions are closely tied to a professional monitoring, supervision, and referral structure. Within such a context, NET can be an important element in a more comprehensive mental health or psychosocial aid structure. Recent randomized trials in Rwanda and the Democratic Republic of Congo demonstrated that local NET therapists successfully trained the next generation of therapists within a train-the-trainer model (Jacob et al., 2014; Köbach et al., 2017), which is a further step toward making expatriate therapists dispensable in the process of providing trauma treatment in low income countries.

SPECIAL TOPICS

To meet the demands of overburdened health care systems, the NET procedure, as well as the application and dissemination, is characterized by maximum pragmatism. A series of randomized controlled trials demonstrated that NET can be successfully applied by trained lay therapists who do not have formal medical or psychological education (e.g., teachers and fellow refugees in a refugee camp; Köbach et al., 2017; Neuner, Onyut et al., 2008; Robjant & Fazel, 2010), even with war victims and refugees who live in unsafe and threatening environments. This idea is consistent with the principle of task shifting from academically trained professionals to trained lay health workers for countries with an insufficient health sector (Jordans & Tol, 2013), as recommended by the World Health Organization.

So far, there is no standardized system of certification of NET. While some educated professional psychotherapists may feel confident in applying NET solely based on studying the manual (Schauer, Neuner, & Elbert, 2011), NET workshops have been provided globally by experienced NET trainers, most of them associated with the developers of NET through the nongovernmental aid organization vivo international (http://www.vivo.org). The duration and intensity of training are flexible, depending on the therapeutic preeducation and experience of the trainees. A more structured approach to training and certification is currently under development in a joint approach by several universities.

DESCRIPTION OF TREATMENT COMPONENTS

NET consists of five components: diagnosis, psychoeducation, lifeline exercise, the narration, and a closing session. In the following sections, each component is described and illustrated with clinical material.

Diagnostics, Inclusion, and Exclusion Criteria

A prerequisite of NET is a thorough diagnostic evaluation that includes a review of the client's life events and monitoring of current suffering. The assessment must include event checklists that reveal the experience of traumatic events, including childhood adversities and child maltreatment. In addition, symptoms of PTSD and depression should be measured with the help of valid instruments. The current evidence supports the application of NET for clients with a diagnosis of PTSD and comorbid disorders. Exclusion criteria are typically associated with the treatment setting rather than the NET procedure itself. For example, some conditions, including severe suicidal ideation, self-harm, or harm of others, may require hospitalization. If current substance use disorder requires detoxification, this should be achieved first. Additionally, NET requires the ability to create elaborated narrations based on memories. NET has not been tested in young children who do not yet possess the necessary cognitive skills.

Case Illustration

The case example has been used with permission of the client. Some details, such as names and locations, are hidden or have been changed to maintain anonymity.

Ahmed is a 29-year-old refugee in Germany. He was raised in a family that belonged to the cultured class of a Middle East country, ruled by a totalitarian and autocratic regime. He had been active in an underground opposition movement that, in part, had turned into a rebel army that fought against the government. After an injury that resulted from combat experience, he fled to Germany. A volunteer refugee worker referred him to a university-based outpatient clinic with substantial expertise in the treatment of refugees. A detailed diagnostic interview conducted by a psychotherapist with the assistance of an interpreter resulted in a diagnosis of PTSD and major depressive disorder with substantial symptom scores. Moreover, no medical cause was found for severe and persistent physical pain. The event checklist indicated that the client had experienced various forms of torture, imprisonment, combat experience, and sexual violence.

Psychoeducation

A psychoeducational introduction is presented to the survivor, focusing on the explanation of his problems and symptoms according to the memory theory of trauma. If appropriate, a statement about the universality of human rights is also presented. This is followed by an outline of the treatment rationale. For participants with a low educational background, psychoeducation is often based on metaphors that allow the illustration of the memory theory, including the emotional pain involved in exposure, such as the metaphor of trauma memory as messy shelves that need to be organized. More educated clients receive a detailed explanation of the theory. In addition, survivors receive an explanation about the motivation of the therapist and her or his ability to listen to the worst stories. This explanation is founded on a professional basis to help the survivor in the recovery process but also emphasizes the readiness for empathic involvement in the treatment process. Psychoeducation closes with an invitation to engage in NET.

Case Illustration

After the interview and the explanation of the diagnosis, the therapist discussed the treatment options with Ahmed. Because of his high educational background, he received a full explanation of the memory theory of PTSD as a basis of the rationale of trauma-focused therapy. He hesitated to agree to participate. This psychoeducation ultimately resulted in the following discussion of the challenge of talking about the past traumatic events.

THERAPIST: Have you ever talked to someone about your bad experiences?

AHMED: Well, no. Not in detail. There are many things I have to hide.

THERAPIST: Who tells you that you have to hide?

AHMED: (blushes, looks down, silent)

THERAPIST: Ahmed, are you still with me?

AHMED: (looks down, nodding)

THERAPIST: Is it difficult to respond to me now?

AHMED: (sighing)

THERAPIST: Does talking about your memories make you silent?

AHMED: Some things, yes.

THERAPIST: Some memories make you ashamed and silent?

AHMED: Yes. You have no idea what happens in the prisons.

THERAPIST: I have never been in a prison in your home country, you are right. Not many people here know what happens in your home country.

AHMED: Yes. This is unfortunate.

THERAPIST: You think it would be good if more people knew about the injustice there?

AHMED: The whole world should know.

THERAPIST: Could you contribute to this?

AHMED: I cannot fight, I am a failure, I am in exile.

THERAPIST: And you are silent.

AHMED: So, you think I should talk in public?

THERAPIST: I am not the one to tell you what to do. But I could help enable you to decide what you want to do. Right now, you think you cannot talk, and you feel that you cannot even explain why. I offer you to try to talk with me and to find out the obstacles and to overcome them. I will be there and listen, whatever it is, I will be with you.

AHMED: Thank you. But I cannot promise.

THERAPIST: You do not need to promise anything but to try.

After this session, Ahmed agreed to participate in NET treatment. Ahmed and the therapist made a plan for intervention in case of urgent crises and decided about potential social support by Ahmed's family members. He received written information about treatment and the formalities, including legal aspects of confidentiality and data protection, and he signed an informed consent sheet.

Lifeline Exercise

The therapy continues with the lifeline exercise, which provides a biographical overview of the life span. This exercise consists of placing positive and negative life events, symbolized by flowers and stones respectively, along a rope in chronological order. The lifeline should reflect good and bad memories of moments or periods in the biography of the individual. With the guidance of the therapist, the client classifies each flower and stone with one or a few words, without going into detail. The purpose of the lifeline is to enable a cursory overview of the times and locations in which events occurred within the overarching context of the individual's life. Because this procedure does not allow a detailed narration that would restore autobiographic memory, the lifeline exercise can be burdening for the client and must be contained within one 90-minute session.

Case Illustration

Guided by the therapist, Ahmed laid his lifeline, starting with some flowers that represented the support by his parents in his childhood and his educational achievements. He placed stones of varied sizes to represent the effects of political persecution for the family early in his life. The father had been arrested several times. Representing later in life, he placed some large stones for three imprisonments, the witnessed killing of a friend, the start of the armed fighting, the injury, and a life-threatening experience during the flight to Germany, and he placed some pebbles for his current situation as an asylum seeker. Already in the lifeline it is observable that a central theme of Ahmed's evaluation of his past life experiences is justice in a political context.

The Narration

In the next session, the narration starts with essential background information and a summary of the first years of life, which the client cannot explicitly remember because of early age. In an active process, the therapist and the client create detailed narrative accounts of the key events of the biography, which are tied to connecting information about the developments between the events. The biography is written down between the sessions by a therapist or, preferably, a cotherapist or student who is present during the sessions.

If available, the pretrauma period in childhood may be used as the time during which a foundation for the therapeutic core process is laid and a good rapport between therapist and client is established. In this phase, for example, the telling of emotional, warm, or exciting moments in the survivor's early life can be a training ground for emotional processing and communication between client and therapist.

Case Illustration

Ahmed started the narrative procedure without further hesitation. Next to the interpreter, a cotherapist (student) joined the session to assist in writing the narration. For research purposes and for monitoring of quality, the sessions were videotaped. Ahmed's main motivation was to continue to contribute against the regime in his home country by telling his life story. He hoped that treatment would make him more functional. His reconstructed narration started as follows:

> My name is Ahmed XX. I was born in 1989 in XX. My father had a shop where they sold food. My mother was a tailor. At home there was also a room as a tailor's shop. I have two brothers and two sisters. I'm the youngest of them all. As children, we used to help in my father's shop. I well remember the colors and the smells of the vegetables and the fruits. We always had fresh fruit and parsley. My mother was a wonderful cook, and we always had the best ingredients. In my school, other children were jealous because I could bring fresh bread with vegetables.
>
> My parents were against the government. At home, my father talked about the regime. My siblings and I were told by him who these people are. My father said he knew that they would ruin our country. Already when I was in elementary school, I used to see people being arrested on the street. I was always told to be careful and to tell no one what I think. The government wanted to destroy the opposition. When I was in middle school, my brother was arrested. Many have been arrested in my family. My father criticized the government and had to go to the police very often. He could not keep quiet and had difficulties again and again. One day he didn't come home at night. We were very scared. My mother told us that he must have said something again and was arrested.

During the narrative procedure, the survivor continues recounting his life story in chronological order. Reestablishing a sequence is especially important for survivors of repeated traumatic experiences, which often result in broken lifelines. When a "stone" (i.e., traumatic incident) occurs, the event is relived strictly chronologically in a slow-motion moment-by-moment reprocessing of the sensory, cognitive, emotional, and bodily details of the traumatic scenes, ensuring the interweaving of hot and cold memory elements, meaning making, and integration. During the telling of the events, the therapist structures the topics and helps to clarify ambiguous descriptions. Inconsistencies in the survivor's report are gently pointed out and often resolved by raising in-depth awareness of recurring bodily sensations or thoughts. The client is encouraged to describe the traumatic events with sensory details and to reveal the perceptions, cognitions, and emotions that were experienced at that time but to refrain from evaluating the event from the current perspective. The survivor is encouraged to relive these experiences while narrating, without losing the connection to the present. The therapist is empathic and nonjudgmental but directs the procedure to prevent avoidance, flashbacks, or dissociation. Using permanent reminders that the feelings and physiological responses result from activation of hot memories, the therapist links these representations to episodic facts related to time, place, and chronology (i.e., cold memory). The imaginal exposure to the traumatic past is not terminated until the related affect decreases. In this way, the therapist is supportive yet directive in eliciting the narrative to recover the implicit information of the trauma in its entirety.

Case Illustration

Ahmed continued treatment regularly and did not miss any sessions. At the fifth NET session, the event that was represented by one of the largest stones on his lifeline was narrated. This session was far more difficult to structure for the therapist. Ahmed's story was initially very confused and fragmented. The narration procedure started like this:

AHMED:	I remember this day. They put me in a prison. There was blood everywhere.
THERAPIST:	Ahmed, sorry, I cannot follow.
AHMED:	It smelled like blood and urine. (looks down)
THERAPIST:	Ahmed, I guess you smell this right now. I think you are right there at the moment.
AHMED:	Yes.
THERAPIST:	Don't go there alone. Take me along. I want to understand.
AHMED:	Hm.
THERAPIST:	Can you look at me for a moment?
AHMED:	(looks up)
THERAPIST:	Thank you. Ahmed, we have time. I need to understand how this evolved piece by piece. So far, I cannot understand. We need it step by step, so that we both can digest it.
AHMED:	Okay.
THERAPIST:	Are you with me again?
AHMED:	Yes.

THERAPIST: So, tell me where it all started. I understand that you were 24 years old, and others had warned you that the police might come. It was a period of fear.

AHMED: Yes, I could not sleep at this time.

THERAPIST: What happened before you were arrested?

AHMED: There was a jeep across the street from my house that day. It looked like a police jeep. I thought the car might be there by accident. But I had to be careful. I went to my uncle's house and not home. When I got back, I didn't see the jeep anymore. So, I went home.

THERAPIST: Were you frightened by the jeep?

AHMED: Well, not more than usual. It was a time of fear. They could be everywhere.

THERAPIST: So, you had to be alert?

AHMED: Yes.

THERAPIST: Can you feel this right now again, the basic tension and alertness you had at this time?

AHMED: Yes. It is always there.

THERAPIST: In your body?

AHMED: My heart is racing. My hands are sweating.

THERAPIST: Like often, at this time, back in your home country.

AHMED: Yes.

THERAPIST: So, what happened next, after you returned home?

The final narration of the arrest was recounted as follows:

At about 2 o'clock that night, someone rang the doorbell. I opened the door. The people outside the door grabbed me even though I was still wearing pajamas. I wasn't allowed to dress. They threw me in a jeep. It was the same jeep I saw the day before. I saw government officials from the village and another car with Secret Service. The jeep was going somewhere; the intelligence guys were always behind us. My heart was beating like hell, but I was stiff and could not move.

The narration eventually arrived at one hot spot (i.e., point of high emotional arousal) of Ahmed's torture experience. The reconstruction of the following short narration took about 20 minutes.

The men tied me to the wall with chains. I was fully naked. I felt so ashamed. They pushed my legs apart with their boots. They tied a large stone, about a kilo, to my testicles. The men from the Secret Service said, "If you write another slogan, we'll rip your balls out." I had known this torture method from other people who were arrested. And now it was my turn. I was in a lot of pain.

One of the men picked up [the weight tied to my testicles] and dropped it again [to the floor]. I couldn't bear it. I screamed loudly. The pain went through my whole body right into my stomach and my heart. I was shaking. As they repeated this, I felt like crying. I wanted to shout my pain. But as they continued, I started to blank out. My vision blurred. I saw everything just like through a veil. It felt like dying from the inside. In front of my eyes I saw my family and was very sad. I thought that the torturers would kill me. At that moment, I hoped they would kill me.

Ahmed's narration continued on this day until this first torture experience ended. Afterward, the therapist asked for a quick report of how Ahmed finally was released, to enable a safe ending of the session. At the end of the session, Ahmed was sad. He explained that on this day he had lost his masculinity. A part of him had died this day. After this, he had never felt close to any woman and never allowed any romantic feelings. The therapist commented that Ahmed had, so far, given up much of what belongs to a private life for resistance and political activity and that the treatment would eventually allow him to decide about his own goals and interests without many of the restrictions of his traumatic past.

In the subsequent sessions, the autobiography is briefly reread to the patient, who is instructed to fill in further information and to correct details. Further emotionally arousing peaks (i.e., the next stones and flowers) are then processed (i.e., additional traumatic experiences are added to the narration). The procedure is repeated in subsequent sessions until a final version of the survivor's autobiography of arousing events across the life span has been completed.

The Closing Session

The final NET session includes the closure of the procedure using rituals. The lifeline is reconsidered as a review of the client's life. The client, the translator, the cotherapist (if present), and the therapist sign the written narration. A copy of the signed document is handed to the client. With the agreement or upon request of the narrator, another copy may be passed on to lawyers or, in anonymized form, to human rights organizations as documentation of the atrocities that have happened. In addition, rituals can be used to ease the mourning and grief related to unresolved losses in the life history. After NET, treatment may continue with different treatment goals and procedures that target present problems (e.g., a refugee adjusting to a new role in the host society, a battered woman coping with further relationships).

Discussion of the Case

At the end of the NET treatment, Ahmed expressed thankfulness to the therapist, the interpreter, and the cotherapist. He felt that his story had been valued because it had been documented with much effort and was now available in written form. He wanted to make his story available for education about the situation in his home country. The therapist advised considering all potential risks of this decision. For the client's protection, he suggested extracting an anonymous testimony from the narration. Ahmed wanted to continue treatment. He could now see that only half of him had been living in recent years and that he might need help to find out how to further overcome his fear and pains related to his intimate life. He also planned to have a new medical examination of his genitals.

SUMMARY

Taken together, a range of randomized trials has tested the feasibility and efficacy of NET across various global contexts. NET can be carried out by specifically trained counselors with little formal education and by licensed psychotherapists who ideally have profited from a few days of workshops. NET has its place in undersupplied mental health structures in low- and middle-income countries as well as in well-developed mental health systems in high-income countries. It is emerging as the treatment of choice for traumatized refugees and may have a place for victims of other chronic forms of abuse, such as child maltreatment. With a clear human-rights focus, the approach can play an important role in the fight against individual symptoms and the causes of trauma related to abuse, persecution, and atrocities.

KEY IDEAS

- Narrative exposure therapy (NET) is a brief treatment (i.e., 6–16 sessions, depending on the setting) of complex PTSD that results from exposure to multiple traumatic events.

- During treatment, the patient (survivor), with support from and guided by the therapist, creates a detailed narration or biography, with a focus on recall of the traumatic events. This process includes contrasting the sensations, cognitions, and emotions felt during the recall with those experienced during the events.

- NET is based on memory theories of PTSD, which assume that PTSD is maintained by a dissociation of associative and contextual memory of traumatic events.

- NET has been developed for traumatized survivors of wars, torture, and persecution who have experienced a series of traumatic events over the life span.

- NET has been successfully tested with survivors from various cultures across the globe, including survivors who continue to live in unsafe regions.

- NET can be applied by trained lay therapists.

REFERENCES

Adenauer, H., Catani, C., Gola, H., Keil, J., Ruf, M., Schauer, M., & Neuner, F. (2011). Narrative exposure therapy for PTSD increases top-down processing of aversive stimuli—Evidence from a randomized controlled treatment trial. *BMC Neuroscience, 12*. http://dx.doi.org/10.1186/1471-2202-12-127

Bisson, J. I., Ehlers, A., Matthews, R., Pilling, S., Richards, D., & Turner, S. (2007). Psychological treatments for chronic post-traumatic stress disorder: Systematic review and meta-analysis. *The British Journal of Psychiatry, 190*, 97–104. http://dx.doi.org/10.1192/bjp.bp.106.021402

Bracha, H. S. (2004). Freeze, flight, fight, fright, faint: Adaptationist perspectives on the acute stress response spectrum. *CNS Spectrums, 9*, 679–685. http://dx.doi.org/10.1017/S1092852900001954

Brewin, C. R. (2014). Episodic memory, perceptual memory, and their interaction: Foundations for a theory of posttraumatic stress disorder. *Psychological Bulletin, 140*, 69–97. http://dx.doi.org/10.1037/a0033722

Brewin, C. R., Dalgleish, T., & Joseph, S. (1996). A dual representation theory of post-traumatic stress disorder. *Psychological Review, 103*, 670–686. http://dx.doi.org/10.1037/0033-295X.103.4.670

Catani, C. (2010). Krieg im Zuhause—ein Überblick zum Zusammenhang zwischen Kriegstraumatisierung und familiärer Gewalt [War in the home: A review of the relationship between family violence and war trauma]. *Verhaltenstherapie, 20*, 19–27. http://dx.doi.org/10.1159/000261994

Catani, C., Kohiladevy, M., Ruf, M., Schauer, E., Elbert, T., & Neuner, F. (2009). Treating children traumatized by war and tsunami: A comparison between exposure therapy and meditation-relaxation in North-East Sri Lanka. *BMC Psychiatry, 9*. Advance online publication. http://dx.doi.org/10.1186/1471-244X-9-22

Cohen, H., Liberzon, I., & Richter-Levin, G. (2009). Exposure to extreme stress impairs contextual odour discrimination in an animal model of PTSD. *International Journal of Neuropsychopharmacology, 12*, 291–303. http://dx.doi.org/10.1017/S146114570800919X

Conway, M. A., & Pleydell-Pearce, C. W. (2000). The construction of autobiographical memories in the self-memory system. *Psychological Review, 107*, 261–288. http://dx.doi.org/10.1037/0033-295X.107.2.261

Craske, M. G., Kircanski, K., Zelikowsky, M., Mystkowski, J., Chowdhury, N., & Baker, A. (2008). Optimizing inhibitory learning during exposure therapy. *Behaviour Research and Therapy, 46*, 5–27. http://dx.doi.org/10.1016/j.brat.2007.10.003

Craske, M. G., Treanor, M., Conway, C. C., Zbozinek, T., & Vervliet, B. (2014). Maximizing exposure therapy: An inhibitory learning approach. *Behaviour Research and Therapy, 58*, 10–23. http://dx.doi.org/10.1016/j.brat.2014.04.006

Crumlish, N., & O'Rourke, K. (2010). A systematic review of treatments for post-traumatic stress disorder among refugees and asylum-seekers. *Journal of Nervous and Mental Disease, 198*, 237–251. http://dx.doi.org/10.1097/NMD.0b013e3181d61258

Eberle-Sejari, R., Nocon, A., & Rosner, R. (2015). Zur wirksamkeit von psycho-therapeutischen interventionen bei jungen flüchtlingen und binnenvertriebenen mit posttraumatischen symptomen [The effectiveness of psychotherapeutic interventions in young refugees and internally displaced persons with post-traumatic symptoms]. *Kindheit und Entwicklung, 24*, 156–169. http://dx.doi.org/10.1026/0942-5403/a000171

Ehlers, A., Bisson, J., Clark, D. M., Creamer, M., Pilling, S., Richards, D., . . . Yule, W. (2010). Do all psychological treatments really work the same in posttraumatic stress disorder? *Clinical Psychology Review, 30*, 269–276. http://dx.doi.org/10.1016/j.cpr.2009.12.001

Ehlers, A., & Clark, D. M. (2000). A cognitive model of posttraumatic stress disorder. *Behaviour Research and Therapy, 38*, 319–345. http://dx.doi.org/10.1016/S0005-7967(99)00123-0

Ehring, T., Ehlers, A., & Glucksman, E. (2008). Do cognitive models help in predicting the severity of posttraumatic stress disorder, phobia, and depression after motor vehicle accidents? A prospective longitudinal study. *Journal of Consulting and Clinical Psychology, 76*, 219–230. http://dx.doi.org/10.1037/0022-006X.76.2.219

Ertl, V., Pfeiffer, A., Schauer, E., Elbert, T., & Neuner, F. (2011). Community-implemented trauma therapy for former child soldiers in Northern Uganda: A randomized controlled trial. *JAMA, 306*, 503–512. http://dx.doi.org/10.1001/jama.2011.1060

Fazel, M., Reed, R. V., Panter-Brick, C., & Stein, A. (2012). Mental health of displaced and refugee children resettled in high-income countries: Risk and protective factors. *The Lancet, 379*, 266–282. http://dx.doi.org/10.1016/S0140-6736(11)60051-2

Fazel, M., Wheeler, J., & Danesh, J. (2005). Prevalence of serious mental disorder in 7000 refugees resettled in western countries: A systematic review. *The Lancet, 365*, 1309–1314. http://dx.doi.org/10.1016/S0140-6736(05)61027-6

Foa, E. B., & Kozak, M. J. (1986). Emotional processing of fear: Exposure to corrective information. *Psychological Bulletin, 99*, 20–35. http://dx.doi.org/10.1037/0033-2909.99.1.20

Halligan, S. L., Michael, T., Clark, D. M., & Ehlers, A. (2003). Posttraumatic stress disorder following assault: The role of cognitive processing, trauma memory, and appraisals. *Journal of Consulting and Clinical Psychology, 71*, 419–431. http://dx.doi.org/10.1037/0022-006X.71.3.419

Hensel-Dittmann, D., Schauer, M., Ruf, M., Catani, C., Odenwald, M., Elbert, T., & Neuner, F. (2011). Treatment of traumatized victims of war and torture: A randomized controlled comparison of narrative exposure therapy and stress inoculation training. *Psychotherapy and Psychosomatics, 80*, 345–352. http://dx.doi.org/10.1159/000327253

Hijazi, A. M. (2012). *Narrative exposure therapy to treat traumatic stress in Middle Eastern refugees: A clinical trial* (Doctoral dissertation). Retrieved from https://digitalcommons.wayne.edu/cgi/viewcontent.cgi?referer=https://scholar.google.com/&httpsredir=1&article=1542&context=oa_dissertations

Hijazi, A. M., Lumley, M. A., Ziadni, M. S., Haddad, L., Rapport, L. J., & Arnetz, B. B. (2014). Brief narrative exposure therapy for posttraumatic stress in Iraqi refugees: A preliminary randomized clinical trial. *Journal of Traumatic Stress, 27*, 314–322. http://dx.doi.org/10.1002/jts.21922

Jacob, N., Neuner, F., Maedl, A., Schaal, S., & Elbert, T. (2014). Dissemination of psychotherapy for trauma spectrum disorders in postconflict settings: A randomized controlled trial in Rwanda. *Psychotherapy and Psychosomatics, 83*, 354–363. http://dx.doi.org/10.1159/000365114

Jelinek, L., Randjbar, S., Seifert, D., Kellner, M., & Moritz, S. (2009). The organization of autobiographical and nonautobiographical memory in posttraumatic stress disorder (PTSD). *Journal of Abnormal Psychology, 118*, 288–298. http://dx.doi.org/10.1037/a0015633

Jordans, M. J., & Tol, W. A. (2013). Mental health in humanitarian settings: Shifting focus to care systems. *International Health, 5*, 9–10. http://dx.doi.org/10.1093/inthealth/ihs005

Karunakara, U. K., Neuner, F., Schauer, M., Singh, K., Hill, K., Elbert, T., & Burnham, G. (2004). Traumatic events and symptoms of post-traumatic stress disorder amongst Sudanese nationals, refugees and Ugandans in the West Nile. *African Health Sciences, 4*, 83–93.

Kindt, M. (2014). A behavioural neuroscience perspective on the aetiology and treatment of anxiety disorders. *Behaviour Research and Therapy, 62*, 24–36. http://dx.doi.org/10.1016/j.brat.2014.08.012

Köbach, A., Schaal, S., Hecker, T., & Elbert, T. (2017). Psychotherapeutic intervention in the demobilization process: Addressing combat-related mental injuries with narrative exposure in a first and second dissemination stage. *Clinical Psychology & Psychotherapy, 24*, 807–825. http://dx.doi.org/10.1002/cpp.1986

Lang, P. J., Davis, M., & Ohman, A. (2000). Fear and anxiety: Animal models and human cognitive psychophysiology. *Journal of Affective Disorders, 61*, 137–159. http://dx.doi.org/10.1016/S0165-0327(00)00343-8

McPherson, J. (2012). Does narrative exposure therapy reduce PTSD in survivors of mass violence? *Research on Social Work Practice, 22*, 29–42. http://dx.doi.org/10.1177/1049731511414147

Metcalfe, J., & Jacobs, W. J. (1996). A hot-system/cool-system view of memory under stress. *PTSD Research Quarterly, 7*, 1–3.

Miller, G. A., Elbert, T., & Rockstroh, B. (2005). Judging psychiatric disorders in refugees. *The Lancet, 366*, 1604–1605. http://dx.doi.org/10.1016/S0140-6736(05)67655-6. http://dx.doi.org/10.1016/S0140-6736(05)67655-6

Morath, J., Gola, H., Sommershof, A., Hamuni, G., Kolassa, S., Catani, C., . . . Kolassa, I. T. (2014). The effect of trauma-focused therapy on the altered T cell distribution in individuals with PTSD: Evidence from a randomized controlled trial. *Journal of Psychiatric Research, 54*, 1–10. http://nbn-resolving.de/urn:nbn:de:bsz:352-289518. http://dx.doi.org/10.1016/j.jpsychires.2014.03.016

Morath, J., Moreno-Villanueva, M., Hamuni, G., Kolassa, S., Ruf-Leuschner, M., Schauer, M., . . . Kolassa, I.-T. (2014). Effects of psychotherapy on DNA strand break accumulation originating from traumatic stress. *Psychotherapy and Psychosomatics, 83*, 289–297. http://dx.doi.org/10.1159/000362739

Nandi, C., Crombach, A., Bambonye, M., Elbert, T., & Weierstall, R. (2015). Predictors of posttraumatic stress and appetitive aggression in active soldiers and former combatants. *European Journal of Psychotraumatology, 6*, 26553. http://dx.doi.org/10.3402/ejpt.v6.26553

Neuner, F., Catani, C., Ruf, M., Schauer, E., Schauer, M., & Elbert, T. (2008). Narrative exposure therapy for the treatment of traumatized children and adolescents (KidNET): From neurocognitive theory to field intervention. *Child and Adolescent Psychiatric Clinics of North America, 17*, 641–664, x. http://dx.doi.org/10.1016/j.chc.2008.03.001

Neuner, F., Kurreck, S., Ruf, M., Odenwald, M., Elbert, T., & Schauer, M. (2010). Can asylum-seekers with posttraumatic stress disorder be successfully treated? A randomized controlled pilot study. *Cognitive Behaviour Therapy, 39*, 81–91. http://dx.doi.org/10.1080/16506070903121042

Neuner, F., Onyut, P. L., Ertl, V., Odenwald, M., Schauer, E., & Elbert, T. (2008). Treatment of posttraumatic stress disorder by trained lay counselors in an African refugee settlement: A randomized controlled trial. *Journal of Consulting and Clinical Psychology, 76*, 686–694. http://dx.doi.org/10.1037/0022-006X.76.4.686

Olema, D. K., Catani, C., Ertl, V., Saile, R., & Neuner, F. (2014). The hidden effects of child maltreatment in a war region: Correlates of psychopathology in two generations living in Northern Uganda. *Journal of Traumatic Stress, 27*, 35–41. http://dx.doi.org/10.1002/jts.21892

Robjant, K., & Fazel, M. (2010). The emerging evidence for narrative exposure therapy: A review. *Clinical Psychology Review, 30*, 1030–1039. http://dx.doi.org/10.1016/j.cpr.2010.07.004

Saile, R., Ertl, V., Neuner, F., & Catani, C. (2016). Children of the postwar years: A two-generational multilevel risk assessment of child psychopathology in northern Uganda. *Development and Psychopathology, 28*, 607–620. http://dx.doi.org/10.1017/S0954579415001066

Saile, R., Neuner, F., Ertl, V., & Catani, C. (2013). Prevalence and predictors of partner violence against women in the aftermath of war: A survey among couples in northern Uganda. *Social Science & Medicine, 86,* 17–25. http://dx.doi.org/10.1016/j.socscimed.2013.02.046

Schauer, M., & Elbert, T. (2010). Dissociation following traumatic stress. *Zeitschrift für Psychologie, 218,* 109–127. http://dx.doi.org/10.1027/0044-3409/a000018

Schauer, M., Neuner, F., & Elbert, T. (2011). *Narrative exposure therapy* (2nd ed.). Seattle, WA: Hogrefe.

Schnyder, U., Bryant, R. A., Ehlers, A., Foa, E. B., Hasan, A., Mwiti, G., . . . Yule, W. (2016). Culture-sensitive psychotraumatology. *European Journal of Psychotraumatology, 7.* http://dx.doi.org/10.3402/ejpt.v7.31179

Schnyder, U., Ehlers, A., Elbert, T., Foa, E. B., Gersons, B. P. R., Resick, P. A., . . . Cloitre, M. (2015). Psychotherapies for PTSD: What do they have in common? *European Journal of Psychotraumatology, 6.* http://dx.doi.org/10.3402/ejpt.v6.28186

ter Heide, F. J. J., Mooren, T. M., & Kleber, R. J. (2016). Complex PTSD and phased treatment in refugees: A debate piece. *European Journal of Psychotraumatology, 7.* http://dx.doi.org/10.3402/ejpt.v7.28687

Zang, Y., Hunt, N., & Cox, T. (2013). A randomised controlled pilot study: The effectiveness of narrative exposure therapy with adult survivors of the Sichuan earthquake. *BMC Psychiatry, 13.* Advance online publication. http://dx.doi.org/10.1186/1471-244X-13-41

10

Pharmacotherapy for PTSD

What Psychologists Need to Know

Matthew J. Friedman and Jeffrey H. Sonis

In addition to recommending multiple psychological interventions for adults with posttraumatic stress disorder (PTSD), the *Clinical Practice Guideline for the Treatment of PTSD* (APA Clinical Practice Guideline; American Psychological Association [APA], 2017) includes four medications as evidence-based treatments for PTSD. Although most psychologists cannot prescribe such pharmacological agents, it is very likely that a significant number of their patients will receive pharmacotherapy before, during, or after their participation in a course of psychotherapy. Because some jurisdictions allow specially trained psychologists to prescribe, we address challenges faced by prescribing as well as nonprescribing psychologists. It is vital for all psychologists to know (a) what medications are effective for PTSD, (b) what side effects may emerge during treatment, (c) what to watch for after reduction or discontinuation of medication, (d) how to gauge the separate contributions of pharmacotherapy and psychotherapy to clinical success or failure, (e) which medications are not recommended for PTSD treatment and why, (f) how medications not recommended for PTSD may be important for treating co-occurring disorders, and (g) when to consult the prescribing clinician about medication-related concerns (e.g., discontinuation or dosage adjustment). Finally, within the construct of shared decision making when developing a course of treatment for a new patient, psychologists should be able to discuss the relative benefits and risks of pharmacotherapy as well as those of psychotherapy.

http://dx.doi.org/10.1037/0000196-010
Casebook to the APA Clinical Practice Guideline for the Treatment of PTSD, edited by
L. F. Bufka, C. V. Wright, and R. W. Halfond

In this chapter, we provide psychologists with information needed for these purposes. Specifically, we begin with a review of evidence supporting the APA Clinical Practice Guideline's favorable recommendation regarding four antidepressants: (a) sertraline, (b) paroxetine, (c) fluoxetine, and (d) venlafaxine. Next, we discuss potential harms (i.e., side effects of these medications). We also present likely scenarios following reduction or discontinuation of medication after a successful course of treatment. We complete this part of our discussion by reviewing other medications that psychologists' patients may be taking that have no demonstrated efficacy for PTSD, may produce significant side effects, or may be indicated for comorbid disorders. Another pertinent issue that we discuss is how to monitor ongoing pharmacotherapy during the initial clinical assessment and afterward. Finally, it is extremely important to know when to notify prescribing clinicians about medication-related concerns. Indeed, because the psychologist may see patients for weekly treatment, whereas the prescriber may have scheduled medication follow-up visits at monthly or longer intervals, the psychologist is often in the best position to observe complications from medication treatment and to make a timely referral to the prescribing clinician for reassessment of pharmacotherapy.

APA *CLINICAL PRACTICE GUIDELINE FOR THE TREATMENT OF PTSD*: MEDICATIONS

The APA guideline development panel made recommendations about a relatively small number of medications. To understand why, it is necessary to review some of the panel's methodology.

At the outset of its deliberations, prior to reviewing evidence for any interventions, the panel decided through a modified Delphi method that PTSD symptom reduction and serious harms were the two critical outcomes that would be the primary determinants of its recommendations. Although other outcomes, such as PTSD remission, reduction in comorbid depression, and daily functioning, are important for making treatment decisions, these were not weighted as heavily in making the guideline recommendations. In addition, the panel decided to make recommendations only for those psychological and pharmacological interventions with at least low strength of evidence (SOE) for either of the two critical outcomes in the systematic review that served as the primary evidence base for its deliberations (Jonas et al., 2013).

The systematic review that served as the evidence base for the guideline development panel included other medications: alpha blockers (e.g., prazosin); anticonvulsants and mood stabilizers other than topiramate (e.g., lamotrigine, tiagabine); atypical antipsychotics other than risperidone (e.g., olanzapine, quetiapine); serotonin–norepinephrine reuptake inhibitor (SNRI) antidepressants other than venlafaxine (e.g., duloxetine); selective serotonin reuptake inhibitor (SSRI) antidepressants other than fluoxetine, sertraline, and paroxetine (e.g., citalopram); tricyclic antidepressants, benzodiazepines, and second-generation antidepressants (e.g., bupropion, mirtazapine, nefazodone, trazodone). However, the APA Clinical Practice Guideline includes no recommendations for those medications because all of them had insufficient or very low SOE for both PTSD symptom reduction and serious harms. Also, because PTSD symptoms as a whole and not individual symptoms were a critical outcome, the panel did not make recommendations about medications that targeted only specific symptoms, such as nightmares or insomnia.

The guideline panel made the following recommendations on medications for treatment of PTSD among adults: Fluoxetine, paroxetine, and sertraline (all of which are SSRIs) each received a conditional recommendation for use based on the panel's conclusion that benefits slightly outweighed harms. Because there were no studies of patient preferences for any of the SSRI anti-depressants compared to placebo, patient preferences did not play a role in the panel's recommendations for fluoxetine, paroxetine, and sertraline. The panel did not make a recommendation for the following SSRIs: citalopram (insufficient SOE for both benefits and harms), fluvoxamine (one randomized clinical trial [RCT] excluded because of high risk of bias), and escitalopram (no RCTs identified).

Although medications sometimes have class effects, the panel did not make recommendations for classes of medications, such as SSRIs, but rather only for individual medications. A *medication class effect* occurs when medications with similar chemical structures (e.g., benzodiazepines, which have a benzene ring and a diazepine ring), as well as similar physiologic mechanisms of action (e.g., SSRIs, which selectively block reuptake of the neurotransmitter serotonin) or pharmacologic effects (e.g., anticonvulsants, which reduce seizure frequency), are believed to have analogous beneficial and adverse treatment effects (McAlister, Laupacis, Wells, & Sackett, 1999; Mills et al., 2014). Medications frequently exhibit class effects, and many clinical practice guidelines in medicine recommend classes of medications rather than individual medications within a class (Stone et al., 2014). However, different medications within the same class may differ significantly with respect to both efficacy and side effect profiles. As a result, analyses comparing harm/benefit ratios for medications within the same class can be complicated and difficult to interpret. Therefore, the panel decided to make recommendations only for specific medications and not for medication classes.

Venlafaxine, an SNRI, also received a conditional recommendation on grounds similar to those for fluoxetine, paroxetine, and sertraline. The panel did not make recommendations for the following SNRIs: duloxetine (insufficient SOE for benefits and harms) and desvenlafaxine (insufficient SOE for benefits and harms).

The panel concluded that there was insufficient evidence to recommend for or against risperidone for three reasons: (a) there was low SOE of a small-magnitude benefit for PTSD symptom reduction rather than moderate SOE as there was for the three SSRIs (fluoxetine, paroxetine, sertraline) and one SNRI (venlafaxine) that received weak recommendations from the panel; (b) none of the important outcomes had at least low SOE for benefit; and (c) adverse effects, including weight gain and dystonic reactions, were posited to be more serious than the adverse effects for the recommended medications. Because the benefits and the harms and burdens were thought to be balanced, the panel concluded that there was insufficient evidence to recommend for or against use of risperidone.

The panel also concluded that there was insufficient evidence to recommend for or against topiramate. There was moderate SOE for a medium- to large-magnitude benefit for PTSD symptom reduction. However, side effects, including memory difficulties and dizziness, were thought to be more serious than adverse effects for the three SSRIs or the one SNRI that were recommended (Jonas et al., 2013). As a result, the panel believed that benefits and the harms and burdens were balanced and concluded that there was insufficient evidence to recommend for or against use of topiramate.

Although several psychological treatments received strong recommendations from the panel while none of the medications did, the panel did not recommend that psychological treatments be used instead of medications because the systematic review identified only one head-to-head trial directly comparing a psychological treatment (eye-movement desensitization and reprocessing [EMDR] therapy) to a medication (fluoxetine) for PTSD (insufficient SOE; van der Kolk et al., 2007). Some other guideline panels have recommended psychological interventions as "first-line" treatment and medications as "second-line" (U.S. Department of Veterans Affairs & U.S. Department of Defense [VA/DoD], 2017) primarily based on larger magnitude effect sizes for PTSD symptom reduction for psychological treatments than for medications. However, the APA guideline development panel believed that the larger effect sizes for psychological treatments than for medications were inappropriate measures to assess comparative effectiveness for several reasons. First, all the trials of recommended medications, but none of the trials of recommended psychotherapies, used blinding of participants to treatment allocation. As Huhn and colleagues (2014) reported, three meta-analyses of treatments for mental disorders demonstrated smaller effect sizes for RCTs with blinding than for RCTs without blinding. Second, all the medication trials used contemporaneous controls, whereas the trials of psychological interventions that used wait-list controls used, by definition, noncontemporaneous controls. Huhn et al. further reported that eight meta-analyses of psychological and pharmacological treatments for mental disorders showed smaller effect sizes for contemporaneous controls than for noncontemporaneous controls. Finally, Huhn et al. reported that, in the research literature for treatment of depression, the effect size for psychological treatments compared to inactive comparators (ES = 0.67) was more than twice the effect size for medication treatments compared to the inactive comparator of placebo (ES = 0.31), but the effect size for the head-to-head comparison of medications to psychological treatments was near null (ES = 0.05). Accordingly, although the APA panel offered strong recommendations for several psychological interventions and only conditional recommendations for individual medications, it did not recommend that psychological interventions be preferred over medications.

Finally, at this time, it is reasonable to assume that the recommendations regarding evidence-based pharmacotherapy for PTSD apply to everyone because there is insufficient evidence to modify selection of pharmacologic agents for treatment of PTSD on the basis of gender, ethnicity, and other demographic characteristics. The recommended dosages of such medications will vary, though, on the basis of age and other personal factors that influence drug metabolism.

Putative Mechanism of Action of SSRIs and SNRIs (S/NRIs)

Serotonin and norepinephrine are two chemical messengers that mediate synaptic transmission in certain neurons. After release from the presynaptic nerve ending, they either activate postsynaptic receptors or are reabsorbed presynaptically (e.g., reuptake). Increasing the postsynaptic availability of either serotonin or norepinephrine is presumed to mediate an antidepressant effect. SSRIs increase the amount of postsynaptic serotonin, whereas SNRIs ease depression by increasing levels of both serotonin and norepinephrine in the brain. As shown in the APA Clinical Practice Guideline, there is also solid empirical evidence that SSRIs and SNRIs ameliorate PTSD as well as depressive symptoms.

Potential Harms From S/NRIs

Many effective medications for the treatment of particular disorders have side effects that must be seriously taken into account. For example, prescribing an S/NRI to a patient with PTSD and co-occurring bipolar disorder raises the risk of precipitating mood instability that might escalate into a manic episode. Because of such concerns, it is usually advisable to prescribe a mood-stabilizing medication (e.g., lithium or an antiepileptic agent) before initiating S/NRI treatment. However, there is evidence that different antidepressants have varying effects on destabilizing mood in bipolar disorder (McElroy et al., 2010).

The toxic or unwanted side effects that may result from S/NRIs are

- sexual dysfunction (e.g., decreased libido, delayed orgasm, anorgasmia);
- significant interactions with hepatic enzymes, producing adverse drug interactions that are sometimes very serious;
- clinically serious interactions for people also taking monoamine oxidase inhibitors;
- insomnia, restlessness, nausea, decreased appetite, daytime sedation, nervousness, and anxiety; and
- exacerbation of hypertension, particularly with venlafaxine.

It is important for psychologists to be aware of side effects from these recommended medications because they may affect their patient's well-being as well as his or her capacity to benefit from psychotherapy. Indeed, the impact of side effects can range from a minor annoyance that can be easily tolerated to a serious medical emergency. Obviously, all discomforts experienced by a patient cannot automatically be attributed to S/NRI medication, but if the side effects are consistent with what has been listed here, the prescribing clinician should be informed. An effective way to monitor potential side effects is to perform a brief check-in at the beginning of each session. There are also standardized self-report side-effect forms that patients might fill out routinely, such as the Antidepressant Side-Effect Checklist, which lists side effects from all categories of antidepressants (Uher et al., 2009). This guidance also applies to nonrecommended medications that the patient is receiving, discussed in the following sections and shown in Table 10.1.

Reduction or Discontinuation of S/NRIs

After a successful course of treatment with S/NRIs, symptom-free patients often want to stop their medication. Although a general rule of thumb is to continue S/NRI pharmacotherapy for 6 to 12 months, it is not unusual for remitted patients to prefer discontinuation much sooner. Given the importance of patient preference and treatment compliance, it is generally advisable to accede to such requests, if the patient is adamant, but to do so gradually in order

TABLE 10.1. Not Recommended, Commonly Used Medications: Comorbid Indications and Side Effects

Medication	Indication	Possible side effects
Citalopram (SSRI)	Depression Anxiety	Cardiac/intraventricular conduction abnormalities
Non-S/NRI antidepressants	Depression Anxiety disorders	Sedation Liver toxicity (nefazadone) Seizures, panic (buproprion) Weight gain (mirtazapine) Anticholinergic/cardiac arrhythmias (tricyclics) Hypertensive crisis/anticholinergic/hypotension (phenelzine)
Antiadrenergic	Hypertension Cardiac arrhythmias	Hypotension (prazosin, clonidine) Bradycardia/depression/asthma (propranolol)
Benzodiazepines	Anxiety Panic disorders	Sedation, ataxia, cognitive impairment Addiction potential May interfere with CBT treatment
Antipsychotics	Psychosis	Weight gain, metabolic syndrome Type 2 diabetes
Mood Stabilizers/ anticonvulsants	Bipolar disorder Seizure disorder	Neurological symptoms, ataxia Dizziness, sedation Teratogenic in pregnancy (valproate)

Note. SSRI = selective serotonin reuptake inhibitor; S/NRI = SSRI and SNRI; SNRI = serotonin–norepinephrine reuptake inhibitor; CBT = cognitive behavior therapy.

to determine whether or not pharmacotherapy is still necessary. For example, a typical protocol for tapering a maintenance dose of 200 mg of sertraline would be a 50-mg reduction every 2 weeks.

The advantage of a gradual dosage reduction is twofold: (a) to determine whether discontinuation is premature because the full dose of medication is still needed; and (b) to attenuate the severity of any discontinuation withdrawal syndrome. In both cases, patients will begin to exhibit PTSD symptoms (or depressive symptoms if comorbid depression had also been present), usually 3 to 7 days after the dose has been reduced. The symptoms will be the same as those that required treatment in the first place (e.g., intrusive recollections, avoidance symptoms, hypervigilance) and may vary from one patient to the next, depending on the original clinical presentation. In addition, a variety of somatic symptoms are common among persons with withdrawal symptoms related to SSRI or S/NRI discontinuation, including flu-like symptoms, imbalance, sensory disturbances, and others. Withdrawal symptoms are believed to be more common among persons discontinuing paroxetine than other SSRIs (Fava, Gatti, Belaise, Guidi, & Offidani, 2015; Jha, Rush, & Trivedi, 2018). If a symptom is a withdrawal syndrome, it will subside and disappear within 3 to 5 days. Patients should be told at the outset that they might experience such withdrawal symptoms, that they will only last a few days, that a symptom does not mean that their PTSD has returned, and that no immediate dosage increase is warranted. If, however, PTSD symptoms persist for more than a week, patients should be told that they still need the medication and that the prediscontinuation or reduction dose should be reinstated.

MEDICATIONS COMMONLY USED BUT NOT RECOMMENDED IN THE APA CLINICAL PRACTICE GUIDELINE

Unfortunately, the list of medications that did not receive recommendations (for or against) is much longer than the list of the four recommended S/NRIs. There are many reasons for this. First, large, rigorous RCTs are difficult and costly. With wavering interest in medications for PTSD by pharmaceutical companies, fewer and fewer RCTs have been conducted in recent years (Krystal et al., 2017). Indeed, there are relatively few rigorous RCTs on the many available medications to guide the APA Clinical Practice Guideline recommendations and decisions about optimal pharmacotherapy. As a result, many new medications, especially antidepressants recently put on the market, have never been tested in PTSD. Therefore, it cannot be assumed that an untested S/NRI has any efficacy for PTSD. Second, results from RCTs with a specific medication are sometimes conflicting or inconclusive where one trial is positive while another shows that the medication is no better than the placebo. Third, clinicians sometimes treat symptoms, rather than PTSD per se. Therefore, they may prescribe antipsychotics for agitation and flashbacks, benzodiazepines for anxiety and insomnia, mood stabilizers for aggression and impulsivity, and antiadrenergic/antihypertensive agents for excessive arousal. The APA Clinical Practice Guideline does not address such symptom-driven prescribing practices. Fourth, the guideline panel did not make recommendations for treatments that received very low or insufficient SOE ratings on the two critical outcomes of PTSD symptom reduction and serious harms. The most common reasons that treatments received very low or insufficient SOE ratings (and therefore did not receive recommendations) were: (a) high risk of bias ratings in the randomized trials of those treatments (i.e., one or more serious methodological flaws that threatened the validity of the study); (b) evidence based on one study with small sample size; and (c) evidence based on two studies with conflicting findings.

Table 10.1 lists major side effects from commonly used medications not recommended in the APA guideline.

Rationale for Prescribing Medications Not Recommended in the APA Clinical Practice Guideline

There are four major reasons why a patient with PTSD may receive a medication that did not receive a recommendation in the APA guideline: (a) low availability of evidence-based psychotherapy, (b) failure of CPG-recommended pharmacotherapy, (c) appropriate treatment of comorbid disorders, and (d) inappropriate pharmacotherapy.

Low Availability of Evidence-Based Psychotherapy

There is a limited pool of psychotherapists who are trained to provide psychological interventions that were strongly or conditionally recommended in the guideline. In many places outside of the U.S. Department of Veterans Affairs (VA) or military settings, relatively few available therapists are trained in one of the recommended psychological interventions. In contrast, there are many prescribing clinicians, including psychiatrists, and primary care clinicians (and, in some states, credentialed psychologists), who may diagnose PTSD and prescribe medication for their patients. Remote residential locales and long waiting lists for recommended psychotherapies can be very discouraging to clinicians and patients who would prefer psychotherapy to pharmacotherapy; however, given a choice between no psychotherapy for 3 months and immediate pharmacotherapy, it is easy to see why patients suffering from PTSD may opt for medication as their initial treatment, even if they prefer a psychological treatment. Given this familiar scenario, it is obviously extremely important that the best medicine be prescribed.

Failure of CPG-Recommended Pharmacotherapy

Following a 12-week trial of treatment with CPG-recommended sertraline, paroxetine, fluoxetine, or venlafaxine, patients may still be symptomatic. Indeed, in two large RCTs with sertraline and paroxetine respectively, remission rates were only 30% (Brady et al., 2000; Marshall, Beebe, Oldham, & Zaninelli, 2001).

Most of the other patients, following an adequate clinical trial, exhibited some improvement, but their level of distress and functional impairment remained substantial. There is little or no evidence-based pharmacotherapy to offer after a patient has been given an adequate trial of sertraline, paroxetine, fluoxetine, or venlafaxine and the trial has been unsuccessful.

Given this scenario and given the possibility of partial or minimal response to first-line pharmacotherapy, it is not surprising that prescribing clinicians may feel that they have no choice but to reach for nonevidence-based medications that they hope will ameliorate persisting distressing or incapacitating PTSD symptoms, scientific evidence notwithstanding. Such medications may include hypnotic and sedative or atypical antipsychotic agents for insomnia; benzodiazepines for anxiety; atypical antipsychotics for agitation, hypervigilance, and flashbacks; mood stabilizers and anticonvulsants for aggression and impulsivity; and antiadrenergic agents for insomnia, traumatic nightmares, or excessive arousal. At other times, they may implement adjunctive treatments in which they keep the patient on the initially prescribed S/NRI and add another medication to augment treatment. Such adjunctive agents often include atypical antipsychotics, prazosin, or benzodiazepines. The problem with both scenarios is that the patient is now receiving medications that do not have demonstrated efficacy and have known adverse effects. For example, up to 37% of PTSD patients receiving VA care are being prescribed benzodiazepines (Lund, Bernardy, Vaughan-Sarrazin, Alexander, & Friedman, 2013). These medications have many serious side effects, such as increased aggression, risk of depression, risk of substance abuse, ataxia (potentially causing falls and bone fractures in the elderly), cognitive blunting, and increasing PTSD severity. In addition, discontinuing benzodiazepines once they have been started may be difficult because of nonspecific anxiolytic effects, physical dependence, or because patients don't want to stop them despite their lack of efficacy for PTSD and potential harms (VA/DoD, 2017). With regard to cognitive blunting, there is strong preclinical evidence that benzodiazepines interfere with fear extinction and some clinical evidence that they interfere with prolonged exposure (PE) treatment (Guina, Rossetter, DeRhodes, Nahhas, & Welton, 2015; Rothbaum et al., 2014). Finally, because individuals with PTSD have a higher risk of chronic pain, benzodiazepines may increase the risk of serious central nervous system depression, respiratory depression, and death among those who are on chronic opiate therapy for chronic pain. Indeed, veterans with PTSD who receive benzodiazepines are more likely than others to also be prescribed opiates, and this trend is significantly higher among women than men (Bernardy & Friedman, 2016). On August 31, 2016, the U.S. Food and Drug Administration (FDA) announced that it was adding its strongest warning (i.e., a *boxed* warning) to the drug labeling of opiates and benzodiazepines.

Appropriate Treatment of Comorbid Disorders

In the general population, 80% of individuals with PTSD have at least one other co-occurring psychiatric disorder; depression and substance use disorder are the most frequent co-occurring problems (Kessler, Sonnega, Bromet, Hughes, & Nelson, 1995). Traumatic brain injury (TBI) may also occur, often sustained within the context of domestic violence, motor vehicle accidents, and sexual assault as well as in the war zone (Vasterling, Verfaellie, & Sullivan, 2009). As a result, many patients seeking psychotherapy may already be receiving appropriately prescribed medications for their co-occurring disorders. There are two important aspects to this. First, the presence of a co-occurring disorder (including a TBI) is not a contraindication for PE, EMDR, cognitive processing therapy, or other forms of therapy. Second, the medications are an appropriate aspect of the clinical picture and should be maintained throughout psychotherapy treatment.

Inappropriate Pharmacotherapy

Unfortunately, compliance with guidelines for treatment of PTSD developed by any organization is variable (Abrams, Lund, Bernardy, & Friedman, 2013; Barnett et al., 2014). For example, (a) less than 15% of veterans with PTSD have received evidence-based psychotherapy (Osei-Bonsu et al., 2017), (b) recommended S/NRIs are underutilized (Kobayashi, Patel, & Lotito, 2015), (c) nonrecommended benzodiazepines are overutilized (Kobayashi et al., 2015), and (d) veterans with PTSD are often prescribed medications not supported by previous guidelines (Abrams et al., 2013). There are many reasons for such findings, ranging from poor implementation of previous guidelines to clinicians' beliefs about the treatments that work and those that do not, based on clinical judgment rather than the rigorous review of scientific evidence that is the cornerstone of every CPG (Jain, Greenbaum, & Rosen, 2012; Wilk et al., 2013). Whatever the reasons, psychologists may often encounter patients who have received medications that not only affect quality of life and overall functioning, especially sedating medications affecting arousal level and motor control among older adults, but also are unlikely to help their PTSD.

This not-infrequent scenario is a serious and delicate challenge to psychologists who are not authorized to prescribe or change any medications, because the patient may be very reluctant to give up a medication (especially a benzodiazepine) and because the prescribing clinician may not welcome having his or her pharmacotherapy questioned by a psychologist. Psychologists credentialed to prescribe medications may also encounter this challenge, since they may have been referred patients who have already been placed on a nonrecommended medication. Ideally, the psychologist has a good working relationship with a prescribing clinician who appreciates any feedback regarding both the positive and the negative impact of medications. When mutual trust and respect do not characterize the relationship between a psychologist and a prescriber, communications about pharmacotherapy may be neither pleasant nor productive. Despite the potential pitfalls in such discussions, our opinion is that it is better to document and communicate such concerns rather than to remain silent about them.

ASSESSMENT OF PHARMACOTHERAPY DURING THE INITIAL EVALUATION AND AFTERWARD

Given the likelihood that a significant number of a psychologist's patients will receive pharmacotherapy at some point, it is important to document and monitor responses to medication throughout treatment. The APA Clinical Practice Guideline states, "monitoring PTSD symptoms across the course of treatment likely provides insight into progress and highlights ongoing clinical targets" (APA, 2017, p. 65). From our perspective, this certainly applies to routinely monitoring the presence or absence of pharmacotherapy within the context of the patient's entire treatment regimen.

During the first visit, medication history should be assessed, and a diagnostic assessment should be conducted.

- Medication history: what medications and dose the patient is receiving, specifically for PTSD; whether such medication is recommended by the APA Clinical Practice Guideline (see Table 10.2); how long the patient has been on this medication, along with a history of other medications previously prescribed for PTSD; side effects or complaints about the medication (see Tables 10.1 and 10.2); and medications currently prescribed for other psychiatric or medical problems.

- Diagnostic assessment: whether the patient has PTSD; symptom severity of PTSD, using a standardized scale such as the PTSD Checklist for *DSM–5* (PCL-5; U.S. Department of Veterans Affairs, National Center for PTSD, 2017; such information is important to establish a baseline by which to gauge any added benefit of psychotherapy); whether the patient has another psychiatric problem; and whether the current medication is appropriate for a comorbid problem, even if it is not recommended for PTSD.

In addition to the routine documentation and longitudinal monitoring of patients receiving psychotherapy for PTSD, clinicians will also want to document

TABLE 10.2. Medications That Received Recommendations in the APA Clinical Practice Guideline

Medication	Category	Recommendation
Fluoxetine	SSRI	Conditional for
Paroxetine	SSRI	Conditional for
Sertraline	SSRI	Conditional for
Venlafaxine	SNRI	Conditional for
Risperidone	Atypical antipsychotic	Insufficient[a]
Topiramate	Anticonvulsant	Insufficient

Note. SSRI = selective serotonin reuptake inhibitor; SNRI = serotonin norepinephrine reuptake inhibitor. The first four medications are listed in rank order. Data from American Psychological Association (2017, p. ii).
[a]Insufficient = insufficient evidence to recommend for or against use.

initial medication assessment as described along with changes in doses and side effects over the course of care.

SHARED DECISION MAKING: CHOOSING THE BEST TREATMENT

Among the four recommended medications for treatment of PTSD, there is essentially no difference in the magnitude of the treatment effects (i.e., the effect sizes for PTSD symptom reduction and the risk differences for binary outcomes, such as loss of PTSD diagnosis) or the strength of evidence for those effects. Accordingly, the choice of medication for treatment of PTSD should be driven by patient preferences and values regarding side effects of medications, other illnesses that the patient might have, other medications (including over-the-counter medications) that the patient is taking, and the cost of medications. We recommend individuals not start psychotherapy and medications simultaneously but rather get on a stable dose of medication for at least 2 months before beginning psychotherapy or have had the active ingredients of psychotherapy before adding medications. Otherwise, the reason for any clinical improvement may be erroneously attributed, and the patient may not be able to feel confident in the distinct contributing effects of each intervention.

Sexual side effects are important to many patients; among the three recommended SSRI medications, paroxetine is less likely to cause these side effects than fluoxetine or sertraline (Gartlehner et al., 2011). Data comparing the incidence of sexual side effects of venlafaxine, the S/NRI recommended by the APA guideline, to the incidence of the three recommended SSRIs are not available. Therefore, for patients for whom sexual side effects are more important than gastrointestinal side effects, paroxetine may be a good choice.

Gastrointestinal side effects are commonly reported among users of the three recommended SSRIs. Diarrhea is more common with sertraline (16%) than with paroxetine, fluoxetine, or venlafaxine (8%; Gartlehner et al., 2011). Because irritable bowel syndrome is more common among persons who have PTSD (Afari et al., 2014), patients with irritable bowel syndrome with predominant diarrhea may prefer paroxetine, fluoxetine, or venlafaxine. Nausea and vomiting are more common with venlafaxine (33%) than with SSRIs (22%; Gartlehner et al., 2011). Thus, for patients with upper gastrointestinal disorders, such as peptic ulcer disease and gastrointestinal reflux disease, or gastrointestinal symptoms, such as nonulcer dyspepsia, one of the three recommended SSRIs (i.e., paroxetine, sertraline, or fluoxetine) may be a better choice than venlafaxine.

Potential medication interactions are important considerations. Among the recommended medications, both paroxetine and fluoxetine are potent inhibitors of the CYP2D6 cytochrome enzyme, which is involved in metabolism of other medications. This may lead to altered blood levels due to greater metabolic elimination of these other medications. Sertraline may, in general, be less likely to cause drug interactions than either paroxetine or fluoxetine, but medication interactions should always be checked. Many online medication-interaction websites are now available, such as the one via WebMD (https://www.webmd.com/interaction-checker/default.htm).

SSRIs have been linked to serotonin syndrome, a potentially lethal condition resulting from overstimulation of serotonergic receptors that presents with changes in mental status (e.g., agitation), neuromuscular changes (e.g., muscle rigidity, tremor), and autonomic system hyperactivity (e.g., increased sweating, fever; Volpi-Abadie, Kaye, & Kaye, 2013). It is believed that this syndrome occurs most commonly as a result of interactions between SSRIs and other serotonergic medications, but it can also be precipitated by SSRI medication alone. It is believed to be relatively uncommon, but because of its potential severity, it should be included in the shared decision-making process between a clinician and a patient. To our knowledge, there is no evidence that any one SSRI is more or less likely to cause serotonin syndrome than any other SSRI.

DIVERSITY CONSIDERATIONS IN PHARMACOLOGICAL TREATMENT OF PTSD

The systematic review that served as the evidence base for the APA guideline, including studies published to May 2012, reported that "Evidence was insufficient to determine whether any treatment approaches are more or less effective for specific subgroups, including victims of particular types of trauma" (Jonas et al., 2013, p. ES-17). Very few of the randomized trials included in the systematic review conducted subgroup analyses to address this question. Indeed, the heterogeneity of enrolled samples, relatively small number of trials for each specific treatment, and covariation of some subgroup characteristics (e.g., gender) with other subgroup characteristics (e.g., rape as the type of trauma) precluded stratified analyses or metaregression by the group that conducted the systematic review. A recently published update to the systematic review, based on studies published to April 2017, also concluded that evidence was insufficient to determine whether there was treatment effect heterogeneity by patient demographic characteristics (e.g., ethnicity or gender), trauma types, psychiatric comorbidities (e.g., depression, substance use disorders), chronicity, or severity of PTSD (Hoffman et al., 2018). Accordingly, we do not believe that there is justification, at this time, for a clinician to select any of the recommended SSRIs over any other SSRI or over venlafaxine (or vice versa) based on such subgroup characteristics alone. Patient preferences and side effect profiles, as described previously, should be important determinants of which medication the patient and clinician select.

Among the three SSRIs and one S/NRI recommended by the APA guideline, paroxetine should be avoided during pregnancy because of the increased risk of congenital heart defects (Bérard et al., 2016). Use of sertraline, fluoxetine, and venlafaxine during pregnancy is a complicated topic and involves weighing the risks of harm to the fetus and neonate due to SSRI or S/NRI use against the risk of harm due to untreated PTSD (or untreated depression), among patients who prefer medications or are unable to access a recommended psychotherapy. Although the American College of Obstetrics and Gynecology and the American Psychiatric Association have not issued joint recommendations for management of PTSD during pregnancy, as they did for management of depression during pregnancy (Yonkers et al., 2009), we believe that similar considerations are likely to apply. We recommend that any woman considering pregnancy or who becomes pregnant while taking sertraline, fluoxetine, or venlafaxine for PTSD should discuss the risks and benefits of using those medications during pregnancy and while breastfeeding with the clinicians treating and managing her PTSD and pregnancy.

CASE ILLUSTRATIONS

Two case illustrations are presented that illustrate practical issues in the use of medications for treatment of persons with PTSD. Some components are drawn from real patients, but other elements, including the names of the patients and clinicians, are fictitious.

Case Illustration 1

Frank James is a 40-year-old self-identified Latino man who saw Dr. Alicia Brunello, his primary care physician (PCP), because he was concerned that he might have PTSD. While driving at night about a year earlier, he had hit a pedestrian who was walking on the side of the road. The pedestrian was severely injured and died shortly after being transported to the hospital by ambulance. Mr. James sought care because he did not want his symptoms to affect his relationship with his wife.

   Throughout the year prior to his seeking treatment, he had been experiencing vivid memories of the pedestrian's injured face multiple times every day. He felt intense anxiety when he got into his car at night, and the anxiety would last for at least an hour. He actively avoided driving anywhere near the scene of the crash. He blamed himself for the crash and could not get rid of the feeling that he is a "terrible" person because he was not careful enough. He reported that although he used to be a "good sleeper," he was currently waking up at least five times every night and was tired all the time. He denied suicidal thoughts. He reported drinking about one or two beers per night and denied using illicit drugs.

   Dr. Brunello performed a brief mental status examination, which was normal except for mildly depressed mood. She asked Mr. James to complete the PCL-5 and the Patient Health Questionnaire 9 (PHQ-9). While he was completing those forms, Dr. Brunello reviewed Mr. James' past medical history on the electronic medical record. She noted that he had a history of irritable bowel syndrome with diarrhea predominance, paroxysmal supraventricular tachycardia (SVT, episodes of rapid heart rate), and borderline high blood pressure. His blood pressure in the office was 135/82. His only medication was the calcium channel blocker, verapamil extended release 180 mg daily, for prevention of SVT. His total symptom score on the PCL-5 was 56, and he met criteria for PTSD based on diagnostic criteria. His PHQ-9 score was 7, consistent with mild depressive symptoms.

Dr. Brunello told Mr. James that he met criteria for PTSD and discussed treatment options. She gave Mr. James the option of reviewing the PTSD Treatment Decision Aid developed by the U.S. Department of Veterans Affairs National Center for PTSD (https://www.ptsd.va.gov/apps/decisionaid/) at home and returning for a second visit to engage in shared decision making, but Mr. James wanted to begin treatment at the first visit. Dr. Brunello presented the treatment options as (a) medication treatment, (b) referral to a psychologist for an evidence-based psychotherapy, (c) both, or (d) no treatment. Mr. James preferred treatment with medication, stating, "That's why I came in today." After reviewing the common and the rare but serious side effects of the SSRIs fluoxetine, sertraline, and paroxetine and of the SNRI venlafaxine, Dr. Brunello prescribed paroxetine 20 mg daily; because sertraline is more likely than other SSRIs to cause diarrhea, Dr. Brunello chose to avoid its use in this patient with diarrhea-predominant irritable bowel syndrome.

At his 6-week follow-up visit, Mr. James reported minimal improvement. He stated that he might be having fewer intrusive memories related to the crash but was otherwise unchanged. He denied nausea, diarrhea, worsening anxiety, suicidal thoughts, erectile dysfunction, and difficulty achieving orgasm. His PCL-5 score was 54, indicating no improvement from the medication. Dr. Brunello recommended increasing the dose of paroxetine to 30 mg daily for 1 week and then 40 mg daily thereafter.

At his follow-up visit 4 weeks later, Mr. James reported substantial improvement. He was waking up only once every night, had fewer intrusive memories, and felt less irritable and "short" with his wife. His PCL-5 score was 40, a drop of 14 points from his last visit. He also noted that the intermittent diarrhea caused by his irritable bowel syndrome had improved. However, he noted that he had difficulty maintaining an erection long enough to complete intercourse (a well-known side effect from SSRIs) and described this as a "deal breaker." His blood pressure was 130/78.

Dr. Brunello discussed the following options with Mr. James: (a) waiting a few weeks to see if the erectile dysfunction (ED) decreased; (b) lowering the dose to 30 mg, recognizing that good clinical response at 40 mg might not be maintained at a lower dose; (c) switching to a medication, venlafaxine, that is in a different chemical class but is a recommended evidence-based treatment for PTSD; (d) adding a medication to improve erectile function, like sildenafil; and (e) stopping paroxetine and being referred to a psychologist for an evidence-based psychotherapy. Mr. James asked whether venlafaxine was less likely to cause ED. Dr. Brunello responded that while the risk of ED is about the same for venlafaxine as it is for paroxetine, some patients who have ED on one medication do not have ED on a medication from a different chemical class. Dr. Brunello also explained that if Mr. James preferred to switch to venlafaxine, his blood pressure would need to be monitored closely because this medication has the potential to increase blood pressure. Mr. James stated that he would like to try venlafaxine. Dr. Brunello recommended tapering paroxetine while gradually increasing the dose of venlafaxine and gave Mr. James a detailed schedule for the process. She asked Mr. James to purchase a home blood-pressure monitor, check his blood pressure daily, and bring the monitor to the next visit in 2 weeks.

At his follow-up visit 4 weeks after starting venlafaxine, Mr. James reported that although his PTSD symptoms worsened during the cross-tapering process, his PTSD symptoms had improved and his ED had resolved since starting venlafaxine ER 75 mg daily. His PCL-5 score was 25, and his average blood pressure from his home monitor over the previous two weeks had been 126/76. He had mild dry mouth and mild dizziness but felt he could live with those symptoms. Dr. Brunello prescribed a 3-month supply of venlafaxine with three refills and recommended follow-up in 3 to 6 months.

Mr. James called Dr. Brunello a year later. His PTSD symptoms were tolerable (PLC-5 score = 15), his blood pressure had remained normal, and he had not had recurrence of ED. However, he didn't want to be on venlafaxine "forever" and was tired of having a dry mouth. Mr. James tapered venlafaxine over a 4-week period, per Dr. Brunello's instructions, and for the next 3 months noticed no recurrence. However, over the following 6 months, he noticed a gradual recurrence of PTSD symptoms, and he returned to see Dr. Brunello. His PCL-5 was 45, and he reported frequent awakenings, recurrence of intrusive memories, and other symptoms. He stated that he didn't want to go back on medications and asked about psychotherapy. Dr. Brunello informed Mr. James that multiple psychotherapies have been shown to be effective for treatment of PTSD and gave him a handout with the URL for the APA website that describes psychotherapies for treatment of PTSD, as noted in the CPG (http://www.apa.org/ptsd-guideline/treatments/index.aspx). She referred him to a psychology practice in town for psychotherapy.

This case illustrates multiple issues with regard to medication use.

Initial Choice of Medication

Because Mr. James had diarrhea-predominant irritable bowel syndrome, Dr. Brunello and the patient chose to avoid sertraline, which is associated with a greater risk of diarrhea than other recommended treatments for PTSD.

Starting Dose and Titrating Up (Start Low, Go Slow)

Dr. Brunello increased the dose of paroxetine when Mr. James did not have a clinical response at the initial dose of 20 mg. It is standard practice to increase the dose of a medication within the therapeutic range if a patient does not have a clinical response at a lower dose. However, a recent meta-analysis for SSRIs for treatment of depression showed only a weak dose–response relationship (Jakubovski, Varigonda, Freemantle, Taylor, & Bloch, 2016). In addition, in the two trials that compared fixed doses of paroxetine (Marshall et al., 2001) and fluoxetine (Martenyi, Brown, & Caldwell, 2007) for treatment of PTSD, the effect sizes for PTSD symptom reduction and depression symptom reduction were similar for lower and higher doses. On the other hand, in all trials of SSRIs for PTSD that used a flexible dose strategy, the mean or median dosage at which treatment response occurred was substantially higher than the starting dose, providing indirect evidence that up-titration of SSRIs when patients do not respond at lower dosages is a reasonable strategy (Brady et al., 2000; Davidson et al., 2006; Davidson, Rothbaum, van der Kolk, Sikes, & Farfel, 2001; Friedman, Marmar, Baker, Sikes, & Farfel, 2007; Martenyi, Brown, Zhang, Prakash, & Koke, 2002; Tucker et al., 2001; van der Kolk et al., 2007; Zohar et al., 2002). There is also evidence that starting low may minimize medication intolerance due to side effects (McCormack, Allan, & Virani, 2011).

How to Address Adverse Effects

In this scenario, Dr. Brunello offered Mr. James multiple options for erectile dysfunction, including watchful waiting, lowering the dose (recognizing that this might lead to worsening of PTSD symptoms), switching to a different medication, adding a medication to treat ED, or switching to a nonmedication treatment (i.e., psychotherapy) for PTSD. Other side effects of recommended medications can be addressed using similar approaches.

How To Address Lack of Response, After Up-Titration

Options typically include switching to a different medication in the same class (e.g., from one SSRI to a different SSRI), switching from one medication class to a medication in a different class (e.g., from an SSRI to an S/NRI), and switching to a nonmedication treatment (i.e., psychotherapy). The research literature on options for treatment-resistant depression is much more robust than for treatment-resistant PTSD. Based on the relative dearth of research literature on best strategies for managing treatment-resistant PTSD, the APA Clinical Practice Guideline did not include any recommendations on this important issue.

Monitoring Symptoms

Use of a self-report instrument, such as the PCL-5, can be very useful for monitoring response to treatment (Weathers et al., 2013). Research on the PCL-5 indicated that a 10-point or greater decrement was indicative of a clinically significant change (Monson et al., 2008). Although clinically significant change in score on the PCL-5 has not yet been identified, it is likely to be in the same range as the PTSD Checklist for *DSM–IV* (U.S. Department of Veterans Affairs, National Center for PTSD, 2017).

**Medical Comorbidities That Need to be Taken
Into Account When Choosing Medications**

In this case illustration, Dr. Brunello needed to monitor the patient's blood pressure because venlafaxine has been associated with increases in blood pressure.

Recurrence of Symptoms After Discontinuation

This case illustration shows that PTSD symptoms may recur after discontinuation of medication. Clinicians should be alert to this possibility and maintain vigilance for symptom recurrence after discontinuation.

Case Illustration 2

Margaret Beeson is a 45-year-old woman of Scottish ancestry who was robbed at gunpoint a year earlier while walking home from a restaurant at night. Immediately after the trauma, she developed nightmares, difficulty concentrating and sleeping, and a feeling that she was not connected to the rest of the world. She had not gone out at night since the attack. She kept thinking that her symptoms would improve, but they did not. Several months later, she started feeling sad all the time and thinking about death constantly. Her appetite was poor, and she lost 10 pounds (going from 130 to 120 pounds). When her best friend noticed how much weight she had lost, she pushed her to see a psychiatrist, Dr. Robert Steel.

Dr. Steel diagnosed Ms. Beeson with PTSD and major depressive disorder (MDD). Because Ms. Beeson did not want to see a therapist on a regular basis, she and Dr. Steel agreed to medication treatment. Her past medical history was significant only for cigarette smoking. At the time of the physical exam, her blood pressure was 124/75 (classified as "elevated blood pressure" by the American Heart Association Guidelines; Whelton et al., 2018).

When Dr. Steel reviewed the side effect profile of the three recommended SSRIs and the one recommended SNRI (venlafaxine), Ms. Beeson was disappointed to learn of the high incidence of sexual dysfunction and side effects with all of them. Because she smoked cigarettes (one pack per day for 10 years) and had considered stopping, she and Dr. Steel agreed to treatment with bupropion XL 150 mg once daily for 3 days, then 150 mg twice daily. Even though it is not recommended in the APA Clinical Practice Guideline, bupropion has shown efficacy in treatment of depression and has been shown to be effective for smoking cessation (Haddad & Davis, 2016).

Ms. Beeson did not keep her 1-month follow-up appointment with Dr. Steel. She continued to take bupropion because it reduced (but did not eliminate) her craving for cigarettes; she also started using a nicotine patch (21 mg/day) that she purchased over the counter. She was having fewer nightmares and was less jumpy than before. She still felt sad most of the time and had poor appetite. Most of her symptoms of PTSD were unchanged. A friend recommended that she see Dr. Selma Schwartz, a psychologist with expertise in psychotherapy for PTSD. At the initial evaluation, Dr. Schwartz concluded that Ms. Beeson met criteria for both PTSD and MDD and felt that she could benefit from one of the psychotherapies recommended by the APA guideline. After discussing risks and benefits of different treatments and exploring Ms. Beeson's preferences for treatments, Dr. Schwartz and Ms. Beeson agreed to a course of prolonged exposure. After eight sessions, Dr. Schwartz concluded that Ms. Beeson's PTSD was improving (her PCL-5 score had decreased from 45 to 25) and her depression was improving. However, Ms. Beeson continued to report difficulty with sleep onset and sleep maintenance. Because Ms. Beeson's PTSD and depression symptoms had improved, Dr. Schwartz wondered if the insomnia was due to bupropion and urged Ms. Beeson to see Dr. Steel.

At her visit with Dr. Steel 2 weeks later, Ms. Beeson reported continued improvement in her PTSD and depression symptoms but also continued difficulty sleeping. She reported that she had been able to stay off cigarettes and attributed her success to the use of a nicotine patch (which she continued at a dose of 21 mg/day) and bupropion. Dr. Steel was surprised to learn of her use of the nicotine patch. Her average blood pressure, based on two readings, was 170/90. Dr. Steel thought that both the sleep difficulties and the treatment-emergent hypertension could be due to the combination of the nicotine patch and bupropion (Jorenby et al., 1999). Dr. Steel discontinued bupropion and asked Ms. Beeson to stop the nicotine patch. He was hopeful that she would maintain improvement in PTSD and depression as she continued with the prolonged exposure treatment. He told her that if she developed cravings for cigarettes in the future, varenicline could be considered. He urged her to see her PCP for follow-up of her blood pressure.

When she saw her PCP, Dr. Anne Shemp, 2 weeks later, her blood pressure on the home blood pressure monitor that she had purchased, averaged over the 2-week period, was 122/72. Her blood pressure in the office was 126/74. However, she still had a little difficulty falling asleep. Dr. Shemp recommended that she reduce salt consumption because of her elevated blood pressure and that she not use the nicotine patch along with bupropion in the future.

Dr. Schwartz continued to see Ms. Beeson for 15 sessions in which she completed prolonged exposure treatment. At a 6-month follow-up visit, she had few symptoms of PTSD or depression. Her blood pressure on her home monitor averaged 124/76. She continued to have some difficulty falling asleep but did not find it bothersome enough to consider medication or psychotherapy (e.g., cognitive behavior therapy for insomnia).

This case also illustrates important issues in the treatment of PTSD.

Comorbidity Is the Rule and May Influence Treatment Choice

A majority of patients with PTSD meet criteria for one other diagnosis, such as major depressive disorder, an anxiety disorder, or substance use disorder. In this case illustration, the patient, Ms. Beeson, had comorbid depression. Based on the dearth of evidence addressing which PTSD treatments are most effective for patients with specific comorbid disorders, the APA Clinical Practice

Guideline did not make recommendations for these circumstances. Dr. Steel, the psychiatrist in this case illustration, prescribed bupropion (which is not a recommended treatment for PTSD included in the guideline) because, in addition to depression, the patient smoked cigarettes and wanted help with smoking cessation. The patient also expressed a strong preference to avoid medications associated with sexual side effects.

Use of Medications Not Recommended in a Guideline

Many patients are treated for PTSD with medications not recommended in a guideline. In this case illustration, Ms. Beeson was treated with bupropion, which is not recommended for PTSD by the APA Clinical Practice Guideline but is recommended in other guidelines for treatment of depression (e.g., the guideline from the American Psychiatric Association; Gelenberg et al., 2010). Ms. Beeson declined all of the four S/NRI medications recommended for PTSD because of concerns about sexual side effects. In this case, bupropion was a good choice to address her non-PTSD-related problems; specifically, it is effective for treatment of depression, and it is also effective for cigarette smoking cessation. Thus, although the choice of bupropion was not unreasonable given the totality of Ms. Beeson's situation, it would be particularly important for the clinician to monitor PTSD symptoms. At the point at which Ms. Beeson saw the psychologist, Dr. Schwartz, she had been on bupropion for at least 8 weeks and still met criteria for PTSD and MDD. However, because Dr. Schwartz had not seen Ms. Beeson prior to initiation of bupropion, Dr. Schwartz could not determine whether she had experienced any symptom improvement since starting bupropion. In addition, Dr. Schwartz knew that bupropion was being used for smoking cessation. Accordingly, Dr. Schwartz did not contact Dr. Steel at that point to discuss whether Ms. Beeson should continue bupropion, but it would have been reasonable if she had. When Ms. Beeson had continued insomnia, despite improvement in PTSD and depression during her prolonged exposure treatment, Dr. Schwartz appropriately recommended that Ms. Beeson see Dr. Steel for reevaluation.

Beware of Over-the-Counter Medications

Over-the-counter medications, just like prescribed medications, can interact in potentially dangerous ways with other medications that the patient is taking (Honig & Gillespie, 1995). In this case illustration, Ms. Beeson added the nicotine patch and did not inform Dr. Steel. This is not an uncommon occurrence and, in this case, led to dangerous increases in Ms. Beeson's blood pressure, due to the interaction between the combination of nicotine and bupropion.

Medication side effects can be physiological responses, such as elevations in blood pressure, although side effects are frequently thought of as symptoms. Physiological parameters, such as blood pressure elevations, are not associated with symptoms. In this case illustration, the elevated blood pressure was detected only by accident when the patient was referred back to the psychiatrist because of the insomnia.

SUMMARY

Many PTSD patients receiving psychotherapy also receive medications. Often the medications have been prescribed before psychotherapy has been initiated. Because it is not unusual for psychotherapists to see patients more frequently than their prescribing practitioners see them, psychotherapists are often in a better position to observe both beneficial and adverse outcomes from medications.

The APA Clinical Practice Guideline includes four S/NRI antidepressants as evidence-based treatments for PTSD: (a) sertraline, (b) paroxetine, (c) fluoxetine, and (d) venlafaxine. There are no additional recommendations for any other medication.

Practitioners should be aware that these medications have side effects that may cause some patients to withdraw from treatment. Therefore, it is useful for prescribing practitioners to discuss the possibility of such side effects before starting treatment so that patients are prepared for the emergence of the side effects. It is also important for nonprescribing clinicians to know about side effects so that they can be discussed adequately during a psychotherapy session. Although these medications have a relatively benign side-effect profile, they sometimes produce sexual symptoms, gastrointestinal symptoms, drug interactions, and a few other symptoms that may affect patients' willingness to take these medications as prescribed.

Patients may also be receiving other medications that are not recommended by the APA Clinical Practice Guideline for PTSD or other guidelines. Psychologists should be sufficiently familiar with such medications so that they can refer the patient back to the prescribing clinician to assess the impact of pharmacotherapy. It is important to monitor and to document medications received as well as their effects throughout treatment; all therapeutic decisions should be made after thorough discussion of risks, benefits, and other options within the context of shared decision making.

KEY IDEAS

- The APA Guideline did not include a recommendation for psychotherapy over pharmacotherapy or vice versa as initial treatment for PTSD. Patient preferences about the following elements should be incorporated into shared decision making about choice of psychotherapy or medications for initial treatment of PTSD: (a) putative mechanism of action, (b) what the patient will need to do, (c) frequency of visits required, (d) time between initiation of treatment and onset of benefit, (e) duration of benefit after cessation of treatment, and (f) risks and adverse effects.

- The APA Guideline suggests one of four medications for pharmacotherapy of PTSD: (a) fluoxetine, (b) paroxetine, (c) sertraline, and (d) venlafaxine.

- Because the recommended medications are equally effective for treatment of PTSD, the choice of medication should be based on patient preferences regarding medication side effects, other medical or psychiatric illnesses, medications that the patient is taking, and the medication costs.

- Medications should be started at the lowest therapeutic dose. If the patient is tolerating the medication but has not had an adequate response at 4 to 6 weeks, the dose may be increased within the therapeutic range. Subsequent dosage changes may be made at 4-week intervals. Self-report instruments, such as the PCL-5, can be useful for monitoring response to treatment.

- Patients who do not respond to the maximal dose of a recommended medication may be switched to another recommended medication in the same class (e.g., from one SSRI to another SSRI), to a medication in a different class (e.g., from an SSRI to venlafaxine, an SNRI), or to psychotherapy.

- When a patient has a good clinical response to a recommended medication but has an intolerable side effect, options include decreasing the dose, switching to another recommended medication, treating the side effect with a medication targeting the side effect (e.g., phosphodiesterase-5 inhibitors to treat erectile dysfunction), and switching to psychotherapy.

- A standard course of medication treatment is 6 to 12 months.

- Somatic withdrawal symptoms, including flu-like symptoms, imbalance, and sensory disturbances, may occur on discontinuation of SSRIs. Withdrawal symptoms are believed to be more common among persons discontinuing paroxetine than other SSRIs.

- Nonprescribing clinicians should be aware of potential side effects of other (non-S/NRI) medications that might be prescribed for PTSD. Nonprescribing clinicians should monitor potential problems so that they can provide such information to the prescribing clinician.

REFERENCES

Abrams, T. E., Lund, B. C., Bernardy, N. C., & Friedman, M. J. (2013). Aligning clinical practice to PTSD treatment guidelines: Medication prescribing by provider type. *Psychiatric Services, 64,* 142–148. http://dx.doi.org/10.1176/appi.ps.201200217

Afari, N., Ahumada, S. M., Wright, L. J., Mostoufi, S., Golnari, G., Reis, V., & Cuneo, J. G. (2014). Psychological trauma and functional somatic syndromes: A systematic review and meta-analysis. *Psychosomatic Medicine, 76,* 2–11. http://dx.doi.org/10.1097/PSY.0000000000000010

American Psychological Association. (2017). *Clinical practice guideline for the treatment of PTSD.* http://dx.doi.org/10.1037/e514052017-001

Barnett, E. R., Bernardy, N. C., Jenkyn, A. B., Parker, L. E., Lund, B. C., Alexander, B., & Friedman, M. J. (2014). Prescribing clinicians' perspectives on evidence-based psychotherapy for posttraumatic stress disorder. *Behavioral Sciences, 4,* 410–422. http://dx.doi.org/10.3390/bs4040410

Bérard, A., Iessa, N., Chaabane, S., Muanda, F. T., Boukhris, T., & Zhao, J. P. (2016). The risk of major cardiac malformations associated with paroxetine use during the first trimester of pregnancy: A systematic review and meta-analysis. *British Journal of Clinical Pharmacology, 81*, 589–604. http://dx.doi.org/10.1111/bcp.12849

Bernardy, N. C., & Friedman, M. J. (2016). How and why does the pharmaceutical management of PTSD differ between men and women? *Expert Opinion on Pharmacotherapy, 17*, 1449–1451. http://dx.doi.org/10.1080/14656566.2016.1199686

Brady, K., Pearlstein, T., Asnis, G. M., Baker, D., Rothbaum, B., Sikes, C. R., & Farfel, G. M. (2000). Efficacy and safety of sertraline treatment of posttraumatic stress disorder: A randomized controlled trial. *JAMA, 283*, 1837–1844. http://dx.doi.org/10.1001/jama.283.14.1837

Davidson, J. R. T., Rothbaum, B. O., Tucker, P., Asnis, G., Benattia, I., & Musgnung, J. J. (2006). Venlafaxine extended release in posttraumatic stress disorder: A sertraline- and placebo-controlled study. *Journal of Clinical Psychopharmacology, 26*, 259–267. http://dx.doi.org/10.1097/01.jcp.0000222514.71390.c1

Davidson, J. R. T., Rothbaum, B. O., van der Kolk, B. A., Sikes, C. R., & Farfel, G. M. (2001). Multicenter, double-blind comparison of sertraline and placebo in the treatment of posttraumatic stress disorder. *Archives of General Psychiatry, 58*, 485–492. http://dx.doi.org/10.1001/archpsyc.58.5.485

Fava, G. A., Gatti, A., Belaise, C., Guidi, J., & Offidani, E. (2015). Withdrawal symptoms after selective serotonin reuptake inhibitor discontinuation: A systematic review. *Psychotherapy and Psychosomatics, 84*, 72–81. http://dx.doi.org/10.1159/000370338

Friedman, M. J., Marmar, C. R., Baker, D. G., Sikes, C. R., & Farfel, G. M. (2007). Randomized, double-blind comparison of sertraline and placebo for posttraumatic stress disorder in a Department of Veterans Affairs setting. *The Journal of Clinical Psychiatry, 68*, 711–720. http://dx.doi.org/10.4088/JCP.v68n0508

Gartlehner, G., Hansen, R. A., Morgan, L. C., Thaler, K., Lux, L., Van Noord, M., . . . Lohr, K. N. (2011). Comparative benefits and harms of second-generation antidepressants for treating major depressive disorder: An updated meta-analysis. *Annals of Internal Medicine, 155*, 772–785. http://dx.doi.org/10.7326/0003-4819-155-11-201112060-00009

Gelenberg, A. J., Freeman, M. P., Markowitz, J. C., Rosenbaum, J. F., Thase, M. E., Trivedi, M. H., & Van Rhoads, R. S. (2010). *Practice guideline for the treatment of patients with major depressive disorder* (3rd ed.). Retrieved from https://psychiatryonline.org/pb/assets/raw/sitewide/practice_guidelines/guidelines/mdd.pdf

Guina, J., Rossetter, S. R., DeRhodes, B. J., Nahhas, R. W., & Welton, R. S. (2015). Benzodiazepines for PTSD: A systematic review and meta-analysis. *Journal of Psychiatric Practice, 21*, 281–303. http://dx.doi.org/10.1097/PRA.0000000000000091

Haddad, A., & Davis, A. M. (2016). Tobacco smoking cessation in adults and pregnant women: Behavioral and pharmacotherapy interventions. *JAMA, 315*, 2011–2012. http://dx.doi.org/10.1001/jama.2016.2535

Hoffman, V., Middleton, J. C., Feltner, C., Gaynes, B. N., Weber, R. P., Bann, C., . . . Green, J. (2018). *Psychological and pharmacological treatments for adults with posttraumatic stress disorder: A systematic review update* (AHRQ Publication No. 18-EHC011-EF; PCORI Publication No. 2018-SR-01; *Comparative Effectiveness Review* No. 207) [Prepared by the RTI International–University of North Carolina at Chapel Hill Evidence-Based Practice Center under Contract No. 290-2015-00011-I for AHRQ and PCORI]. Rockville, MD: Agency for Healthcare Research and Quality.

Honig, P. K., & Gillespie, B. K. (1995). Drug interactions between prescribed and over-the-counter medication. *Drug Safety, 13*, 296–303. http://dx.doi.org/10.2165/00002018-199513050-00003

Huhn, M., Tardy, M., Spineli, L. M., Kissling, W., Förstl, H., Pitschel-Walz, G., . . . Leucht, S. (2014). Efficacy of pharmacotherapy and psychotherapy for adult psychiatric disorders: A systematic overview of meta-analyses. *JAMA Psychiatry*, *71*, 706–715. http://dx.doi.org/10.1001/jamapsychiatry.2014.112

Jain, S., Greenbaum, M. A., & Rosen, C. (2012). Concordance between psychotropic prescribing for veterans with PTSD and clinical practice guidelines. *Psychiatric Services*, *63*, 154–160. http://dx.doi.org/10.1176/appi.ps.201100199

Jakubovski, E., Varigonda, A. L., Freemantle, N., Taylor, M. J., & Bloch, M. H. (2016). Systematic review and meta-analysis: Dose–response relationship of selective serotonin reuptake inhibitors in major depressive disorder. *The American Journal of Psychiatry*, *173*, 174–183. http://dx.doi.org/10.1176/appi.ajp.2015.15030331

Jha, M. K., Rush, A. J., & Trivedi, M. H. (2018). When discontinuing SSRI antidepressants is a challenge: Management tips. *The American Journal of Psychiatry*, *175*, 1176–1184. http://dx.doi.org/10.1176/appi.ajp.2018.18060692

Jonas, D. E., Cusack, K., Forneris, C. A., Wilkins, T. M., Sonis, J., Middleton, J. C., . . . Gaynes, B. N. (2013). *Psychological and pharmacological treatments for adults with post-traumatic stress disorder (PTSD)* (AHRQ Publication No. 13-EHC011-EF; *Comparative Effectiveness Review* No. 92). Rockville, MD: Agency on Healthcare Research and Quality. Retrieved from National Center for Biotechnology Information website: https://www.ncbi.nlm.nih.gov/books/NBK137702/pdf/Bookshelf_NBK137702.pdf

Jorenby, D. E., Leischow, S. J., Nides, M. A., Rennard, S. I., Johnston, J. A., Hughes, A. R., . . . Baker, T. B. (1999). A controlled trial of sustained-release bupropion, a nicotine patch, or both for smoking cessation. *The New England Journal of Medicine*, *340*, 685–691. http://dx.doi.org/10.1056/NEJM199903043400903

Kessler, R. C., Sonnega, A., Bromet, E., Hughes, M., & Nelson, C. B. (1995). Posttraumatic stress disorder in the National Comorbidity Survey. *Archives of General Psychiatry*, *52*, 1048–1060. http://dx.doi.org/10.1001/archpsyc.1995.03950240066012

Kobayashi, T. M., Patel, M., & Lotito, M. (2015). Pharmacotherapy for posttraumatic stress disorder at a Veterans Affairs facility. *American Journal of Health-System Pharmacy*, *72*(11, Suppl. 1), S11–S15. http://dx.doi.org/10.2146/ajhp150095

Krystal, J. H., Davis, L. L., Neylan, T. C., A Raskind, M., Schnurr, P. P., Stein, M. B., . . . Huang, G. D. (2017). It is time to address the crisis in the pharmacotherapy of post-traumatic stress disorder: A consensus statement of the PTSD Psychopharmacology Working Group [Letter]. *Biological Psychiatry*, *82*, e51–e59. http://dx.doi.org/10.1016/j.biopsych.2017.03.007

Lund, B. C., Bernardy, N. C., Vaughan-Sarrazin, M., Alexander, B., & Friedman, M. J. (2013). Patient and facility characteristics associated with benzodiazepine prescribing for veterans with PTSD. *Psychiatric Services*, *64*, 149–155. http://dx.doi.org/10.1176/appi.ps.201200267

Marshall, R. D., Beebe, K. L., Oldham, M., & Zaninelli, R. (2001). Efficacy and safety of paroxetine treatment for chronic PTSD: A fixed-dose, placebo-controlled study. *The American Journal of Psychiatry*, *158*, 1982–1988. http://dx.doi.org/10.1176/appi.ajp.158.12.1982

Martenyi, F., Brown, E. B., & Caldwell, C. D. (2007). Failed efficacy of fluoxetine in the treatment of posttraumatic stress disorder: Results of a fixed-dose, placebo-controlled study. *Journal of Clinical Psychopharmacology*, *27*, 166–170. http://dx.doi.org/10.1097/JCP.0b013e31803308ce

Martenyi, F., Brown, E. B., Zhang, H., Prakash, A., & Koke, S. C. (2002). Fluoxetine versus placebo in posttraumatic stress disorder. *The Journal of Clinical Psychiatry*, *63*, 199–206. http://dx.doi.org/10.4088/JCP.v63n0305

McAlister, F. A., Laupacis, A., Wells, G. A., & Sackett, D. L. (1999). Users' guides to the medical literature: XIX. Applying clinical trial results B. Guidelines for determining whether a drug is exerting (more than) a class effect. *JAMA*, *282*, 1371–1377. http://dx.doi.org/10.1001/jama.282.14.1371

McCormack, J. P., Allan, G. M., & Virani, A. S. (2011). Is bigger better? An argument for very low starting doses. *Canadian Medical Association Journal, 183*, 65–69. http://dx.doi.org/10.1503/cmaj.091481

McElroy, S. L., Weisler, R. H., Chang, W., Olausson, B., Paulsson, B., Brecher, M., . . . Young, A. H. (2010). A double-blind, placebo-controlled study of quetiapine and paroxetine as monotherapy in adults with bipolar depression (EMBOLDEN II). *The Journal of Clinical Psychiatry, 71*, 163–174. http://dx.doi.org/10.4088/JCP.08m04942gre

Mills, E. J., Gardner, D., Thorlund, K., Briel, M., Bryan, S., Hutton, B., & Guyatt, G. H. (2014). A users' guide to understanding therapeutic substitutions. *Journal of Clinical Epidemiology, 67*, 305–313. http://dx.doi.org/10.1016/j.jclinepi.2013.09.008

Monson, C. M., Gradus, J. L., Young-Xu, Y., Schnurr, P. P., Price, J. L., & Schumm, J. A. (2008). Change in posttraumatic stress disorder symptoms: Do clinicians and patients agree? *Psychological Assessment, 20*, 131–138. http://dx.doi.org/10.1037/1040-3590.20.2.131

Osei-Bonsu, P. E., Bolton, R. E., Wiltsey Stirman, S., Eisen, S. V., Herz, L., & Pellowe, M. E. (2017). Mental health providers' decision-making around the implementation of evidence-based treatment for PTSD. *The Journal of Behavioral Health Services & Research, 44*, 213–223. http://dx.doi.org/10.1007/s11414-015-9489-0

Rothbaum, B. O., Price, M., Jovanovic, T., Norrholm, S. D., Gerardi, M., Dunlop, B., . . . Ressler, K. J. (2014). A randomized, double-blind evaluation of D-cycloserine or alprazolam combined with virtual reality exposure therapy for posttraumatic stress disorder in Iraq and Afghanistan War veterans. *The American Journal of Psychiatry, 171*, 640–648. http://dx.doi.org/10.1176/appi.ajp.2014.13121625

Stone, N. J., Robinson, J. G., Lichtenstein, A. H., Bairey Merz, C. N., Blum, C. B., Eckel, R. H., . . . Wilson, P. F. (2014). 2013 ACC/AHA guideline on the treatment of blood cholesterol to reduce atherosclerotic cardiovascular risk in adults: A report of the American College of Cardiology/American Heart Association Task Force on Practice Guidelines. *Circulation, 129*(Suppl. 2), S1–S45. http://dx.doi.org/10.1161/01.cir.0000437738.63853.7a

Tucker, P., Zaninelli, R., Yehuda, R., Ruggiero, L., Dillingham, K., & Pitts, C. D. (2001). Paroxetine in the treatment of chronic posttraumatic stress disorder: Results of a placebo-controlled, flexible-dosage trial. *The Journal of Clinical Psychiatry, 62*, 860–868. http://dx.doi.org/10.4088/JCP.v62n1105

Uher, R., Farmer, A., Henigsberg, N., Rietschel, M., Mors, O., Maier, W., . . . Aitchison, K. J. (2009). Adverse reactions to antidepressants. *The British Journal of Psychiatry, 195*, 202–210. http://dx.doi.org/10.1192/bjp.bp.108.061960

U.S. Department of Veterans Affairs, National Center for PTSD. (2017). *PTSD Checklist for* DSM–5 *(PCL-5)*. Retrieved from https://www.ptsd.va.gov/professional/assessment/adult-sr/ptsd-checklist.asp

U.S. Department of Veterans Affairs, & U.S. Department of Defense. (2017). *VA/DoD clinical practice guideline for the management of post-traumatic stress disorder and acute stress disorder* (Version 3.0). Retrieved from https://www.healthquality.va.gov/guidelines/MH/ptsd/VADoDPTSDCPGFinal012418.pdf

U.S. Food and Drug Administration. (2016). *FDA warns about serious risks and death when combining opioid pain or cough medicines with benzodiazepines; requires its strongest warning*. Retrieved from https://www.fda.gov/downloads/Drugs/DrugSafety/UCM518672.pdf

van der Kolk, B. A., Spinazzola, J., Blaustein, M. E., Hopper, J. W., Hopper, E. K., Korn, D. L., & Simpson, W. B. (2007). A randomized clinical trial of eye movement desensitization and reprocessing (EMDR), fluoxetine, and pill placebo in the treatment of posttraumatic stress disorder: Treatment effects and long-term maintenance. *The Journal of Clinical Psychiatry, 68*, 37–46. http://dx.doi.org/10.4088/JCP.v68n0105

Vasterling, J. J., Verfaellie, M., & Sullivan, K. D. (2009). Mild traumatic brain injury and posttraumatic stress disorder in returning veterans: Perspectives from cognitive neuroscience. *Clinical Psychology Review*, *29*, 674–684. http://dx.doi.org/10.1016/j.cpr.2009.08.004

Volpi-Abadie, J., Kaye, A. M., & Kaye, A. D. (2013). Serotonin syndrome. *The Ochsner Journal*, *13*, 533–540.

Weathers, F. W., Litz, B. T., Keane, T. M., Palmieri, P. A., Marx, B. P., & Schnurr, P. P. (2013). *The PTSD Checklist for* DSM–5 *(PCL-5)*. Retrieved from https://www.ptsd.va.gov/professional/assessment/adult-sr/ptsd-checklist.asp

Whelton, P. K., Carey, R. M., Aronow, W. S., Casey, D. E., Jr., Collins, K. J., Dennison Himmelfarb, C., . . . Wright, J. T., Jr. (2018). 2017 ACC/AHA/AAPA/ABC/ACPM/AGS/APhA/ASH/ASPC/NMA/PCNA guideline for the prevention, detection, evaluation, and management of high blood pressure in adults: Executive summary: A report of the American College of Cardiology/American Heart Association Task Force on Clinical Practice Guidelines. *Journal of the American College of Cardiology*, *71*, 2199–2269.

Wilk, J. E., West, J. C., Duffy, F. F., Herrell, R. K., Rae, D. S., & Hoge, C. W. (2013). Use of evidence-based treatment for posttraumatic stress disorder in Army behavioral healthcare. *Psychiatry*, *76*, 336–348. http://dx.doi.org/10.1521/psyc.2013.76.4.336

Yonkers, K. A., Wisner, K. L., Stewart, D. E., Oberlander, T. F., Dell, D. L., Stotland, N., . . . Lockwood, C. (2009). The management of depression during pregnancy: A report from the American Psychiatric Association and the American College of Obstetricians and Gynecologists. *Obstetrics and Gynecology*, *114*, 703–713. http://dx.doi.org/10.1097/AOG.0b013e3181ba0632

Zohar, J., Amital, D., Miodownik, C., Kotler, M., Bleich, A., Lane, R. M., & Austin, C. (2002). Double-blind placebo-controlled pilot study of sertraline in military veterans with posttraumatic stress disorder. *Journal of Clinical Psychopharmacology*, *2*, 190–195. http://dx.doi.org/10.1097/00004714-200204000-00013

11

Conclusion

PTSD Treatment Themes, Shared Components, and Future Research Directions

Raquel W. Halfond

The purpose of this casebook is to provide illustrative examples of and more detailed information about each of the recommended treatments for adults with posttraumatic stress disorder (PTSD) in the *Clinical Practice Guideline for the Treatment of PTSD* (APA Clinical Practice Guideline; American Psychological Association [APA], 2017) to begin familiarizing the interested provider with these PTSD treatments. Chapter 2 includes a discussion of the foundations of PTSD treatment relevant to the psychotherapy and pharmacotherapy treatments presented in Chapters 3 through 10. This conclusory chapter summarizes themes from this book and discusses common components shared across psychotherapy treatments. Finally, gaps in current knowledge and directions for future research to enhance patient care are discussed.

However, a discussion of an APA clinical practice guideline would not be complete without drawing the reader back to APA's (2005) policy on evidence-based practice in psychology. This policy is illustrated by an overlapping-circle model, with three circles to represent the best available evidence, clinician expertise, and patient's culture, characteristics, and preferences. Decisions are intended to be made at the intersection of these three circles in the context of shared decision making between the patient and provider. Clinical practice guidelines, such as the one for the treatment of PTSD in adults, are tools that synthesize the best available evidence about efficacy and comparative effectiveness of treatments. Together with other relevant evidence, the clinician's expertise and the patient's characteristics, culture, and preferences help

http://dx.doi.org/10.1037/0000196-011
Casebook to the APA Clinical Practice Guideline for the Treatment of PTSD, edited by
L. F. Bufka, C. V. Wright, and R. W. Halfond

inform shared decision making between patient and provider. The material in this book is intended to provide clinical illustrations of various treatments as well as highlight related treatment issues; however, it does not replace clinical judgment.

THEMES

Several themes were highlighted across this book. One theme illustrated throughout the treatment chapters was the individualization of treatment to the needs of the patient. Even in treatments that are traditionally considered to be manualized, the authors illustrated how the patient's characteristics, culture, and preferences were integrated into treatment. For example, in the case example in Chapter 3, cognitive behavior therapy (CBT) began with the patient setting her own goals to individualize the treatment plan. Sessions 2 and 3 of the treatment included an exploration of the impact of the patient's culture and race on her trauma experience and subsequent PTSD symptoms. This information was then used to individualize the patient's CBT by prioritizing certain components of treatment and offering them earlier than they would otherwise be offered. Similarly, in the case example of cognitive therapy (CT) presented in Chapter 5, the therapist obtained information from the patient about meanings attributed to the trauma and strategies that the patient had been using to cope with the trauma memories. The therapist then worked together with the patient to use this information to individualize the case formulation and treatment plan.

Hand-in-hand with individualizing treatment came another theme highlighted in this book: shared decision making. Shared decision making involves the provider and patient working together, using clinician expertise together with patient's preferences, values, and personal characteristics and information about the best available research to guide decision making in treatment (Barry & Edgman-Levitan, 2012; Elwyn et al., 2012; National Learning Consortium, 2013). In Chapter 1, Bufka and Sonis noted a number of reasons that shared decision making is ideal in PTSD treatment, including its principled and ethical nature, evidence that it ultimately results in better decisions, the individuality of patients' treatment preferences, and the desire of patients exposed to trauma to be involved in making decisions about their treatment. Furthermore, shared decision making gives the patient power in making decisions about treatment and can also facilitate trust—two areas that can be considerably impacted by the trauma experience. Bufka and Sonis listed various components that should be included as part of shared decision making, a number of which were highlighted in various treatment chapters. In the case example presented in Chapter 9, after providing psychoeducation about narrative exposure therapy (NET), the therapist invited the patient to engage in deciding whether to participate in NET treatment, and they jointly planned crisis interventions and social support. Chapter 10 also emphasized the importance of shared decision making, particularly given the varying side effects of medications for PTSD in the context of similar magnitudes of effect. Regardless of treatment type, shared decision making allows the patient and provider to optimize the treatment and help ensure the patient is receiving the best possible care.

Attention to diversity issues when delivering care across different populations and subgroups was another theme apparent in this book. There was insufficient evidence in the systematic review (Jonas et al., 2013) underlying the APA Clinical Practice Guideline for treating PTSD for the panel to be able to make definitive conclusions about subgroup effects. However, authors were explicitly asked to attend to diversity issues given the universality of trauma. For example, in Chapter 7, Gersons, Nijdam, Smid, and Meewisse noted that although brief eclectic psychotherapy (BEP) was initially tested in a specific population in one country, it has since been translated into numerous languages and its use broadened for various populations in various countries. Likewise, in Chapter 9, Neuner et al. showed that NET is conducted across cultures and, given the universality of trauma reactions, any modifications are based on the individual patient rather than on a generalization for a cultural background (cf. Schnyder et al., 2016). Incorporating a patient's culture as well as other personal characteristics, values, and preferences comprises an important part of evidence-based practice in psychology (APA, 2005).

Finally, the topic of competency was addressed. In Chapter 2, Wright highlighted the issue of competency and provided an in-depth discussion of core competencies as well as trauma-specific competencies as part of training and practice. Most of the treatment chapters also explicitly discussed training and competency. For example, in Chapter 9, Neuner et al. discussed relevant training resources and the development of a standardized approach to training and certification. Additionally, in Chapter 5, Ehlers and Wild included a note directing interested readers to a detailed manual for further training on cognitive therapy for PTSD. It is hoped that the content in this book combined with other training resources will help the interested provider achieve competency.

SHARED COMPONENTS OF PSYCHOTHERAPY TREATMENTS FOR TRAUMA

Although each psychotherapy presented in this book is unique, many include similar components. First, many of the treatments include some form of psychoeducation in which the patient is given information about the PTSD symptoms, as well as about the particular treatment. For example, in NET (Chapter 9), the patient is provided with an explanation of his or her symptoms, the treatment rationale, the therapist's motivation to help the patient, and finally an invitation to participate in NET. In cognitive processing therapy

(CPT; Chapter 4), the patient is provided psychoeducation focusing on PTSD symptoms, development of the disorder, and the relationship between thoughts and feelings.

The treatments include some form of processing of the trauma, either direct or indirect. For example, prolonged exposure (PE; Chapter 6) includes as its main components imaginal exposure to the trauma as well as in vivo exposure to benign situations the patient has been avoiding. Likewise, BEP (Chapter 7) has an imaginal exposure component of the treatment, which is supplemented by the use of memorabilia and letter writing. In eye-movement desensitization and reprocessing (Chapter 8), the patient participates in a desensitization phase in which she or he concentrates on the trauma memory while being engaged by the therapist in eye movements.

Furthermore, many treatments include an element of meaning making, which is typically a process later in treatment, in which patients reflect on the positive and negative changes in themselves and their views of the world following the trauma. For example, BEP includes a meaning-making phase in which posttraumatic growth and potential negative changes in a patient's world beliefs are discussed (Chapter 7). CT includes a component in which the patient engages in adjusting the personal meaning attributed to the trauma and its aftermath, particularly when the original attributed meaning is not helpful to the patient (Chapter 5). In CPT, the therapist works with the patient to examine the meaning that the patient has attributed to the trauma and returns to examine this again later in treatment to see how the meaning has changed (Chapter 4).

Moreover, numerous treatments include a focus on the rebuilding of one's life after the trauma to include activities that are meaningful to the patient. For example, CT includes a focus on reclaiming one's life via discussion and subsequent homework that involves engaging in activities that were significant to the patient before the trauma (Chapter 5). As part of the conclusion of PE treatment, the patient and therapist discuss ways to move forward with his or her life applying the skills learned in treatment (Chapter 6).

Finally, many of the treatments include a special closing session or farewell ritual to mark the end of treatment. For example, NET has a special closing session in which the lifeline is reviewed, the written narration is signed, and other individualized rituals may be performed (Chapter 9). CBT involves a termination session in which progress is reviewed and skills are identified for moving forward and preventing relapse (Chapter 3).

Altogether, the shared components evident across various psychotherapies for PTSD treatment were striking. Even among treatment approaches that from the outside appear fairly different, there are commonalities. Ideally, the shared components allow for a number of viable treatment options for individuals diagnosed with PTSD. Consideration of these shared components may be informative for future clinical practice guidelines as well as research on the treatment of PTSD with the ultimate goal of enhancing patient care. Table 11.1 summarizes these shared components.

TABLE 11.1. Shared Components of Various Psychotherapy Treatments for Trauma

Shared component	Description
Psychoeducation	The patient is provided information about the PTSD symptoms as well as about the particular treatment.
Trauma processing	A form of processing of the trauma, either direct or indirect.
Meaning making	A process in which patients reflect on the positive and negative changes in themselves and their views of the world following the trauma; typically later in treatment.
Rebuilding of one's life	A focus on the rebuilding of one's life after the trauma to include activities that are meaningful to the patient.
Closing session/ Farewell ritual	Special session or ritual to mark the end of treatment.

PHARMACOTHERAPY

The information presented in the psychotherapy chapters in this book (Chapters 3–9) was complemented by the information presented by Friedman and Sonis in Chapter 10, discussing pharmacotherapy. Although a majority of psychologists are not able to prescribe pharmacotherapy, many psychologists have numerous patients who have taken or will be prescribed pharmacological treatment. Moreover, psychologists with certain credentials in some states (e.g., Idaho, Iowa, Illinois, Louisiana, New Mexico as of 2018) and in some services (e.g., U.S. military) can obtain prescribing privileges. Thus, it is imperative that prescribing and nonprescribing psychologists who work with patients with PTSD have a solid understanding of several considerations regarding pharmacotherapy.

Friedman and Sonis discussed efficacy of medications for PTSD along with possible side effects of those medications, why certain medications are not recommended for treating PTSD but might be helpful for other co-occurring disorders, whether and how much pharmacotherapy or psychotherapy might be contributing to treatment success or failure, and when consultation with the prescribing provider is appropriate for concerns related to the pharmacotherapy. Furthermore, they illustrated why it is important for psychologists, in the context of shared decision making, to discuss with patients the benefits versus the potential harms of pharmacotherapy in addition to psychotherapy.

GAPS AND FUTURE RESEARCH

Although this casebook illustrates treatments that were recommended in the APA clinical practice guideline (APA, 2017), the guideline also notes that additional research is needed in several areas. Furthermore, the guideline notes that additional research that emerges and is summarized in future systematic review could especially impact some of the recommendations that were conditional (i.e., EMDR, NET) and might affect the future strength of those recommendations. Research that addresses the gaps in the knowledge base is critical to enhance patient care.

As is clear from the themes presented across this casebook, more research is needed examining possible subgroup effects of treatment and whether there are moderating effects of treatment based on certain subgroups. In particular, research is needed that focuses on characteristics such as race and ethnicity, gender, sex, differing severity and chronicity levels of PTSD, and trauma type (APA, 2017). As described previously, diversity is a particular theme of this casebook, and authors were explicitly asked to attend to issues of diversity in drafting their chapters. Part of the reason for this request, beyond the importance of diversity, was the dearth of information on subgroup effects and PTSD treatments available in the literature. Although this topic was of interest to the panel while developing the guideline for the treatment of PTSD in adults, the panel was unable to make any definitive statements in the guideline because it had insufficient evidence. Greater attention to possible subgroup effects is critical to enhancing patient care.

Furthermore, research is needed comparing active treatments with other active treatments. Although research evidence suggests the efficacy of some treatments (i.e., compared with inactive control), the guideline noted a paucity of research comparing efficacious psychotherapy treatments with each other, efficacious medications with each other as well as with efficacious psychotherapy, and combinations of efficacious medication and psychotherapy. Future research in this realm would provide clinicians with better information to select a particular treatment over another, including psychotherapy and medication.

Future research should also include more individuals with comorbid disorders, given the frequency with which other conditions can be comorbid with PTSD (APA, 2017). In particular, individuals with comorbid suicidality or substance dependence were excluded from most of the trials in the systematic review underlying the PTSD guideline; this is concerning given the frequent comorbidity of PTSD with these disorders. Several of the chapters in this casebook address the comorbidity issue directly. For example, while discussing PE, Gallagher et al. (Chapter 6) note that abuse of substances can interfere with a patient's ability to learn new material and fully engage in the exposures. As another example, the second case example illustrating CPT (Chapter 4) presents an individual who was drinking alcohol and smoking marijuana as his primary methods of coping with PTSD symptoms. These are only a few examples, but the point is clear: More work is needed to ascertain the role of comorbidities on PTSD treatment.

Moreover, the PTD treatment trials reviewed by the guideline panel included relatively few outcomes that are important to patients (e.g., quality of life; APA, 2017). These patient-centered outcomes, however, were expressed in the patients' goals in various chapters in this casebook. For example, it was important to the patient receiving CBT (Chapter 3) to obtain housing and employment, improve her self-esteem, maintain her sobriety, and stay safe.

TABLE 11.2. Areas for Future Research

Area for future research	Description
Subgroup effects of treatment	Whether there are moderating effects of treatment based on particular subgroup.
Comparative effectiveness of active treatments	Research comparing efficacious psychotherapy treatments to each other, efficacious medications to each other as well as to efficacious psychotherapy, and combinations of efficacious medication and psychotherapy.
Individuals with comorbid disorders	Include more individuals with comorbid disorders to ascertain the role of comorbidities on PTSD treatment.
Patient-centered outcomes	Include outcomes that are important to patients (e.g., quality of life).
Serious harms	Include information on serious harms as well as whether there were no serious harms.

Note. Data from American Psychological Association (2017).

One patient receiving PE (Chapter 6) emailed her therapist to let her know she was engaged and noted that she considered this a sign of successfully moving forward with her life after the trauma. While these outcomes are important to patients and can promote treatment engagement, they are often not reported or, more frequently, not even gathered in research trials. Additional research is needed to understand the impact of treatment on patient-centered outcomes.

The guideline panel also noted a relative dearth of strong evidence regarding potential serious harms, particularly for the psychotherapy trials. This critical gap in the evidence base is common across the treatment literature; however, it is especially apparent in psychotherapy rather than in medication trials. A recent study found that only 38% of all registered systematic review protocols of health care interventions included plans for examining adverse events (Parsons, Golder, & Watt, 2019). Of those studies that planned to include adverse events, more than one third ultimately did not completely report adverse events as had been intended in the protocol. In future research trials, inclusion of information on serious harms is imperative in order to have strong evidence on which to evaluate the relative benefit of a treatment when developing treatment recommendation. Table 11.2 shows a summary of future research areas.

SUMMARY

The purpose of this casebook is to introduce readers to the treatments recommended for adults with PTSD in the *Clinical Practice Guideline for the Treatment of PTSD* (APA, 2017). Several themes were woven throughout the book, including the individualization of treatment, shared decision making, attention to issues of diversity in treatment, and finally competency. It is noteworthy that many of the psychotherapy interventions detailed in the casebook have various components in common, such as psychoeducation about PTSD symptoms and treatment, trauma processing, meaning making, rebuilding of one's life, and a special closing session or farewell ritual. The information in these chapters is rounded out with a chapter devoted to information that psychologists should know about pharmacotherapy. Although it is not expected that simply reading a treatment chapter in this casebook would make a provider competent to provide the particular treatment, it is hoped that each of these chapters will contribute to helping providers identify the treatments that are likely to be most beneficial to their clinical populations and to complement their existing skills so that they can complete other training and obtain competency in the particular treatments.

Finally, several gap areas were noted in the treatment literature for adults with PTSD, including potential subgroup effects of treatment, research comparing active treatments with each other, treatment concerns for individuals with comorbidities, lack of information on patient-centered outcomes, and potential harms of treatment. Although this is not an exhaustive discussion of all possible gap areas in the PTSD treatment literature, it includes several of the most prominent gaps that became apparent while developing treatment recommendations for adults with PTSD. Further research in these areas is critical for enhancing the care of adults with PTSD. Clinicians are encouraged to attend to these areas in their work with patients, and researchers are urged to address these gaps in the refinement of existing treatments and the development of emerging approaches to treatment.

REFERENCES

American Psychological Association. (2005). *Policy statement on evidence-based practice in psychology.* Retrieved from https://www.apa.org/practice/guidelines/evidence-based-statement.aspx

American Psychological Association. (2017). *Clinical practice guideline for the treatment of PTSD.* http://dx.doi.org/10.1037/e514052017-001

Barry, M. J., & Edgman-Levitan, S. (2012). Shared decision making—Pinnacle of patient-centered care. *The New England Journal of Medicine, 366,* 780–781. http://dx.doi.org/10.1056/NEJMp1109283

Elwyn, G., Frosch, D., Thomson, R., Joseph-Williams, N., Lloyd, A., Kinnersley, P., . . . Barry, M. (2012). Shared decision making: A model for clinical practice. *Journal of General Internal Medicine, 27,* 1361–1367. http://dx.doi.org/10.1007/s11606-012-2077-6

Jonas, D. E., Cusack, K., Forneris, C. A., Wilkins, T. M., Sonis, J., Middleton, J. C., . . . Gaynes, B. N. (2013). *Psychological and pharmacological treatments for adults with posttraumatic stress disorder (PTSD).* Rockville, MD: Agency for Healthcare Research and Quality.

National Learning Consortium. (2013). *Shared decision making* [Fact sheet]. Retrieved from https://www.healthit.gov/sites/default/files/nlc_shared_decision_making_fact_sheet.pdf

Parsons, R., Golder, S., & Watt, I. (2019). More than one-third of systematic reviews did not fully report the adverse events outcome. *Journal of Clinical Epidemiology, 108,* 95–101. http://dx.doi.org/10.1016/j.jclinepi.2018.12.007

Schnyder, U., Bryant, R. A., Ehlers, A., Foa, E. B., Hasan, A., Mwiti, G., . . . Yule, W. (2016). Culture-sensitive psychotraumatology. *European Journal of Psychotraumatology, 7.* http://dx.doi.org/10.3402/ejpt.v7.31179

INDEX

ABOUT THE EDITORS

Lynn F. Bufka, PhD, is senior director, practice transformation and quality, at the American Psychological Association (APA) and a Fellow of the APA. The Practice Transformation and Quality Department focuses on the development and implementation of programs and policies related to expanding opportunities for professional psychology. Dr. Bufka's current areas of emphasis are the integration of psychology in the health care delivery system, diagnostic and functional classification, clinical practice guideline development, outcomes measurement and gathering "real world" practitioner data to inform policy and resource development. She presents regularly on these topics and has published over 30 peer-reviewed articles and book chapters. Dr. Bufka worked closely with the APA Guideline Development Panel for the Treatment of Posttraumatic Stress Disorder in Adults that wrote the clinical practice guideline on posttraumatic stress disorder. She has particular experience in the delivery and evaluation of cognitive behavior therapy for all the anxiety disorders. She maintains an active clinical license and regularly serves as a media spokesperson on stress, anxiety, psychology practice, and other issues.

Caroline Vaile Wright, PhD, is senior director, health care innovation, at the American Psychological Association (APA) and a member of APA's Stress in America team. The broad focus of her independent research has been related to the assessment and treatment of the traumatic effects of violence against women and the intersection of the criminal and civil justice system. She has maintained an active line of research with peer-reviewed articles in multiple journals, including the *Journal of Interpersonal Violence, Violence and Victims, Law and Human Behavior,* and the *Journal of Traumatic Stress.* Dr. Wright has been interviewed by television, radio, print and online media—including NBC News, *The Today Show*, CSPAN, *The Washington Post*, *The New York Times*, CNN, and NPR—on a range of topics, including stress, politics, discrimination and harassment, trauma, and #MeToo. Dr. Wright has received extensive training in evidence-based treatment for trauma, including cognitive processing therapy, prolonged exposure, and dialectical behavior therapy. She is licensed in the District of Columbia.

Raquel W. Halfond, PhD, is director, evidence based practice, in the Practice Transformation and Quality Department, at the American Psychological Association (APA). Dr. Halfond oversees the day-to-day activities of the initiative and worked closely with the APA Guideline Development Panel for the Treatment of Posttraumatic Stress Disorder in Adults that wrote the PTSD clinical practice guideline. She actively publishes in peer reviewed journals and books as well as presents on topics relevant to evidence-based practice and more. She has extensive training in evidence-based treatments, particularly for children and adolescents and has special expertise in child trauma and work with Latina/o children and families. Dr. Halfond is a child clinical psychologist and is licensed in Virginia. She received her doctorate in clinical psychology from Virginia Commonwealth University, her master's in experimental psychology from Wake Forest University, and her bachelor's in psychology and Hispanic studies from the College of William and Mary. Dr. Halfond completed her APA-approved clinical internship at Children's Hospital Los Angeles, where she specialized on the child trauma team. She completed her postdoctoral fellowship at Harbor-UCLA Medical Center, where she specialized in the child trauma clinic and the adolescent dialectical behavior therapy and cognitive behavior therapy clinic.